With love & affection.
CR Dharani Murthy

To   Hari prasad.

They Lived With God

They Lived With God

Sri Ramakrishna (1836-1886)
'As many faiths, so many paths'.

They Lived With God

LIFE STORIES OF SOME DEVOTEES OF SRI RAMAKRISHNA

by Swami Chetanananda

Advaita Ashrama
(Publication Department)
5 Dehi Entally Road
Kolkata 700 014

Published by
Swami Mumukshananda
President, Advaita Ashrama
Mayavati, Champawat, Himalayas
from its Publication Department, Kolkata
Email: mail@advaitaonline.com
Website: www.advaitaonline.com

First Indian Edition, August 1991
Third Reprint, January 2002
3M8C

ISBN 81-85301-02-6

Printed in India at
Trio Process
Kolkata 700 014

Contents

Publisher's Note

"In an age so secular that many persons speak of God's death, it is important to have these detailed accounts of individuals who not only experienced God as alive, but who came to a new life themselves through that experience." This comment was made by Huston Smith, a renowned American professor of philosophy, about Swami Chetanananda's book *They Lived with God*.

In this book the author narrates twenty-eight life stories of Sri Ramakrishna's lay devotees, who played a vital role in the unfolding of their Master's mission. They demonstrate how to lead God-centred lives while living as householders. It is inspiring to watch the spiritual transformations of these men and women from all walks of life as they came to know Sri Ramakrishna.

Many who have read *The Gospel of Sri Ramakrishna* and *Ramakrishna: the Great Master* want to know more about the lives and fortunes of these devotees closely associated with him. The present highly interesting and valuable narrative, which abounds with new information and anecdotes, fulfills this need. On the one hand, the reader learns about a God-man, how he lives, how he behaves, and how he communicates with others; and on the other, the reader can see how his teachings on practical Vedanta were translated into action by his devotees. We are pleased to publish this treasured addition to the Ramakrishna-Vedanta literature.

This book has been co-published by Shepheard-Walwyn of London and the Vedanta Society of St. Louis. We express our sincere gratitude to the Vedanta Society of St. Louis for preserving the copyright and granting this valuable book to us for exclusive publication and circulation in India.

ADVAITA ASHRAMA
Mayavati, Himalayas   PUBLISHER
13 July 1991

Preface

While in Southern California (1971-78) I gave a series of lectures on the lay disciples of Sri Ramakrishna under the title 'They Lived With God'. I was happy to know that American audiences were eager to know more about these people who had lived with Sri Ramakrishna — their relationships with him and how their lives had been transformed after coming in contact with him. Each one of these disciples played an important role in the divine drama of Sri Ramakrishna.

The householder disciples of the Master had husbands or wives, children, relatives, and friends; they had jobs, household duties, social commitments, and various problems; still they lived God-centred lives. They learned from their Master 'God first and then the world'. Human life becomes heavy, boring, and painful if materialism is the goal. On the contrary, it becomes meaningful, joyful, and inspiring if spirituality is the goal. This fact has been illustrated in the life stories presented in this book.

During the last five years I have done extensive research, collecting materials from many Bengali books and magazines as well as other sources published in English. Most of the information on which this book is based is unknown to Western readers. As the various facets of a diamond increase its brilliance, so the twenty-eight short biographies in this book will shed new light on the glory of Sri Ramakrishna.

If someone asks about the title of the book *They Lived with God*, my answer is: Krishna mentioned in the Gita that when religion declines and irreligion prevails, God incarnates to reestablish the eternal religion. Thus the same God was born as Krishna, Buddha, Christ at different times to fulfill the need of the age. The Divine Incarnations are always accompanied by a group of special people who carry their messages. In this book I have not tried to prove whether Sri Ramakrishna was God or not; that I leave for the readers to decide.

Some episodes about the Master are included in two or three biographies. I deleted most of the repetitions except for a few necessary to maintain the continuity of thought. Also, for readability I have edited some quotations from *Sri Ramakrishna, The Great Master*.

I am grateful to the Vedanta students who helped edit and type the manuscript of this book.

As Sri Ramakrishna blessed the assembled devotees at the Cossipore garden house on January 1, 1886, saying, 'Be illumined', may he bless us again and again.

St. Louis, U S A   Chetanananda

Sri Ramakrishna
(A Biographical Introduction)

'When religion declines and irreligion prevails, I incarnate myself in every age to establish religion', declared Sri Krishna in the Bhagavad Gita.[1] The lives of Buddha, Christ, Mohammed, Chaitanya, and Ramakrishna justify this statement. That God descends to the earth as a human being to help mankind is not a myth, but a fact. Each *avatar*, or Divine Incarnation, fulfills the need of a particular age and points out the goal of human life. Peace and bliss come through spiritual values, not through materialism.

Sri Ramakrishna was born on February 18, 1836, in Kamarpukur, a small village sixty miles northwest of Calcutta. In the spring of 1835 his father, Khudiram Chattopadhyay, had gone to visit Gaya* to perform a rite for his ancestors. One night, in his sleep, Khudiram had a vision. He saw a luminous Being gazing at him affectionately. The Being said in a sweet voice: 'Khudiram, your great devotion has made me very happy. The time has come for me to be born once again on earth. I shall be born as your son'.[2]

Khudiram was filled with joy until he realized that he did not have the means to carry out such a great responsibility. So he said: 'No, my Lord, I am not fit for this favour. I am too poor to serve you properly'.[3] 'Do not be afraid, Khudiram', said the Lord. 'Whatever you give me to eat, I shall enjoy'.[4] Khudiram woke, convinced that the Lord of the Universe was going to be born into his household. He then left Gaya and returned to Kamarpukur before the end of April.

On his return, Khudiram heard from his wife, Chandra, of an experience she had had in front of the Yogi Shiva temple next to their house. Chandra said: 'I saw that the holy image of Lord Shiva inside the shrine was alive! It began to send forth waves of the most

---

*Gaya is a holy city sacred to Vishnu, the preserver of the universe and the second deity in the Hindu trinity with Brahma the Creator and Shiva the Dissolver. Buddha attained enlightenment (*nirvana*) in 550 B.C. a few miles from the Vishnu temple in Gaya.

beautiful light — slowly at first, then quicker and quicker. They filled the inside of the temple, then they came pouring out — it was like one of those huge flood waves in the river — right towards me! I was going to tell Dhani [a neighbour woman], but then the waves washed over me and swallowed me up, and I felt that marvellous light enter into my body. I fell down on the ground, unconscious. When I came to myself, I told Dhani what had happened, but she did not believe me. She said I'd had an epileptic fit. That cannot be so, because since then I have been full of joy and my health is better than ever. Only — I feel that light is still inside me, and I believe that I am with child'.[5]

Khudiram then told Chandra about his vision, and they rejoiced together. Prayerfully, the pious couple waited patiently for the birth of the divine child the following spring. Owing to Khudiram's experience at Gaya, Sri Ramakrishna was named 'Gadadhar', an epithet of Vishnu meaning 'Bearer-of-the-Mace'. He was the couple's fourth child, born after two sons, Ramkumar and Rameshwar, and a daughter, Katyayani. A second daughter, Sarvamangala, was born when Sri Ramakrishna was three years old.

Sri Ramakrishna grew up in Kamarpukur. He was sent to school where he learned to read and write, but he soon lost interest in this 'bread-earning education'. When he was six or seven years old, he had his first experience of Cosmic Consciousness. 'One morning', he recalled in later life, 'I took some parched rice in a small basket and was eating it while walking along the narrow ridges of the rice fields. In one part of the sky, a beautiful black cloud appeared, heavy with rain. I was watching it and eating the rice. Very soon the cloud covered almost the entire sky. And then a flock of cranes came flying by. They were as white as milk against that black cloud. It was so beautiful that I became absorbed in the sight. Then I lost consciousness of everything outward. I fell down and the rice was scattered over the earth. Some people saw this and came and carried me home'.[6]

Khudiram died in 1843. Sri Ramakrishna keenly felt the loss of his father and became more indrawn and meditative. He began to visit the rest-house in the village where pilgrims, especially monks, would stop on their way to Puri. While serving these holy people he learned their songs and prayers.

When Sri Ramakrishna was nine years old, following the brahminical tradition, he was invested with a sacred thread, which allowed him to perform ritualistic worship. Gradually he began to help the household by conducting the ritual to the family deities. He had some friends with whom he would play, sing, and act out religious dramas. Once, during the Shiva-ratri festival (a spring worship of Lord Shiva), he enacted the role of Shiva and lost outer consciousness. Then on another occasion, while going to worship the Divine Mother in a neighbouring village, Sri Ramakrishna went into samadhi.

In 1850 Ramkumar opened a school in Calcutta, and as a secondary profession he used to perform rituals in private homes. It soon became difficult for him to manage both, so in 1852 he brought Sri Ramakrishna to Calcutta to assist him. Sri Ramakrishna helped his brother in performing the rituals, but when Ramkumar asked him to continue his studies he declined. On May 31, 1855, Ramkumar took the responsibility of officiating at the dedication ceremony of the Kali temple of Dakshineswar, which had been founded by Rani Rasmani, a wealthy woman of Calcutta. Sri Ramakrishna was present on that occasion. Soon afterwards he moved to Dakshineswar and in time became a priest in the temple. Ramkumar died in 1856.

Sri Ramakrishna now began his spiritual journey in earnest. While worshipping the Divine Mother, he questioned: 'Are you true, Mother, or is it all a fiction of the mind — mere poetry without any reality? If you do exist, why can't I see you? Is religion, then, a fantasy, a mere castle in the air?'[7] His yearning for God-realization became more intense day by day. He prayed and meditated almost twenty-four hours a day. Then he had a remarkable experience:

There was an unbearable pain in my heart, because I could not see the Mother. Just as a man wrings a towel with all his strength to get the water out of it, so I felt as if my heart and mind were being wrung. I began to think I should never see Mother. I was dying of despair. In my agony, I said to myself: 'What is the use of living this life?' Suddenly my eyes fell on the sword that hangs in the temple. I decided to end my life with it, then and there. Like a madman, I ran to it and seized it. And then — I had a marvellous vision of the Mother, and fell down unconscious...It was as if houses, doors, temples, and everything else vanished altogether; as if there was nothing anywhere! And what I saw was an infinite, shoreless sea of light; a sea that was consciousness. However far and in whatever direction I looked, I saw shining waves, one after another, coming towards me. They were raging and storming upon me with great speed. Very soon they were upon me; they made me sink down into unknown depths. I panted and struggled and then lost consciousness.[8]

After this vision it was not possible for Sri Ramakrishna to continue the ritual in the temple, so he entrusted his responsibility to Hriday, his nephew, and passed more than two years in a God-intoxicated state. In 1859 he returned to Kamarpukur and lived with his mother for approximately one year and seven months. Chandra arranged his marriage to Sarada Mukhopadhyay, a young girl from Jayrambati, a village just west of Kamarpukur. After the marriage Sri Ramakrishna returned to Dakshineswar in 1860.

After arriving at Dakshineswar the Master was caught up again in that spiritual tempest. He forgot his home, wife, family, body, and surroundings. He described his experience of that period:

> No sooner had I passed through one spiritual crisis than another took its place. It was like being in the midst of a whirlwind — even my sacred thread was blown away, I could seldom keep hold of my dhoti [cloth]. Sometimes I'd open my mouth, and it would be as if my jaws reached from heaven to the underworld. 'Mother!' I'd cry desperately. I felt I had to pull her in, as a fisherman pulls in fish with his dragnet. A prostitute walking the street would appear to me to be Sita, going to meet her victorious husband. An English boy standing cross-legged against a tree reminded me of the boy Krishna, and I lost consciousness. Sometimes I would share my food with a dog. My hair became matted. Birds would perch on my head and peck at the grains of rice which had lodged there during the worship. Snakes would crawl over my motionless body.
>
> An ordinary man couldn't have borne a quarter of that tremendous fervour; it would have burnt him up. I had no sleep at all for six long years. My eyes lost the power of winking. I stood in front of a mirror and tried to close my eyelids with my finger — and I couldn't! I got frightened and said to Mother: 'Mother, is this what happens to those who call on you? I surrender myself to you, and you give me this terrible disease!' I used to shed tears — but then, suddenly, I'd be filled with ecstasy. I saw that my body didn't matter — it was of no importance, a mere trifle. Mother appeared to me and comforted me and freed me from my fear.[9]

In 1861 Bhairavi Brahmani (a nun) came to Dakshineswar to initiate Sri Ramakrishna into Tantric disciplines. The Master practised sixty-four methods of Tantra and attained perfection through all of them. After completing his Tantra *sadhana* (disciplines) he practised *vatsalya bhava* (the affectionate attitude towards God) under Jatadhari, a Vaishnava monk, and then *madhura bhava* (the sweet mood), in which a devotee approaches God as a lover. After these spiritual practices Tota Puri, a Vedanta monk, came to initiate Sri Ramakrishna into *sannyasa* (monastic vows). The Master attained nirvikalpa samadhi, the highest Vedantic experience, in three days.

In 1866 Sri Ramakrishna practised Islam under the guidance of a

Sufi named Govinda Roy. The Master later mentioned to his disciples: 'I devoutly repeated the name of Allah, and I said their prayers five times daily. I spent three days in that mood, and I had the full realization of the sadhana of their faith'.[10]

In 1868 Sri Ramakrishna went on a pilgrimage with Hriday, Mathur, and Mathur's family. He visited Deoghar, Varanasi, Prayag, Vrindaban, and also Navadwip. Mathur, after having served the Master for fourteen years, died in 1871. The following year Sarada Devi came to Dakshineswar and Sri Ramakrishna worshipped her as the Divine Mother.

In 1873 the Master met Shambhu Charan Mallik, who would read to him from the Bible and talk to him about Jesus of Nazareth. One day Sri Ramakrishna visited Jadu Mallik's garden house, which was adjacent to the Dakshineswar temple. In his living room, the Master saw a picture of the Madonna with the child Jesus sitting on her lap. While he was gazing at it, he saw that the figures of the Mother and Child were shining, and that the rays of light coming forth from them were entering his heart.

For the next three days he was absorbed in the thought of Jesus, and at the end of the third day, while walking in the Panchavati, he had a vision of a foreign-looking person with a beautiful face and large eyes of uncommon brilliance. As he pondered who this stranger could be, a voice from within said: 'This is Jesus Christ, the great yogi, the loving Son of God, who was one with his Father and who shed his heart's blood and suffered tortures for the salvation of mankind!'[11] Jesus then embraced Sri Ramakrishna and merged into his body.

After realizing God in different religions as well as in different sects of Hinduism, Sri Ramakrishna proclaimed: 'As many faiths, so many paths'.[12] The jewels of spirituality which he had gathered during three-quarters of his life spent in hard struggle were now ready to be given to humanity. In 1875 Sri Ramakrishna met Keshab Chandra Sen, a famous Brahmo leader, who was a popular hero of the time. Keshab and his followers began publishing the fascinating life and teachings of Sri Ramakrishna in their journals, and as a result many people came to know about the saint of Dakshineswar.

Through direct experience Sri Ramakrishna realized that the form of the Divine Mother was one with the formless Supreme Brahman, like fire and its burning power, like milk and its whiteness. The Divine Mother once said to the Master: 'You and I are one. Let your life in this world be deep in devotion to me, and pass your days for the good of mankind. The devotees will come'.[13]

Sri Ramakrishna was disgusted with the mundane talk of worldly people. In the evening during vespers, when the temples resounded with the ringing of bells and the blowing of conch shells, he would climb up to the rooftop of the kuthi and cry out in a loud voice: 'Come to me, O devotees! Where are you? I cannot bear to live without you'.[14]

In 1879 the devotees started to come to Dakshineswar. First came Ram, Manomohan, then Kedar, Surendra, Chuni, Latu, Nityagopal, and Tarak. In 1881-82 Narendra (Swami Vivekananda), Rakhal, Bhavanath, Baburam, Balaram, Niranjan, M., and Yogin came. In 1883-85 Adhar, Sharat, Shashi, Gangadhar, Kali, Girish, Devendra, Sarada, Kalipada, Upendra, Hari, Subodh, Purna, and other disciples met Sri Ramakrishna. With them the Master played his divine drama. Sri Ramakrishna also met many distinguished people of that time, such as Michael Madhusudan Datta, Dayananda Saraswati, Devendra Nath Tagore, Ishwar Chandra Vidyasagar, Dr. Mahendralal Sarkar, Bankim Chatterjee, Mr. Joseph Cook, Mr. Williams, Mr. Missir, and others.

Sri Ramakrishna trained his disciples to carry out his mission, and he made Swami Vivekananda their leader. When Swami Vivekananda asked the Master, 'Have you seen God?' he replied, 'Yes, I see him just as I see you here, only in a much more intense way'.[15] That impressed Swami Vivekananda at once. Later he carried the message of Sri Ramakrishna to the modern world, saying: 'Do not care for doctrines, do not care for dogmas or sects or churches or temples. They count for little compared with the essence of existence in each man, which is spirituality; and the more a man develops it, the more power he has for good. Earn that first, acquire that, and criticize no one; for all the doctrines and creeds have some good in them. Show by your lives that religion does not mean words or names or sects, but that it means spiritual realization'.[16]

When the flower blooms, bees come of their own accord. People from all over flocked to Sri Ramakrishna and he would sometimes talk about God as much as twenty hours a day. This continued for years. His intense love for mankind would not allow him to refuse to help anyone. In the middle of 1885, this tremendous physical strain resulted in throat cancer. When his disciples tried to stop him from teaching, he said: 'I do not care. I will give up twenty thousand such bodies to help one man'.[17]

Sri Ramakrishna passed away on August 16, 1886, at the Cossipore garden house, located between Calcutta and Dakshineswar. A couple of days before his passing, Sri Ramakrishna said to Vivekananda: 'He who was Rama and He who was Krishna is now Ramakrishna in this body'.[18]

1

Rani Rasmani

God often plays in mysterious ways. Rani Rasmani, a famous wealthy woman of Calcutta, had for a long time planned a pilgrimage to Varanasi. When all arrangements had been made and she was finally ready to start, she had a dream of the Divine Mother who commanded her to build a temple instead of undertaking the pilgrimage. Thus the Dakshineswar temple came into existence.

Sri Ramakrishna once said: 'Rani Rasmani was one of the eight *nayikas* [attendant goddesses] of the Divine Mother. She came down to the world to spread the worship of the Divine Mother'.[1] In the middle of the last century, this great woman of India provided a setting in which Sri Ramakrishna enacted his divine drama for thirty years. The whole story began in that beautiful temple garden on the Ganga, four miles north of Calcutta. As Sister Nivedita pointed out, 'Humanly speaking, without the Temple of Dakshineswar there [would have] been no Ramakrishna; without Ramakrishna, no Vivekananda; and without Vivekananda, no Western mission'.[2]

Rani Rasmani was born in September 1793 at Kona, a small village on the eastern bank of the Ganga, about thirty miles north of Calcutta. Her given name was Rasmani, but her mother nicknamed her Rani (literally, 'queen') when she was one and a half years old. Her father, Harekrishna Das, and her mother, Ramapriya Dasi, were pious and simple, but very poor. Her father maintained the family by farming and by repairing the roofs of cottages in the village.

The children of poor families live through sun and rain as well as cold and lack of nourishment. They must struggle from their very birth; they are labourers from their childhood. When Rasmani was very young she carried food to the field for her father, helped her mother with the household work, and picked vegetables from the garden. Like other poor children she was never demanding, and no one ever heard her say, 'I cannot'. Her favourite pastime was to swing with her friends on a hammock which her father had tied to a branch of a mango tree in their garden.

Rani Rasmani (1793-1861)

Harekrishna, though a farmer, knew how to read and write Bengali, and this he taught to his daughter. He also had a gift for narrating stories from the traditional religious literature. As a village story teller, he played a vital role in spreading mass education, and the villagers took advantage of his talents. In the evenings they would gather at his home and listen to his melodious and dramatic readings from the Ramayana, the Mahabharata, and the Puranas. Rasmani would also listen to those tales and her childhood imagination would carry her mind high.

Rasmani's parents were devout Vaishnavas (followers of Vishnu, a devotional sect), and it was their custom to put special religious marks on their foreheads before practising spiritual disciplines. Rasmani liked to imitate them. Sitting in front of a mirror she would also paint her face with religious marks. Thus was planted in her mind the seed of religion, which later grew to an immense form. She had spontaneous faith and love for God, and her character was a blend of strength, truthfulness, uprightness, contentment, and other noble qualities.

Rasmani was only seven years old when her mother, Ramapriya, died from a high fever. It was a great shock to the little girl. Her relatives tried to console her by saying, 'Your mother has gone to recover her health and she will be back soon'. But eventually she understood that her mother had died, and only time, the great healer, could remove the sorrow from her heart.[3]

Besides his daughter, Harekrishna also had two sons and one sister in his household. Grief and poverty tormented his heart, but his faith in God helped him to survive. Four years passed and then another problem crept in. Harekrishna began to worry about Rasmani's marriage; it would require a great deal of money. Although Rasmani was only eleven years old, she looked older, and she was also a very beautiful girl.

One day in the spring of 1804, Rasmani went to bathe in the Ganga with a few other villagers. She did not know that some people on a boat were watching her from a distance. It was the large pleasure boat of Rajchandra Das, son of Pritaram Das, the great landlord of Jan Bazar, Calcutta. Rajchandra had married twice but both of his wives had died, so he was not willing to marry again. His father, however, wanted him to remarry so that his lineage might continue. Pritaram's eldest son, Harachandra, had died earlier without any children.

Rajchandra often went to Triveni, near Rasmani's village, by boat with his friends for a pleasure trip as well as for a holy bath in the confluence of the three rivers. When Rajchandra's friends showed him Rasmani from a distance he was impressed. With Rajchandra's consent his friends anchored the boat and made inquiries about her. They then returned to Calcutta. Pritaram was delighted to hear the news, and he immediately sent a messenger to Harekrishna with a proposal of marriage. Harekrishna took it as a godsend and gave his approval. The marriage was held at Rajchandra's Calcutta residence in April 1804.

Rasmani's father-in-law, Pritaram, was an intelligent, self-made man. He was born in a poor family in 1753. His parents died when he was young and he was brought up by his aunt. He began his career as a clerk in a salt distributing agency in Calcutta and then became the manager of a large estate in Natore, East Bengal (now in Bangladesh). Later he started his own business in Calcutta. Among his many enterprises was the supplying of various commodities to the ruling English people, and in this way he developed a close relationship with them. Eventually he bought many estates and became a renowned landlord. When Pritaram died in 1817, his son, Rajchandra, inherited 650,000 rupees in cash and a vast amount of property.[4]

Wealth begets wealth. It is said that Rajchandra earned 50,000 rupees in one day through an auction. Like his father, Rajchandra was a very successful man, but he always consulted his intelligent wife, Rasmani, before making any decisions. Although she had very little education, Rajchandra greatly admired and appreciated his wife's perception, common sense, tactfulness, and humility. Wealth generally makes a person proud and haughty, but the simple village girl, Rasmani, remained unchanged. Her quiet nature conquered the hearts of the whole household. She served her husband, supervised the kitchen work and other household activities, and performed worship and spiritual disciplines just as she used to at her village home.

Instead of hoarding their vast wealth, Rajchandra and Rasmani undertook many charitable projects. Their hearts cried out for the poor, the miserable, and the distressed. In 1823, when many places of Bengal were devastated by flood, Rasmani spent money liberally to feed and house the afflicted. In that same year her father died. When she went to the Ganga to perform certain religious rites in connection with his death, she noticed the terrible condition of the bathing ghat. She then requested her husband to construct a new ghat and also a road for the people. Lord Bentinck, Governor General of India, gave Rajchandra permission for the project, and thus Babu Ghat and Babu Road (now Rani Rasmani Road) were built. Rajchandra had another bathing ghat constructed at Ahiritola, in the western part of Calcutta, in memory of his mother, and a home for the dying at Nimtala at the request of Rasmani. They also donated 10,000 rupees for the improvement of the government library, arranged for a free ferry to cross the Beliaghata canal, and in Talpukur, a village fourteen miles north of Calcutta, they had a large pond dug to alleviate the water scarcity.[5]

Rajchandra was known for his truthfulness as well as his generosity. Once, at the request of his brother-in-law, he promised to lend 100,000 rupees to an English merchant. That night he heard the news that the company was going to be liquidated and the merchant would therefore have to return to England. But in the morning when the merchant came to him for the money Rajchandra gave it to him. Someone asked him why he did not refuse when he knew of the merchant's insolvency, and Rajchandra replied, 'I have not learned to say no after having said yes'.[6]

In 1833 Rajchandra was honoured by the British rulers with the title 'Rai Bahadur' (Leader among Men) for his integrity, generosity, and philanthropic activities. Truly, he was one of the elite of Calcutta society in his day. Prince Dwarakanath Tagore (grandfather of Rabindranath Tagore), Akrur Dutta, Kaliprasanna Sinha, Sir Raja Radhakanta Dev, Lord Auckland (Governor General of India), John Bebb, and many other distinguished members of the East India Company were his close friends.

Rasmani and Rajchandra had four daughters — Padmamani, Kumari, Karuna, and Jagadamba. They trained their daughters in a traditional Hindu manner in spite of the fact that they were surrounded by affluence and Western influence.

In 1821 Rajchandra had a new home built for his family in Jan Bazar, Calcutta, at a cost of two and a half million rupees. It has seven sections with three hundred rooms, and it took eight years to complete. This palace is now known as 'Rani Rasmani Kuthi'. The first section of the palace was dedicated to Lord Raghunath (Ramachandra), the family deity. One hot summer day Rajchandra was taking an afternoon nap when a monk with a robust body and matted hair came to see him. The gatekeepers at first tried to ignore the monk, but he finally persuaded them to let him meet the owner of the palace. When Rajchandra was informed that a monk had come to see him, he came to the parlour. The monk presented him with an image of Lord Raghunath and said: 'Please serve the Lord. It will do good to you. I am going to a distant place for a pilgrimage, and I don't know whether I shall be back or not'. Rajchandra offered something in exchange, but the monk smiled and said, 'I am not a beggar monk'. He then quickly left. Rajchandra installed the image of Raghunath in the shrine with great festivity.[7]

One day in 1836 when Rajchandra was travelling in his carriage, he suddenly had an attack of apoplexy and fell unconscious on the seat. The driver rushed home and Rajchandra was carried to his room. All the best doctors of Calcutta were brought in, but to no avail. Rajchandra died at the age of forty-nine.

Rasmani was stricken with grief. It is said that she lay on the floor for three days without taking any food or drink. Afterwards she performed all the rituals according to the injunctions of the scriptures for her departed husband. In addition, she weighed herself against silver coins and had them (6,017 coins) distributed among the brahmins. She also fed the poor and gave them various gifts. At the conclusion of the ceremonies the monk who had given her husband the image of Raghunath came. Rasmani offered expensive gifts to the monk, but he smiled and asked for only two things — a small water pot and a blanket. Tears fell from Rasmani's eyes when she saw the monk's nonattachment and lack of greed. He wanted to pay his homage to Raghunath so Rasmani accompanied him to the shrine. The monk then blessed Rasmani and left. Later this image of Raghunath was stolen from the shrine.[8]

Rasmani now began to manage the vast estate with the help of her three sons-in-law, but she mostly depended on the youngest, Mathur Nath Biswas, who was intelligent, tactful, and well versed in English. Her third daughter, Karuna, had been married to Mathur, but had died in 1833. Rasmani then asked him to marry her fourth daughter, Jagadamba.

One day Prince Dwarakanath Tagore came to Rasmani and said, 'It would be nice if you could engage an efficient manager to look after your vast estate'.

Rasmani was too shy to speak directly to her husband's friend, so she sat behind a curtain and gave her replies through Mathur. She said: 'Yes, you are right. But it is very difficult to get such a faithful person'.

'If you want I shall be your manager'.

'That would be nice. But at present I do not know how much money and property I have, and how much money has been given out in loans. I know that my husband lent you two hundred thousand rupees. If I could get back that money now, it would be very helpful to me'.

'Yes, I shall repay that money soon. Tomorrow I shall let you know about it'.

The next day Prince Dwarakanath said, 'I do not have any cash now, but I shall hand over one of my estates to you in exchange'.

'What is the annual income from that property?' asked Rasmani.

'Thirty-six thousand rupees, but the value is over two hundred thousand rupees'.

Rasmani accepted the property, and when the transaction was over she said to the prince: 'I am a widow and my property is not large. It would be discourteous of me to request a venerable person like you to be my manager. My sons-in-law are the heirs of this estate and they will manage it'. Prince Dwarakanath then understood that Rasmani was a tactful, highly intelligent, and far-sighted woman.[9]

In spite of her responsibility now as owner and custodian of such immense wealth, Rasmani remained as unattached as ever. According to the Hindu custom widows do not remarry. They lead a pure and unattached life like a nun. Rasmani also followed the ancient custom. Early in the morning she would get up and repeat her mantram in the shrine. Then in midmorning she would sit in her office and sign official documents, appoint officers, check accounts, and discuss various problems and projects with Mathur. At noon she would partake of the food which had been offered to the Lord, and then she would rest. Later in the day, after supervising the office work, she would attend the vesper service. She was fond of inviting brahmin scholars and listening to their discourses on the scriptures.

In 1838 Rasmani had a desire to celebrate the Car Festival of the Lord and asked Mathur to order a silver chariot for that purpose. In this festival the image of the Lord is placed in a chariot, which is pulled by the devotees. Mathur suggested the name of the Hamilton Company, a famous English jewellery firm, to make the chariot, but Rasmani disapproved. She advised him to have it done by local silversmiths so that their talents could get an opportunity to be recognized. When the celebration took place thousands of people joined the procession and pulled the chariot through the streets of Calcutta. Rasmani's sons-in-law joined the procession barefooted. Rasmani also arranged a banquet at this time for the foreign dignitaries of Calcutta, who later remarked, 'Our eyes have never seen such a gorgeous, extraordinary celebration as this'.[10]

There is a saying among the Hindus, 'Thirteen festivals in twelve months'. Without festivals life is very dull. As Rasmani led a God-centred life, so her place was the abode of God and the scene of constant religious festivals. Every year Rasmani celebrated the Durga Puja (worship of the Divine Mother), spending fifty to sixty thousand rupees. At this time she would give food and other gifts to the needy. Her devotion for God and love for the poor were manifest side by side. Other festivals — such as Janmashtami (Krishna's birthday), Lakshmi Puja, Jagaddhatri Puja, Kartik Puja, Saraswati Puja, Basanti Puja, Dol Yatra, and so on — would follow, one after another. On these occasions also the poor were fed and clothed, offerings were given to brahmins for maintaining the religious traditions, and singers and musicians were rewarded and appreciated. In addition, weight lifters and wrestlers were encouraged to show their feats and the winners would receive expensive gifts from Rasmani.

Rasmani was highly regarded for her courage and public spirit. Once, on the day preceding the worship of the Divine Mother Durga, her priests went in a musical procession to the Ganga to perform a particular ritual. It was early in the morning and the music disturbed the sleep of an Englishman. He ordered the musicians to stop, but no one paid any attention to him. He then complained to the police and sought immediate action. But Rasmani engaged even more musicians for the next day and, without caring for the protest, the ritual was performed with great enthusiasm. As a result a case was brought to the court against Rasmani, which she lost, and she was fined fifty rupees. Rasmani was infuriated that the government had acted against a religious observance. She paid the fine, but at the same time she ordered barricades to be put up at both ends of Babu Road, from Jan Bazar to Babu Ghat, so that no traffic could pass through. When the government protested, Rasmani replied in a letter: 'The road is mine. Without receiving compensation I shall not allow anyone to pass through it'. The government was helpless to do anything against Rasmani's challenge because legally she was the owner of Babu Road. The news spread quickly all over the city, and the people composed a couplet about this brave woman:

> When the Rani's horses and carriage roll down the street, they say,
> None, even the English Company, dares to stand in her way.

At last, when the British Government reimbursed her the fine and earnestly requested her to open the road for the public, she had the barricades removed.[11]

Rasmani was always ready to help the poor and the persecuted. At one time the government imposed a tax on the fishermen who made their meagre living by fishing in the Ganga. The fishermen requested various prominent people to help them, but no one would come forward to their defence. At last they went to Rani Rasmani and she promised to do something. Paying ten thousand rupees to the government, she discreetly took the lease of the fishing right of the Ganga, from Ghusuri to Metiabruz. She then asked the fishermen to barricade that area of the Ganga, from shore to shore, with bamboo poles and catch fish there without paying any tax. (According to *Sri Ramakrishna, The Great Master,* the barricade was made with chains.) As a result, the water traffic was stopped and the commercial boats could not reach their ports. A 'Show Cause' summons came from the government along with an order to remove the barricades. Rasmani replied that the big steamboats frightened the fish, causing them to run to and fro, and this made it difficult for them to lay their eggs. The poor fishermen were therefore not able to catch many fish, which was their only source of income. Furthermore, she replied, that with a view to protecting the fishermen she had paid the government a large amount of money, and legally she had every right to put up a barricade in her own area. At last the British Government settled the case with Rasmani by returning her money for the lease of the land and rescinding the tax from the fishermen.[12]

Rasmani always fought for a just cause. It was not her intention to embarrass or challenge the government unnecessarily. On the other hand, during the critical time of the Sepoy Mutiny in 1857, she helped the government by providing food, livestock, and other necessities. This benevolent action was much appreciated by the British Government.

Some of the soldiers, however, were not so appreciative. There was a British army barracks near Rasmani's home, some of whose soldiers often robbed and persecuted passers-by and looted neighbourhood shops. One day a few drunken soldiers were molesting a person on the street. Rasmani's sons-in-law noticed it from their roof and they could not bear it. They ordered their guards to drive the drunken soldiers away, and in the process one of the soldiers was wounded. The soldiers then returned to their barracks and reported their plight to their friends. Immediately a group of angry soldiers ran out and attacked Rasmani's palace. Her guards tried to resist them but they failed, as the soldiers were well armed and outnumbered them. Some of the guards were wounded and others ran away. Rasmani ordered all of her relatives to flee through a back door but did not try to save her own life. With an open sword in hand, she stood guard at the door of the shrine. Fortunately the soldiers did not come to that part of the house. They ransacked most of the palace, destroying expensive chandeliers, furniture, pictures, paintings, windows, and musical instruments. They mercilessly killed Rasmani's pet peacock and other birds and animals. The vandalism continued until ten o'clock at night. Mathur was not at home during the attack. When he returned and discovered what was going on inside the palace, he immediately went to the barracks and met the commanding officer, who rushed to the palace with Mathur and sounded a bugle. The soldiers then returned to their barracks. After this terrible incident Rasmani appointed twelve trustworthy English soldiers to protect her palace for two years. She also collected compensation from the British Government for the damage to her property. [13]

In 1850 Rasmani went on a pilgrimage to Puri to visit Lord Jagannath. In those days there was no train or good road to Puri from Calcutta. If pilgrims could afford it, they would travel by boat down the Ganga and then cross the Bay of Bengal. Rasmani started her journey with a large convoy of relatives, friends, guards, servants, food, and other necessities, requiring many boats. It was a long journey. As they reached the Bay of Bengal they were suddenly hit by a cyclone that scattered the boats in different directions. Night came and the ocean was still very dangerous. Rasmani ordered her sailors to anchor their boat near the shore, and then she disembarked with a woman attendant and started looking for some shelter. Seeing a light at a distance, they went towards it and found a tiny cottage belonging to a poor brahmin family. Rasmani did not tell them who she was, but they graciously allowed the two women to pass the stormy night with them. The next morning she gave the family one hundred rupees. In the meantime the convoy had been reunited and Rasmani resumed her journey.

On their way Rani Rasmani noticed that the road to Puri, beyond the Subarnarekha River, was in very bad condition. She later paid for its repair for the convenience of the pilgrims. At Puri she offered three diamond-studded crowns, costing 60,000 rupees to Lord Jagannath, Balaram, and Subhadra, the deities of the main temple. She also gave food and money to the temple priests and the poor. [14]

The next year Rasmani went on a pilgrimage to Gangasagar (the confluence of the Ganga and the sea), Triveni, and Navadwip (the birthplace of Chaitanya). On the way back, near Chandannagore, her boat was attacked by robbers. Rasmani's guards exchanged fire with them and one robber was wounded. She then ordered both groups to cease firing and asked to speak with the robber chief.

The robber said to her: 'Mother, we want money. If you do not fulfill our demand there will be terrible bloodshed'.

Rasmani: 'How much money do you want? How many are there in your group?'

Robber: 'There are twelve of us'.

Rasmani: 'I don't have any cash right now. Tomorrow evening I shall send twelve thousand rupees to you. If you are unwilling to accept this offer then take my gold necklace and these few silver vessels'.

Robber: 'We accept your offer. If we do not get the money by tomorrow evening, your journey will be stopped'.

Rasmani was true to her word. The next evening she sent the robbers twelve thousand rupees through a messenger.[15]

Pilgrims, through their love and devotion, tears and prayers, make a place holy. Their austerities and their longing for God create such an intense spiritual atmosphere that whoever comes to the place where they worship will feel it. Varanasi, the city of light, is one such holy place of India. In 1847 Rasmani had a desire to visit Lord Vishweshvar Shiva and the Divine Mother Annapurna of Varanasi. As there was no train between Calcutta and Varanasi, she decided to go by boat. Her convoy of twenty-five boats got ready with provisions for six months. There were seven boats for food and other supplies, one for herself, three for her three daughters and their families, two for the guards, two for the servants, four for other relatives and friends, two for her estate officials, one for the doctor and for medicine, one for the washerman, one for four cows, and one for fodder.[16]

On the night before Rasmani's departure, the Divine Mother appeared to her in a dream and said: 'You need not go to Varanasi. Install my image on a beautiful spot along the bank of the Ganga and arrange for my worship and offerings there. In this image I shall be constantly present and shall ever accept your worship'. (In another version of this incident it is said that Rasmani started her journey, and on the first night they halted near Dakshineswar, where she had that dream.) Rasmani immediately cancelled her pilgrimage. The articles procured for the journey were distributed among the brahmins and the poor, and the money allotted for the pilgrimage was set aside for purchasing land.[17]

There is a saying, 'The western bank of the Ganga is as holy as Varanasi'. Rasmani first tried to buy some land in the Bally and Uttarpara areas, across the river from Dakshineswar. She offered enormous amounts of money, but the landlords of those places, out of petty jealousy, would not sell any land to her. At last she bought a piece of land, measuring about twenty acres, at Dakshineswar, on the eastern bank of the Ganga, a few miles north of Calcutta. A part of this land, with a bungalow, had belonged to an Englishman, and the other part was an abandoned Muslim graveyard where a Muslim holy man had been buried. The plot of land was in the shape of a tortoise shell, high in the centre and low around the edge, which, according to the Tantras, is auspicious for a place of Shakti worship.[18]

The construction of the temple complex began in 1847, and it took more than eight years to complete it. Besides the main temple, dedicated to the Divine Mother Kali, there was also to be a temple dedicated to Krishna and twelve small temples dedicated to Shiva. Rasmani spent 50,000 rupees for the land, 160,000 rupees for building an embankment along the river, and 900,000 rupees for the temple complex. In addition, she spent 226,000 rupees for some property which was meant to be used as an endowment for the maintenance of the temple.

It was Rasmani's earnest desire to have cooked food offered daily in a temple which she herself had built, and to have holy men come and partake of the offered food. But according to the caste rules, only a brahmin can offer cooked food to a deity in a temple. As Rasmani was not a brahmin, she was excluded from offering this service to God and holy people. She began to wonder if perhaps all her money and effort had been spent in vain. Desperately, she sent out letters to pandits who were expert in the interpretation of the scriptures, which state the proper procedure for ritualistic worship. She hoped that they could somehow find a way for her around the rigid and complex rules of the caste system.

Rasmani received all unfavourable answers except one, which came from Ramkumar Chatterjee, the elder brother of Sri Ramakrishna. Ramkumar was then conducting a Sanskrit school in Calcutta, and Sri Ramakrishna was living with him. His suggestion was: 'Let the Rani make a formal gift of the temple property to a brahmin. Let this brahmin arrange for the installation of the image of Kali in the shrine and for the cooking of the food that is to be offered to her. It will not be any violation of the injunction of the scriptures, and other brahmins will be able to take prasad [offered food] at the temple without losing their social status'.[19]

Rasmani was delighted, and she immediately acted upon Ramkumar's advice. Transferring the temple property to her family guru, she retained only the right to act as his representative in its managerial activities.

Although the temple construction had not yet been completed, Rasmani suddenly felt compelled to dedicate the temple as soon as possible. Sri Ramakrishna told the following story:

> The Rani practised severe austerities according to the scriptures
> from the day on which the making of the image began. She bathed

three times a day, took simple vegetarian food, slept on the floor, and practised japam, worship, and prayer according to her capacity...[In the meantime] the image was kept packed in a box lest it should be damaged. But it suddenly perspired for some reason or other and the Rani got the command in a dream: 'How long will you keep me confined this way? I feel suffocated! Install me as soon as possible'. No sooner had she got that instruction than the Rani became flurried and had the almanac consulted to find an auspicious day. As no such day could be found before the Snanayatra [the bathing festival of Lord Jagannath], she resolved to perform the installation on that day.[20]

It was May 31, 1855. Ramkumar, at the request of Rani Rasmani, had agreed to officiate at the installation and also to continue as priest of the Kali temple until a successor could be found for him. The ceremony was performed with great solemnity and princely splendour. The temples were decorated lavishly and with innumerable lights. Recitation of mantras, devotional singing, and the sounds of conchs and bells reverberated throughout the temple compound. Pandits from all over India came to grace the occasion and were given silk cloths, gold coins, and other lavish gifts, and thousands of people partook of the offered food. Rasmani spent 200,000 rupees for the dedication ceremonies. It was certainly the greatest achievement of her life.

Sri Ramakrishna, who was then just nineteen years old, was present at the dedication ceremony, but he did not eat any of the offered food. Instead, he bought some puffed rice from a market and ate it before walking back to Calcutta to sleep. The next day, when Sri Ramakrishna returned to Dakshineswar, Ramkumar asked him to stay, but he refused. He again went back to Calcutta, expecting his brother to return shortly also. After a week Ramkumar still had not returned, so Sri Ramakrishna went to Dakshineswar. This time Ramkumar told him that he had accepted, at the request of Rasmani, the post of the priest of Kali, and that he would close his school. Sri Ramakrishna at last agreed to stay at Dakshineswar with Ramkumar, but he continued to cook his own food with Ganga water. He followed his caste rules firmly and with great faith at the beginning of his sadhana.

Three months after the ceremonial opening of the temples an accident took place in the Krishna temple. Kshetranath, the priest, slipped and fell while carrying the image of Krishna from the altar to the bedchamber, and as a result, one leg of the image was broken. This accident caused quite a commotion, as it was considered to be an inauspicious omen. The priest was immediately dismissed, and pandits were called together to give their opinions as to what should be done about the image. They unanimously agreed that a broken image cannot be worshipped. Another image should be installed and the old one immersed in the Ganga.

This decision made Rani Rasmani very despondent. She did not want to throw away the image which she had worshipped with love and devotion. At Mathur's suggestion she consulted Sri Ramakrishna, and he answered in an ecstatic mood: 'If any one of the Rani's sons-in-law were to break a leg, would she forsake him and put someone else in his place? Wouldn't she rather have him cured by a doctor? Let it be the same in this case. Mend the image and worship it as before'.[21] This simple, satisfying, and logical answer surprised the pandits, but the Rani and Mathur were delighted. Sri Ramakrishna himself skillfully mended the image. At the request of Rasmani and Mathur, Sri Ramakrishna then agreed to become the priest of the Krishna temple.

Ramkumar's health was now beginning to fail. With Rasmani's approval, he began to teach Sri Ramakrishna the worship in the Kali temple, a more responsible and more difficult duty, while he himself took charge of the Krishna temple. But within a year Ramkumar died suddenly while away on some business for a few days. This unexpected turn of events was a great shock to Sri Ramakrishna. Ramkumar had been like a father to him, for he had been only seven years old when their father had died. Sri Ramakrishna continued to perform the worship of the Divine Mother in the temple, but gradually a God-intoxicating mood possessed him. He felt the transitoriness of the world, and his sole desire was to have the vision of the Mother. His unusual behaviour and strange manner of worship were soon noticed by the temple staff. They were convinced that Sri Ramakrishna had become mad and that he should be removed from his duties. A message to that effect was sent to Rasmani and Mathur.

One day Mathur paid an unexpected visit to the temple and secretly observed Sri Ramakrishna's method of worship. He saw how Sri Ramakrishna decorated the Divine Mother, talked to her, fed her, and fanned her as if she were a living person. Mathur was very much impressed and ordered the temple officials not to disturb or interfere with Sri Ramakrishna's worship in any way. He then reported to Rasmani: 'We have got an extraordinary worshipper. It seems the goddess will be awakened soon'.[22]

The love and respect which Rani Rasmani and Mathur had for Sri

Ramakrishna and the support they gave him were quite amazing when one realizes how strange his behaviour was at that time, and how much criticism about him came to them from other temple officials. Once, for example, Rani Rasmani came to Dakshineswar and, after bathing in the Ganga, entered the shrine of the Divine Mother for japam and meditation. Sri Ramakrishna was also there at that time. Rasmani had heard his devotional singing many times and was very fond of it so she requested him to sing. Sri Ramakrishna began singing, but all of a sudden he stopped and turned towards Rasmani, exclaiming, 'What! Even here you think such thoughts!' Saying this he struck the Rani with the palm of his hand.

Immediately there was a commotion in the temple. The women attendants of Rasmani began to scream, and the temple guards and officials rushed to the shrine to drag Sri Ramakrishna out of the temple. They hesitated, waiting only for the Rani's order. But Rasmani was sitting calmly in an introspective mood. Instead of listening to the song, she had been thinking about a lawsuit. She marvelled at how Sri Ramakrishna had known what she had been thinking. When she became aware of her surroundings she noticed that people were standing around them, ready to punish Sri Ramakrishna, who was sitting quietly and smiling. Rasmani then ordered: 'The young priest is not to blame. Do not take any action against him'.[23]

Rasmani retired to her room. When her attendants complained about Sri Ramakrishna's insolent behaviour towards her, she replied: 'You do not understand it. The Divine Mother herself punished me and thus illumined my heart'.[24] Because of her own highly pure nature, Rasmani was immediately able to understand, accept, and benefit from Sri Ramakrishna's harsh action.

After the dedication of the temple at Dakshineswar, Rani Rasmani began to spend more and more time in spiritual disciplines. She loved to come to Dakshineswar and talk about God with Sri Ramakrishna and to hear him sing devotional songs. But gradually the time came for her departure from Sri Ramakrishna's divine drama. In the early part of 1861 Rasmani became sick with a fever and chronic dysentery. The best doctors of Calcutta tried their utmost to cure her but at last gave up hope. They then suggested that she be moved to a healthier place. It was Rasmani's desire to go to her garden house at Kalighat, in South Calcutta, which was on the bank of the Adi Ganga, a small stream flowing into the Ganga.

Rasmani knew that her death was imminent and there was one task which she had left unfinished. The property which she had bought in

Dinajpur (now in Bangladesh) as an endowment for the maintenance
of the Dakshineswar temple was still not transferred to the temple
trust. She executed the deed of endowment on February 18, 1861, and
died the next day (February 19).

Shortly before her passing away she was brought to the bank of the
Ganga. Seeing some lamps lighted in front of her, she exclaimed:
'Remove, remove these lights. I don't care for this artificial
illumination anymore. Now my Mother has come and the brilliance of
her form has illumined the whole place'.* After a short pause she
passed away, saying, 'Mother, you have come!'[25]

---

*In another version of Rani Rasmani's death it is said that just before she
passed away all lights of the Kalighat temple were blown out by a strong gust
of wind, and then the Divine Mother appeared to her.[26]

2

Mathur Nath Biswas

'It was written in Mathur's horoscope that his *Ishta* [Chosen Deity] would always be gracious to him — nay, would even accompany him wherever he went and protect him, assuming a human form'.[1] Thus Sri Ramakrishna described Mathur Nath Biswas's wonderful good fortune to the devotees who came to him long after Mathur had passed away.

One day Sri Ramakrishna was pacing back and forth on the northeastern verandah of his room in Dakshineswar. He was in a spiritual mood, completely oblivious of his surroundings. Mathur was then seated alone in a room of the kuthi (bungalow) near the nahabat, and was watching him through a window. All of a sudden Mathur ran out of the house, threw himself down at Sri Ramakrishna's feet, and began to cry profusely.

'What are you doing?' said Sri Ramakrishna in alarm. 'You are an aristocrat and Rani Rasmani's son-in-law. What will people say if they see you acting like this? Calm yourself. Please, get up!'

Mathur gradually got control of himself and said: 'Father [as he called Sri Ramakrishna], I was watching you just now as you walked back and forth — I saw it distinctly: As you walked towards me you were no longer yourself. You were the Divine Mother Kali from the temple! Then, as you turned around and walked in the opposite direction, you became Lord Shiva! At first I thought it was some kind of optical illusion. I rubbed my eyes and looked again, but I saw the same thing. As often as I looked I saw it!'

Sri Ramakrishna then said, 'But I know nothing about it'.

Mathur again became overwhelmed and started crying. This made Sri Ramakrishna very nervous. He thought that if Rani Rasmani would hear about it she might misunderstand and think that he had put a spell on Mathur. At last he was able to console Mathur and calm him down.[2]

Very little is known about Mathur's early life. His parental home was in the Khulna district of East Bengal (now Bangladesh), and he

17

Mathur Nath Biswas (1817-1871)

studied at the Hindu College with Devendra Nath Tagore, father of
the great poet Rabindranath Tagore. Both Rani Rasmani and her
husband, Rajchandra, recognized Mathur's capabilities from
observing his intelligence and tactfulness. Hence they asked him to
marry their third daughter, Karunamayi. She died in 1833, however,
leaving Mathur with a son. In order to keep Mathur in the family,
Rasmani then married her fourth daughter, Jagadamba, to him. After
Rajchandra's death in 1836, Mathur became the steward of Rasmani's
vast estate.

The Dakshineswar temple garden, built by Rani Rasmani, was
dedicated on May 31, 1855. Sri Ramakrishna's elder brother,
Ramkumar, officiated as priest of the Kali temple. Although Sri
Ramakrishna was present on that occasion and was greatly attracted
to the beautiful temple garden on the bank of the Ganga, he did not
decide to live there permanently with his brother until several days
had passed. Mathur was immediately impressed when he met Sri
Ramakrishna and observed his gentle, pure, and simple nature. Sri
Ramakrishna was just nineteen years old at the time. Mathur asked
Ramkumar to engage him in some temple work, such as decorating
the image of Kali, but Ramkumar told him that his younger brother
was unwilling to accept any job. About this same time Hriday, a
nephew of Sri Ramakrishna, came to Dakshineswar looking for
employment.

One day Sri Ramakrishna made an image of Shiva out of clay from
the riverbank and worshipped it. Mathur happened to notice the
image while walking by and asked Hriday to give it to him when the
worship was over. After getting the image Mathur took it to Rani
Rasmani. Both were amazed with Sri Ramakrishna's talent and
obvious devotion. Shortly after this Mathur approached Sri
Ramakrishna and persuaded him to help his elder brother dress the
image of the Divine Mother. Sri Ramakrishna agreed, but on the
condition that Hriday would be responsible for looking after the
Mother's jewellery.

Three months after the dedication ceremony, the image of Krishna
in the Vishnu temple was broken and the priest of the temple was
dismissed. Sri Ramakrishna was then appointed to take his place. But
within a year he was asked to take over his brother's position as priest
of the Divine Mother Kali, and his spiritual adventure began. Mathur
played a very important role in Sri Ramakrishna's life for the next
fourteen years. Sri Ramakrishna later said: 'In that state of divine
exaltation I could no longer perform the formal worship. "Mother", I
said, "who will look after me? I haven't the power to take care of

myself. I want to listen only to talk about thee. I want to feed thy
devotees. I want to give a little help to those whom I chance to meet.
How will all that be possible, Mother? Give me a rich man to stand by
me''. That is why Mathur Babu did so much to serve me'.[3]

The temple officials soon began to notice Sri Ramakrishna's strange
behaviour and manner of worship. He would climb on the altar and
caress the Divine Mother; he would sing, laugh, joke, and talk with
her. Sometimes he would partake of the food before offering it to the
Mother, or he would feed it to a cat — a very blasphemous act.

When the officials complained to Mathur, he asked them not to
interfere with Sri Ramakrishna's actions in any way. He wanted to
see things for himself. One day Mathur paid an unannounced visit to
Dakshineswar and secretly observed Sri Ramakrishna in the temple.
From what he saw he was convinced that Sri Ramakrishna was not
crazy, but that his worship was the result of heartfelt and profound
love for the Divine Mother. Mathur himself actually felt that the
temple was filled with an intense manifestation of divinity.
Immediately he told Rani Rasmani that they had an extraordinary
worshipper, and sent a message to the temple officials telling them to
let Sri Ramakrishna perform the worship in whatever way he liked.

But still he was concerned about Sri Ramakrishna's safety. As his
love and adoration for the Master grew day by day, so also did his
worry and anxiety for him. One day Sri Ramakrishna entered one of
the Shiva temples and began to recite the *Shiva Mahimnah-stotra*, a
hymn in praise of Shiva, which includes the following verse:

> O Lord, if the blue mountain be the ink, the ocean the inkpot,
> the biggest branch of the heavenly tree be the pen, the earth the
> writing-leaf, and by taking these, if the goddess of learning writes
> forever, even then the limit of thy glory could never be reached.[4]

As Sri Ramakrishna recited this verse he became overwhelmed
with emotion. Tears poured down his cheeks and he cried aloud, 'O
Lord, how can I express thy infinite glory?' The temple servants and
officials quickly gathered around him, joking and saying such things
as: 'He's even crazier than usual today', and 'Is he going to ride on
Shiva's shoulders? There is still time to pull him out of the temple'.
Meanwhile Mathur had come. One of the officials seriously
suggested that Sri Ramakrishna be forcibly removed from the shrine
as he was very close to the deity. 'Touch him if you don't value your
head!' said Mathur furiously. After a short time Sri Ramakrishna
regained consciousness of the outer world. Seeing Mathur and the
others standing around him, he became like a fearful child and asked,
'Did I do anything wrong?' 'Oh no', said Mathur. 'You were just

reciting a hymn. I came here to make sure that no one disturbed you'.[5]

But Mathur questioned Sri Ramakrishna's sanity when he slapped the Rani for thinking about a lawsuit when she was sitting in the Mother's shrine. Mathur was not sure whether Sri Ramakrishna's unusual behaviour was caused by mental eccentricity or by divine intoxication, so with the consent of Rasmani, he engaged a well-known physician, Ganga Prasad Sen, to give the Master a thorough checkup and prescribe medicine. Mathur also arranged a special diet and cold drinks for him, hoping to restore his system to a normal condition. But Mathur and Rasmani did not stop there. One day they brought a prostitute to his room, 'in order to test me and also to cure my madness', as Sri Ramakrishna later told the devotees. 'She was beautiful to look at, with pretty eyes. I cried, "O Mother! O Mother!" and rushed out of the room. I ran to Haladhari and said to him, "Brother, come and see who has entered my room!" I told Haladhari and everyone else about this woman'.[6]

Mathur's doubts still remained. With the idea of testing him further, he one day said to the Master: 'Even God has to obey his own laws. Once a law is set up by God, not even he can overrule it'. Sri Ramakrishna replied: 'What do you mean? He who makes a law can unmake it if he so desires, or he can replace it with another law'. But Mathur refused to accept this opinion, saying: 'It is God who made the law that a red flower tree will produce only red flowers and never white ones. Let me see if he can produce a white flower on a red flower tree'. Sri Ramakrishna answered confidently, 'Yes, he can do everything — even that'.

The next day, on the way to the pine grove, Sri Ramakrishna saw two flowers, one red and the other dazzling white, on the same branch of a red hibiscus tree. He immediately broke off the branch and took it to Mathur. Naturally Mathur was very much amazed and he said to Sri Ramakrishna, 'Yes, Father, I am defeated'.[7]

Soon after Rani Rasmani passed away in 1861, Bhairavi Brahmani, a woman teacher of the Tantra, came to Dakshineswar. She quickly recognized the spiritual condition of Sri Ramakrishna and declared him to be an avatar (Incarnation of God). Mathur protested and quoted the scriptures which said that there could not be more than ten avatars. But the Brahmani replied that the Bhagavatam had mentioned twenty-four avatars, and it had also left room for countless others. Mathur could not argue with the Brahmani further because she was well versed in the scriptures. Then Bhairavi Brahmani asked Mathur to convene a conference of scholars with

whom she would hold a debate and establish her view that Sri
Ramakrishna was an avatar. Torn between faith and doubt, Mathur
was thoroughly confused. However, he agreed to invite the scholars
in order to settle the matter and to satisfy his own curiosity.

It was decided to invite Vaishnavcharan and Pandit Gauri to take
part in the debate. Vaishnavcharan was a famous spiritual leader and
scholar of the Vaishnava sect. Gauri was a scholar of the Tantra and a
man of remarkable occult powers. Since Gauri could not come to
Dakshineswar right away the Brahmani first presented her case to
Vaishnavcharan and a few other scholars. She elaborately described
the spiritual experiences of the Master and then verified them by
quoting the scriptures and by comparing his experiences with those
of other illumined souls. Vaishnavcharan heartily subscribed to all of
the conclusions of the Brahmani, and furthermore, he declared, from
his own understanding, that *mahabhava* (supreme devotion) was fully
manifest in Sri Ramakrishna. This verdict made the Brahmani jubilant
and created a sensation among the people. Mathur was
dumbfounded, but Sri Ramakrishna took it calmly. Like a boy, he
said to Mathur: 'So he really thinks that! Well, anyway, I'm glad it's
not a disease!'[8]

A few days later Pandit Gauri came to Dakshineswar unannounced
and entered the Kali temple, repeating a mantram loudly. This was
one of his occult powers which made him invincible in debate. But Sri
Ramakrishna, without knowing about this power, began shouting
the mantram louder than Gauri. After a few exchanges, each one
louder than the last, Sri Ramakrishna won the shouting match and
absorbed Gauri's occult power. Gauri understood Sri Ramakrishna's
greatness. Later, when he heard that Vaishnavcharan had declared
the Master to be an Incarnation of God, he said, 'I consider that to be
an understatement! I believe that you are He by a fraction of Whose
power the avatars come forth and accomplish their mission'.[9]

Most probably it was during this period that Mathur once more
tested Sri Ramakrishna to see whether or not he had truly conquered
lust. He secretly engaged Lakshmibai, a famous courtesan of
Calcutta, to tempt Sri Ramakrishna. One day Mathur picked up Sri
Ramakrishna and Hriday in his carriage for what was supposed to be
a pleasure trip. Instead they went to Lakshmi's quarters in
Mechuabazar, Calcutta. According to plan, Mathur and Hriday
entered a sitting room and sent Sri Ramakrishna, who was unaware
of the plot, to Lakshmi's room, where she was waiting to receive him.
As soon as the Master saw Lakshmi he addressed her as 'Blissful
Mother', bowed down to her, and merged into samadhi. Lakshmi

had never before seen a person like this. Calling the other girls, she said, 'Look, this man is free from lust'.

One of them said, 'It seems to me that he is a god-man'. Another girl remarked, 'Our profession may be sinful, but what a great good fortune for us that we have seen such a great soul!' Still another said: 'Sister, what a hell we have invited by trying to tempt this holy man! It is an unpardonable sin'.

Lakshmi and the other girls bowed down to Sri Ramakrishna and took the dust of his feet. Just then Mathur and Hriday came to the room. The women severely reprimanded Mathur for encouraging them to tempt a god-man — an act that could ruin their lives. Sri Ramakrishna gradually returned to the normal plane of consciousness and Mathur took him back to Dakshineswar.[10]

During her lifetime Rasmani had made Mathur the custodian of the Dakshineswar temple, and after her death he became the sole executor of her vast estate. Naturally this placed on him a great deal of responsibility, which he took very seriously. One day a thief stole the ornaments from the image of Krishna. When Mathur found out about it he went to the temple and said to the deity, 'What a shame, O God! You couldn't save your own ornaments!' Sri Ramakrishna, who was also there, sharply rebuked him, saying: 'The idea! Does he who has Lakshmi [the goddess of fortune] for his handmaid and attendant ever lack any splendour? Those jewels may be precious to you, but to God they are no better than lumps of clay. Shame on you! You shouldn't have spoken so meanly. What riches can you give to God to magnify his glory?'[11]

Although Mathur was normally a miserly person, his generosity knew no bounds when it came to Sri Ramakrishna, and he never hesitated to feed and clothe even the wandering holy men who came to Dakshineswar. Sometimes at the bidding of the Master he would lavishly offer other gifts also to the monks, such as blankets or water-pots.

Once Mathur and the Master were watching a *yatra* (a folk play based on a sacred story). Mathur placed one hundred rupees, arranged in stacks of ten, in front of the Master so that he could reward the various actors with a stack each. But Sri Ramakrishna had no sense of money. He would simply push the entire amount to the first actor who pleased him with a song or speech. Without the least irritation Mathur praised the royal mood of the Master and replaced the money. Again, Sri Ramakrishna gave it all away to another actor. Then, wishing to reward a third actor and finding no money laid out for him, he took off his own clothes and gave them to the actor.

A few years before this, in order to free himself from attachment for money, Sri Ramakrishna had one day taken money in one hand and clay in the other and thrown both into the Ganga, saying, 'Rupee is clay and clay is rupee'.[12] Even though Mathur knew about this, he loved to offer expensive things to the Master. Sometimes he would bring Sri Ramakrishna to his Calcutta residence so that he could enjoy his holy company and serve him to his heart's content. As it is the nature of a person to offer the very best to someone he loves, so Mathur one day bought a new set of dishes, made of gold and silver, just for the Master to use. To Sri Ramakrishna, however, a leaf plate and a gold plate were just the same. He came to Mathur's house and used those expensive dishes without any wonder or awe. Then Mathur dressed the Master in elegant clothes and said: 'Father, you are the owner of everything, including the estate. I am nothing but your steward. Look, you have just finished your meal from a gold plate and have drunk from a silver vessel, and then you have left without giving them a backward glance. Now it is my duty to have them cleaned and put in a safe place so that you can use them again'.[13]

One day Mathur presented a very expensive shawl to the Master. Sri Ramakrishna cheerfully accepted it, put it on, and walked around the temple garden, showing it off to people like a jubilant boy. He did not forget to mention the price, which was one thousand rupees at that time. But after a short while his mood changed. His discriminating mind started to ponder: 'What is there in this shawl? Nothing but sheep's wool. Like everything else it is a modification of matter. It protects one from cold, no doubt, but this can be done as well by a blanket or quilt. And like other material things it does not help one to realize God. Rather it makes the owner assume an air of superiority. He thinks himself rich and is proud. So it takes a man away from God'. This idea was unbearable to Sri Ramakrishna. Immediately he threw the shawl on the dusty ground and began to trample and spit on it. Then he got a match and was about to burn it. In the meantime someone grabbed it and took it away. Hearing about the sad fate of the shawl, Mathur smiled and said, 'Father did the right thing'.[14]

Sri Ramakrishna once prayed to the Divine Mother: 'Mother, don't make me a dry monk. Let me enjoy the fun and felicity of your creation'.[15] In spiritual life it is not good to cherish desires, but Sri Ramakrishna used to play with them, while Mathur was the playfellow and onlooker. In later years Sri Ramakrishna was fond of telling the devotees about these desires and how he had dealt with them. He said: 'Once the idea came to me to put on a very expensive robe embroidered with gold and to smoke a silver hubble-bubble. Mathur Babu sent me the new robe and the hubble-bubble. I put on the robe. I also smoked the hubble-bubble in various fashions. Sometimes I smoked it reclining this way, and sometimes that way, sometimes with head up, and sometimes with head down. Then I said to myself, "O mind, this is what they call smoking a silver hubble-bubble". Immediately I renounced it. I kept the robe on my body a few minutes longer and then took it off. I began to trample it underfoot and spit on it, saying, "So this is an expensive robe! But it only increases a man's rajas" '.[16]

It is quite amazing that whenever Sri Ramakrishna wished to take up a particular spiritual discipline, an adept or teacher of that discipline would come to Dakshineswar and help him. At the same time Mathur unfailingly stood by, supplying all the necessary articles that the Master required so that he could practise those rituals and disciplines according to the injunctions of the scriptures. When Sri Ramakrishna started to practise the *madhura bhava* (the spiritual discipline in which one identifies oneself with Radha in her devotion to Krishna), he asked Mathur for some women's clothes. Mathur provided him with a lovely and costly sari from Varanasi, a scarf, a skirt, and a bodice. To complete the transformation, Mathur adorned him with a set of gold ornaments and a wig. Needless to say, this strange sadhana of the Master created some scandal, but both he and Mathur ignored it.

Sri Ramakrishna wore women's clothes for six months, and during this period people were surprised to see that his way of walking and speaking, his gestures, and even his smallest actions were exactly like a woman's. Once Mathur took Sri Ramakrishna to his home in Jan Bazar, Calcutta. The women of the family loved the Master very much and immediately took him to their own quarters. Mathur then brought Hriday to that section and asked him to find his uncle among the women. But Hriday had a hard time identifying his uncle even though he lived with him and served him daily.

Shortly after this sadhana, Tota Puri, an illumined monk of the nondualistic school of Vedanta, came to Dakshineswar and initiated Sri Ramakrishna into *sannyasa* (monasticism). Within three days he attained nirvikalpa samadhi, the culmination of Vedantic experience. The Master also took initiation from Govinda, a Sufi, and devoutly repeated the name of Allah. Within three days he realized the goal of Islamic Sufism. During this particular sadhana Sri Ramakrishna would not look at the images of Hindu gods and goddesses. He also wore clothes like the Arab Muslims and said the Muslim prayer five times a day. But when he asked to eat Muslim food Mathur begged him not to, since this would include beef. As a compromise, Mathur engaged a Mohammedan cook to instruct a Hindu cook to prepare food for the Master in the Muslim manner.

Some time before Sri Ramakrishna started to practise nondualistic Vedanta, his mother moved to Dakshineswar from Kamarpukur. Mathur had great regard for her and would call her 'Grandma'. Mathur was very much concerned about Sri Ramakrishna's future welfare. Earlier he had discussed it with Hriday and had decided to offer Sri Ramakrishna an estate. But as soon as the Master heard about it he became mad and rushed to hit Mathur, shouting, 'Rascal, you want to make me a worldly man?' Since this plan did not work, Mathur devised another. He went to Chandramani, the Master's mother, and begged her to ask of him anything she wanted. But the guileless old lady was perplexed. She said: 'My son, you have already removed all my wants. I shall inform you if I need anything in the future. I have enough clothing, and you have provided plenty of food. So what else do I need?' When Mathur insisted, she thought a while and said, 'Well, if you really want to give me something, please buy me an anna [one sixteenth of a rupee — equivalent to less than one cent] worth of tobacco leaves. I want to make some tooth powder'. Mathur was moved to tears. He saluted her and remarked, 'Who but such a mother could give birth to a son like Sri Ramakrishna?'[17]

About this same time an incident happened in Mathur's family which greatly strengthened his faith in the Master. His second wife, Jagadamba, contracted severe dysentery. The doctors tried their utmost to cure her but finally declared the case to be beyond treatment. Mathur was panic-stricken. He knew that if his wife died he would lose control over Rani Rasmani's estate. Desperately he rushed to Sri Ramakrishna, his last refuge, and wept, saying, 'Father, not only am I threatened with a terrible personal loss, but if the management of the estate passes into other hands, I shall be unable to continue my services to you'. Seeing Mathur's agony, Sri Ramakrishna's mind was filled with compassion. He said in an ecstatic mood: 'Don't be afraid. Your wife will recover'. These words greatly reassured Mathur. He returned home and found that Jagadamba's illness had taken a dramatic turn for the better. Referring to this incident later, Sri Ramakrishna said: 'From that day, Jagadamba slowly started to recover and the disease was transferred to this body [meaning himself]. As a result of this cure, I suffered for six months from dysentery and other complaints'.[18]

As mentioned before, Mathur had tested Sri Ramakrishna in many ways before he surrendered himself to him and sought his guidance. He offered money, gold, and property to the Master, but they were all rejected. Sri Ramakrishna's mind was free from greed. He engaged beautiful girls to tempt the Master and found that his mind was far above lust. Mathur treated Sri Ramakrishna like a god, offering him the utmost honour. This did not in the least affect Sri Ramakrishna, who was free from ego. Observing the Master's superhuman nature, Mathur one day declared: 'Hriday, my wife, children, wealth, position, and everything are unreal. Sri Ramakrishna alone is real'.[19]

Mathur and Sri Ramakrishna developed an unusual relationship. Mathur would sometimes regard Sri Ramakrishna as his spiritual father and other times as an innocent, carefree boy. On the other hand, Sri Ramakrishna would often treat Mathur as his son or disciple, and at other times he would consider himself to be a child of the Divine Mother and Mathur to be the caretaker of her property. In this mood he gave orders to Mathur, who actually was his employer and he, Sri Ramakrishna, the employee.

However, whenever Mathur was in trouble he would go straight to Sri Ramakrishna in Dakshineswar for help. Once he ordered his guards to take part in a brutal gang fight with the guards of a rival landlord. When the news reached him that several men had been killed, Mathur came to his senses and realized that he would be prosecuted. He pleaded with the Master to save him. Sri Ramakrishna scolded him, saying: 'Rascal, you will create a row every day and come and cry, "Save me!" What can I do? Go and suffer the consequences'. But at last, seeing Mathur's deep anguish, the Master said, 'Well, it will be as Mother wills'. Mathur escaped arrest.[20]

Another time, when Mathur was involved in a lawsuit, he asked Sri Ramakrishna to offer a flower to the Divine Mother for him without telling the Master his intention. He firmly believed that he would receive the Mother's blessings through Sri Ramakrishna. The Master offered the flower unsuspectingly and Mathur won the case.

The Master always protected Mathur in his difficulties, but some days, like a child, it was he who would run to Mathur for help. The scriptures say: 'An illumined soul, established in the Self, wanders in the world, sometimes like a madman, sometimes like a child, and at other times like an unclean spirit. Sometimes he behaves like a fool, and sometimes like a wise man. Sometimes he seems splendid as a king, and sometimes he is a penniless mendicant'.[21] One day the

Master became greatly worried because a worm had come out of his
body with the urine, and he told Mathur about it. Now Mathur was
very intelligent and had great presence of mind. He quickly reassured
the Master: 'It is good, Father, that it happened. Everyone has a
worm in his body that generates lust. It is this lust-worm which
creates various bad thoughts in the mind and forces a person to
commit evil actions. It is the grace of the Mother that the lust-worm
has left your body. Why are you so worried about it?' Mathur's reply
greatly relieved and comforted the Master.[22]

Sri Ramakrishna sometimes would ask for Mathur's opinions about
his spiritual visions, as if to verify them. One day he told Mathur that
the Divine Mother had shown him that she would play through him
and that many devotees would come to him and receive spiritual
experiences and devotion. 'Is it a hallucination or is it true?' asked the
Master.

Mathur: 'Who says it is a hallucination? Father, the Divine Mother
has never before shown you anything false, so how can this not be
true? Why are they so late in coming? Let them come soon and we
shall be happy in their company'.

The Master: 'I don't know when they will come. But the Mother
told me about it and showed it to me in a vision. Everything happens
at her will'.[23]

Mathur would often take Sri Ramakrishna out in his magnificent
phaeton for a ride or to visit different people. Whenever Sri
Ramakrishna heard of any person who had sincere longing for God,
he wanted to go and see him. If a man moves one step towards God,
God comes ten steps towards him. Many times on these occasions Sri
Ramakrishna was humiliated and put in embarrassing situations, but
he did not care, as his mind was above praise and blame. On one
such occasion, having heard that Devendra Nath Tagore (the leader
of the Adi Brahmo Samaj) liked to meditate and chant the name of
God, he asked Mathur to take him to Tagore's home. Devendra
received them very cordially and they had a pleasant spiritual
conversation. Then Devendra, out of courtesy, invited Sri
Ramakrishna to attend the annual Brahmo festival, which was to be
held in a few days. Devendra added, however, that Sri Ramakrishna
should wear both an upper and a lower garment for the sake of
propriety. 'That's impossible', said the Master. 'I can't be dressed
like a dandy'. Both Devendra and Mathur laughed heartily at this.
But the next day Devendra wrote a letter to Mathur and cancelled the
invitation, explaining that he could not have Sri Ramakrishna attend
the festival without proper clothes.[24]

'Another day', Sri Ramakrishna told the devotees, 'I learnt of a good man named Dina Mukherjee, living at Baghbazar near the bridge. He was a devotee. I asked Mathur to take me there. Finding me insistent, he took me to Dina's house in a carriage. It was a small place. The arrival of a rich man in a big carriage embarrassed the inmates. We too were embarrassed. That day Dina's son was being invested with the sacred thread. The house was crowded, and there was hardly any place for Dina to receive us. We were about to enter a side room, when someone cried out: "Please don't go into that room. There are ladies there". It was really a distressing situation. Returning, Mathur Babu said, "Father, I shall never listen to you again". I laughed'.[25]

Swami Turiyananda once told the following story about a strange experience Mathur had while riding in his carriage with Sri Ramakrishna. It shows how even the subtle thoughts of Sri Ramakrishna could produce an effect in the gross plane.

One day Mathur Babu was returning to Jan Bazar in his deluxe phaeton and was bringing Sri Ramakrishna with him. When the carriage reached Chitpore Road, the Master had a wonderful vision. He felt that he had become Sita and that Ravana was kidnapping him. Seized by this idea, he merged into samadhi. Just then the horses, tearing loose from their reins, stumbled and fell. Mathur Babu could not understand the reason for such a mishap. When Sri Ramakrishna came back to the normal plane of consciousness, Mathur told him about the accident. Sri Ramakrishna then said that while he was in ecstasy he had perceived that Ravana was kidnapping him and that Jatayu [the great bird who had attempted to rescue Sita] was attacking Ravana's chariot and was trying to destroy it. After hearing this story Mathur Babu said, 'Father, how difficult it is even to go with you through the street!'[26]

The same year that Sri Ramakrishna practised madhura bhava, Mathur held a large celebration at the time of the Durga Puja and brought the Master to his Calcutta home. This celebration includes an elaborate and expensive ritualistic worship done with a clay image, which is immersed in the nearest river or lake when the worship is over. During the festival the Master was most of the time in an ecstatic mood. He would usually sit next to the priest while the worship was being performed. Once, when the priest was offering food to the deity, the Master started eating from the plate. The priest was shocked because such a thing is considered blasphemy, but Mathur was happy. He was convinced that it was the Divine Mother who took the food through the Master.[27]

One evening at this time the Master was in deep samadhi in the women's section of the house. He was then wearing women's clothes. Jagadamba wanted to attend the vesper service, but she was reluctant to leave the Master by himself as once before he had fallen onto a pan of live charcoal while in ecstasy and had been badly burned. Like her husband, she had tremendous love and regard for Sri Ramakrishna. Suddenly, out of inspiration, she thought of a way to bring the Master to outer consciousness. Putting some of her precious jewellery on him, she began to say: 'Father, it's time to wave the lights. Won't you come and fan Mother Durga?' The Master slowly regained normal consciousness and went with Jagadamba to the shrine. Mathur noticed from a distance that an unknown aristocratic woman was standing near his wife and fanning the image. When the vesper service was over he asked his wife about the lady. Jagadamba smiled and said: 'You didn't know? That was Father'. 'No one can know Father', said Mathur, 'if he doesn't allow himself to be known'.[28]

Mathur and his family were carried along on a current of bliss during the five days of this festival. As it was coming to its conclusion, the priest sent a messenger to Mathur Babu, requesting him to say his final prayer to the Mother before the immersion ceremony. This came as a shock to Mathur. It was unbearable for him to think of disrupting that joyful festival, and he cried out: 'I won't allow anyone to immerse the image of the Mother. Let her worship be continued as it is. If anyone immerses the image against my will, it will lead to a terrible disaster — even bloodshed'.

Since everyone else was afraid to say anything more to Mathur, Jagadamba asked the Master to save the situation. Sri Ramakrishna went to Mathur's room and found him pacing back and forth with a grim face and red, tearful eyes. Seeing the Master, Mathur said: 'Father, whatever others may say, I won't allow the Mother to be immersed in the Ganga. I have ordered the worship to be continued daily. How shall I survive in this world without the Mother?' Sri Ramakrishna stroked Mathur's chest and said: 'Oh, is this what makes you afraid? Who has told you that you will have to live without the Mother? And where would she go even if you consign her image to the Ganga? Can the Mother stay away from her son? For the last three days she has accepted your worship in the puja hall, but from today she will accept your worship, sitting constantly in your heart'. That magic touch of the Master transformed Mathur's mind and convinced him that his fears were meaningless. He became happy again and the immersion ceremony was performed.[29]

Seeing Sri Ramakrishna in samadhi many times, Mathur became eager to know more about this mysterious phenomenon. He knew very well that the Master had the power to transmit samadhi to others, so one day he asked to experience it himself. At first Sri Ramakrishna tried to dissuade him from this desire, but after repeated requests from Mathur he finally said: 'Well, I'll ask Mother about it. She will do as she thinks best'.

A few days later Mathur experienced bhava samadhi (a state in which the mind is neither in the absolute plane nor in the relative plane) while at his home in Calcutta. Sri Ramakrishna described what happened next: 'He sent for me; and when I went there I found him altogether changed — he wasn't the same man. Whenever he spoke of God, he shed floods of tears. His eyes were red from weeping, and his heart was pounding. When he saw me, he fell down and clasped my feet. ''Father'', he said, ''I admit it — I'm beaten! I've been in this state for the past three days. I can't apply my mind to worldly affairs, however hard I try. Everything is going wrong. Please take back the ecstasy you gave me. I don't want it''. ''But you begged me for ecstasy'', I said. ''I know I did. And it is indeed a blissful state — but what's the use of bliss when all my worldly affairs are going to pieces? This ecstasy of yours, Father, it only suits you. The rest of us don't really want it. Please take it back!'' Then I laughed and just rubbed Mathur's chest with my hand and he was himself again'.[30]

Mathur had a family priest named Chandra Haldar who was very jealous of Sri Ramakrishna because of Mathur's devotion to him. He was convinced that Sri Ramakrishna held some charm over Mathur, and he wanted to know his secret. One evening Sri Ramakrishna was lying in a state of ecstasy in Mathur's Calcutta residence. There was no one else in the room and Chandra found his opportunity. Shaking the Master several times, he demanded: 'Hey, tell me, how did you capture Mathur Babu? Don't pretend you can't talk! How did you hypnotize him?' The Master could not speak because his mind was not in the physical plane of consciousness. But this made Chandra extremely angry. 'So you won't tell me, you scoundrel!' he cried. Kicking the Master three times, he left the room in disgust.

Sri Ramakrishna said nothing about this incident to Mathur at that time. Later Chandra was dismissed for some other reason, and one day, in the course of conversation, Sri Ramakrishna told Mathur what Chandra had done to him. Mathur became furious and said, 'Father, if I had known that then, he would have been killed'.[31]

On January 27, 1868, Mathur and Jagadamba left on a pilgrimage to the main holy places of northwestern India with a party of about one hundred and twenty-five people, including the Master and Hriday. One second-class and three third-class railroad cars had been reserved for them with an arrangement with the railroad company that they could be detached at any station. Mathur spent over one hundred thousand rupees on this pilgrimage.

The party first stopped for a few days at Deoghar to visit a famous shrine of Shiva. One day Sri Ramakrishna was overcome with compassion, seeing the miserable condition of the people in a nearby village. He said to Mathur: 'You are a steward of Mother's estate. Give these poor people one piece of cloth and one good meal each, and also some oil for their heads'. But Mathur was reluctant. He said: 'Father, this pilgrimage is going to cost a great deal, and there are many people here. If I give them what you ask I may find myself short of money later'. Sri Ramakrishna cried bitterly. 'You wretch!' he said. 'I'm not going to Varanasi. I'm staying here with these people. They have no one to care for them. I won't leave them'. Mathur, of course, yielded. He had cloth brought from Calcutta and fulfilled all of the Master's other requests. Then they continued their journey to Varanasi.[32]

Along the way, however, there was one slight mishap. At a station near Varanasi, Sri Ramakrishna and Hriday got off the train for a few minutes, and it left without them. Mathur became very upset. He sent a wire from Varanasi that they should be sent there by the next train. But soon afterwards an official of the railway company happened to come there by a special train and cordially offered them a ride with him to Varanasi.

Mathur rented two houses on the Kedarghat, near the Kedarnath temple in Varanasi, and lived there in a royal style. Whenever he went out to visit the temples, a servant would hold a silver umbrella over his head. Since he knew that Sri Ramakrishna might fall while going into ecstasy, Mathur thoughtfully arranged to have a palanquin carry him so that he could visit the temples with ease. One day Mathur gave a feast to the local brahmins and also presented them with gifts. The Master noticed how those pandits quarrelled among themselves for petty things. Mathur also began indulging in worldly conversation with another landlord. All this worldliness greatly pained Sri Ramakrishna, and he wished that he were back in Dakshineswar.

On another day Mathur took Sri Ramakrishna on a boat trip for a view of the city from the Ganga. As they approached the Manikarnika cremation ground, Sri Ramakrishna had a vision. He rushed to the edge of the boat and then went into samadhi. The boatmen were afraid that he would fall and they ran to catch him, but the Master stood there motionless. Mathur and Hriday stood by him without touching him. Sri Ramakrishna later described his vision: The Divine Mother was sitting next to the funeral pyre, untying the knots that bound the soul to the world, while Shiva was whispering in the ear of the departed person a mantram giving immediate liberation. The pandits were amazed when they heard about this vision, which went beyond even the description in the scriptures.[33]

After a week in Varanasi, the party went to Allahabad for a few days and bathed in the holy confluence of the Ganga and the Jamuna, and then returned to Varanasi. Next, they went to Vrindaban, the playground of Krishna. Here, too, Mathur arranged to have a palanquin take Sri Ramakrishna to the holy places. He also gave away large sums of money in charity. Ganga Mata, a highly revered Vaishnava woman who lived in Vrindaban, believed that Sri Ramakrishna was an Incarnation of Radha. She wanted the Master to live there also and almost convinced him to stay. Mathur was heartsick. He did not know how he could return to Calcutta without the Master. However, Sri Ramakrishna finally changed his mind when he remembered that his old mother, Chandra, was living in Dakshineswar.

The pilgrims again returned to Varanasi, after two weeks in Vrindaban, and stayed until the end of May. Mathur wanted to visit Gaya on the way back, but the Master refused to go. He knew about his father's vision at Gaya and the mysterious nature of his birth, and he was convinced that if he went there he would become merged in his divine origin and leave the body before his mission was accomplished. After four months the party returned to Calcutta.

It was hard for Mathur to live without Sri Ramakrishna's holy company, so wherever he went he took the Master with him. Once they took a pleasant boat trip on the Ganga to visit one of Mathur's estates near Ranaghat, in West Bengal. At Ranaghat Sri Ramakrishna was overwhelmed with grief when he saw the miserable condition of the villagers, and he asked Mathur to feed and clothe them. At first Mathur was reluctant, but later he carried out the Master's wishes. During this excursion they also visited Mathur's birthplace at Khulna, where they stayed a few weeks. From there they returned to Calcutta.

In 1870 Mathur took the Master by boat to visit Navadwip, the birthplace of Chaitanya. On the way they stopped at Kalna, in the district of Burdwan, where they met Bhagavan Das, a Vaishnava saint. Mathur donated some money to Bhagavan Das's ashram to have a special festival held on an auspicious day.

For fourteen years Mathur moved with Sri Ramakrishna like a shadow, and as a result a great transformation came over his life. His haughtiness and pride of wealth and learning slowly left him through the Master's spiritual influence. His deep love and regard for Sri Ramakrishna gradually brought his mind to a higher state.

Once Mathur had a large abscess and was bedridden for a long time in his Calcutta residence. He desperately wanted to see the Master, but Sri Ramakrishna would not come. The Master told the messengers that he had no power to cure the abscess, so his visit would be of no avail. At last, after repeated requests from Mathur, he came. When Mathur saw him he said, 'Father, give me a little dust of your feet'.

Sri Ramakrishna: 'What good will it do? Will it cure your abscess?'

Mathur: 'Father, am I so mean? Do you think I want the dust of your feet to cure my abscess? Doctors are there for that purpose. I want the dust of your feet in order to cross the ocean of maya'.

Hearing this, Sri Ramakrishna merged into samadhi. Mathur then put his head on the feet of the Master and received his blessing. He recovered a short time later.[34]

Once, while in an ecstatic mood, Sri Ramakrishna said to Mathur, 'As long as you are alive I shall be in Dakshineswar'. Mathur was startled to hear that because he knew it was the Divine Mother herself who was protecting not only him, but his family also. He humbly said: 'Why do you say so, Father? My wife and son Dwaraka are also very much devoted to you'. 'All right', said the Master, 'I shall remain as long as your wife and Dwaraka live'.[35] And, as a matter of fact, they had all passed away by the time Sri Ramakrishna left Dakshineswar in 1885.

Soon Mathur's part in Sri Ramakrishna's divine drama came to an end. On July 14, 1871, he died of typhoid fever after a short illness. Sri Ramakrishna did not go to see him while he was ill but sent Hriday every day except the last. That day Mathur was taken to Kalighat, a holy place in South Calcutta. Sri Ramakrishna meanwhile became absorbed in deep samadhi in his room for a couple of hours while his spirit went forth to help Mathur attain the goal. At five o'clock Sri Ramakrishna came out of samadhi and said to Hriday, 'The companions of the Divine Mother took Mathur with love and care into their celestial chariot and his soul has ascended to the sphere of the Mother [Deviloka]'. Later that night the news reached Dakshineswar that Mathur had passed away just at five o'clock.[36]

Mathur's service to the Master is now a legend. In later years Sri

Ramakrishna was never tired of telling the devotees about him. Once one of the devotees asked the Master: 'Sir, what became of Mathur after death? Surely he wouldn't have to be born again, would he?' The Master replied: 'Perhaps he has been born as a king somewhere. He still had a desire for enjoyment'. Then he changed the subject.[37]

But no matter what happened to Mathur after his death, he undoubtedly loved and served the Master with all his heart. And, more important, he realized who the Master was. Once he said to Sri Ramakrishna, 'Father, there is nothing inside you but God'.[38]

Sri Ramakrishna standing in ecstasy during a *kirtan* at Keshab Sen's house
in Calcutta. He is surrounded by Brahmo devotees, with Hriday,
his nephew, supporting him.
(Photo taken on September 21, 1879)

3

Hridayram Mukhopadhyay

The birth, life, and actions of an avatar are divine and therefore inscrutable to the ordinary mind. Moreover, avatars do not seek publicity or write autobiographies. They love to remain hidden, carrying out their missions in an inconspicuous way. From time to time they may tell the stories about their early struggles and experiences to close disciples. Only in this way do people come to know about their divine lives. It is extremely important for the seekers of God to know of the avatar's detailed personal life — his quest for the Infinite, his spiritual struggles and fulfillment. Unfortunately, very little is known about the spiritual quest of Krishna, Buddha, Christ, or Chaitanya.

However, M., the recorder of *The Gospel of Sri Ramakrishna*, heard directly from the Master about his spiritual journey, and what he heard he published almost verbatim in the *Gospel*. Swami Saradananda, a monastic disciple of Sri Ramakrishna, wrote *Sri Ramakrishna, The Great Master*, an authentic and authoritative biography of the Master. He himself witnessed many incidents in Sri Ramakrishna's life. He also heard directly from the Master about many episodes and spiritual experiences of his early life, and he collected still other incidents from those persons who had been eyewitnesses. While writing the second part of *The Great Master* (Sri Ramakrishna 'As the Spiritual Aspirant'), Swami Saradananda was helped tremendously by Hridayram Mukhopadhyay, who was with the Master almost constantly for twenty-five years (1855-1881).

Hriday was a grandson of Sri Ramakrishna's paternal aunt and was therefore a cousin of the Master, or according to the Hindu view of relationships, a nephew. He was four years younger than Sri Ramakrishna, so it seems he was born in 1840. His birthplace, Sihar, was only four miles from Kamarpukur, where Sri Ramakrishna was born. As a boy, Sri Ramakrishna often visited Sihar, and thus he and Hriday knew each other well. In 1852 Sri Ramakrishna moved to Calcutta and then in 1855 to Dakshineswar. When Hriday was about

37

sixteen, he tried but failed to get a job at Burdwan, a town near his village. When he found out that his maternal uncle, Ramkumar, had been appointed priest in the new temple of Rani Rasmani in Dakshineswar, he went there without delay. Sri Ramakrishna was delighted to see Hriday, his boyhood companion.

Hriday was tall, handsome, and muscular. He was also bold, good-humoured, and extremely energetic. Hard work did not bother him. Highly resourceful, he easily adapted himself to changing circumstances, often inventing unique solutions when faced with problems. Over and above these qualities, he had genuine affection for his young uncle, Sri Ramakrishna, and spared no pains to make him happy, even at his own expense. In spite of all these good qualities, Hriday was not notably spiritual. Given the opportunity, he fully enjoyed the world, and greatly longed for worldly prosperity.

It was through Divine Providence that Hriday came back into Sri Ramakrishna's life when the Master was about to begin his spiritual journey, forgetting his body, surroundings, and everything else. During this long and arduous period Hriday became his caretaker, bodyguard, cook, nurse, companion, and adviser. Inevitably Hriday imbibed many good qualities as a result of his holy association with the Master. Sri Ramakrishna said many times that without Hriday it would have been impossible for him to protect his body during the period of his spiritual disciplines. For this wonderful selfless service Hriday will always be gratefully remembered by Sri Ramakrishna's followers.

Hriday later described his feelings for Sri Ramakrishna: 'Many a time I felt an indescribable attraction towards the Master, and I always remained with him like a shadow. Even a moment's separation from him was painful to me'.[1] Before his acceptance of the post of priest, Sri Ramakrishna used to cook his own meal under the Panchavati tree with Hriday's help. But Hriday would take his lunch in the temple kitchen. Then at night they would take prasad of the Divine Mother together. After lunch, Hriday observed that the Master would invariably disappear for a couple of hours, and he would search for his uncle here and there. When asked later about where he had gone, Sri Ramakrishna would answer, 'I was just near about this place'. One day Hriday found the Master coming from the direction of the Panchavati grove, so he thought perhaps he had gone there to answer calls of nature and did not question him anymore.[2]

Rasmani and Mathur were eager to engage Sri Ramakrishna for temple service, but when the offer was made to him through his brother Ramkumar, the Master declined, saying, 'I will not serve anyone but God'.[3]

Ramkumar was more than thirty years older than Sri Ramakrishna, and gradually it became difficult for him to manage the worship of the Divine Mother alone. This provided Mathur with an excuse to request the Master to help his brother. One day Sri Ramakrishna and Hriday were walking in the temple garden. Seeing them from a distance, Mathur sent a messenger to Sri Ramakrishna with a request that he come and see Mathur. Knowing what was in Mathur's mind, the Master told Hriday, 'As soon as I go there, he will ask me to remain here and take service'. Hriday asked: 'What is the harm in that? It can only be good to be appointed to work under a great man in such a holy place. Why are you reluctant?' The Master replied: 'I have no intention of being tied down to service all my life. Besides, if I agree to perform the worship here, I will have to be responsible for the ornaments on the goddess. That is a difficult task, and it will not be possible for me. But if you stayed here and took that responsibility, then I would have no objection to performing the worship'. Hriday had originally come to Dakshineswar seeking a job, so he gladly agreed.[4]

Sri Ramakrishna then went to Mathur and when the latter requested that he work in the Kali temple, he consented on the condition that Hriday would take care of the ornaments. Mathur agreed to this condition, and from that day, Sri Ramakrishna started the dressing of the Divine Mother with Hriday taking responsibility for the jewellery. Within three months of the temple dedication at Dakshineswar, an accident took place in the Krishna temple when the priest fell while carrying the image, breaking one of Krishna's legs. Immediately the priest was discharged and Sri Ramakrishna was appointed to worship Krishna. Hriday had to take on the Master's duty in addition to his own. Within a year Sri Ramakrishna became the priest of the Kali temple, and Hriday was transferred to the Krishna temple.

Hriday used to say that the Master's worship was an event worth seeing. Indeed, whoever saw it was amazed. Sri Ramakrishna would sing in his sweet, melodious voice with exuberant devotion. While singing, profuse tears would flow from his eyes. Those who heard these songs could never forget them. At the time of worship the Master became so absorbed that he would be totally unaware of anyone who approached him or called him.[5]

In 1856 Ramkumar died suddenly. He had been like a father to Sri Ramakrishna, and his death was a terrible shock. The fire of renunciation was kindled in the Master's mind, and he realized the transitoriness of the world. He became indifferent to food and sleep.

When the door of the temple was closed at midday and at night, he went off by himself, entered the jungle around the Panchavati, and spent his time in contemplation of the Mother of the Universe. This worried Hriday. He was very fond of his young uncle and thought that if the Master passed sleepless nights, he would not be able to stand the hard labour involved in the divine service in the temple.

One night Hriday followed Sri Ramakrishna without his knowledge and saw him enter the jungle near the Panchavati. He knew that if he went near him the Master would be annoyed, so in order to frighten him, he threw stones into the bushes. Finding that this did not bring the Master back, he returned to his room. The next day Hriday asked the Master, 'What do you do when you enter the jungle at night?' 'I meditate there', replied Sri Ramakrishna, 'under an amalaki tree. The scriptures say that if anybody meditates desiring something under an amalaki tree, his desire is fulfilled'. Hriday continued to throw stones as usual but could not deter the Master from passing the nights in meditation in the jungle.[6]

One night Hriday mustered his courage, determined to see for himself what was going on in the dead of night in the jungle. He was startled to find his uncle seated under the tree in deep meditation, without clothes or sacred thread. He thought, 'Has Uncle gone mad?' He then called to him desperately: 'Uncle, what is this? Why have you taken off your cloth and the sacred thread?' At first there was no answer. Then, having regained outer consciousness, Sri Ramakrishna answered: 'Why, don't you know that this is the way one should think of God, free of all ties? From our very birth we have the eightfold fetters of hatred, shame, lineage, pride of good conduct, fear, secretiveness, caste, and grief. This sacred thread means that I am a brahmin and therefore superior to all. When calling upon the Mother, one has to set aside such ideas. So I have removed the sacred thread, which I shall put on after I have finished meditation'. Hriday was dumbfounded and quietly left the place.[7]

Later on, after his first vision of Kali, Sri Ramakrishna lived in a state of God-intoxication. Hriday was puzzled watching the astonishing behaviour of the Master. He used to say: 'You felt awestruck when you entered the Kali temple in those days, even when Uncle wasn't there — and much more so when he was. Yet I couldn't resist the temptation of seeing how he acted at the time of the worship. As long as I was actually watching him, my heart was full of reverence and devotion; but when I came out of the temple, I began to have doubts and would ask myself: "Has Uncle really gone mad? Why else should he do such terrible things during the worship?'' I was afraid of what the Rani and Mathur Babu would say when they came to hear of it. But Uncle never worried...I didn't venture to speak to him much any longer; my mouth was closed by a fear I can't describe. I felt that there was some kind of barrier between us. So I just looked after him in silence, as best as I could. But I was afraid he would make a scene someday'.[8]

About Sri Ramakrishna's method of worship, Hriday said: 'I would notice that Uncle, taking flowers and bel leaves in his hand, touched his own head, chest, in fact the whole body, including the feet, with them and then offered them at the feet of Kali.[9] I saw how Uncle's chest and eyes were always red like those of a drunkard. He'd get up reeling from the worshipper's seat, climb onto the altar, and caress the Divine Mother, touching her affectionately under the chin. He'd begin singing, laughing, joking, and talking with her, or sometimes he'd catch hold of her hands and dance.

'I saw how, when he was offering cooked food to the Divine Mother, he'd suddenly get up, take a morsel of rice and curry from the plate in his hand, touch the Mother's mouth with it, and say: "Eat it, Mother. Do eat it!" Then maybe he'd say: "You want me to eat it — and then you'll eat some afterwards? All right, I'm eating it now". Then he'd take some of it himself and put the rest to her lips again, saying: "I've had some. Now you eat".

'One day, at the time of the food offering, Uncle saw a cat. It had come into the temple, mewing. He fed it with the food which was to be offered to the Divine Mother. "Will you take it, Mother?" he said to the cat'.[10]

Actions such as these are deemed sacrilegious in Hindu ritual. Gradually the temple officials came to know about the apparently deranged behaviour of Sri Ramakrishna, and they sent a message of complaint to Mathur in Calcutta. One day he arrived unannounced at the temple, and what he saw convinced him that the Master was not insane but living in a higher plane of consciousness. However, Sri Ramakrishna could not continue the daily ritualistic worship in that state of divine intoxication. One day Mathur and Hriday were present while he was worshipping in the Kali temple. Suddenly the Master in ecstasy rose from his seat and said to Mathur: 'Hriday will perform the worship from now on. Mother says that she will accept his worship in the same manner as mine'.[11] The devout Mathur accepted the words of the Master as a command of the Mother.

Sri Ramakrishna had now reached a point where he was being swept away by a spiritual tempest. Both Mathur and Hriday worried about him. Mathur brought in the best physicians of Calcutta to treat his unusual symptoms — a burning sensation, sleeplessness, excessive gas, etc. — but they could not help him. One wise physician did mention that the Master had a yogic disease. Then in 1858 Sri Ramakrishna went to Kamarpukur for a visit. His mother and brother, thinking it would steady his mind, arranged his marriage, which took place in 1859.

In 1861 Bhairavi Brahmani, a sannyasini (nun), came to Dakshineswar to initiate Sri Ramakrishna into Tantric disciplines. She was in her late thirties and extremely beautiful. Seeing her at the chandni (bathing ghat), the Master returned to his room and asked Hriday to call her to him. Hriday was rather surprised, for he had never before seen his uncle eager to speak to any strange woman. He said: 'She is a stranger. Why should she come even if invited?' 'Go and tell her my name, and she will come', replied the Master.[12] Hriday brought the Bhairavi to Sri Ramakrishna and was amazed when she burst into tears of joy and surprise, as if she had at last found her long-lost treasure. Sri Ramakrishna was also moved.

In 1863 Sri Ramakrishna completed his Tantric sadhana with the help of Bhairavi Brahmani, and then began some Vaishnava sadhanas, such as *vatsalya bhava* (affectionate attitude towards God) and *madhura bhava* (wife-husband attitude towards God). When Sri Ramakrishna was practising madhura bhava, he dressed like a woman. He considered himself to be Radha, a gopi, and became completely absorbed in the thought of Krishna. 'One day during this time', said Hriday, 'Mathur took me into the women's quarters of his Calcutta residence and said, "Can you tell me which of them is your uncle?" And although I'd been living with him so long and serving him daily, I couldn't, at first. Uncle used to collect flowers every morning in the garden of Dakshineswar, with a basket. We'd watch him and we'd notice that he always stepped out left foot first as a woman does'.[13]

In 1864 Tota Puri, a Vedanta monk, having stopped at Dakshineswar in the course of his travels, initiated Sri Ramakrishna into sannyasa (monastic vows). The Master attained nirvikalpa samadhi (the highest nondualistic experience) within three days and remained in that mood for six months. One day Sri Ramakrishna was at the chandni, watching the Ganga in an ecstatic mood. Two boats were at the ghat and the boatmen were quarrelling over something. Suddenly the stronger one gave the weaker one a heavy blow on the back. Sri Ramakrishna immediately cried out in pain. Hriday heard it from the Kali temple, came running, and saw that the Master's back had become red and swollen. Beside himself with anger, Hriday repeatedly said, 'Uncle, show me the man who has beaten you; I will chop off his head'. After a while when the Master calmed down a little, Hriday was amazed to hear from him how he felt the pain and got the marks on his back from the boatmen's fight.[14] This incident illustrates Sri Ramakrishna's experience of oneness, which is the goal of Vedanta.

In 1867 Sri Ramakrishna went to Kamarpukur with the Bhairavi and Hriday. Through the years the Bhairavi had grown egotistic, thinking she was the teacher of Sri Ramakrishna, and she tried to control him by keeping his wife away from him. Then, when she started to disrupt the social customs of the village, the villagers became upset. At this point Hriday asked the Bhairavi to leave Kamarpukur, and a furious quarrel ensued. Later on, the Bhairavi understood her mistake, and begging forgiveness from Sri Ramakrishna, she left for Varanasi.

While at Kamarpukur Sri Ramakrishna visited Sihar, Hriday's village. Hriday invited some well-known Vaishnava devotees to meet Sri Ramakrishna and hold religious discourses with him. His mother, Hemangini Devi, revered Sri Ramakrishna as her Chosen Deity and worshipped his feet with flowers. One day she prayed to the Master for a boon so that she could die in the holy city of Varanasi. In a state of samadhi, the Master blessed her with that boon and later she actually died in Varanasi.[15]

After spending seven months in Kamarpukur, Sri Ramakrishna returned to Dakshineswar with Hriday via Burdwan. Then in 1868 Sri Ramakrishna and Hriday went to Deoghar, Varanasi, Prayag, Vrindaban, and other holy places with Mathur and his family. In Varanasi they took a boat trip one day, and while the boat was passing near the Manikarnika ghat, Sri Ramakrishna had a vision of Shiva. He stood near the edge of the boat and went into samadhi. The boatman, fearing that the Master might fall into the Ganga, cried to Hriday, 'Catch hold of him! Catch hold of him!'[16] Immediately Hriday and Mathur jumped up to keep the Master from falling.

From Varanasi the party went to Vrindaban. From there Sri Ramakrishna went to visit Mount Govardhan, Shyamkunda, and Radhakunda by palanquin. On the way the Master wept bitterly, saying: 'O Krishna! Everything here is as it was in the olden days. You alone are absent'.[17] Hriday followed him and warned the bearers to be careful about the Master.

In Vrindaban, Gangamayi, an old Vaishnava woman saint, saw Sri Ramakrishna as an embodiment of Radha. She persuaded the Master to stay at Vrindaban and offered to serve him. This turn of events

worried Mathur and Hriday. One day Hriday decided to drag the
Master away from the place, and took hold of his hand. But
Gangamayi caught hold of the other hand. At that moment the
Master remembered his own mother living alone at Dakshineswar, so
he said to her, 'No, I must go'.[18]

In 1870 Mathur, Sri Ramakrishna, and Hriday set out by boat to
visit Navadwip, Chaitanya's birthplace. On the way they stopped at
Kalna, near Burdwan, where the Master and Hriday met Bhagavan
Das, a Vaishnava saint.

During the Master's twelve years of sadhana Hriday was his
faithful attendant, and later, wherever the Master went, he followed
as his bodyguard and companion. Hriday was a down-to-earth
person with little sentiment in his heart. His main concerns were the
prosperity of his little family and as much enjoyment of life as
possible. Constant association with Sri Ramakrishna at times created
a little sattva (spiritual) quality in his mind, but it never lasted long.

Shortly after their return from the pilgrimage in 1868, Hriday's wife
died, and as a result his outlook on life changed. Passion was
transformed into dispassion and he yearned for God. He began to
worship the Divine Mother more intensely and meditated now and
then, casting off his cloth and holy thread as the Master had done. He
also tried to persuade Sri Ramakrishna to give him visions and
mystical experiences. The Master kept assuring him that this was
unnecesary in his case, but when Hriday insisted, he said: 'All right.
Let Mother's will be done. My wish is of no avail. It was she who
revolutionized my mind and made me pass through all these stages
of realization. If she wills, you too shall have them'.[19]

A few days later Hriday began to have visions and even
occasionally experience the stage of semi-consciousness during
meditation and worship. One day, seeing Hriday in that state,
Mathur asked the Master, 'What is going on, Father?' Sri
Ramakrishna replied: 'Hriday is not feigning these states. He
earnestly prayed to the Mother for some visions and this is the result.
She will very soon calm him down'. 'No, Father', said Mathur with a
smile, 'this is all your play. You have put Hriday in that state. Now
please bring him down so that we may both serve you. These
spiritual states are not for us'.[20]

One night Hriday saw Sri Ramakrishna going towards the
Panchavati. Thinking that the Master needed his waterpot and towel,
Hriday took them and followed him. Suddenly he saw a wonderful
sight. His uncle's ordinary human body was transformed into a
luminous form which radiated light in all directons. The shining feet

did not touch the earth at all. Hriday rubbed his eyes again and again to make sure it was not a hallucination. He looked around and found that the Ganga, the trees, and the cottage were as usual, but he repeatedly saw the Master in that luminous form. Hriday then looked down at his own body and saw that it, too, was shining and full of light, and he became aware that this light was no other than the light which formed Sri Ramakrishna. He experienced that he was a part and parcel of that luminous God, but he now had a separate entity in order to serve him. This revelation overwhelmed him with joy, and forgetting himself and his surroundings he shouted frantically again and again: 'O Ramakrishna, we are not men. Why are we here? Let us go from place to place and save human beings from bondage. You and I are the same!'[21]

Sri Ramakrishna immediately turned to him and begged him to be silent. He told Hriday that if he continued shouting that way the people of the temple garden would come running to see what was wrong. But Hriday did not stop. Sri Ramakrishna then touched his chest and prayed, 'Mother, make this rascal dull and stupid again'. Immediately Hriday lost that vision and joy. He came down with a jolt into the worldly plane. Sobbing, he protested: 'Why did you do that to me, Uncle? You've taken that blissful vision away from me. Now I'll never have it again!'

'I didn't say you would never have it again', Sri Ramakrishna told him. 'I only wanted to calm you down. You were making such a fuss over that little vision of yours — that's why I had to ask Mother to make you dull. If you only knew how many visions I have every day! And do I raise such a racket? You're not ready for visions yet. The time will come for them'.[22]

Hriday became pacified for the time being, but he felt terribly hurt. Privately he resolved to get back his visions and experiences. So he went to the Panchavati alone at dead of night and sat down for meditation in the same spot where Sri Ramakrishna was accustomed to meditating. Fortunately for Hriday, Sri Ramakrishna soon felt an impulse to go to the Panchavati. Scarcely had he reached it when he heard Hriday calling out piteously to him: 'Uncle, save me! I'm being burned to death!' The Master rushed to Hriday and asked, 'What is the matter?' 'Uncle, no sooner had I sat down here to meditate', replied Hriday, 'than it was as if a plate of live charcoal had been thrown right over me! Oh, the pain is unbearable!' Sri Ramakrishna then gently stroked his nephew's body, cooling it at once. 'You will feel all right again', said Sri Ramakrishna. 'Tell me, why do you do all these things? Didn't I tell you that you will gain everything by serving me?' After that Hriday never went back to the Panchavati for meditation.[23]

In spite of the Master's reassurances, Hriday longed for more spiritual adventure, a longing which later proved to be his undoing. Sri Ramakrishna narrated for his disciples how a monk once came to Dakshineswar who was drunk with divine knowledge. He looked like a ghoul — almost naked, with dust all over his head and body, and long hair and nails. He stood in front of the Kali temple, fixed his eyes on the image, and recited a hymn with such power that the temple seemed to shake. He was not allowed to eat with the other monks and pilgrims because of his dirty appearance, so he went to the garbage heap and shared the leftover scraps with the dogs. Recognizing his high spiritual state, Sri Ramakrishna went to Hriday's room and told him about the monk.

Immediately Hriday ran to see the unusual monk and found that he was leaving the garden. He followed him a long way and kept asking, 'Holy sir, please teach me how I can realize God'. At first the monk didn't answer, but at last he said to Hriday, pointing to the sewer water around a drain in the road, 'When this water and the water of the Ganga seem equally pure to you, then you will realize God'. Hriday said, 'Sir, please make me your disciple and take me with you'. But the monk did not reply. He went on. Again, when he looked back and saw Hriday still following him, he made an angry face and picked up a brick, threatening to throw it at Hriday. When Hriday fled, he dropped the brick, left the road, and disappeared.[24]

Hriday was a person of exceptional energy and activity, and it was hard for him to be satisfied with only the regular routine of daily temple duties. In 1868 he decided to celebrate the Durga Puja in the new shrine in his home. Sri Ramakrishna gave his approval and Mathur gave Hriday the necessary money. Hriday wanted the Master to go with him, but Mathur insisted that Sri Ramakrishna attend the worship in his Calcutta home. The Master comforted Hriday, saying: 'Don't grieve. I shall be there in a subtle body every day to watch your worship. You alone will see me. Get another brahmin to read out the mantras to you and conduct the worship in your own fashion. Don't fast altogether, but take milk, Ganga water, and rock candy syrup at noon. If you follow my instructions, the Divine Mother will certainly accept your worship'.[25]

Hriday went home with a joyous heart and performed the worship accordingly for three days. Each day during the time of vespers, and at the time of the sandhi puja (a special worship held between the second and third days of worship), he was astonished to see the

Master in a shining body by the side of the image. Shortly afterwards he returned to Dakshineswar and told the Master what he had seen. Sri Ramakrishna admitted: 'Yes, at the time of the vesper service and again at the sandhi puja time, I was very eager to watch your worship. In samadhi I felt myself carried along a path of light, and was present at your shrine in a luminous form'.[26] Once in an ecstatic mood, Sri Ramakrishna had told Hriday to worship Mother Durga three times. Disregarding the Master's words, he secretly tried to celebrate the worship a fourth time but a series of obstacles baffled his plans.[27]

In spite of all the spiritual experiences and visions Hriday had had by the grace of Sri Ramakrishna, he was basically a family person. Shortly after the first year's Durga celebration, he married a second time and again devoted himself to the worship of Kali and the service of his uncle in Dakshineswar. Yet even while working as a priest in the temple, his thoughts were on his wife and home. Sri Ramakrishna told this incident to his devotees:

> Once Hriday brought a bull-calf here. I saw, one day, that he tied it with a rope in the garden, so that it might graze there. I asked him, 'Hriday, why do you tie the calf there every day?' 'Uncle', he said, 'I am going to send this calf to our village. When it grows strong I shall yoke it to the plough'. As soon as I heard these words I was stunned to think: 'How inscrutable is the play of the divine maya! Kamarpukur and Sihar are so far away from Calcutta! This poor calf must go all that way. Then it will grow, and at length it will be yoked to the plough. This is indeed the world! This is indeed maya!' I fell down unconscious. Only after a long time did I regain consciousness.[28]

Lust and gold are maya. They are the two great obstacles to God-realization. In the beginning of his spiritual sadhana, Sri Ramakrishna took money in one hand and clay in the other, and through discrimination he came to the conclusion that both are the same. He then threw both into the Ganga.[29] Hriday did not like this action of the Master's. He had tremendous greed for money. He used to flatter the rich devotees of Sri Ramakrishna and would try to exploit them at the expense of his uncle. Once Mathur wanted to give the Master an estate and consulted Hriday about it. Sri Ramakrishna overheard the whole discussion and said to him: 'Please don't harbour any such thought. It will injure me greatly'.[30]

Temptation is the test of renunciation. All great teachers of the world have had to face temptation. Sri Ramakrishna was no exception. Hriday once conspired secretly with Lakshminarayan

Marwari to get ten thousand rupees. Sri Ramakrishna later told the
following story:

Lakshminarayan Marwari, a Vedantist, used to come here
[Dakshineswar] very often. One day he saw a dirty sheet on my
bed and said: 'I shall invest ten thousand rupees in your name.
The interest will enable you to pay your expenses'. The moment he
uttered these words, I fell unconscious, as if struck by a stick.
Regaining consciousness I said to him: 'If you utter such words
again, you had better not come here. It is impossible for me to
touch money. It is also impossible for me to keep it near
me'...Lakshminarayan then wanted to leave the money with
Hriday. I said to him: 'That will not do. If you leave it with Hriday,
then I shall instruct him to spend it as I wish. If he does not
comply, I shall be angry. The very contact of money is bad. No,
you can't leave it with Hriday'.[31]

Sri Ramakrishna was simple and guileless like a child. Therefore
whatever he was told, he believed wholeheartedly. Hriday knew
that his uncle had direct contact with the Divine Mother, and he also
knew that he could influence the Master. He used to pester him to
pray for occult powers from Mother so that he could get some benefit
from them. Sri Ramakrishna narrated his experience:

Once, a long time ago, I was very ill. I was sitting in the Kali
temple. I felt like praying to the Divine Mother to cure my illness,
but couldn't do so directly in my own name. I said to Her,
'Mother, Hriday asks me to tell You about my illness'. I could not
proceed any farther. At once there flashed into my mind the
Museum of the Asiatic Society, and a human skeleton strung
together with wire. I said to Her, 'Please tighten the wire of my
body like that, so that I may go about singing Your name and
glories'. It is impossible for me to ask for occult powers.[32]

People of small intellect seek occult powers — power to cure
disease, win a lawsuit, walk on water, and such things. But the
genuine devotees of God don't want anything except His Lotus
Feet. One day Hriday said to me, 'Uncle, please ask the Mother for
some powers, some occult powers'. I have the nature of a child.
While I was practising japa in the Kali temple, I said to Kali,
'Mother, Hriday asked me to pray to You for some occult powers'.
The Divine Mother at once showed me a vision. A middle-aged
prostitute, about forty years old, appeared and sat with her back to
me. She had large hips and wore a black-bordered sari. Soon she
was covered with filth. The Mother showed me that occult powers
are as abominable as the filth of that prostitute. Thereupon I went
to Hriday and scolded him, saying: 'Why did you teach me such a
prayer? It is because of you that I had such an experience'.[33]

Whenever Sri Ramakrishna had occasion to travel he needed a companion, because no one, including the Master himself, knew when he might go into samadhi. In such an event someone had to be ready to hold him, if necessary, to prevent him from falling. In March of 1875 Sri Ramakrishna and Hriday went to meet Keshab Chandra Sen, a famous Brahmo leader, at a garden house in Belgharia where he was conducting a retreat. They drove there in a horse carriage and arrived early in the afternoon. Hriday went alone to speak to Keshab in order to introduce his uncle. 'My uncle is a great lover of God', he said. 'He loves to hear talk and songs about the Lord. When he hears them, he goes into samadhi. He has heard that you are a great devotee, and he has come to listen to you talk about God and his glories. With your kind permission, I'll bring him to you'. Keshab of course agreed, and Hriday brought the Master to where Keshab's group was seated. At first sight, Keshab and the sceptical Brahmos saw nothing out of the ordinary in Sri Ramakrishna.

'Is it true, gentlemen', Sri Ramakrishna asked humbly, 'that you have the vision of God? I want so much to know what it's like. That's why I've come to see you'. Then the Master sang a song of Ramprasad: 'Who knows what Kali is? The six philosophies cannot explain her'. Immediately after singing, he went into samadhi.[34] The Brahmos had no concept of samadhi, so they took it as a kind of brain sickness or a trick of Sri Ramakrishna's to impress them. Hriday then started to repeat Om in the Master's ear in order to bring him back to the normal plane. Gradually the Master's face beamed with joy, and in an ecstatic mood he charmed Keshab and his disciples by telling them parables. On September 21, 1879, Sri Ramakrishna again visited Keshab, this time at his Calcutta home. There, during the time of kirtan, Sri Ramakrishna stood up and went into samadhi, and Hriday immediately held him. Keshab had a photographer take a picture of Sri Ramakrishna and Hriday, while the Master was in samadhi. This was the first photograph of the Master.

Once Sri Ramakrishna went with Hriday to Kalighat (South Calcutta) to visit the Divine Mother. On the northern side of the pond near the temple there were *kachu* shrubs. Sri Ramakrishna saw the Divine Mother there in the guise of a girl, wearing a red-bordered cloth. She was playing with some other girls, catching grasshoppers. Seeing her, the Master cried out, 'Mother, O Mother!' and lost all outer consciousness. Coming back to normal consciousness, he went inside the temple and found the same cloth on the image of the Mother as she had worn while playing as a girl in the bushes. Listening to this story from the Master, Hriday asked: 'Uncle, why didn't you tell me then and there? I would have run and caught hold of her'. Sri Ramakrishna smilingly replied: 'Is it so easy? If Mother does not want to be caught, who has the power to catch her? Without her grace, nobody can see her'.[35]

On another occasion in Calcutta there was a big exhibition to which many maharajas (rulers) sent precious articles such as gold couches and ornaments for display. Some devotees talked about it with the Master. Sri Ramakrishna understood human psychology. Those who desire wealth, talk about wealth. He said to them with a smile: 'Yes, you gain much by visiting those things. You realize that those articles of gold and the other things sent by maharajas are mere trash. That is a great gain in itself. When I used to go to Calcutta with Hriday, he would show me the Viceroy's palace and say: "Look, Uncle! There is the Viceroy's palace with the big columns". The Mother revealed to me that they were merely clay bricks laid one on top of another. God and His splendour. God alone is real; the splendour has but a two-days existence'.[36]

In 1879 Sri Ramakrishna visited Kamarpukur for the last time with Hriday. On that occasion he went to Sihar and Phului Shyambazar (a few miles from Sihar) to attend a Vaishnava festival. People came from all around and stayed day and night there. Here the Master manifested the attraction of Yoga-maya. When God incarnates himself on earth, he attracts people through this power and holds them spellbound. Sri Ramakrishna later narrated: 'The rumour spread everywhere that a man had arrived who died [referring to his samadhi] seven times and came back to life again. Hriday would drag me away from the crowd to a paddy field for fear I might have an attack of heat apoplexy. The crowd would follow us there like a line of ants. Again the cymbals and the never-ending "Takuti! Takuti!" of the drums. Hriday scolded them and said: "Why do you bother us like this? Have we never heard kirtan?" '[37]

Whenever Sri Ramakrishna visited Kamarpukur, both the men and the women of his village and those from distant places would flock to him day and night. The women would bring him various kinds of sweets, fruits, and cooked food. Some would finish their household duties early so they could talk to the Master a little longer on their way to bathe in the Haldarpukur (a pond). The men generally came after the women had returned home to do their daytime cooking. Thus the Master had very little time to rest. He would make people happy with his jokes, songs, and stories. When Mathur was alive he would give money to Hriday for the Master's personal expenses, but Sri Ramakrishna would always distribute a portion of it among the poor villagers.

On one occasion Sri Ramakrishna wanted to visit Jayrambati, his father-in-law's village, which was three miles away from Kamarpukur. The Master's body was so delicate that he could not walk such a long distance, so Hriday arranged for a palanquin to carry him. After lunch that day, Sri Ramakrishna put on a scarlet silk cloth and a gold amulet around his arm. His lips were crimson from chewing betel. As he was about to get into the palanquin, he noticed that a large crowd had gathered, and he asked Hriday the reason for it. 'Well', said Hriday, 'you are going away and they won't see you for some days. They have come to have a parting look at you'. 'But they see me every day', said the Master. 'What new feature has attracted them in such large numbers today?' Then Hriday told him: 'The thing is, you look so handsome in that silken cloth, and your lips shine with a crimson colour. That is why they want to see you'. Sri Ramakrishna was shocked to hear that the people were attracted by his physical beauty, which was external and ephemeral, instead of wanting to see God within. 'What!' he exclaimed. 'People are crowding to see a man! I won't go. Wherever I may go, people will crowd about like this!' The Master returned to his room and took off the silk cloth in utter disgust. In spite of the entreaties of Hriday and others, he did not go out that day.[38] Afterwards they returned to Dakshineswar.

Hriday became a personal attendant of Sri Ramakrishna in 1855, and he devoted much of his adult life to serving his uncle with affection and loyalty. As a young man he had his faults, such as foolishness and impulsiveness, but the Master overlooked them. However, by the age of forty Hriday's character had changed. Gradually he had become a despotic, jealous, and unkind guard who behaved at times like a jailer. Anyone who wanted to see Sri Ramakrishna had to go to Hriday first and give him money, for otherwise he would not allow that person to see his uncle. When the Master came to know about this he scolded Hriday, but Hriday paid no attention and continued in his own way. He made it clear to everyone that his uncle was completely dependent on him. He would speak rudely to the Master in front of others and would laugh at him behind his back. Sometimes he would try to charm people by imitating the gestures Sri Ramakrishna made when he was in samadhi, and he would try to sing and dance just as the Master did.

Once Sri Ramakrishna was in bed with a fever. Some devotees from Calcutta came to see him, bringing a cauliflower for him. The Master was very pleased but said hastily, 'Please hide it and don't tell

Hriday, or he will abuse me'. He went on to defend Hriday, however, praising his past services and adding: 'Mother has rewarded him richly for his faithfulness. He has been able to buy some land for himself. He can afford to lend out money to people. And he's a very important personage in this temple — highly honoured'. No sooner had the Master finished saying this than Hriday entered the room and spotted the cauliflower. Sri Ramakrishna seemed dismayed, and he said to Hriday: 'Look, I never asked them to bring this to me. They brought it of their own accord. Believe me. I never asked them to!' But Hriday flew into a rage and scolded the Master severely. Sri Ramakrishna appealed to the Divine Mother, weeping, 'Mother, you freed me of all worldly ties and yet you let Hriday humiliate me like this!' Then, suddenly his melancholy mood changed, and he added with a smile: 'Hriday loves me dearly and therefore scolds me. He is a mere boy and knows not what he does. You mustn't be angry with him, Mother'. After this, he went into samadhi.[39]

Pride must have its fall, and Hriday's pride was swelling day by day. The temple officials were disgusted with his behaviour and were just waiting for a reason to dismiss him. Sri Ramakrishna knew this and kept warning Hriday to be less aggressive. In March 1881 Sarada Devi came from Jayrambati to see her husband at Dakshineswar with her mother and some neighbours. The moment they arrived Hriday treated them rudely and told Sarada Devi that she was not wanted. With tearful eyes she and her mother left for Jayrambati on the same day. Sri Ramakrishna was helpless. He was afraid to irritate Hriday and kept quiet. But later Sri Ramakrishna warned Hriday: 'Look here. You may insult me, but don't hurt her feelings. If He who dwells in this [his own body] hisses, you may somehow get by; but if He who dwells in her [Sarada Devi] hisses, no one — not even Brahma, Vishnu, or Shiva — will be able to protect you'.[40]

Soon after this incident Hriday arranged his own downfall. In May 1881 Trailokya, one of Mathur's sons, arrived at Dakshineswar with his wife and children to take part in the annual dedication festival of the temple. At one point his eight-year-old daughter — unaccompanied by her parents — was present in the Kali temple while Hriday was performing the worship. Suddenly Hriday was seized with a desire to worship the Goddess in the person of this little girl, and following the Tantric rites offered flowers and sandal paste at her feet. It was the sandal paste that betrayed Hriday. Trailokya's wife noticed it as soon as her daughter returned from the ceremony. When she heard what Hriday had done, she was horrified, for there was a superstition that if a brahmin worshipped a girl of a lower caste, she would be widowed soon after marriage. Seeing his wife crying and learning the cause, Trailokya became furious and ordered Hriday to leave the temple precincts immediately.[41]

Hriday rushed to Sri Ramakrishna and told him what had happened. He tried to persuade the Master to leave with him, but Sri Ramakrishna refused, so Hriday left the garden with a heavy heart, alone. It appeared that Trailokya, in the first flush of his rage, had made some remark against Sri Ramakrishna, implying that it would be well to get rid of him too. Accordingly, a temple official came to the Master and asked him to leave at once. Immediately the Master put a towel over his shoulder and walked out of his room towards the gate. Trailokya saw him from a distance and came rushing to him, saying, 'Sir, where are you going?' 'But didn't you want me to go away?' asked the Master. 'No, they misunderstood. I never meant that. I beg you to stay!' At this Sri Ramakrishna smiled and returned to his room, as if nothing had happened.[42]

Hriday did not go far away. He took shelter at Jadu Mallik's garden house, adjacent to the temple grounds. Sri Ramakrishna used to send meals to him and also went to see him. Hriday requested the Master again and again to leave Dakshineswar, proposing to establish a Kali temple elsewhere where the two might live happily together. But Sri Ramakrishna always refused, and Hriday finally went away to his country home to take care of his farm. Later the Master said to the devotees: 'The Divine Mother removed him from Dakshineswar. He pestered visitors for money. If he had stayed with me, all these people could not have come. That is why the Mother removed him'.[43]

On August 19, 1883, Sri Ramakrishna received a letter from Hriday which he mentioned to M.: 'You see, I am very much depressed today. Hriday has written me that he is very ill. Why should I feel dejected about it? Is it because of maya or daya?' Then the Master continued: 'Do you know what maya is? It is attachment to relatives — parents, brother and sister, wife and children, nephew and niece. Daya means love for all created beings. Now what is this, my feeling about Hriday? Is it maya or daya? But Hriday did so much for me: He served me wholeheartedly and nursed me when I was ill. But later he tormented me also. The torment became so unbearable that once I was about to commit suicide by jumping into the Ganga from the top of the embankment. But he did much to serve me. Now my mind will be at rest if he gets some money. But whom shall I ask for it? Who likes to speak about such things to our rich visitors?'[44]

On October 26, 1884, Hriday came to visit Sri Ramakrishna at Dakshineswar. M. recorded in the *Gospel*:

A man entered the room and told the Master that Hriday was waiting to see him in Jadu Mallik's garden, near the gate.

The Master said to the devotees: 'I shall have to see Hriday. Please don't leave the room'. He put on his slippers and went towards the east gate of the temple garden, M. accompanying him.

At the sight of the Master, Hriday, who had been standing there with folded hands, prostrated himself before him. When the Master told him to get up, he rose and began to cry like a child. How strange! Tears also appeared in the Master's eyes. He wiped them away with his hands. Hriday had made him suffer endless agonies, yet the Master wept for him.

Master: 'Why are you here now?'

Hriday (weeping): 'I have come to see you. To whom shall I tell my sorrows?'

Sri Ramakrishna smiled and said to him by way of consolation: 'One cannot avoid such sorrows in the world. Pleasure and pain are inevitable in worldly life. (Pointing to M.) That is why they come here now and then. They get peace of mind by hearing about God. What is your trouble?'

Hriday (weeping): 'I am deprived of your company and so I suffer'.

Master: 'Why, was it not you who said to me, "You follow your ideal and let me follow mine"?'

Hriday: 'Yes, I did say that. But what did I know?'

Master: 'I shall say good-bye to you now. Come another day and we shall talk together. Today is Sunday and many people have come to see me. They are waiting in my room. Have you had a good crop in the country?'

Hriday: 'It isn't bad'.

Master: 'Let me say good-bye. Come another day'.

Hriday again prostrated himself before the Master, who started back to his room with M.

Master (to M.): 'He tormented me as much as he served me. When my stomach trouble had reduced my body to a couple of bones and I couldn't eat anything, he said to me one day: "Look at me — how well I eat! You've just taken a fancy that you can't eat". Again he said: "You are a fool! If I weren't living with you, where would your profession of holiness be?" '

M. became speechless at these words of the Master. For such a man he had shed tears a few minutes before!

Master (to M.): 'Well, he served me a great deal; then why should he have fallen on such evil days? He took care of me like a parent bringing up a child. As for me, I would remain unconscious of the world day and night. Besides, I was ill for a long time. I was completely at his mercy'.[45]

As far as the record goes, this was the last meeting between Sri Ramakrishna and Hriday. Hriday must have heard that his uncle was suffering from cancer and living either in Calcutta or Cossipore, but he never went to see him. After the passing away of Sri Ramakrishna, Hriday came to Calcutta to find a job. Ram Chandra Datta, a devotee of the Master, had installed the relics of Sri Ramakrishna in his garden house at Kankurgachi Yogodyana, and had begun daily worship there. He asked Hriday to perform the worship of the Master in exchange for a monthly salary and free board and lodging. Hriday accepted, but within a few days he started disrupting things as before. He would eat butter and rock candy in the morning before offering them to the Master, and again in the evening he would eat the food which was meant for offering. Ram was disgusted and sent him packing.[46]

Then Hriday became a hawker and started to sell clothes from door to door in Calcutta. Sometimes he would visit the Alambazar monastery where the monastic disciples of the Master had installed the shrine of Sri Ramakrishna. Hriday used to have his lunch there and would relate to the disciples stories of Sri Ramakrishna's spiritual sadhanas, pilgrimages, meetings with distinguished people, and about the old days of Dakshineswar, Rasmani, Mathur, and also about Kamarpukur. Since none of the disciples of Sri Ramakrishna had known the Master until after 1879, without Hriday it would have been almost impossible for Swami Saradananda to complete the biography of the Master. Hriday was able to recount in detail about the Master's personal and public life, because he had been Sri Ramakrishna's companion longer than anyone else.

Some time in the 1890s, Nag Mahashay, a great devotee of the Master, visited Dakshineswar along with Suresh Chandra Datta and Sharat Chandra Chakrabarty. It was the first visit of Sharat Chandra, who later wrote in his *Saint Durga Charan Nag*: 'Hriday Mukhopadhyay, a nephew of the Master, also happened to come to the garden that day. [It seems the temple officials overlooked him or simply did not pay any attention.] He had a pack of clothes with him and he looked very sad. Hriday was at that time earning his livelihood by hawking clothes. He was known to Nag Mahashay, and both began to talk about Sri Ramakrishna. Hriday sang a few songs about the Divine Mother. Nag Mahashay said that the Master used to sing those songs. After a long conversation, Hriday said: ''What a transformation has come to your lives through the grace of the Master! But alas! I have still to walk from door to door as a street hawker for my bread. Uncle did not extend his grace to me''. Saying this, he cried bitterly like a child'.[47]

When the light of the full moon reflects on the shallow water, the small fish become happy and they play, thinking the moon is their companion. But when the moon sets they become miserable, missing their luminous friend. In a similar way Hriday missed the Master terribly. His body was in the world but his mind was on his beloved uncle at Dakshineswar. Again in 1895 during the birthday celebration of Sri Ramakrishna, Hriday was present in the temple garden of Dakshineswar and told the devotees many stories about the Master. He lamented: 'When nobody came I served the Master; and now nobody cares for me. If a cat spoils the master's milk, does the master throw the cat away?'[48] Knowing Hriday's pitiable condition, some devotees of the Master began to help him financially.

While Hriday was living with the Master at Dakshineswar, he was strong and quite healthy. But in later years his health slowly broke down under the pressure of hawking clothes all day and practising left-handed Tantric disciplines at night.[49] Brokenhearted, Hriday at last returned to Sihar, his country home, where he died in 1899 (Vaisakh 1306).[50] One day before he left for home, Hriday came to the Alambazar monastery and bowed down to the Master in the shrine. Swami Niranjanananda (a disciple of the Master) greeted him, saying, 'Hello, Mukherjee. How are you?' Hriday answered: 'Brother, I am living-dead! Those days are gone. Uncle passed away, and my heart has also gone with him. I am moving in this world with this lifeless body'.[51]

4

Lakshmi Devi

When God incarnates as a human being, other gods and goddesses, yogis and illumined souls, incarnate with him. He does not come by himself, because he needs some companions who can appreciate his divine play and help him to fulfill his mission. It is not possible for ordinary people to understand the omniscient, omnipotent, omnipresent Lord, just as an ant cannot comprehend the strength of an elephant. But these *nityasiddhas*, or ever-free souls, are immediately able to recognize the avatar, or Incarnation of God, since they themselves are endowed with divine qualities. They feel a particular relationship with him and with each other, as their own divine nature is revealed to them. Each one becomes aware of his goal and the role he will have to enact under the direction of the main actor, the avatar.

Lakshmimani Devi, a niece of Sri Ramakrishna, was an incarnation of the goddess Shitala. One day at the Udbodhan house Holy Mother was talking to a devotee about Khudiram, her father-in-law: 'He had fervent faith in God and was devoted to the goddess Shitala, who was ever by his side. It was his custom to get up before dawn to pick flowers [for worship]. One day he had gone to the Lahas' garden when a little girl of about nine came to him there, saying: "Come this way, Father. These branches over here are loaded with flowers. Let me hold them down while you pick the blossoms". He asked, "Who are you, my child, and why are you out here so early?" Then she told him, "It is I, Father, from the Haldar's house". Because of his [Khudiram's] piety and devotion, God himself was born in his house, and along with him came all his campanions'.[1]

Khudiram had three family deities — Raghuvir, or Sri Rama, Rameshwar Shiva, and the goddess Shitala. The symbol of Shitala which he worshipped is actually a pot full of water with a mango twig on the top and red vermillion marks on the outside. The goddess is meditated on as wearing a red cloth and using the twig to sprinkle water for peace and prosperity. Now it so happened that when Sri

Lakshmi Devi (1864-1924)
Sri Ramakrishna's niece

Ramakrishna was living in Dakshineswar, he often received various kinds of sweets and fruits from the devotees. One day a thought came to his mind: 'I get so many nice things to eat here and Mother Shitala at Kamarpukur does not get any of them'. A few days later he had a dream in which Mother Shitala told him: 'I dwell in one form in the water pot and in another form in your niece Lakshmi. It will be equivalent to feeding me if you feed her'. After that, whenever Sri Ramakrishna was given any good food, he would feed Lakshmi with his own hands.[2]

Lakshmi was born at Kamarpukur in February 1864. Her father, Rameshwar, was Sri Ramakrishna's second elder brother. Lakshmi had two brothers, Ramlal and Shivaram. As a little five-year-old girl, Lakshmi would help with the worship of the family deities by making sandal paste and picking flowers. Her playtime was mainly spent in performing her own worship, and she was very fond of solitude. Lakshmi started to read the first primary book in the village school. When she came home she shared her lessons with her aunt, Sri Sarada Devi, who was ten years older. Later in Dakshineswar they learned the second primary book from a young boy named Sharat Bhandari, who was appointed by the Master for that purpose.

During the rainy season Dakshineswar became very unhealthy, so at that time Sri Ramakrishna would generally visit Kamarpukur, Jayrambati, and Sihar and would take Hriday with him. On one occasion while he was there the special rice, which was used for the food offering to Raghuvir, was all gone. Rameshwar's wife asked her daughter, Lakshmi, to go to Mukundapur and buy some. Lakshmi was then ten years old, a thin girl wearing a short cloth. It was raining. Putting a bamboo basket on her head, she left through the back door with half a rupee. The Master was then talking with some villagers near the main gate. After some time Lakshmi returned without any rice and met the Master at the gate. He asked, 'Lakshmi, where did you go?' The little girl burst into tears and said, 'I went to Mukundapur to buy rice for the Lord, but I couldn't get any'. The Master's heart went out to her in her predicament and he said, 'Oh, what suffering there is for the people of the world!' He then called his sister-in-law, who explained that though they had rice for their meals they had no special rice for the offering.

Immediately the Master took decisive steps to end the family's food problem. He called his neighbour, Sri Ram Yogi, and his boyhood friend, Gayavishnu, and asked them to buy some land.[3] After a long search, six acres of land were found. In order to make the purchase official, the Master went one day to the court at Goghat by palanquin.

As he described it: 'Once I went to the Registry Office to register some land, the title of which was in the name of Raghuvir. The officer asked me to sign my name; but I didn't do it, because I couldn't feel that it was "my" land'.[4] After returning to Kamarpukur, the Master said to Lakshmi: 'Henceforth you won't suffer from lack of food. And you won't have to run to Mukundapur for rice anymore either'.[5]

Lakshmi had heard from the Master that Krishna lives under a kadamba tree, so one day while Sri Ramakrishna was resting after his midday meal she left home to look for a kadamba tree to see Krishna. She could not find one in Kamarpukur, but she kept searching until she found one in a neighbouring village. For a long time she waited under that tree, but Krishna did not come. She finally returned home. When the Master saw her, he asked, 'Where did you go?' Lakshmi explained that she had gone to find Krishna under a kadamba tree but she had not seen him. Then the Master said to her: 'That kadamba tree is not outside. It is within'.[6]

Lakshmi's stories of the Master are firsthand and full of details. Many years later she related to an American devotee the following incident:

When Thakur [Sri Ramakrishna] was in his village, every evening he was in the habit of sitting by the door of his mother's home, watching the people as they passed along the street outside. All the women had to go that way to bring water from the tank [pond]. They would come with their jugs and seeing him at the door, they would sit down in the little yard in front with their water jugs beside them and forget everything in the joy of hearing him talk or sing of God. Fearing lest they might be neglecting their duties he asked concerning them. One girl said: 'I have a cow. When I heard that you were coming I cut straw enough to last a month and filled my room with it'. To another he said, 'How is your baby?' 'Oh! I forgot', she exclaimed. 'I left it with a neighbour'. She had walked more than a mile to come.

One day Thakur said, 'Now, today you must sing and I will listen'. They all remained silent. Not one dared utter a sound. But there was one girl whom Thakur loved very much, so much that whenever she did not come, he would send for her. As soon as she saw that no one else would sing, she sang a song in a weak, high-pitched, quavering voice. All the girls began to laugh at her, but when she had finished Thakur was delighted. 'See how great is her devotion', he exclaimed. 'Just because I asked her she has sung so frankly and simply. She alone among you has true devotion'.[7]

Another story was told by Lakshmi to some Calcutta devotees: 'Sri

Ramakrishna could not bear to hear any worldly talk. Once at Kamarpukur he overheard from his home the conversation of some village women who were at the bathing ghat of the Haldarpukur [pond]. They were discussing their menus for that day. The Master said to Hriday: "Look, those women are talking only about how they prepared different fish dishes. Shall I go and tell them not to talk such nonsense?" Hriday discouraged the Master because the aristocratic women from the Haldar family were there. But as soon as Hriday left, the Master rushed to the pond and said to the women, "Do you want to pass your precious life talking only about fish preparations or about God?" '8

Lakshmi was married at the age of eleven to Dhanakrishna Ghatak of Goghat village. The marriage had been arranged by her father, Rameshwar, before his passing away in 1873. When Ramlal brought the news of her marriage to the Master, who was then at Dakshineswar, Sri Ramakrishna immediately said, 'Lakshmi will be a widow', and went into samadhi. Hriday was shocked. After a while the Master came back to the normal plane of consciousness and Hriday said to him: 'You have so much affection for Lakshmi. Hearing the news of her marriage you are supposed to bless her, but instead of that, what an awful thing you have said!' Sri Ramakrishna replied: 'What can I do? The Divine Mother spoke that through me... Lakshmi is a partial incarnation of Shitala, who is a spirited goddess, while the person who has married her is an ordinary human being. It is not possible for him to enjoy Lakshmi. Only if Lord Shiva would incarnate as a man then she could be his wife. Now she is definitely going to be a widow'.9

A couple of months after the marriage Dhanakrishna went to see Lakshmi at Kamarpukur before leaving on a journey in search of work. He never returned. Following the Hindu custom, Lakshmi waited for twelve years and then went to her husband's home to perform the shraddha ceremony (a ritual for the departed soul). Sri Ramakrishna forbade Lakshmi to accept any part of her husband's property, so she gave away her share to other members of his family.

After the disappearance of her husband, Lakshmi continued to live in Kamarpukur for three years, and then she moved to Dakshineswar, where Sri Ramakrishna and Holy Mother were staying. She was then a beautiful young girl of fourteen. Sri Ramakrishna advised her: 'Do your duties and practise religion at home. Do not travel to the holy places by yourself. Who knows who might harm you? Live with your aunt [Sri Sarada Devi]. Life in the world is not safe'.10

Lakshmi narrated her memorable days with the Master at Dakshineswar: 'We [Holy Mother and Lakshmi] used to live in the nahabat [a small concert tower at the temple garden]. The Master used to refer to the nahabat as a cage and to us as *Shuk-Sari* [two birds in Indian folklore who were adept in talking about Krishna's glories]. When fruits and sweets that had been offered to the Divine Mother were brought to the Master, he would remind Brother Ramlal: "Don't forget that there are two birds in that cage. Give them some fruits and peas". Newcomers would take the Master's words literally. Even Master Mahashay [the recorder of *The Gospel of Sri Ramakrishna*] did so at first.

'How we managed in that tiny room of the nahabat, I sometimes wonder. It was the divine play of the Master! Usually it was shared by Holy Mother, another girl, and myself; and sometimes Gopaler-ma, who was a large woman, or other women devotees from Calcutta, would stay with us. Moreover, we had to store our groceries, cooking vessels, dishes, and even the water jar in that room. Since the Master had a weak stomach we also had to store the food for his special diet.

'All through his life the Master had stomach trouble. When Grandma [Sri Ramakrishna's mother] was living in Dakshineswar, the Master would salute her every morning. Grandma was a large woman and very beautiful, but she was also old-fashioned and very shy. Even before her youngest son [Sri Ramakrishna] she would cover her face with a veil. When he came she would ask him, "How is your stomach?" The Master would reply, "Not very good". Grandma would then advise: "Don't take the prasad of Mother Kali. [It was very spicy food.] As long as your stomach is not all right your wife will cook plain soup and rice for you. Please eat only that".

'Sometimes the Master would get tired of eating invalid's food every day and would ask his mother to cook one or two dishes and season them as she used to do in Kamarpukur. So occasionally Grandma cooked for him and the Master enjoyed it.

'The Master used to encourage women to cook. "It is a good occupation for the mind", he would say. "Sita was a good cook, and so were Draupadi and Parvati. Mother Lakshmi [the goddess of fortune] would herself cook and feed others".

'After the death of her two older sons, Grandma became somewhat passive and withdrawn. Furthermore, she would not take her lunch until she had heard the noon whistle of the Alambazar Jute Mill. As soon as it sounded she would exclaim: "Oh! There is the whistle of heaven. That is the signal for offering food to Lakshmi and Narayana". A problem would arise on Sundays, however, when the jute mill was closed; no whistle was blown at noon and consequently she would not eat. This worried the Master very much, and he would lament: "Oh dear! My old mother will refuse her food today and she will be weak". Brother Hriday would say to the Master: "Don't be anxious, Uncle. When Grandma is hungry she will eat of her own accord". But the Master would reply: "Oh no. I am her son. It is my duty to look after my old mother". With much coaxing the Master would persuade his mother to eat the prasad of Krishna.

'One day Brother Hriday made a high-pitched sound by blowing through a pipe. He then said to Grandma: "There, Grandma, did you hear the whistle of heaven? Now please eat your food". But Grandma laughed and said: "Oh no. You made the sound with your pipe". Everyone laughed.

'When Grandma passed away the Master wept.[11]

'One night the Master was filled with the spiritual mood of Radha and had so identified himself with her that he decided to go to the arbour to meet Krishna. Coming out of his room, he entered the rose garden. He had no outward consciousness. He soon got caught in the rose bushes and was scratched all over from the thorns, and there he stood. The night watchman found him and woke us. At once I went to the temple manager and brought him there. Many others, awakened by the noise, crowded around. Aunt also came there and burst into tears. This was the first time that she was seen in public. When the Master was carried to his room he said: "I am going to the arbour. Why are you troubling me? Let me go". After this, Aunt and I began to sleep in his room. A couple of days later, however, he said to us: "Why are you suffering this way? It is so hot now. You had better sleep in the nahabat". We obeyed'.[12]

In *Days In An Indian Monastery*, Sister Devamata recorded the following stories, which Lakshmi had told her:

One morning Sri Ramakrishna disappeared altogether. Holy Mother, Lakididi, his niece [Lakshmi], and another devotee went to the banyan tree to find him, but he was gone. They searched for him everywhere — in the garden, by the temple pools, in his room, in the temple, in the hut. At last Holy Mother concluded that he had gone into samadhi [deep meditation] on the Ganga side and had fallen into the water. They all began to weep bitterly. It so happened that a cow went astray that day and the gardener, unable to find it, plunged into the thorny undergrowth of the jungle in the corner of the temple compound. There near the boundary wall under a bel tree he saw Sri Ramakrishna sitting in samadhi, wholly unconscious of the grief he was causing.

The Master explained afterwards that as he sat under the banyan tree, he was so disturbed by the many women who on their way to their bath in the Ganga stopped to prostrate before him and beg him to bless them with a child or some worldly advantage, he determined to seek out a more inaccessible retreat and had found the bel tree. As he pushed his way through the thick brambles, his feet must have been scratched and torn; for when we went to the tree along a partial clearing, our feet, bared in reverence, were sore and bleeding.[13]

The other story is in Lakshmi's own words:

One day I went with [Holy] Mother to carry Thakur [Sri Ramakrishna] his food. Rakhal, and others who were with him, at once left the room, leaving us alone there. Thakur was lying on his bed in samadhi, but he looked so devoid of life that Mother, having long been anxious for his health, began to weep thinking he had left the body. Then she remembered that he had once said to her that if she ever found him in this state she was just to touch his feet and that would bring him back; so she began to rub his feet. Rakhal and the others hearing the weeping had also hurried back into the room and they too began to rub him vigorously.

This brought him back to consciousness, and opening his eyes he asked with surprise what was the matter. Then realizing their fears, he smiled and said: 'I was in the land of the white people. Their skin is white, their hearts are white and they are simple and sincere. It is a very beautiful country. I think I shall go there'.[14]

Sri Ramakrishna's fascinating life and universal message have spread all over the world, but how the Master trained his disciples is not so well known. Lakshmi was among those fortunate few who were very close to the Master and free with him. As the following stories show, he trained her with love and affection:

'Once the Master asked me', said Lakshmi, 'to eat some of Mother Kali's prasad. I was reluctant to eat a piece of fish [generally a Hindu widow is a strict vegetarian], but the Master insisted [knowing that Lakshmi was the goddess Shitala]. He said to me: "It is prasad. Don't hesitate. Eat. If you don't listen to me you will have to be born again. You may get an ugly, fat husband who will force you to lead a worldly life against your will". "Well", I said, "I certainly don't want to be involved in maya again. Perhaps it is better to eat this nonvegetarian prasad".

'The Master did not sleep much at night. When it was still dark outside he would move around the temple garden, and while passing near the nahabat he would call: "O Lakshmi, O Lakshmi. Get up. Ask your aunt to get up also. How long will you sleep? It is almost dawn. The crows and cuckoos are about to sing. [This is a sign of daybreak in tropical countries.] Chant the name of the Divine Mother''.

'Sometimes in winter, when the Master would call, Mother, while lying under her quilt, would whisper to me: "Keep quiet. He has no sleep in his eyes. It is not the right time to get up, and the birds have not yet started singing. Don't respond''. But if the Master did not get any response, he would pour water under the doorsill, and since we slept on the floor, we had to get up without delay. Even so, sometimes our beds got wet.

'Whenever there was kirtan [devotional singing] in his room, the Master would ask Brother Ramlal to open the door facing the nahabat. He would say: "A current of devotion and bliss will flow here. If the women do not see or hear, how will they learn?'' Mother used to watch through a tiny hole in the bamboo screen, and that made her happy. Sometimes the Master would comment with a laugh, "O Ramlal, the opening in your aunt's screen is getting bigger and bigger''.

'The Master used to tell Aunt and me stories from the Ramayana and the Mahabharata, such as the story of King Nala, and he would then question us to see if we had understood them. He also would make me repeat them, and afterwards he would remark with satisfaction, "That is why I call you a shuk [parrot]'' '.[15]

One night Holy Mother and Lakshmi were softly singing a devotional song in the nahabat. The Master heard them from his room, and the next morning he said to them: 'Last night you were singing with joy. That is very good'.[16]

Sri Ramakrishna one day asked Lakshmi, 'What deity do you love most?' 'Radha-Krishna', answered Lakshmi. With a seed, the Master wrote that mantram on her tongue and uttered it to her audibly. She had a rosary of tulsi (basil) beads, which the Master approved for her use. Previously Lakshmi had received initiation into a Shakti mantram from a monk named Swami Purnananda. When Holy Mother mentioned this to the Master, he said: 'It does not matter. I gave the right mantram to Lakshmi'.[17]

On a certain occasion the Master, standing on the semi-circular verandah of his room, said that he would be born again after a hundred years. Holy Mother, however, expressed her unwillingness to come again. Lakshmi also vehemently opposed the idea. She said that she would never come again — even if she were chopped into shreds like tobacco leaves! The Master then laughed and told them: 'If I come here, where will you stay? Your hearts will pine for me. Our roots are twined together like the *kalmi* plant [a creeper that grows on the surface of a pond] — pull one stem and the whole clump comes forward'.[18]

In order to facilitate the Master's cancer treatment, he was moved from Dakshineswar to Calcutta and then to Cossipore. Holy Mother and Lakshmi moved with the Master to serve him. At Cossipore the Master one day worshipped Lakshmi as the goddess Shitala. He also asked Girish Ghosh to feed her with sweets. About this same time the Master expressed a wish to give Lakshmi a pair of bangles and a necklace. But Lakshmi told him that she did not care for jewellery and that she would be happy to visit Vrindaban with that money. Later, when some of the devotees heard about the Master's wish, they had the jewellery made for her. Lakshmi put them on once and then gave them away out of renunciation.[19]

One day the Master sent Lakshmi and M.'s wife (M. was Mahendranath Gupta, the recorder of *The Gospel of Sri Ramakrishna*) to beg food. 'Go from door to door and spread the Lord's name', he said to them. 'People may criticize you, but still their homes will get the touch of your blessed feet, and this will bring good to them'. The Master also told them to beg from the homes of the poor and not from the rich. Lakshmi was a beautiful young woman, and seeing her begging, a compassionate lady said to her: 'Why are you begging? Why don't you stay at my home as my daughter-in-law? I shall give you ornaments'. Later, when that lady found out that Lakshmi was Sri Ramakrishna's niece, she was quite embarrassed and sent vegetables and other articles to her at the Cossipore garden house.[20]

Sri Ramakrishna blessed Lakshmi at Cossipore, saying: 'Don't worry about yourself. Many people will come to you to hear about God, and they will look after you'.

Lakshmi's account of the Master's last day is very moving: 'He was reclining against a pillow on his bed. There was silence all around, and all were worried about him. Earlier he could not speak, but when Mother and I went to him, he feebly whispered: "You have come. You see, I feel I am going somewhere, to a distant land through water". Mother started to cry. Then the Master said to her: "Don't worry. You will live as you are living now. As Naren and the others are serving me, so they will also take care of you. Look after Lakshmi and keep her with you. She will manage herself and will not be a burden" '.[21]

After Sri Ramakrishna's passing away in 1886, Lakshmi travelled with Holy Mother to different holy places in India and then moved back to Kamarpukur. But sometimes she would visit Calcutta and stay at the Kankurgachi Yogodyana or with Holy Mother. Sister Nivedita met Lakshmi in 1898 at Holy Mother's Calcutta residence and described her in *The Master As I Saw Him*:

Sister Lucky, or Lakshmididi as is the Indian form of her name, was indeed a niece of his [Sri Ramakrishna], and is still a comparatively young woman. She is widely sought after as a religious teacher and director, and is a most gifted and delightful companion. Sometimes she will repeat page after page of some sacred dialogue, out of one of the jatras, or religious operas, or again she will make the quiet room ring with gentle merriment, as she poses the different members of the party in groups for religious tableaux. Now it is Kali, and again Saraswati; another time it will be Jagaddhatri, or yet again, perhaps, Krishna under his kadamba tree, that she will arrange, with picturesque effect and scant dramatic material.[22]

Lakshmi was a very talented woman and had a captivating personality. She could sing, dance, act, mimic, and inspire. She was a wonderful storyteller, and her childlike simplicity deeply impressed people. Sometimes in a gathering she would dress as a gopi and in her melodious voice would sing kirtan or some devotional songs of Ramprasad. On one occasion she acted as the goddess Jagaddhatri and had Sister Nivedita act as her carrier lion. The ladies laughed and laughed as the two moved around the room. Nivedita wrote, 'Amusements like these were much approved of, it is said, by Ramakrishna, who would sometimes himself, according to the ladies, spend hours in reciting religious plays, taking the part of each player in turns, and making all around him realize the utmost meaning of the prayers and worship uttered in the poetry'.[23]

One day in Kamarpukur, nearly forty village women gathered together on the roof of the Lahas' house to listen as Lakshmi sang kirtan. After a while the women became so absorbed in the devotional mood that they forgot what time it was and where they were. Their husbands and relatives called to them from downstairs but did not get any response. In order to give the women a good lesson, then, the men locked the door of the stairway and left. When the singing was over the ladies tried to go downstairs, but finding the door locked, they understood that the men had played a prank on them. They then climbed down to the adjoining low roof over the kitchen and from there jumped onto some piles of ashes on the ground, thus spoiling the men's mischievous plot.[24]

When Ramlal lost his wife in 1905 he asked his sister, Lakshmi, to come back to Dakshineswar. She stayed with him there for ten years. Gradually she began initiating people and formed a group of disciples who helped build a house for her. From the roof of this house she could see the Ganga, and it was close to the temple garden of Dakshineswar.

Lakshmi was very sweet and kind but at the same time very strong and powerful. Once she went to Varanasi on a pilgrimage with some devotees. She was then forty years old. One evening, while she was attending the vesper service of Kedarnath Shiva, a young man touched her. At first she thought he was a pickpocket, so she simply pushed his hand away. But when he again touched her, she understood his motive. Grabbing his hair with her left hand, she started hitting him hard with her right hand. The vesper service immediately stopped. The priests came to her with folded hands and said: 'Mother, you have given the right punishment. That rascal always disturbs the women in the temple. Today Lord Kedarnath has given him a good lesson'.[25]

A certain monk was very devoted to Lakshmi and served her like a disciple. She was also very fond of him. After a while, however, she noticed that he was becoming too free and friendly with women, and that he had begun to attend marriage ceremonies. Such behaviour did not suit a monk, and she was concerned about him. One day Lakshmi said to him: 'Brother, you are supposed to be like a lion, but you are behaving like a jackal. Shame on you! You are always around women. As a monk you must stay away from women. Being a child of Sri Ramakrishna, how could you forget his teachings?' The monk became indignant, and after some time he left. But Lakshmi was not offended. She prayed to the Master for his welfare.[26]

Lakshmi visited many holy places of India, such as Gaya, Varanasi, Prayag, Vrindaban, Navadwip, and Gangasagar, but she was particularly fascinated by Puri. Knowing this, some devotees built a house for her near the seashore there and named it 'Lakshmi Niketan' (the abode of Lakshmi). In February 1924 she moved to Puri.

Lakshmi's daily routine was very simple. She got up at three o'clock in the morning and after washing sat for meditation and japam. Afterwards she ate a little prasad, and at ten o'clock went for her bath. Then she again repeated her mantram until noon, when she took her lunch. At three o'clock, after resting, she either talked to the devotees about the Master or practised japam. From six to eight in the evening she repeated her mantram, and then the devotees sang kirtan and read a chapter from the Srimad Bhagavatam. After taking some prasad and milk for supper she went to bed at ten o'clock.[27]

Frequently Lakshmi experienced bhava samadhi and had visions of different gods and goddesses. Once she had a vision of Sri Ramakrishna on the altar of the Jagannath temple. She was convinced after that that the Master and Jagannath were the same. One day she went alone to bathe in the ocean, near Swargadwara, but was suddenly carried away by the strong undertow. About a mile away, near Chakratirtha, a cowherd boy rescued her and then disappeared. After returning home, Lakshmi went to see Lord Jagannath in the temple. She was amazed when she saw on the image of Balaram the smiling face of that cowherd boy. She realized then that it was Lord Balaram who had saved her life.[28]

The Master had once told Lakshmi: 'If you cannot remember God, think of me. That will do'.[29] This great assurance remained in Lakshmi's mind the rest of her life. Her love and devotion for Sri Ramakrishna was deep and unfathomable, and she was never tired of telling others about the divine play which she had witnessed. In her own unique way she spread the Master's message and inspired many souls. The other disciples of Sri Ramakrishna greatly loved and respected Lakshmi, but Holy Mother especially had much affection for her.

In Puri, even though Lakshmi's health began failing day by day, she continued to go into ecstasy. But despite the excellent care given by her disciples, she passed away on February 24, 1926, at the age of sixty-two. Once, before she passed away, she described to Swami Saradananda a vision she had had: 'I saw a mountain of dazzling mica. On one side of that mountain were Lakshmi and Narayana, and on the other side was Sri Ramakrishna. I saw that the Master was surrounded by Holy Mother, Swamiji, Rakhal Maharaj, and others. Then I saw Yogin-didi and Golap-didi, and they told me: "O Lakshmi, here there is no problem of food and sleep or disease and grief. Living with the Master gives us uninterrupted bliss" '.[30]

Shambhu Charan Mallik (?-1877)

5

Shambhu Charan Mallik

It is remarkable that in this present age a person can live in the world without having or even touching money, without building a home or even owning any possessions. Sri Ramakrishna demonstrated through his life the ideal of renunciation to modern man. Once he said: 'A man cannot realize God unless he renounces everything mentally. A sadhu cannot lay things up. "Birds and wandering monks do not make provision for the morrow" '.[1] Indeed, those who depend wholly on God are provided with everything they need. This was also verified in Sri Ramakrishna's life: 'The Divine Mother showed me in a vision the five suppliers of my needs: first, Mathur Babu, and second, Shambhu Mallik, whom I had not then met. I had a vision of a fair-skinned man with a cap on his head. Many days later, when I first met Shambhu, I recalled that vision; I realized that it was he whom I had seen in that ecstatic state'.[2]

Very little is known about Shambhu Charan Mallik. His father's name was Sanatan Mallik, and their home was in the Sinduriapati section of Calcutta. Shambhu also had a garden house in Dakshineswar, just a few hundred yards south of the Kali temple. Shambhu was married to a devout woman. They had no children. As an agent of a British firm, he earned a good salary, which he used wisely. In fact, he was well known for his generosity and noble character. Because of his philanthropic activities, Kamalnayan Street, where Shambhu's parental home was located, was later renamed Shambhu Mallik's Lane.

Shambhu's interest in God brought him to the Brahmo Samaj, where he developed a close friendship with Keshab Chandra Sen. Once he took Keshab to Sri Ramakrishna for a visit. Shambhu's faith in God was extraordinary. Although he was wealthy and could well afford a carriage, he used to walk from Calcutta to his garden house in Dakshineswar. Once a friend said to him: 'It is risky to walk such a long distance. Why don't you come in a carriage?' Hearing this, Shambhu's face became red and he exclaimed: 'I set out repeating the name of God! What danger can befall me?'[3]

After Mathur's passing away in 1871, Manimohan Sen of Panihati served the Master for a short while. Shambhu then took the responsibility of being Sri Ramakrishna's supplier. Because he lived close to the Kali temple, he came to know the Master very well. The Master would often go for a walk towards Shambhu's house and meet him in his garden, where they would talk about God. Since the Master came to him on his own, Shambhu considered himself very special. One day he proudly said to the Master: 'You come here frequently. Yes, you come because you feel happy talking with me'.[4] As Shambhu's love and devotion for Sri Ramakrishna increased, he started to call him 'Guruji'. But Sri Ramakrishna could not bear to be addressed as 'Guru', 'Father', or 'Master',* because these terms generally inflate a person's ego and bind him. He said to Shambhu: 'Who is the guru and who is the disciple? You are my guru'.[5] Nevertheless, Shambhu continued to address Sri Ramakrishna that way.

Shambhu's wife was also very devoted to Sri Ramakrishna and Sri Sarada Devi. Whenever Holy Mother was in Dakshineswar, Shambhu's wife would invite her to their garden house every Tuesday (an auspicious day for the worship of the Divine Mother) to worship her as a goddess.

Holy Mother came to Dakshineswar for the second time, probably in the middle of 1874. There she lived in a tiny room of the nahabat, where the Master's mother also stayed. Wanting to see her more comfortable, Shambhu bought a piece of land near the temple garden and had a small cottage built for her. Captain Vishwanath Upadhyay, an officer of the Nepal government, was also a devotee of Sri Ramakrishna. When he heard from Shambhu about the building project, he offered to supply all the timber for the cottage. Holy Mother stayed there for a year. She cooked for the Master in that cottage and from there carried food to him at the temple garden. A woman was appointed to help her with the house work. Sometimes the Master visited the cottage to keep her from becoming too lonely. When Holy Mother fell sick with dysentery, Shambhu engaged Dr. Prasad to treat her. In order to convalesce, she was sent to her village home in Jayrambati, probably in 1876.

Shambhu had a charitable dispensary in his garden house. One day while the Master was at his garden house Shambhu found out that

---

*In the Bengali language there are several words meaning 'Master'. The word Sri Ramakrishna was referring to is Karta, which literally means 'doer' or 'agent'. Many people called him Thakur, which also means 'Master'.

Sri Ramakrishna often suffered from stomach trouble, caused by the irregular food and impure water at the temple garden. Shambhu advised him to take small doses of opium as an antidote and offered to give him a package from the dispensary before he left. In the course of conversation, however, both forgot about it. After taking his leave the Master started down the road and then remembered about the opium. He returned and found out that Shambhu was busy in the inner apartment, so without disturbing him, the Master went to the dispensary supervisor and got some opium from him. But as soon as he left Shambhu's garden he could not find his way back to the temple garden. He felt as if someone was pulling his legs in the opposite direction. Yet when he turned around he could clearly see Shambhu's place. Then he realized that Shambhu had said to take the opium from *him* — not from the supervisor, who had no right to give it without Shambhu's permission. Thus, Sri Ramakrishna's action was wrong on two counts — falsehood and theft. Therefore the Divine Mother deterred him. The Master immediately returned to the dispensary, but by now the supervisor had also left. He then threw the package through a window, calling loudly, 'Hello, here I am returning your opium'.[6] Setting out again for the temple garden, he could see the way clearly, and he reached there without further difficulty.*

On another day when Sri Ramakrishna was visiting Shambhu's garden house, Shambhu found out that the Master was not feeling well. Thinking that some sweet pomegranates would be good for him, Shambhu bought some and offered them to the Master before he left for the temple garden. Sri Ramakrishna accepted the gift to fulfill the desire of the devotee, but as he turned to leave he could not find the gate. He began roaming around Shambhu's garden like a drunkard. Shambhu noticed it and could not understand what was wrong. Finally he came out of his house and brought the Master inside. Sri Ramakrishna then returned the pomegranates to Shambhu and became normal again. Explaining to Shambhu, the Master said that if he carried anything with him or hoarded anything, his mind

---

*There is another version of this incident mentioned in *The Gospel of Sri Ramakrishna*: 'Master (*to the doctor*): "...It is impossible for me to lay up anything. One day I visited Shambhu Mallik's garden house. At that time I had been suffering badly from stomach trouble. Shambhu said to me: 'Take a grain of opium now and then. It will help you'. He tied a little opium in a corner of my cloth. As I was returning to the Kali temple, I began to wander about near the gate as if unable to find the way. Then I threw the opium away and at once regained my normal state. I returned to the temple garden" '.[7]

became confused and his nervous system recoiled. Shambhu was amazed to hear of the Master's renunciation.[8]

Once Sri Ramakrishna went with Girija, a disciple of Bhairavi Brahmani, to visit Shambhu in his garden house. The three of them became absorbed in conversation about God, and did not notice the passing of time until the sun had set. Bidding good night to Shambhu, the Master and Girija went to the road. It was pitch dark, and neither of them could find the way back to the Kali temple. Girija had a supernatural power, however, and he told the Master to wait. After a moment's pause, Girija illumined the whole road with a long stream of light emanating from his own body. He then escorted the Master back to the temple garden.[9]

Shambhu had a catholic view of religions. He used to read the Bible to Sri Ramakrishna, and in this way the Master learned about Christ and Christianity. Although the Master did not care for the Christian emphasis on sin, the desire came to him to realize God through the Christian path. One day he went to Jadu Mallik's garden house, which was adjacent to the temple garden. In the parlour of this house there were many pictures of holy persons, including one of Virgin Mary with the child Jesus sitting on her lap. While the Master was looking at it, he felt that the figures of the Mother and Child were awakened, and that rays of light emanated from them and entered his heart. He returned to the temple garden in an entirely new mood and for three days was permeated by the ideal and personality of Christ. During this period he did not even go to the temple to salute the Divine Mother. Near the end of the third day, while he was walking in the Panchavati, he saw a tall foreign-looking man walking towards him. The man had a beautiful face with large, brilliant eyes, while the tip of his nose was a little flat. At first the Master wondered who this person could be. Then a voice from within told him, 'This is Jesus Christ, the great yogi, the loving son of God, one with his Father, who shed his heart's blood and suffered tortures for the salvation of mankind'. Jesus then embraced Sri Ramakrishna and merged into his body. This vision convinced the Master that Jesus was a Divine Incarnation.[10]

Although Sri Ramakrishna had very little formal education and did not read books, still, educated people would come to listen to his words. He demonstrated to the modern world that without reading books and studying scriptures one can have the knowledge of God. The Divine Mother herself revealed to him what was in the scriptures. From his keen observation and his own experiences, he fashioned tales and parables to illustrate his teachings, and these teachings were so practical and full of wisdom that many scholars were deeply impressed. One day Shambhu pointed to the Master and said to someone, 'Here is Shantiram Singh, a great hero, quite able to beat anyone without a sword or shield'.[11]

Shambhu was a good devotee as well as a karma yogi, and Sri Ramakrishna's influence made him even more unattached and unselfish. One day Shambhu expressed a desire to the Master: 'Please bless me, sir, that I may spend all my money for good purposes, such as building hospitals and dispensaries, making roads, and digging wells'. We find this wonderful philanthropic idea of Shambhu's mentioned a number of times by the Master in the *Gospel*. But Sri Ramakrishna never fully approved of it. He said to Shambhu: 'It will be good if you can do all these things in a spirit of detachment. But that is very difficult. Whatever you may do, you must always remember that the aim of this life of yours is the attainment of God and not the building of hospitals and dispensaries. Suppose God appeared before you and said to you, "Accept a boon from me". Would you then ask him, "O God, build me some hospitals and dispensaries?" Or would you not rather pray to him: "O God, may I have pure love at your Lotus Feet! May I have your uninterrupted vision!"? Hospitals, dispensaries, and all such things are unreal. Furthermore, after realizing God one feels that he alone is the doer and we are but his instruments. Then why should we forget him and destroy ourselves by being involved in too many activities? After realizing him, one may, through his grace, become his instrument in building many hospitals and dispensaries'.[12]

Shambhu thought that the main purpose of human life was to offer everything one had to God and to help the poor. One day he said to Sri Ramakrishna, 'Please bless me, that I may die leaving my riches at the Lotus Feet of God'. The Master replied: 'These are riches only to you. What riches can you offer God? To him these are mere dust and straw'.[13]

Although Shambhu was generous, he was also careful about his charity. The Master's nephew Hriday one day asked Shambhu for some money. Shambhu told him: 'Why should I give you money? You can earn your livelihood by working. Even now you are earning something. The case of a very poor person is different. The purpose of charity is fulfilled if one gives money to the blind or the lame'. Hriday then said: 'Sir, please don't say that. I don't need your money. May God help me not to become blind or deaf or extremely poor! I don't want you to give, and I don't want to receive'.[14]

Shambhu served Sri Ramakrishna and Holy Mother for four years, but he gradually became bedridden with diabetes. The Master went with Hriday to see him while he was ill and found that he was quite cheerful and had no fear of death. Shambhu said to Hriday, 'Hridu, I have packed my things and am ready for the journey'. When the Master told him not to say such ominous words, Shambhu replied, 'No, please bless me that I may cast aside all these possessions and go to God'.[15] While returning to Dakshineswar the Master told Hriday, 'The oil in Shambhu's lamp has run out'.[16] Shambhu died in 1877.

One day several years later, while talking about Shambhu, Sri Ramakrishna said to the devotees: 'God's devotees have nothing to fear. They are his own. He always stands by them'.[17]

6

Ram Chandra Datta

Faith and devotion are two important milestones on the path towards God. Faith removes worry, anxiety, and fear, while devotion makes life smooth and joyous. Human life becomes very painful and burdensome if a person has no one to trust and love. Spiritual seekers who put their trust in God and love him wholeheartedly, surrender themselves to him, and as a result God, the Eternal Father, takes care of them. Just as children enjoy a carefree life in their own homes, so spiritual seekers live happily in this world. Truly, God provides whatever his devotees need.

Ram Chandra Datta, a householder disciple of Sri Ramakrishna, had unflinching faith in the Master and his love and devotion for him was exuberant. He used to say that any place Sri Ramakrishna visited even for a day became a holy place, and that whoever came to the Master and served him once was blessed. Ram further asserted that the horse carriage which Sri Ramakrishna took to visit the Calcutta devotees, along with its coachman and horses, were all sanctified by the touch of the Master.

Ram's attitude was considered extreme by many, and once someone sarcastically remarked: 'If that is true then what is there to fear? So many people have seen Sri Ramakrishna on the street and so many coachmen have driven him. Do you think all these people will get liberation?' Ram Chandra's face turned red, and he vehemently replied: 'Go and take the dust of the feet of the coachman who drove the Master. Go and take the dust of the feet of the sweeper of Dakshineswar who saw the Master. This will make your life pure and blessed'.[1]

Ram Chandra Datta was born in Calcutta on October 30, 1851. His father, Nrisimha Prasad Datta, was devoted to Krishna, and his mother, Tulasimani, was known for her piety and kindness. All of these good qualities Ram imbibed from his parents. When he was two and a half years old his mother died and some women relatives in their home looked after him. Ram's favourite pastime when he was

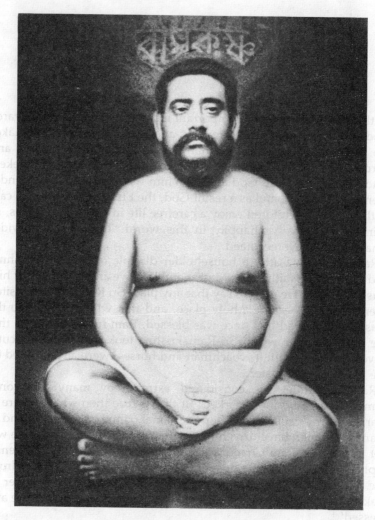

Ram Chandra Datta (1851-1899)

young was to worship Krishna. Sometimes he would arrange a festival and invite playmates with whom he would share prasad. Other times he would dress himself as a gopi and dance in front of the deity. Ram also liked to visit a hermitage near his home where he came in contact with monks of different orders. These monks loved the young boy for his devotion and religious fervour.

From his boyhood Ram was very bold and straightforward about his convictions, and no one could persuade him to act contrary to them. When he was ten years old, he visited the home of a relative who lived about twenty-five miles from Calcutta. This relative knew that Ram was a strict vegetarian, but in spite of this he served Ram a nonvegetarian meal and tried to persuade him to eat it. Ram became furious and immediately left the house. He did not have any money to buy a train ticket, but a generous person bought one for him so that he could return home. Even in the later part of his life, in spite of his education in science, he remained firm in his convictions. Once a doctor prescribed meat soup for his ailing wife, but Ram would not approve of it. He said, 'Let my wife die but I won't allow meat to enter my house'. Fortunately his wife recovered without the soup.[2]

Eventually Ram's father remarried, but Ram did not get along with his stepmother. Shortly after this, Ram's father was forced to sell the parental home due to financial difficulties, and Ram moved to a relative's home. Although Ram suffered various kinds of hardships in his early life, he persevered in his education. He studied at the General Assembly's Institution and later was admitted to the Campbell Medical School in Calcutta. Some time after his graduation he was appointed as an assistant to the Government Quinine Examiner. He also married about this time. Later, when he became financially solvent, he bought a house for his family at Simla, in the central part of Calcutta.

Ram was deeply interested in science and studied chemistry under his English supervisor with great diligence. Having learned this subject thoroughly, Ram extracted from an indigenous medicinal plant an antidote for blood dysentery. This drug was approved by the government and was recommended by leading doctors. As a result, Ram's fame spread and he was appointed a member of the Chemist Association of England. He was also promoted to the post of Government Chemical Examiner and was asked to teach the military medical students at the Calcutta Medical College.

Ram's great enthusiasm for science and modern knowledge made him an inspiring lecturer to the students, but it also made him an atheist. In his own words: 'In those days we did not believe in God.

We considered that everything happens, changes, or dissolves by the force of nature. We were rank materialists, and we held the view that eating, sleeping, and creature comforts were the summum bonum of life'.[3] Ram was fond of debating with others about God and religion and found great satisfaction in defeating his opponents. This ardour for atheism lasted five years.

Grief is an eye-opener which forces a person to face the harsh realities of life. The death of his young daughter was a terrible shock to Ram, and a great change came over his life. On the Kali Puja evening, some time after his daughter's death, he went up to the roof of his house and observed the houses of Calcutta glittering with lights. Above, the dark, clear sky was studded with twinkling stars. His grief-stricken heart seemed to be searching for something meaningful in that panorama of nature. All of a sudden he noticed some clouds passing overhead, driven by the wind. They quickly disappeared. Ram asked himself: 'Where do they come from and where do they go? Does God exist? If so, can he be seen?'[4]

He started to visit different religious leaders of the Brahmo, Christian, and Hindu faiths, but no one could answer his questions about God and religion. During this time Ram's family guru came to his house and wanted to initiate him. Ram was forthright. He said: 'Sir, I don't believe in God. Moreover, I have terrible doubts about his existence. Can you tell me the way to realize God?' The guru kept quiet. He did not know what to say.[5]

'The great inquiry' began to possess Ram. He became more and more determined to have his doubts removed and to satisfy his hunger for God. He studied many religious books but could find no satisfactory answers to his questions. At last he came to know about Sri Ramakrishna from the writings of Keshab Chandra Sen, a Brahmo leader of Calcutta.

On November 13, 1879, Ram went by boat to Dakshineswar with Gopal Chandra Mittra and a cousin, Manomohan Mittra. As soon as they reached the Dakshineswar temple garden, they inquired about Sri Ramakrishna and were directed to his room. But when they reached there they found that the door was shut, and their Western education made them hesitate to call out or knock. Just then Sri Ramakrishna opened the door himself from the inside and asked them to come in. Ram noticed that Sri Ramakrishna did not look like the traditional ochre-clad monk with matted hair and ash-smeared body. On the contrary, the Master was the embodiment of simplicity.

Sri Ramakrishna saluted them, addressing them as *Narayana*, and asked them to sit down. Then he smiled at Ram and said: 'Hello, are you not a doctor? [*Pointing to Hriday*] He is suffering from fever. Could you check his pulse?'[6] Ram was astonished that Sri Ramakrishna knew that he was a doctor. After examining Hriday, Ram reported that his body temperature was normal.

From the very beginning Sri Ramakrishna made Ram his own and would often inquire about his personal life and mental conflicts. Ram felt greatly attracted to the Master and started to visit him every Sunday, returning home in the evening. Soon Ram felt bold enough to ask the questions that had been haunting him.

Ram: 'Does God exist? How can one see God?'

Sri Ramakrishna: 'God really exists. You do not see any stars during the day, but that does not mean that the stars do not exist. There is butter in milk, but can anyone know it merely by sight? In order to get the butter you must churn the milk in a cool place before sunrise. If you want to catch fish in a pond, you have to learn the art of fishing from those who know it, and then you must sit patiently with a fishing rod, throwing the line into the water. Gradually the fish will grab your bait. Then, as soon as the float sinks, you can pull the fish to the shore. Similarly, you cannot realize God by a mere wish. Have faith in the instructions of a holy man. Make your mind like a fishing rod and your prana, or life-force, like a hook. Your devotion and japam are like the bait. Eventually you will be blessed by the vision of God'.[7]

Ram had recently been connected with the Brahmo Samaj, whose members did not believe in a God with form, so he was wondering how one could see a formless God. The Master read his mind and said: 'Yes, God can be seen. Can God, whose creation is so beautiful and enchanting, be imperceptible?'

Ram: 'Is it possible to realize God in this life?'

Sri Ramakrishna: 'You get what you desire. Faith alone is the key to success'. Then he sang a song:

As is a man's meditation, so is his feeling of love;
As is a man's feeling of love, so is his gain;
And faith is the root of all.
If in the Nectar Lake of Mother Kali's feet
My mind remains immersed,
Of little use are worship, oblations, or sacrifice.

The Master continued: 'The more you advance in one direction, the more you leave behind the opposite direction. If you move ten steps towards the east, you move ten steps away from the west'.

Ram: 'But one must have tangible proof. Unless we have direct

experience of God, how can our weak and doubting minds have faith
in his existence?'

Sri Ramakrishna: 'A typhoid patient in a delirious state clamours to
take gallons of water and heaps of rice. But the physician pays no
heed to these entreaties, nor does he prescribe medicine at the
patient's dictation. He knows what he is doing'.[8]

Ram was very much moved and impressed with Sri Ramakrishna's
simple, convincing answers. He would become so intoxicated
listening to these divine discourses that he would be reluctant to
return home. He would forget all about the world, his family, and his
duties.

Yet in spite of Ram's close contact with the Master, his mind was
not content. His doubts persistently clung to him, even though his
longing for God increased more and more. One night he dreamed
that he took his bath in a familiar pond, and that Sri Ramakrishna
then initiated him with a sacred mantram and asked him to repeat it
one hundred times every day after his bath. As soon as Ram woke up
he felt that his whole body was pulsating with bliss. The next
morning he rushed to Dakshineswar and related his dream to the
Master. At this Sri Ramakrishna joyfully said, 'He who receives
divine blessings in a dream is sure to attain liberation'.[9]

Although Ram heard these hopeful words of the Master, his mind
was not satisfied with a holy dream. He was very sceptical, and to
him a dream was just a fantasy. His mind again started to waver. He
found no pleasure in worldly enjoyments, yet he was not convinced
about the existence of God. A few days passed this way. Then one
morning as Ram was standing at the corner of College Square in
Calcutta, explaining his mental conflicts to a friend, a tall stranger
approached Ram and whispered to him: 'Why are you so anxious?
Have patience'. Ram was stunned. After a few moments he turned to
see who this person was who had consoled him with these welcome
words, but the person had vanished. Although both Ram and his
friend had seen and heard the man, now they could not find him
anywhere. Ram felt that it had not been an illusion but a direct
message from God. Later he related this incident to Sri Ramakrishna,
who smiled and said, 'Yes, you will see many such things as
that'.[10]

Gradually Ram began to get a taste of divine bliss because of his
holy association with the Master, and worldly pleasures became more
and more insipid to him. He expressed to the Master his desire to
become a monk, but Sri Ramakrishna dissuaded him, saying:
'Nothing should be done on the spur of the moment. God alone

knows what he means to do through a particular person. Where will your wife and children be if you leave the world? You must not try to upset the arrangement God has made for you. Everything will come in time'. This simple advice satisfied Ram temporarily, but later he raised the subject again. At this Sri Ramakrishna became stern: 'What will you gain by renouncing the world? Living a family life is like living in a fort. It is easier to fight an enemy from inside a fort than from outside. You will be in a position to renounce the world when you can bestow three-fourths of your mind on God, but not before that'.[11] Ram was silenced. He resolved then to be an ideal householder devotee of God.

Soon after Ram met Sri Ramakrishna, he started to read *Sri Sri Chaitanya Charitamrita*, an authoritative biography of Sri Chaitanya, written in Bengali. The more Ram read about that God-intoxicated life, the more he felt that Sri Ramakrishna and Sri Chaitanya were the same person. But again he would have doubts. Once, at the request of the Master, Ram spent a night at Dakshineswar. When he was alone with the Master, he started looking at him in wonder.

'What are you looking at?' asked Sri Ramakrishna.

'I am looking at you'.

'What do you think of me?'

'I consider you to be Chaitanya'.

Sri Ramakrishna was silent for a moment and then said, 'Well, Bhairavi Brahmani used to say the same thing'.[12]

As the days went by Ram saw more and more of Sri Ramakrishna's extraordinary spiritual powers, and his scepticism was replaced by faith. One day on the way to Dakshineswar, Ram bought some *jilipis*, a sweet which the Master liked very much. While crossing a bridge a little boy begged for one of them. Ram tried at first to ignore him, but then he thought that perhaps the boy was God in disguise and he gave a piece to him. After arriving in Dakshineswar, Ram put the sweets in the Master's room and spent the day there. In the afternoon Sri Ramakrishna asked for some refreshments and Ram immediately placed the jilipis in front of him. Sri Ramakrishna touched them and looked up. He then broke a few and, shaking his head, expressed his unwillingness to eat them. After this he washed his hands. Ram was mortified. He could not understand why the Master had refused his sweets. He was so upset that he threw the jilipis away and returned home. After a few days Ram came to Dakshineswar again and the Master said to him: 'When you bring something for me, don't give any of it to anyone else beforehand. I can't take anything without offering it to God, and I can't offer anything to him that has been defiled by being offered to someone else first'. This incident convinced Ram that the Master was omniscient.[13]

Doubt is a terrible disease, and a doubting soul suffers very much. But it is hard to uproot doubt from the mind completely. Every spiritual seeker has to pass through this 'dark night of the soul'. In spite of all that Ram had seen and heard, his old doubts and scepticism reappeared, making him restless and miserable. The world seemed to him like a desert. He went to the Master to tell him his sad tale and to seek consolation as before, but this time the Master cut him short with a curt reply: 'What can I do? It all depends on the will of God'.

'Sir, all these days I have been looking to you for help. Now if you treat me like this what shall I do?'

'I don't owe you anything. If you like, you may come. If not, don't'.

The Master's shock treatment immediately threw Ram into deep despair. His first impulse was to put an end to his life by drowning himself in the Ganga, but as he left the room he thought: 'Why should I commit suicide? I have heard that the name of the Lord is greater and more powerful than the Lord himself. And the Master said that it was my good luck to have had initiation in a dream. I shall test the efficacy of that mantram today'. He lay down on the northern verandah of Sri Ramakrishna's room and began to repeat that mantram silently. At dead of night the Master suddenly came out of his room, sat down near Ram, and gave him some advice. Ram was very happy. The Master emphasized that Ram should serve the devotees of God, and that this would give him joy and peace. Then the Master returned to his room.[14]

Quite often the devotees of Sri Ramakrishna would arrange festivals in their homes and invite the Master and other devotees to come. At these gatherings the Master would talk about God and sing and dance in ecstasy, filling the whole house with an intense atmosphere of spirituality. The host generally bore all the expenses of the feast, including paying the carriage fare of the Master and sometimes hiring a musician. Now Ram was known for his miserliness, and when he started to calculate the expenses involved, he hesitated to invite the Master and the devotees. But when Sri Ramakrishna set a date to visit his home, he had a change of heart and gladly began to make the necessary preparations.

On Saturday, June 2, 1883, the full moon day of the Bengali month of Vaisakh, Sri Ramakrishna came to Ram's house. Ram felt so blessed on this occasion that later he would arrange a festival every year to celebrate that auspicious day. After this Ram invited the Master to his house many times and became so expert in festival management that other devotees would consult him before inviting the Master to their homes. Slowly the Master uprooted Ram's miserliness and made him a generous devotee.

The day after Sri Ramakrishna's first visit to Ram's house (June 3, 1883), Ram went to Dakshineswar and received various spiritual instructions from the Master. At ten o'clock that night Ram took leave of the Master and went out. It was dark and cloudy. While he was still on the verandah he noticed that the Master was coming out of his room. Sri Ramakrishna suddenly came up to Ram and asked, 'Well, what do you want?' Ram was utterly amazed. He felt as if his whole body was charged with electricity. Although he realized that Sri Ramakrishna was standing in front of him like a kalpataru (wish-fulfilling tree), ready to grant any boon that he wanted, he was at a loss to know what to ask for from the Master. In the presence of Sri Ramakrishna's spiritual magnitude, he felt how petty it would be to ask for wealth or supernatural powers. Finally, overwhelmed with emotion, Ram replied: 'Lord, I don't know what to ask for. You decide for me'. 'Give me back the mantram I gave you in the dream', said Sri Ramakrishna as he entered into samadhi. Immediately Ram prostrated himself before the Master and offered the mantram mentally at his feet like a flower. Sri Ramakrishna touched Ram's head with his right foot and Ram also lost outward consciousness. He did not know how long they stayed in that state. Gradually the Master came back to the normal plane of consciousness and took his foot away. Ram stood up. 'If you wish to see anything', said the Master to Ram, 'look at me'. Ram looked and saw that Sri Ramakrishna had taken the form of his Chosen Deity, the form of God that was dearest to his heart. Then Sri Ramakrishna told him: 'You do not need to practise any more spiritual disciplines. Just come here and see me now and then, and bring with you a pice worth of something as a present'.[15]

After this Ram was free of all his restlessness. Moreover, his experience convinced him that Sri Ramakrishna was an Incarnation of God. Once, in Dakshineswar, the exuberant Ram expressed his belief to the great devotee, Girish Chandra Ghosh: 'Do you understand, Brother Girish? This time all three — Sri Chaitanya, Nityananda, and Advaita — are united in the form of Sri Ramakrishna. Love, devotion, and knowledge are equally manifested in this present Incarnation'.[16]

A true disciple carries out to the letter his teacher's instructions, proving thereby his love for his teacher. The Master had said, 'Those who serve the devotees, serve me'.[17] Ram strictly observed this commandment of the Master, serving the followers of Sri Ramakrishna with great devotion until the end of his life. He used to say, 'He who calls on Sri Ramakrishna is my nearest relative'.[18] His wife, Krishnapreyasi, who was also very devout, cheerfully helped her husband in his spiritual path. Ram, furthermore, had heard the Master cautioning the devotees about money: Just as water under a bridge is constantly flowing and as a result it never becomes stagnant and foul, so also the money earned by a real devotee should be spent for a noble cause rather than be accumulated. The desire for accumulation breeds the poison of attachment.[19] Ram, therefore, did not save his earnings, but spent money freely for the good of others, especially for the poor, the needy, and the afflicted. He helped many students financially, even to the extent of providing free board and lodging in his own home. But Ram's main interest was in arranging kirtan (devotional singing) every evening in his home and feeding the thirty or so participants.

Spiritual life is not always smooth. Ram and the devotees would become absorbed in their singing until late hours of the night, but this naturally caused much disturbance and Ram's neighbours began to complain. Ram then decided to buy a secluded garden house where he could hold kirtans and practise spiritual disciplines. When he informed the Master of his intention, Sri Ramakrishna advised him, 'Buy such a solitary garden house that if a hundred murders were committed there no one would know it'.[20] Accordingly, in the middle of 1883 Ram purchased a garden house at Kankurgachi, an eastern suburb of Calcutta.

After a few months the Master said to Ram: 'How is it that you have not yet taken me to the new garden you have purchased for holding kirtan? Let us go one day to your garden to see what it is like'.[21] Ram was exuberant. Immediately he arranged everything for the Master's visit. On Wednesday, December 26, 1883, M. recorded in *The Gospel of Sri Ramakrishna*:

> Sri Ramakrishna, accompanied by Manilal Mallik, M., and several other devotees, was in a carriage on his way to Ram's new garden...
> Master (*to Manilal*): 'In order to meditate on God, one should try at first to think of Him as free from *upadhis*, limitations. God is beyond upadhis. He is beyond speech and mind. But it is very difficult to achieve perfection in this form of meditation.
> 'But it is easy to meditate on an Incarnation — God born as man

Yes, God in man. The body is a mere covering. It is like a lantern with a light burning inside, or like a glass case in which one sees precious things'.

Arriving at the garden, the Master got out of the carriage and accompanied Ram and the other devotees to the sacred tulsi-grove. Standing near it, he said: 'How nice! It is a fine place. You can easily meditate on God here'.

Sri Ramakrishna sat down in the house, which stood to the south of the lake. Ram offered him a plate of fruit and sweets which he enjoyed with the devotees. After a short time he went around the garden.[22]

In sacred memory of Sri Ramakrishna's visit to the garden and because he had mentioned it as an ideal place for meditation, Ram named the place 'Yogodyana' (garden for practising yoga). Ram gave the mango tree the name 'Ramakrishna-bhog' (delight to Ramakrishna), and to the lake where the Master had washed his hands and feet he gave the name 'Ramakrishna-kunda'. In the northeast corner of the garden Ram planted a Panchavati (a grove of five trees) at the Master's suggestion. After the passing away of the Master, his relics were enshrined on the spot near the tulsi-grove where the Master had bowed down. A temple was later erected there.[23]

Even during his boyhood, Ram was strong, assertive, and manly. He was a leader in the local gymnasium, the theatre club, and other social organizations, and people respected him for his character and integrity. Knowing Ram's faculty for leadership, Sri Ramakrishna called him 'Captain', and he also sometimes consulted with him. Once Girish Ghosh, while in a drunken state, humiliated the Master. The devotees were furious with Girish. But when Sri Ramakrishna told Ram about it, Ram defended Girish, suggesting to the Master that Girish was like the serpent Kaliya who had nothing to offer Sri Krishna but its venom. Immediately the Master forgot the affront and went with Ram to Girish's house to forgive him.

Ram was free and frank with the Master, but he was also very outspoken and easily piqued. Once Adhar Sen arranged a recital of the Chandi at his house in Calcutta and invited the Master and many of the devotees. Ram, somehow, was overlooked. He became very upset when he heard about it and complained to the Master. But Sri Ramakrishna replied: 'Suppose he didn't invite you to his house. Why such a fuss about going to a place where the name of the Lord was sung? One may go unasked to participate in religious music. One doesn't have to be invited'.[24]

The Master had a wonderful sense of humour and would sometimes remove the seriousness of a situation or the misunderstandings of the devotees through a joke or by teasing them. On one occasion Ram was trying to prove the superiority of the Master in his presence. While Ram, with all his vigour, was denouncing the Brahmos, the Master said to him: 'Now tell me why my arm was hurt. Stand up and deliver a lecture on that'.[25] Everyone laughed. Another time (September 28, 1884), the Master in a deep spiritual mood was talking to the devotees at Ram's house. But Ram did not hear the talk because he was busy making arrangements to feed the devotees on the roof. When he finally came downstairs the Master asked him, 'Where have you been?' 'I was upstairs, sir'. Immediately the Master reminded him to be humble: 'Isn't it better to stay down below than to be high up? Water accumulates in low land but flows down from a high mound'.[26]

On Sundays and holidays many devotees would visit the Master at Dakshineswar and ask him questions about spiritual life. Ram had a desire to preserve the Master's words so he always carried a pencil and paper with him. While Sri Ramakrishna was answering the devotees' questions, Ram would write down what he was saying. Seeing Ram's enthusiasm and sincerity, the Master one day said to him: 'Why do you take so much trouble? Later your mind will be your guru and will give you the proper guidance whenever you are faced with life's problems'.[27] After receiving this blessing from the Master, Ram stopped taking notes.

When a flower blooms, bees come of their own accord. In the later part of the 1870s people began to hear more and more about Sri Ramakrishna, and in the 1880s many newcomers came. Forgetting his body, the Master helped the seekers of God. But one day at Dakshineswar he complained to the Divine Mother like a child: 'How is it that you are bringing such a crowd here? I find no time even to bathe or eat. [Pointing to his own body] This is but a perforated drum, and if you beat it day and night, how long will it last?'[28] Then, on another occasion, he prayed to the Mother, 'Please give a little power to Vijay, Girish, Kedar, Ram, and Mahendra (M.), so that they may, to a certain extent, prepare the newcomers before they come to me'.[29] Thus Ram was commissioned to teach by the Master. About this same time Ram also received permission from the Master to give a lecture at the Konnagar Hari Sabha on 'What is True Religion?'

In May 1885 Ram compiled some of Sri Ramakrishna's important teachings that he had noted down and brought them out in a Bengali book entitled Tattvasara. A few of the devotees, however, objected to this and even reported it to the Master. Sri Ramakrishna called Ram aside one day and said: 'Look here, some devotees informed me that you were publishing a book. What have you written?' Ram replied that he had collected some of his (Sri Ramakrishna's) teachings and put them together in a book. Ram then read some of it to the Master, who said: 'Oh, you have written those teachings? Very good. Listen, if you think that you have written them you will get very little response from others; but if you think that the Lord is working through you then it will be in great demand'. Sri Ramakrishna further cautioned Ram: 'Do not publish my biography now. If you do, my body will not last long'.[30] Ram obeyed, but after the Master had passed away he wrote the first biography, *Sri Sri Ramakrishna Paramahamsadever Jivanvrittanta*. Later he enlarged *Tattvasara* and published it as *Tattva-Prakashika* (The Teachings of Sri Ramakrishna). He also began to publish a Bengali magazine, *Tattvamanjari*, in order to spread the Master's teachings.

In September 1885 Sri Ramakrishna moved to Shyampukur, in the northern section of Calcutta, for his cancer treatment. Ram took an active part in the arrangements that were made for the Master's care. As the day of the Kali Puja approached, the Master expressed a desire to celebrate the occasion with a worship of the Divine Mother and asked the devotees to collect the necessary materials. Accordingly, they procured flowers, fruits, sweets, sandal paste, incense, and candles. When the auspicious time came they placed them in front of the Master, thinking that he would perform the worship. There was no image. The devotees sat around the Master silently waiting, but he remained absorbed in meditation. All of a sudden the thought came to Ram's mind: 'It is needless for the Master to perform worship. We shall worship him'. Ram whispered this idea to Girish, who responded: 'What did you say? Is the Master waiting to accept our worship?' Immediately Girish took some flowers and offered them to the Master, saying, 'Victory to Sri Ramakrishna! Victory to Mother!' The hair of the Master's body stood on end and he entered into samadhi. His face was radiant with a divine smile. The rest of the devotees also offered flowers to the Master and were blessed.[31]

The stuffy, polluted atmosphere of Calcutta aggravated Sri Ramakrishna's illness. In accordance with the doctor's advice, the devotees moved him to a garden house in Cossipore, a northern suburb of Calcutta. Ram, as usual, took the managerial role there and also contributed money towards the Master's living expenses according to his means. One day, hearing that the Master needed a tongue scraper, Ram bought a silver one and presented it to him. But the Master would not accept it, saying: 'What have you done? Take it away. Please buy a one-pice brass tongue scraper for me'.[32] Sri Ramakrishna was very much against luxury. Ram remembered this and later followed the Master's example.

On January 1, 1886, Sri Ramakrishna went into an extraordinary spiritual mood and blessed many devotees, saying 'Be illumined'. Ram was one of those present on that occasion. Later he celebrated that day every year as 'Kalpataru Day' (Wish-Fulfilling Day) at his garden house.

Sri Ramakrishna passed away on August 16, 1886, at the Cossipore garden house. After his cremation the major part of his sacred relics was preserved and worshipped by his young disciples who later became monks. The remaining portion was installed at the Kankurgachi Yogodyana on Janmashtami (the birth anniversary of Sri Krishna, which fell that year a week after the Master's passing away). Ram took the initiative and immediately arranged for regular worship of the relics. Since then Janmashtami has been observed every year as the main festival day at Yogodyana.

It is noteworthy that Ram was the first person to publish a biography of Sri Ramakrishna, to build a temple for the worship of the Master's relics, and to preach publicly that Sri Ramakrishna was an avatar. His burning faith, devotion, renunciation, erudition, and his power to convince people made him an ideal evangelist. And more important, he had the blessings of his guru, Sri Ramakrishna. From 1893 to 1897, he gave eighteen lectures on Sri Ramakrishna's life and teachings at the Star, City, and Minerva Theatres. They created a sensation in Calcutta. At first some of Sri Ramakrishna's devotees objected to these lectures, but Ram would not listen to them. On Good Friday, 1893, he began a series of lectures, the first of which was 'Is Ramakrishna Paramahamsa an Avatar?' Ram substantiated his view through scriptural quotations, reasoning, empirical evidence, and incidents from his own personal experience.

Ram realized that people would not listen to his lectures on Sri Ramakrishna, who was the embodiment of renunciation and purity, if he himself did not renounce lust and greed. True religion, according to Sri Ramakrishna, is in uniting the mind and speech, and Ram sincerely endeavoured to translate the Master's teachings into his own life. Though he held a good position in his office, he was never proud of it, and he never allowed himself to crave for a higher position or for worldly objects. About food and clothing, he followed the simple path. In spite of the many duties connected with his job and his family, Ram's mind was always on the Master and the Kankurgachi Yogodyana. He lived with his wife and children at their Simla home, but he used to visit Kankurgachi every day. Later he moved to Yogodyana and took care of the worship service, gardening, and cleaning by himself. Sri Ramakrishna had taught his disciples, 'If you desire to live in the world unattached, you should first practise devotional disciplines in solitude for some time'.[33]

God tests his devotees in many ways. A real lover of God is he who can overcome all temptations. Once a Calcutta merchant imported four shiploads of kerosene oil from England. Before marketing the oil, however, he had to bring a sample to Ram for chemical analysis. Ram tested the sample three times and found that it was short by three points, so he would not approve the kerosene for marketing. The merchant was deeply distressed, for it meant the loss of millions of rupees. He offered Ram a bribe of forty thousand rupees to approve the merchandise, but Ram refused to accept the money and told the merchant that he could never write a false certificate.[34] Although Ram received many such offers in his life, he never deviated from the truth.

Ram's surrender to the Master was phenomenal. During the later part of his life someone asked him why he had not saved some money for his wife and children. He replied: 'If I had wanted I could easily have saved a lot of money, but I never felt that I was maintaining my family. I know the Lord provides everything for my wife and children, and after my death he will continue to do so'.[35] When one of Ram's young daughters died on December 7, 1886, from burns suffered in an accident, he endured that terrible grief, and to those who came to offer consolation, he said: 'The Lord gave me that daughter and he took her away. Why should I lament?'[36]

Ordinarily, when people get together, they love to chat, gossip, or criticize others. But to Ram worldly conversation was like deadly poison, and he would not allow anyone in his presence to talk about anything other than the Master or spiritual life. When he would talk about Sri Ramakrishna his face would beam with joy and tears would flow from his eyes. His faith and devotion were palpable. He had some initiated disciples and he changed quite a few lives through his spiritual power. Every Sunday Ram and his followers would sing kirtan and dance barefoot through the streets of Calcutta. Through the grace of his guru, Ram tasted the bliss of God and eagerly shared it with each and all.

Ram's strenuous ascetic life at Yogodyana eventually affected his health. In 1898 he had a severe attack of dysentery which, along with his diabetes and a painful carbuncle, made it necessary for him to move back to his Simla residence for treatment. His wife, friends, and disciples devotedly served him, and other disciples of Sri Ramakrishna were able to visit him more easily. One day Swami Vivekananda came to see him. It was a wonderful meeting of these two great disciples of Sri Ramakrishna. While they were talking about their old days with the Master, Ram had to go to the bathroom. Since there was no one else present, Swami Vivekananda helped him put on his slippers. Seeing Swami Vivekananda's humility, tears came to Ram's eyes and he said: 'Bille [Swami Vivekananda's family nickname], I thought that after travelling to America and becoming famous you would have forgotten us. But now I see that you are my same little brother Bille'.[37] (Ram Chandra Datta and Swami Vivekananda were cousins.)

In spite of the best available treatment and care, Ram's physical condition deteriorated. He developed heart disease and experienced severe breathing difficulty which led to chronic asthma. He would pass sleepless nights chanting the name of the Master. After a month and a half at his Calcutta residence he had a premonition that he would not live long. He asked his wife and family to send him back to Yogodyana so that he could die in that holy place where Sri Ramakrishna's relics had been installed, but they were reluctant to let him go. Ram finally ordered a palanquin and left for Kankurgachi with his disciples. When he arrived there he said, 'I have come here to have my final rest near my guru, Sri Ramakrishna'.[38] He lived only five more days.

On January 17, 1899, at 10:45 P.M., Ram breathed his last. His body was cremated on the bank of the Ganga and the relics were placed next to Sri Ramakrishna's temple at Yogodyana. Before he passed away he told his disciples: 'When I die please bury a little of the ashes of my body at the entrance to Yogodyana. Whoever enters this place will walk over my head, and thus I shall get the touch of the Master's devotees' feet forever'.[39]

7

Manomohan Mittra

Bliss is the source of existence, and again, it is also the goal of all human endeavours. That bliss is God. Human beings are constantly seeking bliss in everything they do. They get married for bliss, have children for bliss, earn money for bliss, eat food for bliss, and move in this world only for bliss. In the last half of the nineteenth century Sri Ramakrishna opened a market of bliss in Dakshineswar, and just as bees flock to a flower for honey, so people came from all directions to the Master for bliss.

One day a devotee asked Sri Ramakrishna, 'Sir, people come to you from distant places and become blessed, but why do the people of Dakshineswar not come?' The Master answered: 'You see, a dark shadow always remains under a lighted oil lamp. Look at a cow tied by a rope on the bank of the Ganga. She is dying of thirst, but she cannot drink the nearby Ganga water because she is bound. On the other hand, stray cows come from afar and drink the water. Bound souls do not like to hear about God. As long as maya, or ignorance, exists they remain forgetful of him'.[1]

Manomohan Mittra, a devotee of Sri Ramakrishna, once described how maya was shattered for him in a dream:

> It was a Saturday night in the fall of 1879. I saw in a dream that the whole world had been flooded with water. All of the tall buildings of Calcutta, including the Ochterloney Monument, were swept away by the terrible current. In whatever direction I looked I saw only water and not a single human being. I was drifting helplessly in the current. All of a sudden the thought came to my mind: 'Where is my mother? Where are my wife, daughter, and sisters?' Immediately I heard a voice: 'There is no one left in this world who is your own. All are dead'.
> 'Then what is the use of my living?'
> 'Suicide is a great sin'.
> 'Then where shall I go? I don't find any human habitation'.
> 'No one is alive in this world. All are dead'.
> 'When none is alive, then with whom shall I stay?'

93

Manomohan Mittra (1851-1903)

'They only have survived from this deluge who have realized God. You will meet them very soon and live with them'.

'I see only water all around. What shall I eat?'

'Search below your heart. You will get food'.

I put my hand below my chest and found a piece of plank, which was helping me to float in the current. I was surprised to witness the play of God. Without my knowing about it he had sent a piece of plank to save my life. I did not know how to swim well, so it would have been impossible for me to float for such a long time.

I woke up at four o'clock in the morning, but I lay there perplexed for some time. Then, seeing my wife, I cried out: 'Where am I? Who are you?' Hearing this, she was dumbfounded. When I regained my normal consciousness I realized that what I had seen was a dream.[2]

Later that morning Manomohan went to see his cousin Ram Chandra Datta and told him about the dream. Ram said: 'What you have seen is true. To tell you the truth, all beings are submerged in maya. They are the living dead'.[3] Manomohan had read about the spiritual life of Sri Ramakrishna in the *Indian Mirror*, *Sulabh Samachar*, and other newspapers, so he suggested that they visit him in Dakshineswar. Ram immediately agreed. It was this dream that brought Manomohan to Sri Ramakrishna.

Manomohan Mittra was born in September 1851 at Konnagar, in the district of Hooghly, which is nine miles north of Calcutta and on the other side of the Ganga. He was greatly influenced by his parents. His father, Bhuban Mohan Mittra, was a successful physician and well versed in history, science, and English literature. At that time Indian society was under the sway of Western culture. But in spite of his education, Bhuban Mohan was against imitating Western hedonism and was a great defender of the traditional Hindu culture. His wife, Shyama Sundari, was very pious and would observe the Hindu rituals and festivals with steadfast devotion. Once Shyama Sundari was absorbed in deep meditation. One of her relatives, in order to test the genuineness of her meditation, dropped a scorpion on her lap. The woman thought that if Shyama's meditation was just a show, she would cry out. But the relative was surprised when she found that Shyama was completely oblivious of her surroundings and unaware of the scorpion, which walked over her lap without stinging her.

Manomohan first studied at the Konnagar School and then went to the Calcutta Hindu School. He was not a brilliant student, but every year he won the prize for good conduct. Through his uncle Rajendra Nath Mittra, he met Devendra Nath Tagore, the leader of the Adi

Brahmo Samaj, and Keshab Chandra Sen, the leader of the
Navavidhan Brahmo Samaj. Manomohan's grandfather noticed
Manomohan's close association with the Brahmos and his excessive
religious inclinations. Fearing that Manomohan would renounce the
world and become a monk, he arranged the boy's marriage.
Manomohan was then seventeen years old and still a student at the
Hindu School. After his marriage Manomohan went to Dhaka, in
East Bengal, with his father, and there he continued his education.

When Bhuban Mohan became ill a few years later, he and
Manomohan returned to Calcutta. In 1873 Bhuban Mohan died of a
heart attack, leaving his wife, four daughters, and one son.
Manomohan was then twenty-one years old, and the whole
responsibility for the family was on him. His wise mother advised
him to rent their Calcutta home and move to their home in Konnagar.
Manomohan could not think of continuing his college education
because he was desperately looking for a job. At last he got a clerical
position at the Bengal Government Secretariat in Calcutta, but he
had to commute to work daily from Konnagar.

Soon after this Manomohan lost a seven-year-old daughter and
became greatly distraught. Whenever he could find a little time he
would visit the spot where his daughter had been cremated. His
mother soon found out about it and persuaded him to move the
family back to Calcutta. With the passage of time Manomohan
overcame his grief.

Rajmohan, a friend of Manomohan's, had become a disciple of
Keshab Chandra Sen. Both of them liked to talk about God and the
greatness of Keshab, who by then had become quite famous as an
evangelist. It was due to Rajmohan's influence and his own mother's
encouragement that Manomohan began to practise the spiritual
disciplines of the Brahmos. Sitting on a tiger skin, he would play on a
one-stringed instrument and say some prayers. He later wrote in his
autobiography: 'At that time I knew nothing about prayer. I used to
add some bombastic adjectives before the word *Brahman* and would
consider that a prayer... I felt that without lamentation and tears the
impurities of the mind would not be washed away. And if the mind
is not pure, one cannot realize God, who is purity itself'.[4]

Just as a cookbook does not appease the hunger of the stomach, so
also scriptural study, dry religious discussions, and lifeless,
mechanical prayers cannot satisfy the spiritual hunger of the heart.
Manomohan at last found the spiritual food that he was seeking from
Sri Ramakrishna.

On Sunday, November 13, 1879, the day after Manomohan's

strange dream, he, Ram Chandra Datta, and Gopal Chandra Mittra, who was a friend of theirs, left for Dakshineswar by boat to visit Sri Ramakrishna, Manomohan had the idea that Sri Ramakrishna Paramahamsa would be like other monks — with shaven head, wearing an ochre cloth, and sitting on a tiger skin. He was very much surprised when an ordinary looking man in a plain, white cloth welcomed them to his room and motioned for them to sit on his bed. Manomohan was deeply impressed with Sri Ramakrishna's simplicity and humility.

Since Manomohan was an ardent devotee of Keshab Chandra Sen and the Brahmo Samaj, he was averse to idol worship. Sri Ramakrishna understood Manomohan's attitude and said to him: 'As an imitation custard apple reminds one of the real fruit, so the divine images enkindle the presence of God. He is all-powerful. It is possible for him to manifest in anything'.[5] Manomohan, Ram, and Gopal had a long conversation with Sri Ramakrishna, and they returned to Calcutta in the evening full of peace and joy.

Manomohan decided after that first visit to see the Master every Sunday. On his second visit he asked Sri Ramakrishna: 'Some people say God is formless, others say he is with form, and again others call him Krishna, Shiva, or Kali. Could you tell us what the real nature of God is?'[6]

Sri Ramakrishna smiled and said: 'He is sometimes with form, he is sometimes formless, and again he is beyond both. He is all-pervading. It is difficult to ascertain his real nature. Just as there is nothing to compare gold with except gold, so there is nothing equal to God. He is the cause of the gross objects as well as of the subtle mind and intellect. For example: The same substance in its solid form is ice, in its liquid form is water, and in its gaseous form is vapour. According to the mental attitude of the spiritual aspirant, God manifests himself. A jnani experiences God as all-pervading, formless space, and a devotee perceives God with a particular form. So, if you sincerely want to know the real nature of God, meditate on him in solitude. Have patience. Surrender yourself to him and pray. When the right time comes you will see him'.[7]

Manomohan: 'We get peace when we feel the presence of God in our hearts; otherwise mere intellectual understanding of God and atheism are the same'.

Sri Ramakrishna: 'In the beginning one should move forward on the spiritual path holding to an initial faith [i.e., faith in the words of the scriptures and the guru]. One then attains direct perception. There are two kinds of faith — initial faith and real faith [i.e., faith that comes from direct experience]. Be steadfast in the first one and then you will see God'.[8]

Another day Sri Ramakrishna said in a gathering, 'This world is a "framework of illusion" '. Manomohan laughed at this, but the Master's words penetrated into his heart and he realized the truth of them -- that the world is indeed impermanent. Sri Ramakrishna continued, 'This world again is a "mansion of mirth", but one should know how to get joy here.[9]

'Try to live in God, and then you will not suffer from misery. Living in God means that one offers one's body and mind to him. Have constant recollectedness of God. Life in the world is fraught with fears, and moreover there are many ways in which the mind can get polluted. But if you can somehow keep your mind in God, all obstacles will go away. There is tremendous power in the name of God. Sing his name and glories'.[10]

Manomohan: 'Does God listen to our prayers?'

Sri Ramakrishna: 'What are you saying? You will call on God and he will not listen? He is omnipresent and omniscient. How do you know that he does not listen to your prayers? You have no faith, so you are doubting him'.

Manomohan: 'Sir, would you tell us how to increase our longing for God?'

Sri Ramakrishna (with a smile): 'As hunger and thirst arise spontaneously, so does longing for God. Everything depends upon time. Mere thinking cannot make a person hungry. In the same way longing for God does not come simply by saying, "Let there be longing". Yearning is awakened in the mind automatically when a person feels the need for God. Yearning for God does not come until and unless a person has satisfied his cravings for mundane objects, renounced all attachment to lust and gold, and shunned worldly comforts and enjoyments like filth. How many people are restless for God-realization? People shed jugfuls of tears for their wives, children, or money, but who weeps for God? He who longs for him certainly will find him. Cry to him. Call on him with a longing heart. You will see him'.[11]

Manomohan: 'Sir, I do not know God, but I have taken refuge in you. Please accept my responsibility'.

Sri Ramakrishna was quiet for some time. It was evening and Manomohan would be returning home soon. The Master went into an ecstatic mood and said: 'Listen. He who comes here for God-realization or to attain knowledge, his desire will be fulfilled. Let me say again: his desire will definitely be fulfilled'.[12]

Sri Ramakrishna's words made Manomohan jubilant, and in great relief he fell at the Master's feet. Thenceforth he accepted Sri Ramakrishna as his guru.

Manomohan soon began to realize that Sri Ramakrishna was not just an ordinary human being, but was an Incarnation of God. After a few visits a desire came to Manomohan's mind to serve the Master. One day he came to Dakshineswar and found the Master seated on his bed with his legs hanging down over the edge. Seeing Manomohan, Sri Ramakrishna drew up his feet and sat cross-legged. This hurt Manomohan and he said to the Master: 'Why did you withdraw your feet? Please extend them as before. If you don't I shall cut them off and carry them to my home so that the devotees may worship your blessed feet'.[13] Sri Ramakrishna smiled and allowed Manomohan to massage his feet.

Manomohan was a very emotional and touchy person. As the only son of his parents he was used to getting a lot of attention, and he expected the same from the Master. Furthermore, he was proud of his devotion. One day the Master praised Surendra's devotion in front of everyone and did not say anything about Manomohan. Manomohan became so upset that he stopped visiting Sri Ramakrishna. When another devotee asked him why he was no longer coming to Dakshineswar he said: 'Let the Master be happy with his devotees. I am nobody there'. The Master sent message after message to Manomohan to come to see him, but Manomohan refused. He finally asked a devotee to report to the Master that he would visit him after attaining devotion. In order to avoid Sri Ramakrishna's messengers Manomohan even moved back to Konnagar and again commuted to his office in Calcutta. But strangely enough, the more he tried to banish all thoughts of Sri Ramakrishna from his mind, the greater became his mental turmoil. It gradually became impossible for him to attend to his day-to-day business. Whenever he tried to put his mind on his work, it automatically turned to Dakshineswar. In despair he realized that Sri Ramakrishna possessed his whole heart.

One day, when Manomohan went to the Ganga for a bath, he saw a country boat anchored near the bathing ghat. Seeing Balaram Babu, another devotee of the Master, on the boat, Manomohan said to him, 'It is my good fortune that today I have met a devotee!' Balaram informed him that the Master himself had come to see him. Meanwhile Niranjan came out on the deck and said to Manomohan: 'Why don't you come to Dakshineswar? The Master is extremely worried about you'. Sri Ramakrishna then appeared and, looking at

Manomohan, went into samadhi. Tears rolled from Manomohan's eyes as he silently watched this scene. 'Ah, he has taken so much trouble for my sake', he thought. 'How greatly I must have wronged him'. Overwhelmed with emotion, Manomohan was about to fall into the water when Niranjan jumped from the boat and caught him. By this time Sri Ramakrishna had regained normal consciousness, and he asked Niranjan to bring Manomohan on board. The Master said most affectionately, 'I have been very anxious about you, so I have come for you'. Manomohan prostrated himself before the Master and said, 'Sir, it was all due to my wounded vanity'. He began sobbing like a child and could say no more. Manomohan then took the Master to his home for a visit and returned with him to Dakshineswar. After this he resumed his regular visits to Sri Ramakrishna.[14]

Manomohan and his cousin Ram Datta got together every evening to sing devotional songs, and gradually many people joined them. Sri Ramakrishna encouraged Manomohan and Ram. He told them one day: 'Holy company is essential. As one gets heat sitting near a fire, so holy company raises the mind to a higher plane. One gets peace and inspiration in the company of the holy'.[15]

When Manomohan became drawn to Sri Ramakrishna and his teachings, his mother, four sisters, and three brothers-in-law also became devoted to the Master. Rakhal, who was later known as Swami Brahmananda, was married to Vishweswari, Manomohan's third sister. It was Manomohan who brought Rakhal to the Master. One of Manomohan's aunts, however, could not understand their attitude. Seeing Manomohan's great dependence on Sri Ramakrishna, she one day warned Manomohan's mother: 'Please don't allow your son to visit Dakshineswar so frequently. What will you do if he renounces the world?' Shyama Sundari replied, 'Will such a blessed day come when my son will dedicate his life to the service of holy people?'

Manomohan overheard their conversation, and when he arrived in Dakshineswar Sri Ramakrishna said to him: 'Look, a devotee visits me, but his aunt does not like it, and she is trying to incite his mother so that he may not come here. Can you tell me whether he will stop coming here or not?' Manomohan was dumbfounded and understood that the Master was all-knowing.[16]

One day Manomohan was coming from Konnagar to Dakshineswar by a passenger boat when a severe rainstorm came up very suddenly. Some of the passengers asked the boatman to return to the shore at once, while others, out of fear, started to cry and pray. Seeing the pitiable condition of these people, Manomohan laughed. This irritated an old man, who exclaimed: 'What a fool you are! You are going to die and you are laughing!' Manomohan smiled and said: 'Sir, I am laughing because I shall die. Why should I die crying? I have reached the other shore of the ocean of maya, and I am going to him who took me there, so I have no fear of death'. The old man frowned. In the meantime the boat reached Dakshineswar.

The Master was surprised to see Manomohan. He said to him: 'You have come to see me in the midst of a cyclone! It proves that you love me'.

Manomohan: 'Sir, if I do not love you then whom else shall I love?'

Sri Ramakrishna: 'Why? Who am I to you?'

Manomohan: 'You are the saviour of my soul. I have no fear when I come to you'.

Sri Ramakrishna smiled.[17]

On Saturday, December 3, 1881, Sri Ramakrishna visited Manomohan's Calcutta home. Manomohan had arranged a festival to celebrate the occasion. M. included an account of that memorable visit in *The Gospel of Sri Ramakrishna*:

In the afternoon Sri Ramakrishna paid a visit to his householder disciple Manomohan, at 23 Simla Street, Calcutta. It was a small two-storey house with a courtyard. The Master was seated in the drawing room on the first floor. Ishan of Bhawanipur asked him: 'Sir, why have you renounced the world? The scriptures extol the householder's life as the best'.

Master: 'I don't know much about what is good and what is bad. I do what God makes me do and speak what he makes me speak'.

Ishan: 'If everybody renounced the world, they would be acting against God's will'.

Master: 'Why should everybody renounce? On the other hand, can it be the will of God that all should revel in "woman and gold" like dogs and jackals? Has he no other wish? Do you know what accords with his will and what is against it?

'You say that God wants everybody to lead a worldly life. But why don't you see it as God's will when your wife and children die? Why don't you see his will in poverty, when you haven't a morsel to eat?'...

Keshab arrived with some Brahmo devotees and respectfully saluted the Master... For some time a reader recited from the Bhagavata and explained the text.

Master (*to the devotees*): 'It is very difficult to do one's duty in the world. If you whirl round too fast you feel giddy and faint; but there is no such fear if you hold on to a post. Do your duty, but do not forget God.

'You may ask, "If worldly life is so difficult, then what is the way?" The way is constant practice. At Kamarpukur I have seen the women of the carpenter families flattening rice with a husking machine. They are always fearful of the pestle's smashing their fingers; and at the same time they go on nursing their children and bargaining with customers. They say to the customers, "Pay us what you owe before you leave".

'An immoral woman goes on performing her household duties, but all the time her mind dwells on her sweetheart.

'But one needs spiritual discipline to acquire such a state of mind; one should pray to God in solitude every now and then. It is possible to perform worldly duties after obtaining love for God. If you try to break a jackfruit, your hands will be smeared with its sticky juice. But that won't happen if, beforehand, you rub them with oil'.

The kirtan began. Trailokya was singing. The Master danced, Keshab and the other devotees dancing with him... After the music he wanted something to eat. A plate of sweetmeats was sent from the inner apartments. Keshab held the plate before Sri Ramakrishna and the Master ate. When he had finished, Keshab poured water on his hands and then dried the Master's hands and face with a towel. Afterwards he began to fan the Master.

Master (*to Keshab and the other devotees*): 'They are heroes indeed who can pray to God in the midst of their worldly activities. They are like men who strive for God-realization while carrying heavy loads on their heads. Such men are real heroes. You may say that this is extremely difficult. But is there anything, however hard, that cannot be achieved through God's grace? His grace makes even the impossible possible. If a lamp is brought into a room that has been dark a thousand years, does it illumine the room little by little? The room is lighted all at once'.

These reassuring words gladdened the hearts of Keshab and the other householder devotees.[18]

Although Manomohan was normally a quiet, peace-loving person, he could sometimes be very outspoken, as it was unbearable for him to see or hear anything unjust or improper. One day on his way to Dakshineswar a man made some false and disrespectful remarks about Sri Ramakrishna in front of him. Manomohan became furious and told the man, 'One more word and I'll knock you to the ground'.

As soon as Manomohan arrived at Dakshineswar Sri Ramakrishna said to him: 'Everyone thinks that his faith is the greatest. If anyone says a word against his faith, he first argues, then becomes angry, and at last loses control and becomes violent'. Manomohan understood that the Master knew everything and that it was impossible to hide anything from him. He humbly explained, 'Sir, I cannot bear to hear anyone criticize you'. The Master replied: 'Whether somebody criticizes me or praises me, that is no one else's business. I am a most insignificant person, so what will that man gain by criticizing me? I have neither the power to give ten jars of gold coins to a person who praises me, nor the power to give ten lashes to a person who censures me. I am a child of the Divine Mother. I live in this world as she wishes'.

Honour and dishonour are the same to an illumined soul, because his mind is constantly absorbed in the Atman, beyond the pairs of opposites. Manomohan had learned a good lesson from the Master, but he became downcast and sat in a corner hiding his face. After some time the Master said to him: 'Why are you so unhappy? Did I scold you? If you are hurt, I shall be in pain. Anger is horrible! I can't touch an angry person, and I can't even bear his presence. The scriptures say that next to lust, anger is the greatest enemy of man. Anger originates from rajas'.[19]

Through trials and tribulations God tests the faith of his devotees. Once Manomohan's eldest daughter, Manikprabha, was seriously ill, so he decided not to go as usual to Dakshineswar. His mother asked him, 'Will you not go to visit the Master today?' 'How can I go, Mother?' Manomohan replied. 'You are going to the Master', said Shyama Sundari, 'whose name removes all evil. I can assure you that while you are visiting him no disaster will happen here. Please go to him right now. Who can stop death? This is the time for you to show your faith. He who remains unperturbed, surrendering everything to God, is a man of faith. Please don't misuse the time. Go to the Master'.

When Manomohan's wife noticed that he was getting ready to leave for Dakshineswar, she became very upset and scolded him, saying, 'Our daughter is dying and you are going off to Dakshineswar!' But Manomohan was not deterred since he had tremendous respect for his mother's words. As he was about to leave, his mother said to him, 'Please inform the Master of your daughter's illness and bring a little dust from that place where the Master meditates'.

'How can I talk about my daughter's illness to the Master?'

'What are you so afraid of? You are a child of God. You are supposed to tell him of your sufferings so that he can remove them'.

'How can I discuss these mundane things with the Master?'

'You won't have to tell him verbally. Go to him and mentally inform him. He is all-knowing. He will understand your pain and then everything will happen according to his will'.

When he arrived at Dakshineswar, Manomohon bowed down to the Master and seated himself among the devotees. In the course of conversation the Master said, 'Today while a man was getting ready to come here, his wife angrily said some harsh words to him'. That day Sri Ramakrishna talked for some time about renunciation. This helped to take Manomohan's mind off the thought of his sick daughter and give him strength. He had felt that his daughter would not live, but by the grace of the Master she recovered.[20]

Once Manomohan and a friend decided to attend the Car Festival of Jagannath at Mahesh, which is a few miles north of Dakshineswar and across the Ganga. Since they had a great desire to take Sri Ramakrishna with them, they rented a boat that morning in Calcutta and stopped first at Dakshineswar. When the Master saw them he asked them where they were going. 'Sir, we are going to see Lord Jagannath at Mahesh', replied Manomohan. To Manomohan's surprise and joy, the Master said, 'Then I shall go with you'. The Master immediately began to get ready and asked his nephew Ramlal to accompany them. At Mahesh, seeing Lord Jagannath on the chariot, Sri Ramakrishna went into samadhi. Manomohan and the others brought him to a safe place away from the crowd. Afterwards they visited the twelve Krishna temples at Ballabhpur and the Annapurna temple at Barrackpore.[21]

Manomohon sincerely tried to follow the teachings of Sri Ramakrishna. He used to cry to God profusely, but still he did not get any vision of God, nor did he have peace of mind. Hearing of his mental agony, Sri Ramakrishna one day said to him: 'Why are you so impatient? Everything happens in course of time. It takes time for fruit to ripen or for an abscess to mature. Divert all of your attachments towards God and he will be revealed to you'.[22]

Sri Ramakrishna was once invited to attend the festival of the Hari Sabha in Konnagar, Manomohan's village, but since he could not go he sent Ram and Manomohan there. Ram gave a lecture entitled 'What is True Religion?' This was followed by devotional singing, which lasted until midnight. A large crowd sang and danced in an inspired mood, encircling Ram and Manomohan. Manomohan lost outward consciousness and did not regain it until the next day. Later Ram and Manomohan came to know that the Master had transmitted spiritual power to them.[23]

Once, on a certain festival day, Manomohan's mother, Shyama

Sundari, was about to lose body-consciousness while listening to the evening kirtan at Ram's house. Immediately she called Manomohan to her and told him privately: 'Listen, my son. Today during the festival I shall give up my body. I shall leave this world while listening to the Lord's name. Please don't tell this to anyone, and let there be no obstruction to the festival'. Manomohan bowed down to his mother and then rejoined the kirtan. In obedience to her last wishes he did not express to anyone the terrible grief he was feeling. Meanwhile Shyama Sundari passed away. Ram and a few neighbours heard the sad news when the festival was over.[24]

There is a saying, 'If a person wants God, God takes away everything from him. And if that person continues to love him, God becomes his slave'. Manomohan passed through ordeal after ordeal. Shortly after his mother passed away, one of his daughters also died. When one of his friends tried to console him he replied: 'Everything happens according to the Master's will. What do we know about his will? He knows what is good for us. Bless me so that I may never go against his will'.[25]

When Sri Ramakrishna was ill at the Cossipore garden house, Manomohan remained in Calcutta so that he could visit him and serve him as far as possible. According to his means he gave money for the Master's support. Once, in a letter to his wife, who was living at their home in Konnagar, Manomohan wrote: 'Be careful how you spend money. Don't misuse a single penny. Otherwise we shall not be able to serve the Master properly. We now need a lot of money for his maintenance. It is a joy to see how the young disciples of the Master are serving him with heart and soul, and it is our duty now to look after this noble task so that it may not collapse from lack of money'.[26] After the Master's passing away Manomohan often visited Dakshineswar and also the Baranagore monastery, where the monastic disciples of the Master were then living.

Since Ram Chandra Datta wanted to write a biography of Sri Ramakrishna, he sent Manomohan to the Master's village home in Kamarpukur to collect information from people who had known him personally. Like Ram, Manomohan had an evangelical spirit, and wherever he went he would preach about the Master. Sometimes he took a leave of absence from his office and travelled to different cities and villages. Many people were stirred by his burning faith and exuberant devotion, and in due course he started centres at Ghatal, Jessore, Dhaka, Navadwip, and Murshidabad. He also wrote many inspiring articles for *Tattvamanjari*, a Bengali magazine published by Ram.

Manomohan's family was a religious one and Sri Ramakrishna was its central figure. With the Master in his heart, Manomohan carried on all the duties of a householder. At first his wife, Adharmohini, had not been in favour of his close association with the Master, but eventually her attitude changed. During her worship she would pray to Sri Ramakrishna: 'Master, I did not have an opportunity to receive initiation from you, but please do not give me up for that reason. Endow me with faith and devotion for you as my husband has. Give me strength so that I can be a true wife to him and a helper in his spiritual pursuit'.[27] One day Manomohan overheard his wife's prayer and saw her crying. It moved him greatly, and he felt the Master's grace. He then realized the truth of Sri Ramakrishna's teaching, that God makes everything favourable for a person who loves him.

Adharmohini went with her husband on a pilgrimage to Puri and died there on March 23, 1900, while Manomohan repeated the name of the Lord at her side. In the Jagannath temple at Puri, Manomohan had a vision of Sri Ramakrishna on the altar in place of Lord Jagannath. This experience uplifted his soul and kept him above earthly grief and pain at the death of his wife.

After this, Manomohan returned to Calcutta and passed his days talking about the Master and giving spiritual discourses. He also helped with the management of Yogodyana, Ram's retreat house, where a portion of the Master's relics had been installed. Although he spent long hours at night in meditation, he would go out early in the morning to visit the devotee's homes which had been sanctified by the blessed feet of the Master. Then he went to the Ganga for a bath. He had many visions and was most of the time in an ecstatic mood. He one day became overwhelmed when he had a vision of Sri Ramakrishna's smiling face in the shrine of the Kankurgachi Yogodyana. Once in his meditation he saw Holy Mother as the goddess of fortune. Another day, while walking on a street in Konnagar, he saw a flock of white cranes slowly disappear in the blue sky. His mind soared to the Infinite, beyond space and time, and he lost outward consciousness. Some of his neighbours carried him home.

Manomohan had tremendous love and respect for the monastic disciples of Sri Ramakrishna. When he heard of Swami Vivekananda's death, he was brokenhearted, and he somehow sensed that he would not be living much longer either. In 1903, after attending the first birth anniversary for Swami Vivekananda at Belur Math, he returned home and never again got up from his bed. The doctors said that he had apoplexy, but according to Swami

Premananda, Manomohan was immersed in yoga until the end. The last three days he continuously repeated the name of Sri Ramakrishna. On the final day, January 30, 1903, he lost his voice, but the devotees noticed that his lips were moving, and they started to repeat aloud the Lord's name for him. Immediately the hair on his body stood on end, his prana merged into the Divine, and he was gone.

Surendra Nath Mittra (1850-1890)

8
Surendra Nath Mittra

There is a saying, 'Sin and mercury cannot be digested'. They come to light either today or tomorrow. When a person does something wrong his conscience begins to bite him and a mist of shame covers his face. At that time it is extremely difficult to stop the momentum of his bad tendencies. He loses discrimination, self-esteem, and even his family members do not trust him. He slowly becomes isolated from others and leads a lonely life, himself a victim of his own evil actions. When compunction is aroused, he broods, laments, and cries in solitude. Some people then, out of desperation, try to take their lives. Others go to a holy person and surrender themselves to him. Surendra Nath Mittra tried both.

Surendra seemed to be a typical young man of his day — open-minded, carefree, and indifferent to religion. He was handsome and well built. As a commercial agent of the Dost Company, a large British firm in Calcutta, he had a well-paying job. He was married but had no children. Most of his friends were of the bohemian type, and like them, he often got drunk and was promiscuous. At the same time, however, he was frank, outspoken, largehearted, and extremely generous. Surendra was born probably in 1850 and met Sri Ramakrishna when he was thirty.

Although Surendra was quite affluent, his licentious conduct was ruining his mental peace. He even thought of killing himself with poison. One day during this period, a Bhairavi (a Tantric nun) of imposing appearance accosted him in passing, saying, 'My son, God alone is true and everything else is false'.[1] These words touched Surendra's heart and gave him strength to rouse himself from his hell of mental agony.

Ram Chandra Datta was a neighbour of Surendra's, and he knew about his mental anguish. Ram had been visiting the Master at Dakshineswar for some time, and, wanting to help Surendra, he asked him many times to accompany him. But Surendra always refused. He said: 'Look, it is very good that you respect him, but why should you take me there? I shall be a misfit there — like a crane

among swans.* I have seen enough of that'. Ram was hurt by this
sarcastic remark about his guru, but he did not give up. After much
persuasion Surendra finally said: 'All right, I shall go. But if that holy
man of yours is a fake, I shall twist his ears'.[2] Such was the attitude
with which Surendra approached Sri Ramakrishna.

It was probably in the middle of 1880 when Surendra first went to
Dakshineswar with Ram and Manomohan. That day the Master's
room was full of devotees. Surendra was determined to preserve his
critical attitude, so he sat down without showing any sign of respect
to Sri Ramakrishna. The Master was saying: 'Why does a man behave
like a young monkey and not like a kitten? The monkey has to cling to
its mother by its own efforts as she moves around. But the kitten just
goes on mewing until its mother comes and picks it up by the scruff of
its neck. The young monkey sometimes loses its hold on its mother;
then it falls and is badly hurt. But the kitten is in no such danger,
because the mother herself carries it from place to place. That's the
difference between trying to do things for yourself and giving
yourself up to the will of God'.

The Master's words made a deep impression on Surendra, and this
meeting became a turning point in his life. 'I behave like the young
monkey', he thought, 'and that's the cause of all my troubles. From
now on I'll be satisfied with any condition the Divine Mother puts me
in'. He then felt great relief and inner strength. When he was about to
leave, the Master said to him, 'Be sure to come again'. Surendra had
by this time been humbled, and he willingly bowed down to the
Master. On the way home he said to his companions: 'Ah, how he
turned the tables on me! It was *he* who twisted *my* ears! How could I
have dreamed that there could be such a man? He read my innermost
thoughts. Now at last I feel that my life has some meaning'.[3]

From the very first meeting with Sri Ramakrishna, Surendra
became extremely devoted to him and went to Dakshineswar almost
every Sunday. His friends were amazed to see the change in him and
his yearning for God. But this did not mean that Surendra
immediately gave up his old bad habits. He would still visit houses of
ill-fame from time to time, and then he would be so ashamed of
himself that he would stay away from the Master, pretending to be
busy at work. When someone reported to the Master what Surendra
had really been doing, Sri Ramakrishna did not seem to be at all
worried or shocked. 'Oh yes', he said, 'Surendra still has some

---

*Surendra was making a pun on the word *hamsa*, which means either a swan
or the soul. The word *parama-hamsa*, means a sannyasin of a high order, or,
sarcastically, a great swan.

desires. Let him enjoy them for a while longer. He will become pure soon enough'.[4] Surendra heard from a friend what the Master had said about him, and he was bold enough to return to Dakshineswar the following Sunday. Since he was a little hesitant to sit in front of the Master, he took his seat in a corner of the room. Sri Ramakrishna affectionately called him: 'Why don't you come and sit near me? Why do you sit aloof, like a thief?' Surendra obeyed. Then, in an ecstatic mood, the Master said: 'Well, when a man goes to a bad place, why doesn't he take the Divine Mother with him? She would protect him from many evil actions'.[5] Surendra was probably the only one there who understood for whom the Master had made that remark. His conscience was stinging him like hornets. The Master continued: 'A little manliness is necessary for everyone'. At this Surendra thought to himself: 'But that is my disease. Lord, save me from it'. The Master suddenly turned to him and said: 'I do not mean that struggle for pleasure which only debases a man, and which lower animals have. I mean the manliness of a great hero like Arjuna — to be able to stick to an ideal to the last breath of one's life!'[6] Surendra was afraid that the Master might expose his faults before the group of devotees, but Sri Ramakrishna stopped there and said nothing further. This advice greatly helped Surendra to fight against his passions.

Surendra was very devoted to the Divine Mother Kali. He set up a shrine to her in his home and worshipped her with much love. One day the Master said to Surendra: 'The devotee of the Divine Mother attains dharma [righteousness] and moksha [liberation]. He enjoys artha [wealth] and kama [fulfillment of desire] as well. Once I saw you in a vision as the child of the Divine Mother. You have both — yoga and bhoga [enjoyment]; otherwise your countenance would look dry'.[7]

Although Surendra had now diverted his energies to spiritual practices, he could not stop his drinking habit. Ram Chandra did not like the idea that one of Sri Ramakrishna's prominent devotees was a drunkard. He thought the Master's reputation would be tarnished if this became known. But whenever he tried to talk to Surendra about it, he was rebuffed. Surendra was a worshipper of Shakti, so to him it was not a sin to drink liquor. One day he said to Ram: 'Why are you so bothered about it? The Master would certainly warn me if he thought that it was bad for me. He knows all about it'. 'Very well', said Ram, 'then let's go and visit him today. He will surely tell you to give it up'. Surendra agreed to this, but he asked Ram not to bring up the subject. He said, 'If the Master refers to it of his own accord and tells me to stop, then I promise I will stop'.

Both of them arrived at Dakshineswar and found the Master sitting under the bakul tree in an exalted mood. As soon as they greeted the Master, he said to Surendra: 'Well, Suresh, why, when you're drinking wine, do you have to think of it as ordinary wine? Offer it first to Mother Kali and then drink it as her prasad. Only you must be careful not to get drunk. Don't let yourself stumble or your mind wander. At first you'll feel only the kind of excitement you usually feel, but that will soon lead to spiritual joy'.* Both Ram and Surendra were astonished.[8]

The Master never asked Surendra to give up drinking altogether, but thenceforth he could not drink at parties or whenever he felt like it. Following the Master's advice, he offered a little wine to the goddess every evening before drinking it himself. Curiously enough, this action filled him with devotion. After a while he began to cry plaintively like a child for the Divine Mother, and wanted to talk only of her. He would often become absorbed in deep meditation. Sri Ramakrishna's subtle spiritual influence gradually transformed Surendra, and the bad effects of wine could not harm him anymore.

What happens when God holds a person? First, his sensitive ego is crushed and he becomes humble; second, he does not enjoy mundane things and his mind dwells in God; and third, he feels an irresistible attraction for God and holy company. It was obvious that the Master had taken responsibility for Surendra. He knew that Surendra was a gem covered with worldly mud. A little washing removed the mud, and he then took Surendra into his inner circle. The Master never scolded Surendra for his bad habits. By pouring out his love and affection on this disciple, he conquered his heart.

One day while Surendra was meditating in his shrine, an idea came to him. He decided to test Sri Ramakrishna's divinity. He thought if the Master would appear before him in the shrine, he would consider him to be an avatar. Strangely enough, Surendra clearly saw the Master three times in the shrine. All his doubts were dissolved.[10]

Surendra had a very responsible position in his office, but from time to time he would feel an overwhelming desire to leave

---

*In *The Gospel of Sri Ramakrishna*, in the entry for September 28, 1884, M. gives the following version of the Master's advice to Surendra: 'Look here, Surendra! Whenever you drink wine, offer it beforehand to the Divine Mother. See that your brain doesn't become clouded and that you don't reel. The more you think of the Divine Mother, the less you will like to drink. The Mother is the giver of the bliss of divine inebriation. Realizing her, one feels a natural bliss'.[9]

everything and go to the Master. One day he left his office to go to Dakshineswar even though he had not finished his work. When he arrived he found that Sri Ramakrishna was preparing to go to Calcutta. Seeing Surendra, the Master said: 'It is good that you have come. I was anxious about you and was going to Calcutta to see you'. Surendra was amazed and delighted to know that Sri Ramakrishna had been thinking about him. He humbly said, 'If you were going out to see me, then please come to my house'. The Master agreed and went with Surendra to bless his house.[11]

Surendra's love for the Master grew deeper and deeper. The Master also loved Surendra dearly. Swami Saradananda wrote in *Sri Ramakrishna, The Great Master*: 'The Divine Mother showed him [the Master] that four suppliers of provisions for him had been sent to the world... Surendra Nath Mittra, whom the Master called Surendar and sometimes Suresh, was, he said, a "half supplier"...And Surendra...used to make arrangements for the food and bedding for those devotees who spent nights with the Master at Dakshineswar to serve him'.[12]

There is a saying: 'If you have money, give in charity. If you don't, repeat your mantram'. Sri Ramakrishna appreciated Surendra's largehearted nature. On February 22, 1885, M. recorded the following conversation in *The Gospel of Sri Ramakrishna*:

Master (*to Surendra*): 'Come here every now and then. Nangta used to say that a brass pot must be polished every day; otherwise it gets stained. One should constantly live in the company of holy men.

'The renunciation of "woman and gold" is for sannyasis. It is not for you. Now and then you should go into solitude and call on God with a yearning heart. Your renunciation should be mental...

'For you, as Chaitanya said, the disciplines to be practised are kindness to living beings, service to the devotees, and chanting the name of God.

'Why do I say all this to you? You work in a merchant's office. I say this to you because you have many duties to perform there.

'You tell lies at the office. Then why do I eat the food you offer me? Because you give your money in charity; you give away more than you earn. "The seed of the melon is bigger than the fruit", as the saying goes.

'I cannot eat anything offered by miserly people. Their wealth is squandered in these ways: first, litigation; second, thieves and robbers; third, physicians; fourth, their wicked children's extravagance. It is like that...'

The devotees listened with great attention to Sri Ramakrishna's words.

Surendra: 'I cannot meditate well. I repeat the Divine Mother's name now and then. Lying in bed, I repeat her name and fall asleep'.

Master: 'That is enough. You remember her, don't you?'[13]

Surendra observed that some of Sri Ramakrishna's disciples were practising spiritual disciplines under his guidance at Dakshineswar. Naturally the desire to do likewise came to him. After informing the Master about his plan, he came one day to Dakshineswar with a bed and other personal things and spent a couple of nights there. This greatly upset his wife, however. She said to him, 'You may go anywhere you like during the daytime, but at night you must not leave home'.[14] Although Surendra's wife prevented him from spending nights at Dakshineswar, his mind was crying for God. His body was at home, but his mind was with the Master.

It is not easy to become a disciple of an Incarnation of God such as Sri Ramakrishna. The way such great teachers discipline their followers is often difficult to understand. Sometimes it is through love, sometimes through indifference, and sometimes through harshness. The lives of these teachers are established in truth, and they preach the truth, which is God himself. Therefore they always insist that their disciples be steadfast in truth. Once Surendra told the Master about a pilgrimage he had just taken:

Surendra: 'We were there [at Vrindaban] during the holidays. Visitors were continually pestered for money. The priests and others asked for it continually. We told them that we were going to leave for Calcutta the next day, but we fled from Vrindaban that very night'.

Master: 'What is that? Shame! You said you would leave the place the next day and ran away that very day. What a shame!'

Surendra (embarrassed): 'Here and there we saw the babajis [Vaishnava holy men] in the woods practising spiritual discipline in solitude'.

Master: 'Did you give them anything?'

Surendra: 'No, sir'.

Master: 'That was not proper of you. One should give something to monks and devotees. Those who have the means should help such persons when they meet them'.[15]

Surendra was rich, aristocratic, and extremely sensitive. M. described how one day in 1881 the Master crushed Surendra's ego at his own home:

Surendra approached the Master with a garland and wanted to put it around his neck. But the Master took it in his hand and threw it aside. Surendra's pride was wounded and his eyes filled with tears. He went to the west porch and sat with Ram, Manomohan, and the others. In a voice choked with sadness he said: 'I am really angry. How can a poor brahmin know the value of a thing like that? I spent a lot of money for that garland, and he refused to accept it. I was unable to control my anger and said that the other garlands were to be given away to the devotees. Now I realize it was all my fault. God cannot be bought with money; he cannot be possessed by a vain person. I have really been vain. Why should he accept my worship? I don't feel like living any more'. Tears streamed down his cheeks and over his chest.

In the meantime Trailokya was singing inside the room. The Master began to dance in an ecstasy of joy. He put around his neck the garland that he had thrown aside; holding it with one hand, he swung it with the other as he danced and sang. Now Surendra's joy was unbounded. The Master had accepted his offering. Surendra said to himself, 'God crushes one's pride, no doubt, but he is also the cherished treasure of the humble and lowly'...

When the kirtan was over, everyone sat around the Master and became engaged in pleasant conversation. Sri Ramakrishna said to Surendra, 'Won't you give me something to eat?' Then he went into the inner apartments, where the ladies saluted him. After the meal Sri Ramakrishna left for Dakshineswar.[16]

On another occasion, on April 15, 1883, Surendra invited the Master and the devotees to attend a festival to the Divine Mother Annapurna in his home. The courtyard had been covered with a beautiful carpet, over which was spread a white linen sheet. Bolsters were placed here and there. The Master was asked to lean against one of them, but he pushed it away, since they were mostly used by rich, aristocratic people for comfort. Sri Ramakrishna practised what he taught. He said to the devotees: 'To lean against a bolster! You see, it is very difficult to give up vanity. You may discriminate, saying that the ego is nothing at all; but still it comes, nobody knows from where...Perhaps you are frightened in a dream; you shake off sleep and are wide awake, but still you feel your heart palpitating. Egotism is exactly like that. You may drive it away, but still it appears from somewhere. Then you look sullen and say: "What! I have not been shown proper respect!"'.[17]

One day in January 1882, Kedar, one of Sri Ramakrishna's devotees, pointed to Surendra, Ram, and Manomohan and said to the Master: 'Sir, when you have graciously given shelter to these souls, why do you put them into more trials and tribulations? Please be merciful to them so that they may be saved forever'. 'What can I do?' replied the Master. 'What power do I have? If the Mother wills, she can do so'. With total indifference he walked away and sat down in the Panchavati. It was evening. Surendra could not bear such indifference from his beloved Master. He went to Sri Ramakrishna and began to cry. He confessed all of his moral lapses and sought the Master's help. Sri Ramakrishna saw that these tears of repentance had washed away the impurities from Surendra's mind. He blessed him, saying, 'May the blissful Mother make your life blissful'.[18]

Just as a fresh breeze clears away the stuffiness of a room, so also the presence of a holy person removes the worldly atmosphere from a house. It is a common custom in India to invite a holy person to one's home and feed him. Whenever Surendra had an opportunity he invited the Master to his home or to his garden house at Kankurgachi, which was right next to Ram's. Surendra's Calcutta home gradually became one of Sri Ramakrishna's parlours, where he would meet the Calcutta devotees. Once the Master came there unexpectedly. Surendra was not at home then, and the cab fare had to be paid. He would have taken care of it if he had been there. The Master said to the devotees: 'Why don't you ask the ladies to pay the fare? They certainly know that their master visits us at Dakshineswar. I am not a stranger to them'.[19] This guileless remark made the devotees laugh.

The Gospel of Sri Ramakrishna records two visits made by Sri Ramakrishna to Surendra's garden house — one on December 26, 1883, and the other on June 15, 1884. On the first occasion he met a monk there and had some refreshments. On the second occasion Surendra arranged a festival and invited many people. It was a grand affair, and the Master went into deep samadhi several times during the devotional singing. Surendra loved to give joy to others in this way. That day the Master said: 'What a nice disposition he [Surendra] has now! He is very outspoken; he isn't afraid to speak the truth. He is unstinting in his liberality. No one that goes to him for help comes away empty-handed'.[20]

An avatar's words, actions, and behaviour are inscrutable to ordinary human beings, because they are divine. M. described what happened when the festival was over: 'After resting a little the Master was ready to leave for Dakshineswar. He was thinking of Surendra's welfare. He visited the different rooms, softly chanting the holy name of God. Suddenly he stood still and said: "I didn't eat any *luchi* [fried bread] at mealtime. Bring me a little now". He ate only a crumb and said: "There is much meaning in my asking for the luchi. If I should remember that I hadn't eaten any at Surendra's house, then I should want to come back for it" '.[21] This is the way the avatar plays with his devotees. Sometimes he is the magnet and the devotee is the needle, and at other times the devotee is the magnet and he is the needle.

Surendra was one of the important householder disciples of Sri Ramakrishna. Not only was he one of the Master's suppliers, but he also had many 'firsts' to his credit. In 1881 Surendra inaugurated the birthday festival of Sri Ramakrishna at Dakshineswar. The first two years he bore all the expenses himself, but from the third year other devotees shared them with him. It was through Surendra that Swami Vivekananda first met Sri Ramakrishna in November 1881 at Surendra's Calcutta home. Again, it was Surendra who first took Vivekananda to Dakshineswar.

Surendra also had the first oil painting of Sri Ramakrishna made. In it the Master is pointing out to Keshab Chandra Sen the harmony of Christianity, Islam, Buddhism, Hinduism, and other religions. When Keshab saw the picture, he said, 'Blessed is the man who conceived the idea'.[22] Sri Ramakrishna also saw the painting and observed: 'Yes, it contains everything. This is the ideal of modern times'.[23]

On December 10, 1881, Surendra took the Master to the studio of the Bengal Photographers in Radhabazar, Calcutta, as Sri Ramakrishna had expressed an interest in the mechanics of photography. The photographer explained his art and showed him how glass covered with silver nitrate takes an image. Later the Master used this example to illustrate how one can retain the impression of God if one's mind is stained with devotion. While they were there, Surendra had the photographer take a picture of the Master. As Sri Ramakrishna was being photographed he went into samadhi.[24] This studio portrait was the second of the three photographs taken of the Master while he was living.

Sri Ramakrishna had to move from Dakshineswar to Shyampukur, Calcutta, in September 1885, for his cancer treatment. About that same time Surendra got permission from the Master to perform the worship of Mother Durga in his house, a celebration previously held every year but discontinued after some mishaps had occurred. His brothers were apprehensive and superstitious about holding the worship, but Surendra was determined to carry it out anyway by himself. His only regret was that the Master could not come because of his illness. At the time of the sandhi puja (an auspicious period between the second and third days of the worship), however, the Master entered into deep samadhi in his room in the presence of his disciples and Dr. Sarkar. About a half an hour later he returned to outer consciousness and said: 'I saw a luminous path open up between here and Surendra's house. Through Surendra's devotion the Mother was manifest in the image there and her third eye was emitting a divine light. The usual series of lamps were burning before her, and Surendra, sitting in the courtyard, was weeping piteously and calling, ''Mother, Mother''. All of you go to his house now. He will feel much comforted to see you'. Accordingly, Swami Vivekananda and other devotees went to Surendra's house and were amazed to find that the Master's vision had corresponded to the external events in every detail.[25]

Gradually Sri Ramakrishna's condition grew worse, so the doctors advised the devotees to move him out of the city, since the polluted air of Calcutta was harming him. A garden house was found in Cossipore, but the rent was eighty rupees a month, a large amount in those days. When Sri Ramakrishna heard this he called Surendra to him and said: 'Look, Surendra, these devotees are mostly poor clerks and have large families to maintain. How can they pay the high rent of the garden? Please bear the whole of it yourself'.[26] Surendra gladly agreed. Moreover, he contributed for other expenses as well, and now and then bought things, such as straw screens for the windows of the Master's room to reduce the sun and heat coming in.

Surendra was now a wholly changed person. M. several times described his devotion and divine intoxication. On April 13, 1886, the first day of the Bengali year, M. wrote:

It was eight o'clock in the evening. Sri Ramakrishna sat on his bed. A few devotees sat on the floor in front of him. Surendra arrived from his office. He carried in his hands four oranges and two garlands of flowers. Now he looked at the Master and now at the devotees. He unburdened his heart to Sri Ramakrishna.

Surendra (*looking at M. and the others*): 'I have come after finishing my office work. I thought, ''What is the good of standing on two boats at the same time?'' So I finished my duties first and then came here. Today is the first day of the year; it is also Tuesday, an auspicious day to worship the Divine Mother. But I didn't go to Kalighat. I said to myself, ''It will be enough if I see him who is Kali herself, and who has rightly understood Kali'' '.

Sri Ramakrishna smiled.

Surendra: 'It is said that a man should bring fruit and flowers when visiting his guru or a holy man. So I have brought these...(*To the Master*) I am spending all this money for you. God alone knows my heart. Some people feel grieved to give away a penny; and there are people who spend a thousand rupees without feeling any hesitation. God sees the inner love of a devotee and accepts his offering'.

Sri Ramakrishna said to Surendra, by a nod, that he was right.

Surendra: 'I couldn't come here yesterday. It was the last day of

the year. But I decorated your picture with flowers'.
Sri Ramakrishna said to M., by a sign, 'Ah, what devotion!'[27]

On April 17, 1886, M. wrote:

It was about nine o'clock in the evening. Surendra and a few other
devotees entered Sri Ramakrishna's room and offered him
garlands of flowers...

Sri Ramakrishna put Surendra's garland on his own neck. All sat
quietly. Suddenly the Master made a sign to Surendra to come
near him. When the disciple came near the bed, Sri Ramakrishna
took the garland from his neck and put it around Surendra's.
Surendra saluted the Master. Sri Ramakrishna asked him, by a
sign, to rub his feet. Surendra gave them a gentle massage.

Several devotees were sitting on the bank of the reservoir in the
garden singing to the accompaniment of drums and cymbals...The
music was over. Surendra was almost in an ecstatic mood.[28]

Sri Ramakrishna passed away on August 16, 1886, at the Cossipore
garden house. Some of his young disciples had to return to their
homes against their wishes, while others had no place to go. They
were like orphans. One evening, early in September, while Surendra
was meditating in his shrine, Sri Ramakrishna appeared to him and
said: 'What are you doing here? My boys are roaming about without a
place to live. Attend to that before anything else'.[29] Immediately
Surendra rushed to Swami Vivekananda's house and said to some of
the disciples: 'Brothers, where will you go? Let us rent a house. You
will live there and make it our Master's shrine; and we householders
shall come there for consolation. How can we pass all our days and
nights with our wives and children in the world? I used to spend a
sum of money for the Master at Cossipore. I shall gladly give it now
for your expenses'.[30]

Accordingly, a house was rented at Baranagore, near the Ganga, at
eleven rupees per month. Surendra paid the rent and provided food
and other necessities for the monastic disciples of the Master. M.
mentioned in the *Gospel*: 'Surendra was indeed a blessed soul. It was
he who laid the foundation of the great Order later associated with Sri
Ramakrishna's name. His devotion and sacrifice made it possible for
those earnest souls to renounce the world for the realization of
God'.[31]

Surendra did not live long, however. He died of dropsy on May 25,
1890, at the age of forty. When he was seriously ill, Swami
Adbhutananda and Swami Ramakrishnananda went to see him.
Surendra at that time offered them five hundred rupees to build a
shrine for the Master, but Swami Ramakrishnananda told him: 'Wait

until your health is better. Later we shall talk about it'.[32] But Surendra never recovered. Before his death, though, he set aside one thousand rupees to be used for purchasing land near the Ganga for a monastery dedicated to the Master. Because of the great love the monastic disciples had for Surendra, they decided to keep this money for something special. When Belur Math was built, this money was used to purchase the marble flooring for the original shrine room where Sri Ramakrishna was installed to do good to humanity.[33]

9

Balaram Basu

Usually Sri Ramakrishna would see his devotees and disciples in a vision or in ecstasy before they came to him. One day he had a vision of Chaitanya and his followers singing and dancing near the Panchavati, between the banyan tree and the bakul tree. As soon as the Master met Balaram Basu for the first time, he received him affectionately, as if he was already familiar with him. He later said: 'He [Balaram] was a devotee of the inner circle of Chaitanya. He belongs to this place [meaning himself]. I saw in ecstasy how Chaitanya along with his main disciples, Advaita and Nityananda, brought about a flood of divine love in the country and inspired the masses through their enchanting kirtan. In that party I saw him [Balaram]'.[1]

Balaram was born in December 1842, in a wealthy Vaishnava family of North Calcutta. His grandfather Guruprasad Basu had established a Radha-Shyam temple in his home, and because of this that section of the city came to be known as Shyambazar. He also built a Shyamsundar temple on the bank of the Jamuna in Vrindaban, at a cost of one hundred thousand rupees. It is called 'Kala Babu's kunja [grove]'. Balaram's father, Radhamohan, and uncle, Bindumadhav, together bought a large estate in the Baleswar district of Orissa and established an office for its management at Kothar. Bindumadhav had three sons: Nimaicharan supervised the estate, Harivallabh was a lawyer in Cuttack, and Achyutananda lived in their house in Calcutta. Radhamohan also had three sons, Jagannath, Balaram, and Sadhuprasad, and two daughters, Vishnupriya and Hemalata.

Radhamohan entrusted the management of their joint estate in Orissa to his brother and nephews, and stayed mainly in Vrindaban. There in that solitary holy place he would look after the temple management while practising spiritual disciplines. Following a family custom, he would repeat his mantram standing in the courtyard in front of the temple and then meditate there. The rest of the day he would study devotional scriptures and arrange for the feeding of the devotees of Krishna.

Balaram Basu (1842-1890)

Balaram imbibed from his father a devotional nature and an indifference towards the world. Like Radhamohan, Balaram spent several hours every morning in japam and meditation. He also entrusted the management of the estate to his cousins and remained satisfied with what they gave him as a monthly allowance. Balaram was married to Krishnabhavini, a sister of Baburam (Swami Premananda), and they had two daughters and one son.

Balaram suffered very much from digestive troubles, and for twelve years he had to live on milk and gruel. In order to regain his health, he lived most of this period in Puri, the holy place of Jagannath on the coast of the Bay of Bengal. There he became acquainted with many Vaishnava monks, and this stirred his interest in spiritual life even more. His father and cousins began to worry lest Balaram renounce his family and become a mendicant. When Balaram came to Calcutta to attend his elder daughter's marriage, his cousins urged him to stay. In order to further persuade him, Harivallabh even bought a house at 57 Ramkanta Bose Street, which he offered to Balaram. Balaram did not want to accept it. If he lived in Calcutta, he would not be able to make his daily visit to Lord Jagannath and have the company of holy people. But to satisfy his cousins, he decided to remain in Calcutta for a while and then return to Puri.

While he was still living in Puri, Balaram had read about the life and teachings of Sri Ramakrishna in the *Sulabh Samachar*, a journal edited by Keshab Chandra Sen. He had also received a letter from one of his family's priests, Ramdayal, giving a detailed account of Sri Ramakrishna's holy life. Ramdayal had met the Master personally and wrote Balaram to come immediately to see him.

The day after he arrived in Calcutta, Balaram went with Ramdayal to Dakshineswar. It was probably January 1, 1881. They reached there late in the afternoon and found Sri Ramakrishna's room crowded with Brahmo devotees, including Keshab. Balaram did not get a chance to introduce himself, but sat down in a corner and listened to the Master. Sri Ramakrishna was saying: 'God cannot be seen without yearning of heart, and this yearning is impossible unless one has finished with the experiences of life. Those who live surrounded by "woman and gold", and have not yet come to the end of their experiences, do not yearn for God'.[2]

As soon as the Brahmos left the room to have some refreshments, Sri Ramakrishna turned to Balaram and said, 'Is there anything you want to ask me?'

'Yes, sir. Does God really exist?'

'Certainly he does'.

'Can a person see him?'

'Yes, he reveals himself to the devotee who thinks of him as his nearest and dearest. Because you do not get any response by praying to him once, you must not conclude that he does not exist'.

'But why can't I see him when I pray to him so much?'

Sri Ramakrishna then smiled and asked, 'Do you really consider him to be as dear to your heart as your own children?'

'No, sir', Balaram admitted. 'I never felt that strongly for him'.

The Master then said in a sweet, convincing voice: 'Pray to God, thinking of him as dearer than your own self. Truly I tell you, he is extremely fond of his devotees. He cannot but reveal himself to them. He comes to a person even before he is sought. If a person comes one step towards God, God comes ten steps towards that person. There is none more intimate and more affectionate than God'.[3]

Balaram was very much impressed. Every word of the Master's penetrated his heart. He returned home that night, but the next morning he came back to Dakshineswar on foot. This time Sri Ramakrishna was alone in his room. Seeing Balaram, the Master said: 'Oh, you have come! Very good. Sit down and have some rest. I was just thinking of you. Where do you live?' 'At Baghbazar', replied Balaram. The Master then inquired in detail about the members of his family, about his children, and other matters, and finally said: 'Look here, the Divine Mother has told me that you are my very own. You are one of her suppliers. Many things are stored up for this place [meaning himself] in your house. Buy something and send it here'.[4] Balaram considered this to be his good fortune and gladly obeyed. Often Sri Ramakrishna would advise the devotees for their own welfare to bring a small present — even if it was just a pice worth of something — whenever they visited a temple or a monk.

It seemed to Balaram that the Master was his very own relative. He had never in his life met such a remarkable person. He noticed that there were similarities between the lives of Sri Chaitanya and Sri Ramakrishna, and he pondered: Such a sweet nature and repeated bhava samadhi (divine ecstasy) are not found in ordinary human beings. Can it be that Sri Chaitanya has incarnated himself again? With these thoughts in mind, Balaram went back to Calcutta and personally selected some food and other things for the Master. He then returned in a carriage to Dakshineswar. Sri Ramakrishna greeted him warmly and asked his nephew Hriday to put the things away. From this time until the Master's death Balaram supplied all of his foodstuff, such as rice, sugar candy, farina, sago, barley, vermicelli, tapioca, and so forth.

The Master used to say: 'Balaram's food is very pure. The members of his family have for generations been devotees and have been hospitable to monks and beggars. His father is living a retired life at Vrindaban, where he passes his time calling upon the Lord. Not only can I take Balaram's food, but I take it with pleasure'. Again: 'All the members of his family are attuned to the same ideal. From the master and mistress down to the children, all are devoted to God. They never take a drop of water without saying their prayers. They are as hospitable as they are pious'.[5]

Needless to say, Sri Ramakrishna was always welcome at Balaram's home. The Master visited his home a hundred times, and Balaram kept a record of all those visits.[6] Whenever necessary the Master would stay overnight at Balaram's and there partake of the prasad of Jagannath, their family deity, who was worshipped every day in their home. The Master sometimes jokingly referred to the temple of Dakshineswar as 'Mother Kali's fort'. Balaram's home was thus his Calcutta fort, or, as he sometimes called it, his 'parlour'.

M. wrote in *The Gospel of Sri Ramakrishna:*

Balaram's house in Calcutta had been sanctified many times by the Master's presence. There he frequently lost himself in samadhi, dancing, singing, or talking about God. Those of the Master's disciples and devotees who could not go to Dakshineswar visited him there and received his instructions. He often asked Balaram to invite young disciples such as Rakhal, Bhavanath, and Narendra to his house, saying: 'These pure souls are the veritable manifestations of God. To feed them is to feed God himself. They are born with special divine attributes. By serving them you will be serving God'. And so it happened that whenever the Master was at Balaram's house the devotees would gather there. It was the Master's chief vineyard in Calcutta. It was here that the devotees came to know each other intimately.[7]

Every year Balaram would celebrate the Car Festival of Lord Jagannath in his home. The Master's presence greatly enhanced the joy of the occasion. The devotees would decorate Lord Jagannath's small wooden chariot with cloth, flowers, and flags, and then place the image in it. There was a small courtyard in the middle of the house around which overhung the verandahs of the upper floors. After the worship the car would be pulled round and round by devotees on these verandahs while a kirtan party would follow, singing devotional songs. This went on for hours. Swami Saradananda described the Car Festival of 1885:

A kirtan party came. The Master and the devotees joined in their

singing as the chariot was drawn. Where else could one experience
and witness such a flow of bliss, of exuberant devotion, of divine
ecstasy, and such sweet, graceful dancing of the Master? Pleased
with the pure love of the pious family, Lord Jagannath did indeed
manifest himself in the image on the chariot and in the body of Sri
Ramakrishna. It was a rare sight! Carried away by the current of
that overflowing devotion, even the heart of an atheist would melt
— what to speak of the devotees! After a few hours of such kirtan,
cooked food was offered to Jagannath. The Master would then
partake of the prasad, followed by the devotees. That fair of bliss
came to an end late at night.[8]

At Balaram's repeated request, his father, Radhamohan, came to
Calcutta from Vrindaban to meet the Master. Sri Ramakrishna knew
that Radhamohan was a steadfast member of the Vaishnava sect, but
he wanted to broaden his religious outlook. Thus the Master said to
him: 'He is indeed a real man who has harmonized everything. Most
people are one-sided. But I find that all opinions point to the One. All
views — the Shakta, the Vaishnava, the Vedanta — have that One for
their centre. He who is formless is, again, endowed with form. It is he
who appears in different forms'.[9] On another occasion the Master
said to Balaram's father: 'The whole thing is to love God and taste his
sweetness. He is sweetness and the devotee is its enjoyer. The
devotee drinks the sweet Bliss of God. Further, God is the lotus and
the devotee the bee. The devotee sips the honey of the lotus. As a
devotee cannot live without God, so also God cannot live without his
devotee. Then the devotee becomes the sweetness, and God its
enjoyer. The devotee becomes the lotus, and God the bee. It is the
godhead that has become these two in order to enjoy Its own Bliss.
That is the significance of the episode of Radha and Krishna'.[10]

All of his life Balaram, like other Vaishnavas, was a believer in
ahimsa, noninjury. He had even thought it wrong to kill the
mosquitoes which disturbed his meditation. But after associating
with Sri Ramakrishna for a couple of years he realized that the most
important thing in spiritual life is to keep the mind in God, and
therefore, killing a few mosquitoes for the sake of steady meditation
should not be considered a sin. His orthodox upbringing, however,
made him doubt this reasoning, and he found himself in a real
dilemma. He immediately left for Dakshineswar to lay the problem
before the Master.

Arriving at Sri Ramakrishna's room, he noticed to his great surprise
that the Master was busy killing bedbugs. As Balaram approached
him and bowed down, the Master said: 'There are many bedbugs

breeding in the pillow. They bite me day and night, create distraction of the mind, and keep me from sleeping, so I am killing them'. Thus Balaram's question was answered by the Master.[11] Furthermore, he understood that though he had been visiting the Master for two or three years and observing him closely day and night, the Master had never done anything which might hurt his feelings or his faith. He had waited to teach Balaram this lesson until he knew that Balaram had enough faith in him to be able to accept it.

One day Balaram decided to test Sri Ramakrishna's power of omniscience. As he carried a tray of sweets to the Master, he mentally selected two of them for the Master to take. Balaram was amazed when the Master smiled at him and took those very two sweets.[12]

As Balaram did not take any active part in the management of the family estate, he was somewhat under the control of his father and cousins, who apportioned to him his monthly share of the income. Because of this he was very careful about his spending, and some people took this to be miserliness. Although he wanted to serve Sri Ramakrishna lavishly, he could not. But the Master looked more to the heart of his devotee than to the amount he could spend.

Sometimes out of fun, however, the Master would tell jokes at Balaram's expense, turning them into lessons for others. One day Sri Ramakrishna observed that since there were no musical instruments to accompany the singing, no atmosphere could be created. He said: 'Do you know how Balaram manages a festival? He is like a miserly brahmin raising a cow. The cow must eat very little but give milk in torrents. Sing your own songs and beat your own drums. That's Balaram's idea!'[13] And on another day: 'Balaram says to me, "Please come to Calcutta by boat; take a carriage only if you must". You see, he has given us a feast today; so this afternoon he will make us all dance! One day he hired a carriage for me from here to Dakshineswar. He said that the carriage hire was twelve annas. I said to him, "Will the coachman take me to Dakshineswar for twelve annas?" "Oh, that will be plenty", he replied. One side of the carriage broke down before we reached Dakshineswar. Besides, the horse stopped every now and then; it simply would not go. Once in a while the coachman whipped the horse, and then it ran a short distance'.[14]

Mahendranath Datta, one of Swami Vivekananda's brothers, told an interesting story revealing Balaram's miserliness as well as his sense of humour. Balaram had a servant who was not well paid, so from time to time he would steal things. That servant also had a bad temper, and the family members were not happy with him. One day

Swami Yogananda tried to persuade Balaram to get rid of that servant. Balaram replied: 'Look, Yogin, servants generally come from poor, uncultured families, and it is taken for granted that they will steal something. Moreover, if I throw him out, where will he go? Can you tell me where I can find a servant who has renounced "lust and gold" and who will work but not steal?' Sri Ramakrishna's disciples later made a joke out of this remark, saying, 'We shall have to find an all-renouncing servant for Balaram'.[15]

Although Balaram belonged to a rich, aristocratic family, one would never know it from his demeanour. He was the embodiment of the Vaishnava attitude: 'Be humbler than a blade of grass and be patient and forbearing like a tree. Take no honour to thyself. Give honour to all. Chant unceasingly the name of the Lord'. M. gave a couple of descriptions of Balaram's self-effacing nature in the *Gospel*. On March 11, 1882, he wrote:

> About eight o'clock in the morning Sri Ramakrishna went as planned to Balaram Basu's house in Calcutta. It was the day of the Dola-yatra [a spring festival associated with Krishna]... The devotees and the Master sang and danced in a state of divine fervour. Several of them were in an ecstatic mood... When the music was over, the devotees sat down for their meal. Balaram stood there humbly, like a servant. Nobody would have taken him for the master of the house.[16]

On August 5, 1882, Sri Ramakrishna went to visit Ishwar Chandra Vidyasagar, and he talked with him about God until late in the evening. M. described the following incident:

> Sri Ramakrishna then took leave of Vidyasagar, who with his friends escorted the Master to the main gate... As soon as the Master and the devotees reached the gate, they saw an unexpected sight and stood still. In front of them was a bearded gentleman of fair complexion, aged about thirty-six. He wore his clothes like a Bengali, but on his head was a white turban tied after the fashion of the Sikhs. No sooner did he see the Master than he fell prostrate before him, turban and all.
>
> When he stood up the Master said: 'Who is this? Balaram? Why so late in the evening?'
> Balaram: 'I have been waiting here a long time, sir'.
> Master: 'Why didn't you come in?'
> Balaram: 'All were listening to you. I didn't like to disturb you'.[17]

Love is reciprocal. If you love, you will be loved. We read about the devotees' love for God in the biographies of the saints, but God's boundless love for the devotees has seldom been recorded, because it is not possible for ordinary human beings to comprehend it. Sri Ramakrishna's niece, Lakshmi Devi, told the following story of the Master's love for Balaram and his family:

> Once Balaram Babu came to Dakshineswar by boat with his wife and children. They visited with the Master for a while, and they all left for Calcutta in the afternoon. The Master himself went to the chandni ghat to see them off. Smiling at them, he said, 'Come back again'.
>
> Their boat pulled out into the river, and the Master stood there watching until they had gone quite a distance. In the meantime a storm began to blow and the sky quickly became dark with clouds. I noticed that the Master was quite worried. He started pacing back and forth like a restless boy, his anxiety increasing as he watched the progress of the violently rocking boat.
>
> Impatiently he was asking everyone: 'What will happen? Will Balaram and his family survive this storm? Alas! What will happen? People will say that Balaram went to see that worthless, unfortunate holy man in Dakshineswar and lost his life coming back. Tell me, what will happen?'
>
> Gradually the boat disappeared from sight. The Master returned to his room, his face gloomy, his mind very much disturbed, and he resumed his restless pacing, lamenting: 'Mother, will you tarnish my face? Won't you hear my prayer? Mother, what will happen?'
>
> Seeing the Master's state of mind, Yogin, without saying anything, set out for Calcutta in the midst of the storm to get what news he could of Balaram Babu. He took a share-carriage from Alambazar, and within a few hours he was back (by then night had fallen) and was able to report to the Master that Balaram Babu and his family had arrived home safely. The Master was overjoyed.[18]

On another occasion Balaram's wife, Krishnabhavini, was seriously ill. When the news reached the Master in Dakshineswar, he immediately said to Holy Mother, 'Please go and see her'. 'How shall I go? There is no conveyance', Holy Mother replied. 'What!' said the Master. 'Balaram's family is on the verge of a disaster, and you will not go to see them because you can't get a vehicle! Walk! Go on foot!' Fortunately a palanquin was found, and Holy Mother went in that to see her.[19]

Krishnabhavini, like her husband, was extremely devoted to the Master. Sri Ramakrishna once said that she was 'one of the eight main companions of Radha'.[20] Ramlal a nephew of the Master's, told the following story: One afternoon Sri Ramakrishna said: 'Ramlal, I don't have any taste for the milk which comes from the temple kitchen. Could you get some pure, sweet milk for me?' After trying in vain at the market, Ramlal went to a milkman, but he could not get any pure milk. When he returned empty-handed the Master said, 'Well, what can be done?' Meanwhile, Krishnabhavini was boiling milk in her kitchen in Calcutta. Yogin-ma was also there, and Krishnabhavini lamented to her: 'Look, Sister, it is my bad luck that I could not feed the Master with this pure, sweet milk. Only the people of the household will enjoy it. If you could accompany me, then both of us could go to Dakshineswar and feed the Master with it. It is dark now and nobody will know if we leave through the back door'. Both of them then left on foot for Dakshineswar with a small jar of milk. As they entered the Master's room, he said: 'Oh, you have brought milk for me? Ever since this afternoon I have been thinking of having some pure, sweet milk'. Krishnabhavini and Yogin-ma were surprised and delighted to be able to fulfill the Master's wish in this way. Sri Ramakrishna then sent them back to Calcutta by a carriage. He also asked Ramlal to accompany them and explain to Balaram that they went to see the Master. He did not want Balaram to misunderstand them.[21]

Obstacles in spiritual life make a devotee strong. For those who surrender themselves to God, God removes all obstacles and makes everything favourable. Balaram was happy to be able to serve the Master. In the later part of 1885, however, about the same time that Sri Ramakrishna was transferred from Dakshineswar to Shyampukur for treatment of his cancer, Balaram's cousin Harivallabh came to Calcutta. Harivallabh was disturbed over the news he was getting about Balaram. He had heard from different people that Balaram was very much involved with Sri Ramakrishna, that Sri Ramakrishna visited their home quite often, and that the women of their family even took the dust of the Master's feet, a custom considered beneath the dignity of their family. Balaram continued to visit Sri Ramakrishna every day, but he was worried that this cousin might make trouble and force him to move away at this crucial time of the Master's life.

It was hard to hide anything from Sri Ramakrishna's eyes. Seeing Balaram's worried and gloomy face, the Master asked him some questions and found out that this cousin was the cause of his anxiety. Then the Master asked: 'What sort of man is he [Harivallabh]? Can you bring him here some day?' Balaram said: 'Sir, as a man he is good, learned, intelligent, magnanimous, and charitable, but he has misunderstood me on the basis of the report of others. He is displeased with me only because I come here. Therefore I doubt if he would come here at my request'. The Master then said: 'You need not ask him then. Please call Girish here'. Girish came and gladly agreed to bring Harivallabh to the Master, as they had been classmates at school.[22]

The next afternoon Harivallabh came with Girish. The Master greeted him warmly and touching him said, 'You seem to be my very own'. Then Sri Ramakrishna talked about faith in God, devotion, and self-surrender. One of the Master's disciples began to sing a song, and Sri Ramakrishna gradually went into samadhi. Seeing the loving form and hearing the inspiring words of the Master, Harivallabh was so moved that tears welled up in his eyes. At dusk he reverently took the dust of the feet of the Master and left. Thus Sri Ramakrishna changed Harivallabh's mind and relieved Balaram from further worry and anxiety.[23]

Before Sri Ramakrishna went to live at the Shyampukur house, in North Calcutta, he stayed for a week at Balaram's house. During the Master's illness Balaram continued to provide all of his food, since the Master did not care for the food which was bought from the subscription money. After the Master's passing away on August 16, 1886, Holy Mother moved to Balaram's house, and Balaram then arranged her pilgrimage to Varanasi, Vrindaban, and other holy places. His home was always open to Holy Mother and the disciples of Sri Ramakrishna.

The monastic disciples eventually established a monastery at Baranagore, and Balaram visited them regularly. One day he noticed that the monks were eating only rice and spinach. After returning home he told his wife that he would have only rice and spinach for his meal. She at first thought that he was asking for such plain food because of his weak stomach, but when she later heard the whole story she immediately sent food and other articles to the monastery. Thenceforth Balaram would give one rupee every day for the food offering to the Master, and moreover he would keep track of the food situation in the monastery through his brother-in-law Swami Premananda and through the cook.[24]

Swami Adbhutananda mentioned the following incidents in his memoirs about Balaram:

> Balaram Babu would save money from his household budget and use it to serve the monks. His relatives thought he was a miser. I never knew how rich he was! One day, seeing him lying on a narrow bed, I said: 'Why don't you find yourself a larger bed? This one is too narrow for you'. Do you know what he said? 'This earthly body will one day return to the earth. Why should money

be spent for my bed when it can be much better spent in service to holy people?'[25]

The wedding banquet for Balaram Babu's younger daughter, Krishnamayi, was held on a grand scale. [It had been arranged by Balaram's brothers.] Balaram Babu had not been in favour of spending so much money, however. He used to say, 'A feast for relatives is equal to a feast for ghosts'. At last he got some satisfaction when Swami Yogananda by coincidence visited his home that day. Balaram Babu said to him, 'I know that monks do not participate in marriage festivals, but if you eat at least a sweet I shall consider this huge spending worthwhile'. Swami Yogananda ate a little on his request.[26]

Swami Vivekananda had tremendous love and regard for Balaram. Swamiji once said to him: 'Our relationship with you is different. If you push us out of the front door, we shall enter again through the back door'.[27] Balaram always stood beside the disciples of the Master and served them wholeheartedly. One day, however, Balaram lamented to Swamiji: 'You and I both went to the Master, but now you have renounced your home and become a monk. You are practising japam and meditation and making tremendous progress in a short time, whereas I remain the same bound soul. I have achieved nothing'. 'Look, Balaram', answered Swamiji, 'three generations of your family have given service to holy people. Do you think such a thing could be fruitless? As the result of such virtuous actions you have had a chance to serve a great soul like Sri Ramakrishna. This will glorify your dynasty. You don't need to practise renunciation or hard austerities. It is the result of your virtuous deeds that you met and served the Master. And you know how much the Master liked to visit your home and was fond of your offerings. What will you do with heaven or liberation? Is it [the Master's love] not enough?' Balaram was happy to hear that. He realized that his service to the Master was equal to meditation and austerity.[28]

In 1890 there was an epidemic of influenza in Calcutta, which took the lives of many people. Balaram also became a victim of that epidemic and died on April 13, 1890. Swami Shivananda told the following story of Balaram's death:

The passing away of each of the devotees of the Master is a wonderful event in itself. The departure of Balaram Babu was equally wonderful. His disease had taken a serious turn, and all were anxious. One day he went on repeating, 'Well, where are my brothers?' When this news reached us we hurried to his house at Baghbazar [in Calcutta]. We ourselves stayed by him and nursed him. For about two or three days before his passing away he would not allow any of his relatives to come near him; he wanted only us to be near at hand. The little that he talked was about the Master alone. One day, before the final departure, the doctor came in and declared that he was beyond cure.

At the last moment we were seated around him, while his wife, stricken with unspeakable grief, was in the inner apartment with Golap-ma, Yogin-ma, and others. Just then she noticed something like a piece of black cloud in the sky, which became denser by stages and began to descend. Soon it assumed the shape of a chariot and alighted on the roof of Balaram Babu's house. The Master came out of that chariot and proceeded towards the room where Balaram Babu lay. Soon after, he issued forth, taking Balaram Babu by the hand, and entered the chariot again, which then ascended and vanished in the sky. This vision raised her mind to a very high plane where there could be no touch of grief or sorrow. When she returned to normal she related this to Golap-ma, who came to apprise us of the fact. Balaram Babu had passed away just a little while before.[29]

Chunilal Basu (1849-1936)

10
Chunilal Basu

What is needed in spiritual life? Longing for God. And this longing does not dawn in the heart until the desire for worldly enjoyment ceases. One might have plenty of money, a luxurious home, vast property; one might have a beautiful wife or a handsome husband, wonderful children, good friends and relatives; one might have excellent health, handsome looks, erudition, name and fame, power and position — but everyone realizes sooner or later that these material acquisitions and personal qualities and relationships do not last. It is a wise person who seeks that which is eternal, who seeks God.

Chunilal Basu was born in Baghbazar, North Calcutta, in 1849. After completing school at the age of twenty-two, he secured a job at the Calcutta Corporation. Chunilal had a wife and children, yet he still felt an emptiness within. Whenever he had the time and opportunity, he used to visit monks and other holy people. Once in a while, he would sit on the bank of the Ganga simply to enjoy the sacred river's pure and serene atmosphere. Chunilal was searching desperately for something or someone.

One day one of his colleagues, who was aware of his state of mind, said: 'If you want to meet a real holy man, go to Sri Ramakrishna Paramahamsa at the Kali temple of Rani Rasmani'.[1] Then he told Chunilal that the temple garden of Dakshineswar was on the bank of the Ganga and that one could go there by boat from Calcutta.

A couple of weeks later, on a Sunday afternoon, probably in March 1881, Chunilal left for Dakshineswar by boat. Anxious about journeying to an unknown place, he landed at the Dakshineswar ghat and wandered around until he met a brahmachari in a cottage who asked him: 'What do you want? Medicine?' 'No. I have come to see the paramahamsa', replied Chunilal. The brahmachari pointed out the way, 'There is a paramahamsa in that corner room'.[2]

Chunilal went to the door of the northern verandah and saw someone alone in the room. Entering, he saluted the Master. Sri

Ramakrishna asked, 'Why are you here?' 'I have come to see you', answered Chunilal.[3] The Master asked him to sit on a bench to the north of his cot. Then he began to get acquainted with Chunilal, asking him many questions and treating him as his own. On that day Sri Ramakrishna did not talk about devotion or renunciation. The Master simply gave Chunilal a piece of rock candy as prasad when he was ready to return to Calcutta.

Under the grip of a restless mind, Chunilal decided to visit the holy cities of Varanasi, Vrindaban, and Hardwar. Also, he wanted to live for some time in Rishikesh, a place for hermits in the Himalayas. One of Chunilal's friends, who was familiar with those places, expressed a desire to join him. Taking his March salary and two hundred rupees from home, Chunilal submitted an application for a one-month leave from work and left Calcutta without telling anyone.

They travelled for nearly two weeks, visiting several places on the way. But Chunilal found the aimless wandering not to his liking, so he left his friend and went to Rishikesh. After discovering, however, that Rishikesh was only for mendicants, Chunilal's pseudo-renunciation died down within a few days, and he returned home before the month was over.

When Chunilal reported back to his office, the superintendent informed him that he had been discharged for leaving work without permission. But Chunilal was mentally prepared for this. He went to a friend of his, Shyam Biswas, the vice-chairman of the corporation, and told him the whole story. The executive overruled the superintendent's decision and reappointed Chunilal to his post, allowing him one month's leave without pay.

A few days later Chunilal returned to Dakshineswar. This time, in Sri Ramakrishna's room, he met Balaram Basu, his next-door neighbour. Chunilal previously had had no occasion to talk with Balaram, who was a wealthy aristocrat. Sri Ramakrishna brought them together by telling Balaram: 'Chunilal lives very close to your house. Whenever you come, please bring him along with you'.[4] Almost every Sunday Balaram used to hire a boat and accompany the Calcutta devotees when they visited the Master.

In this way, travelling to and from Dakshineswar, Balaram and Chunilal became good friends. Chunilal was not well-to-do, and whenever he was sick or in need, Balaram would step forward to help him. This made Chunilal's neighbours jealous, and they taunted him, calling him a 'snob'. But he paid no attention to their criticism.

Before he met Sri Ramakrishna, Chunilal had received initiation from his family guru, and he used to practise yoga according to the Shiva

Samhita, an authoritative text on spiritual life. He continued his yoga sadhana (yoga disciplines) — eating vegetarian food and secretly practising pranayama in a secluded place — even after meeting the Master.

Chunilal did not realize that it was dangerous to practise pranayama without the help of a guru. As a result, he developed various kinds of physical ailments, including asthma, which prevented him from visiting the Master for some time. One day when he felt a little better, Chunilal went to Dakshineswar alone. No one else was in the Master's room, and seeing him, Sri Ramakrishna said immediately: 'Why do you practise all those things? You are a householder. That yoga sadhana is not for you. Have faith and love for God. When you return home, please take three doses of medicine from Brahmachari Gopal, and never again practise pranayama'.[5]

Hearing these words of the Master, Chunilal was dumbfounded because no one knew that he had been practising intense yoga sadhana or that it was the cause of his illness. Later, he was even more amazed when he recovered from the ailment after taking the three doses of medicine. From then on, Chunilal had complete faith in the Master as an avatar.

Chunilal was eager to serve the Master, but his poverty was an obstacle. Seeing his mental agony, Sri Ramakrishna said to him: 'My hand becomes paralyzed if I touch anything metallic. Why don't you buy a regular glass for me?'[6] Delighted, Chunilal bought him one.

According to orthodox Hinduism a nonbrahmin should not utter the pranava mantram (OM) unless he is initiated, so this also was a source of great mental affliction for Chunilal. But Sri Ramakrishna soothed him by saying, 'It is enough to repeat any name of God; there is no need to utter the pranava mantram'.[7] From that time on, Chunilal followed the spiritual instruction of the Master and practised japam and meditation accordingly.

Chunilal's wife was also a devotee of Sri Ramakrishna. Once when she was suffering from stomach trouble, Chunilal decided to give her a change. He took her on a pilgrimage to Vrindaban where they stayed at Balaram's retreat house. Gauri-ma was then living at that holy place, and she showed them around. Later Swami Brahmananda and Balaram, along with his wife, joined them.

After some time, Chunilal returned to Calcutta alone, leaving his wife in Vrindaban. On September 21, 1884, he went to Dakshineswar to tell the Master about his pilgrimage. There are many entries in *The Gospel of Sri Ramakrishna* regarding Chunilal's visits to the Master. As he was a self-effacing, humble devotee, he always tried to remain in the background as a spectator at these gatherings of devotees.

Sri Ramakrishna had a high opinion of Chunilal. On August 9, 1885, the Master revealed one of his experiences to the devotees, saying: 'I had a vision of the indivisible Satchidananda. Inside it I saw two groups with a fence between them. On one side were Kedar, Chuni, and other devotees who believe in the Personal God. On the other side was a luminous space like a heap of red brick dust. Inside it was seated Narendra immersed in samadhi'.[8] On December 23, 1885, Sri Ramakrishna said, 'Chuni's spiritual consciousness has been awakened by frequent visits to me'.[9] The Master once, out of compassion, even visited his home.

On the Kalpataru Day, January 1, 1886, Sri Ramakrishna blessed many devotees on the lawn of the Cossipore garden house, and lifted their souls up to a higher realm of consciousness. The Master was suffering from cancer, and moreover, by taking the bad karma of the devotees, he was in much pain. He returned to his room for a rest, and Swami Niranjanananda took the responsibility of gatekeeper so that no one could disturb him.

Chunilal arrived at Cossipore late that afternoon and heard the whole story. He felt sad and unfortunate that he had not received the blessings of the Master that day. Swami Vivekananda, who was a close friend of Chunilal, told him privately: 'The Master will not live long. If you have anything to ask, please go right now to the Master'.[10] Chunilal knew that it was impossible to pass by Swami Niranjanananda, so he waited for an opportunity. As soon as Swami Niranjanananda left his post on urgent business, Swami Vivekananda advised Chunilal to go to the Master. Seeing Chunilal, Sri Ramakrishna asked, 'What do you want?' Chunilal could not say a single word. Then the Master said: 'Have love and faith in this place [pointing to his body]. You will also achieve everything'. Excited, Chunilal went downstairs and related the Master's words to Swami Vivekananda, who said: 'Wonderful! You have nothing more to fear or worry about!'[11] Those few words of the Master became the mainstay of Chunilal's life.

After the passing away of Sri Ramakrishna, Chunilal kept in close contact with the disciples of Sri Ramakrishna. As a token of their friendship, Swami Vivekananda used to call him 'Narayana', and he helped Chunilal financially while he was in America. All through his life, Chunilal remained a faithful devotee of the Master and a well-wisher of the Ramakrishna Order. During his last illness, Swami Bhagavatananda served him. Chanting the name of Sri Ramakrishna, Chunilal passed away at his home on May 30, 1936, at the age of eighty-seven.

11

Yogin-Ma
(Yogindra Mohini Biswas)

'Austerity is the source of strength and also the means to liberation', says a Hindu scripture.[1] The gods attain godhood by practising austerity; the sages achieve perfection through austerity; human beings overcome obstacles and attain success in life by the power of austerity. Spiritual life and the practice of austerity always go together. It would be hard to believe that a person has realized God without having practised austerities and spiritual disciplines. Yogin-ma's life is a glowing example of the ancient Indian ideal of womanhood and austerity. She combined in her personality great poise and sweetness with a spirit of service and rare spiritual wisdom. She was one of Sri Ramakrishna's prominent women disciples. Once the Master said about her, 'She is a gopi, perfected by God's grace'.[2]

Yogindra Mohini Mittra, or Yogin-ma for short, was born on January 16, 1851, at Baghbazar, in North Calcutta. Her family's home was very close to that of Balaram Basu, a householder disciple of Sri Ramakrishna. Prasanna Kumar Mittra, Yogin-ma's father, was a well-known physician and specialist in midwifery. Besides his regular practice, he also lectured at the Calcutta Medical College on that subject. Prasanna was quite wealthy and owned a large house with a garden, on one side of which there was a Shiva temple. Yogin-ma was his second daughter by his second marriage.

When Yogin-ma was seven she was married to Ambika Charan Biswas, who was an adopted son of a rich and prominent family of Khardah, a village twelve miles north of Calcutta. The Biswas family was noted for its piety and philanthropy, and some of its members were well versed in Tantric rites. One of their ancestors, Prankrishna Biswas, had compiled the *Pranatoshini Tantra*, a famous treatise on Tantra scriptures. Like many wealthy families, the Biswas family wanted to become renowned by building a shrine containing one hundred thousand Shalagrama shilas (sacred stone emblems of Lord Vishnu). Their undertaking was not successful, however, for they

Yogin-ma (Yogindra Mohini Biswas)
(1851-1924)

were able to collect only eighty thousand. Damodar (Vishnu) was their family deity.[3]

Yogin-ma's parents were very happy that their daughter had been married into a pious and wealthy family. Although child marriage was then the custom of society, Yogin-ma did not go to live with her husband at the time of their marriage. Only after she had grown up did she go with great hope and expectation to Khardah to join Ambika Charan. But to her dismay she very soon discovered that this rich young man was a drunkard and libertine. Although Ambika Charan had inherited much property and wealth from his father, he squandered it in a very short time. He was so extravagant that one day he asked a servant to light the tobacco in his hubble-bubble with five hundred rupees in bills. He soon became virtually a beggar.[4] Yogin-ma lived with him for a few years and tried in vain to change his life. She bore him one daughter named Ganu and a son, who lived only six months. But patience has its limits. Disgusted with her husband's immoral life, she at last severed her relationship with him and returned to her parental home, bringing with her their daughter. By then Yogin-ma's father had died, but her mother welcomed them warmly. When Ganu grew up Yogin-ma arranged her marriage.

The romantic picture of a peaceful, happy married life had been shattered, and Yogin-ma felt a great void in her mind. Tormented by anxiety and restlessness, she agonized over how she would spend the rest of her life. Just when she was passing through this mental storm, divine grace opened up a new life for her.

In 1882 Yogin-ma met Sri Ramakrishna for the first time at Balaram Basu's house. As she said in her memoirs: 'Balaram Babu was related to me, being my husband's maternal uncle. One day Sri Ramakrishna came to his house and we went to see him. It was the first time I saw him. The Master was standing at one side of the hall in deep samadhi. He had no outer consciousness. Since no one dared touch him, people bowed down to him from a distance. We also did the same. At that time I had no idea what samadhi was. I at first thought that he was a drunken devotee of Kali. I could not understand the Master at my first meeting. Moreover, it immediately came to my mind that my married life had been ruined by a drunken husband, and again should I undo my spiritual life through the influence of this seemingly drunken person? But gradually I became acquainted with the Master'.[5]

It is interesting to note that Yogin-ma's grandmother (her mother's mother) had met Sri Ramakrishna at Dakshineswar probably in the late 1870s. At that time Keshab Chandra Sen was writing about Sri

Ramakrishna in his newspapers and magazines and had made the Calcutta people aware of him. Yogin-ma's grandmother read about the Master in the newspaper and went to Dakshineswar to meet him. Strangely enough, on arriving there the first person she encountered was Sri Ramakrishna himself. She did not know who he was, since there was nothing unusual about his dress or appearance. Addressing the Master, she asked, 'Can you tell me where Ramakrishna Paramahamsa is and how I can see him?' The Master replied: 'What do I know about him? Some people call him ''Paramahamsa'', some call him ''Young Priest'', and others call him ''Gadadhar Chatterjee''. Please ask someone else to help you find him'. Unfortunately Yogin-ma's grandmother did not press the matter further. Thinking that perhaps Sri Ramakrishna was not so important after all, she lost interest. She walked around the temple garden for a while and then returned home.[6]

Balaram would often go to Dakshineswar by boat and would invite other devotees to go along with him. Yogin-ma went with him a few times, and then she started to visit the Master with some other devotees. In her memoirs she said: 'Gradually I began to feel an attraction for the Master. Just the thought of visiting him would make my mind dance with joy. On the day that I planned to go there I would get up early and finish my household duties as quickly as possible. My longing to see him knew no bounds. After arriving at his room I would forget everything, sitting in his presence. The Master used to experience samadhi off and on, and at that time we would look at his face with wonder. He was so compassionate! Whenever I brought him some ordinary preparations he would relish them like a young boy, saying joyfully, ''Very tasty! Delicious!'' And always at the time of our departure he would say, ''Come back again''.

'When I returned home after my visit with the Master, I would spend the whole week in an intoxicated mood. This established a strong relationship. I cannot express the joy I felt. Even while I was engaged in cooking or other household activities, my mind was with the Master. After some days, when I would feel my intoxication diminishing, my mind would again long to see him'.[7]

Yogin-ma had been initiated into a Devi mantram (a name of the Divine Mother) by her husband's family guru, and she used to repeat it twice daily. When Sri Ramakrishna heard about it he confirmed her mantram and told her to continue repeating it. Then he said to her: 'Look, your Chosen Deity is in this place [pointing to his body]. If you think of me, that will bring recollectedness of your Chosen Deity'. Later, whenever Yogin-ma sat for meditation, she would feel the

Master's presence. Sri Ramakrishna also taught her how to practise japam, showing how the four fingers of the right hand must be kept tightly together. 'The result of japam goes away', said the Master, 'if there is any gap between the fingers'. Another time he said, 'In this Kali yuga a Gopala mantram [a name of Baby Krishna] or a Kali mantram produces quick results'.[8]

After some time Yogin-ma also met Holy Mother, and the two were immediately drawn to one another. They were about the same age. Holy Mother once said, 'Yogin is my Jaya [an attendant of the goddess Durga] — my friend, companion, and attendant'.[9] Yogin-ma described her relation with Holy Mother at Dakshineswar: 'Whenever I went there Holy Mother would take me into her confidence, tell me her secrets, and seek my counsel. I used to visit Dakshineswar every seven or eight days, sometimes spending the night there. Then Holy Mother would not let me sleep anywhere else, but would ask me to sleep in her room at the nahabat.

'Some time after my first visit Holy Mother left for her country home. I stood on the bank of the Ganga and watched her departure, waiting until the boat was no longer visible. After that I returned to the nahabat and wept bitterly. The Master, on his way back from the Panchavati, noticed me crying, and after returning to his room he sent for me. "Her leaving caused a great deal of pain for you", he said tenderly. He then began to console me by recounting the marvellous spiritual experiences he had had during his days of Tantric sadhana. When Holy Mother returned after about a year and a half, he told her: "That girl with nice large eyes, who comes here frequently, loves you very much. She wept a lot at the nahabat when you left for home". Mother replied: "Yes, I know her very well. Her name is Yogin" '.[10]

Whenever Yogin-ma came to Dakshineswar she would serve the Master and Holy Mother. Holy Mother was so fond of the way that Yogin-ma braided her hair that she would not undo it, even at the time of taking her bath, but would wait for Yogin-ma to come again so that she could rebraid it. Holy Mother was extremely shy and would not visit or talk to the Master publicly. One day she said to Yogin-ma: 'All of you have attained bhava samadhi, but nothing has happened to me. Would you tell the Master about it?' Yogin-ma did as she was told, but when the Master heard what she had to say, he remained silent. Yogin-ma returned to Holy Mother and found her seated on her asana (prayer carpet), performing worship. She was in an ecstatic mood. One moment she was laughing, another moment she was crying, and again another moment she was sitting motionless. Yogin-ma was surprised to see her in ecstasy. When Holy Mother came down to the normal plane of consciousness, Yogin-ma asked her, 'You complained that you do not experience samadhi, but what is all this?' Holy Mother smiled.[11]

Yogin-ma's association with the God-intoxicated lives of Sri Ramakrishna and Holy Mother created a spiritual hunger in her mind. She now diverted most of her energy to spiritual pursuits, spending the greater part of her day in worship, study, japam, and meditation. Although the Master discouraged her from reading too many books, he did suggest that she study the devotional scriptures. She had had very little education when she was young, but she now began to study every afternoon one of the main Puranas, the Ramayana, the Mahabharata, the Bhagavad Gita, some Tantric scripture, or the life of Chaitanya.

Many aspirants do not know that spiritual discontent is often a good sign. It indicates that the soul is longing for more and more spiritual experiences. Once Yogin-ma was passing through a dry period and decided to complain about it to Sri Ramakrishna. She left for Dakshineswar on foot very early in the morning, but as soon as she saw the Master she forgot everything. After a little while she went to the garden, picked some flowers, and carried them in the corner of her cloth. Sri Ramakrishna was at that time standing on the northern verandah of his room and saw Yogin-ma coming with something. He asked her, 'What are you carrying?' Yogin-ma showed him the flowers and then bowed down and offered them at his feet. Immediately the Master went into an ecstatic mood and blessed her, touching his foot to her head.[12]

Once Yogin-ma said: 'Several times I noticed that whenever a question arose in my mind, someone else would ask the Master the same question. Thus, in answering that person's question, the Master would remove the doubts in my mind also. He was all-knowing'.[13]

Yogin-ma one day brought her aged mother and her daughter to the Master. They were both very happy to hear his inspiring words. Through Yogin-ma's influence her husband, Ambika Charan, also began trying to change his way of life and to associate with holy people. On November 15, 1882, Balaram brought Ambika Charan to his house to meet Sri Ramakrishna and be blessed by him. But the Master knew how he had ill-treated his wife, and after Ambika Charan had left he said: 'He is an unfortunate wretch. A householder has his duties to discharge, his debts to pay: his debt to the gods, his debt to his ancestors, his debt to the rishis, and his debt to his wife and children. If a wife is chaste, then her husband should support her; he should also bring up their children until they are of age'.[14]

Yogin-ma did not give up, however. She persuaded her husband to associate with the Master, so he met Sri Ramakrishna again, this time at Dakshineswar. This meeting seemed to make a deep impression on him. Unfortunately, not long after this Ambika Charan was bitten by a dog and became bedridden with a fever. When Sri Ramakrishna heard about it he told Yogin-ma to take care of him. He said that as a wife she had a duty towards her husband, even if he had been immoral. Accordingly, Yogin-ma brought her husband to her parental home during his last days and carefully nursed him until his death.

Pleased with Yogin-ma's devotion, Sri Ramakrishna visited her home on July 28, 1885, along with a few devotees. Some musicians entertained them in her parlour, and then the Master was asked to go to Yogin-ma's room in the inner apartment for some refreshments. Golap-ma, Yogin-ma's neighbour, said to Sri Ramakrishna: 'Ganu's mother [Yogin-ma] requests you to bless the room with the dust of your feet. Then the room will be turned into Varanasi, and anyone dying in it will have no trouble hereafter'.[15]

In his reminiscences Swami Akhandananda described an interesting incident that occurred that day at Yogin-ma's house:

Once Sri Ramakrishna went to Yogin-ma's house at Nebubagan, Baghbazar. Hiralal, a brother of Yogin-ma's, did not like the fact that his sister went to Dakshineswar. We heard that when Yogin-ma invited the Master to her house, Hiralal brought a famous gymnast and wrestler named Manmatha, who lived in Gosainpara, to frighten him. After Manmatha saw the Master and heard a few words from him, he fell at his feet and said to him, weeping: 'My Lord, I am guilty. Please forgive me'. The Master replied: 'All right. Come one day to Dakshineswar'.[16]

According to Swami Akhandananda, Manmatha was a ruffian and an expert fighter. Some days later Manmatha asked Swami Akhandananda to accompany him to Dakshineswar to see the Master. Sri Ramakrishna blessed Manmatha, touching his body, and that touch transformed his life.

In the middle of 1885 Yogin-ma and a few other women devotees went by boat with the Master to attend a Vaishnava festival at Panihati, a few miles north of Calcutta. They watched the Master as he sang and danced among the huge crowd. A few days later they again enjoyed his holy company during the Jagannath Car Festival at Balaram Basu's house. The Master spent that night at Balaram's

house, and the next morning he returned to Dakshineswar. Before he
left, the women devotees saluted him and bade him farewell, but
Yogin-ma, feeling an irresistible attraction for the Master, followed
him. Seeing her behind him, the Master said in an ecstatic mood,
'Blissful Mother! Blissful Mother!' and saluted her. Yogin-ma bowed
down to him. Then the Master said to her, 'Why don't you come, O
Mother, why don't you come with me?'

While the Master went to the boat that had been hired for him,
Yogin-ma hurried back to Balaram's house and informed Balaram's
wife that she was going to Dakshineswar with the Master. Another
woman asked to accompany her, and they both ran through the street
so they could reach the boat before it left. On the way to
Dakshineswar Yogin-ma said to the Master: 'I want to call on God
more and put my mind wholly on him, but it is hard to control the
mind. What shall I do?' Sri Ramakrishna replied in a sweet voice:
'Why don't you surrender to him? Be like a cast-off leaf in a gale. Do
you know what that is like? A cast-off leaf lies on the ground and flies
away as the wind carries it. Similarly, one should depend on God.
Let the mind move as the power of divine consciousness moves it.
That's all'.[17]

When the boat reached Dakshineswar, Yogin-ma and her
companion went to the nahabat to see Holy Mother, and the Master
went to bow down to the Divine Mother in the temple. After
returning to his room he learned from Holy Mother that there were
no vegetables for their meal. The Master asked Yogin-ma and the
other woman, 'Could you go to the market?' They immediately
agreed. At that time in India aristocratic women did not go out for
shopping. If they went anywhere they would be carried in a
palanquin or driven in a carriage, their faces covered by a veil. But
because Sri Ramakrishna had asked them, they walked to the market
and bought some vegetables, which Holy Mother cooked for the
Master and the devotees. In the evening Yogin-ma and her
companion returned home on foot. Sri Ramakrishna used to say, 'A
person cannot be perfect as long as he is subject to shame, hatred,
and fear'.[18] In this way the Master freed his women devotees from
such feelings.

In *The Gospel of Sri Ramakrishna* the Master is often quoted as saying,
'Woman and gold is maya', and this is a shock to many women
readers. Yogin-ma associated very closely with the Master, and one
day she talked about the Master's relationship with the women
devotees: 'Sometimes when I was with him I would feel that he was
not a man but one of us [women]. Although it is natural for us to feel

a certain shyness before men, we had no such feeling in the Master's presence. If perchance that feeling would arise, it would disappear immediately, and we would be free to open our hearts to him. We used to speak to him about very intimate things without any scruple or hesitation. And how kind, how affectionate, the Master was to us! When strangers, casually reading the life of Sri Ramakrishna, jump to the conclusion that he did not like women, we simply laugh'.[19]

Once Yogin-ma asked the Master, 'What will happen to us?' 'What more do you want?' replied Sri Ramakrishna. 'You have seen me, fed me, and served me. What else do you need? Don't worry. The thousand-petalled lotus of your seventh plane [sahasrara] will bloom at the time of your death'. He further said, 'At the devotees' last moment I shall have to appear before them. Otherwise, how will they get liberation?'[20]

Yogin-ma was a woman of strong determination. Whatever she undertook she carried through to perfection. After practising spiritual disciplines for some time according to the Master's instructions, she decided that Calcutta was not a suitable place for such practices. The sacred atmosphere of Vrindaban, she thought, would be better. Sri Ramakrishna was then staying at the Cossipore garden house for his cancer treatment. When Yogin-ma asked his permission to go to Vrindaban he readily agreed, but he asked her if she had talked to Holy Mother about it. Holy Mother was present then and said: 'Whatever was to be said has been said by you already. What is there to add?' Nevertheless, the Master said to Yogin-ma: 'My dear child, go, after obtaining her consent. You will get everything'.[21]

The next day Yogin-ma came back to Cossipore to take leave of the Master and Holy Mother. She and Golap-ma had brought some food for Sri Ramakrishna, but since there were some young boy disciples in his room they waited downstairs. When the Master heard that they were there he sent for them and told them that those boys were like his sons. Sri Ramakrishna blessed them, touching their heads, and then asked them to go to Holy Mother. Yogin-ma waited, however, and Swami Brahmananda said to the Master, 'She always salutes you by placing her head on your feet, so she is waiting'. Immediately the Master, out of compassion, took his feet from underneath the cover of his bed, and Yogin-ma bowed down as she used to. This was her last meeting with him.[22] Yogin-ma then went to bow down to Holy Mother. As a blessing, Holy Mother put her hand on Yogin-ma's head and silently repeated her mantram, counting it on her fingers.

When Sri Ramakrishna passed away in August 1886, Yogin-ma was staying at Kala Babu's kunja, a retreat house in Vrindaban belonging to Balaram's family. Hearing of the Master's death, she was overwhelmed with grief for not having seen him again. Holy Mother joined her there soon after. Yogin-ma said: 'The moment Holy Mother saw me she hugged me and began to shed profuse tears over her separation from the Master. Both of us became so disconsolate that our days passed in lamentation, and we could hardly attend to our daily needs. One night the Master appeared to us in a vision and said: "Why are you crying so much? Here I am. Where have I gone? It is just a change from one room to another, isn't that so?" These words reassured us and lessened the intensity of our grief to a considerable extent'.[23]

Yogin-ma spent most of her time at Vrindaban in japam and meditation. One evening, while meditating at Lala Babu's temple, she became so absorbed that she went into samadhi. Long after the evening service was over she still sat there motionless like a statue. The temple attendants tried to bring her back to normal consciousness, since it was time to close the temple gate, but all their efforts were in vain. In the meantime Holy Mother sent Swami Yogananda to find Yogin-ma. Since he knew where she usually went for meditation, he came with a lantern to that temple and found her in samadhi. He began to repeat the Master's name in her ear, and after some time she came down from her exalted state. Later Yogin-ma described her experience, 'I was then in such a high spiritual mood that I even forgot whether the world existed or not'.[24] Holy Mother once said that in Vrindaban Yogin-ma would become so absorbed in meditation that she would not notice when flies sat on her eyes and caused sores in them.

It was also in Vrindaban that Sri Ramakrishna appeared to Holy Mother and told her to initiate Swami Yogananda. When Holy Mother replied that she did not know what to do, the Master told her what mantram to give and also advised her to get Yogin-ma's help.

After spending a few months with Holy Mother in Vrindaban, Yogin-ma returned to Calcutta to look after her aged mother. In her room, which had been sanctified by Sri Ramakrishna, she installed a shrine with an image of Baby Krishna. The four walls of the room were full of pictures of gods, goddesses, and saints. She would perform ritualistic worship every day with great devotion, as a result of which she had many divine visions. Later she spoke highly of the value of ritual as one of the easiest ways to establish a relationship with God and lead one to deep spiritual experiences. 'Once I was in such a high spiritual attitude', she said, 'that wherever I turned my eyes, I would see my Ishta [Chosen Deity]. That state lasted for three days'.[25]

The disciples of Sri Ramakrishna had great love and regard for Yogin-ma. In 1896 Swami Vivekananda wrote from America to his brother disciples to start a convent for women with the help of Yogin-ma, Gauri-ma, and other women disciples of the Master. After Swamiji returned to India he learned one day that Yogin-ma had experienced samadhi in her Calcutta residence. He said to her: 'Yogin-ma, you will pass away in samadhi. Once a person experiences samadhi, the memory of it is revived at the time of death'.[26]

Yogin-ma looked on the monastic disciples as her own children, and they in turn were very free with her. One day Swamiji saw her in Calcutta and said: 'I want to have lunch with you. Please cook a curry for me'. On another occasion he said: 'Today is my birthday. Please feed me well. Prepare some rice pudding for me'.[27] She was an expert cook. Holy Mother and the direct disciples all liked her cooking very much, as had Sri Ramakrishna. When the Maharaja of Khetri visited Swami Vivekananda in Calcutta, Swamiji asked Yogin-ma to prepare his meals with various vegetarian and nonvegetarian dishes. Every year Yogin-ma would celebrate the Jagaddhatri Puja at her house with much festivity and grand feasts. Holy Mother and many of the direct disciples would attend that function.

In 1893 Holy Mother and Yogin-ma performed the *panchatapa*, the austerity of five fires, at Nilambar Babu's garden house near what is now Belur Math. According to the custom, one sits and repeats one's mantram from sunrise to sunset surrounded by four blazing fires, which are placed six feet apart. The fifth fire is the scorching sun above. They practised this austerity for seven consecutive days.

One winter Yogin-ma lived on the bank of the confluence of the Ganga and the Jamuna at Allahabad and observed *kalpavasa*, a spiritual vow. On another occasion she gave up drinking water for six months, taking milk instead. Her whole life was full of fasts and vigils.

Although Yogin-ma apparently was a householder, actually she was a nun. On November 20, 1900, she was initiated along with Swami Saradananda into *purna-abhisheka*, a special Tantric rite, by Ishwar Chandra Chakrabarty. She learned from him the secrets of Tantric sadhana. Later, at Puri, she was initiated into Vedic sannyasa by Swami Saradananda in the presence of Swami Premananda. She was too modest to make a show of her renunciation, however, and wore the ochre cloth only at the time of worship. At other times she wore the usual white cloth.

Yogin-ma had a deep respect for the monastic ideal. One day

Swami Saradananda was dictating some letters to a young monk in his room when Yogin-ma entered. Her foot accidently touched the monk's cloth, and she immediately put her hands together and saluted him. The monk said: 'The touch of your foot is a blessing, Yogin-ma. Please don't feel embarrassed'. Yogin-ma replied: 'You are a monk. Your ochre robe is a symbol of renunciation. It is this renunciation that made Sri Ramakrishna great, and you are following in his footsteps. A little cobra is as poisonous as a big cobra'.[28] Her words made the monk realize what a great responsibility lies in the wearing of the monk's robe.

Yogin-ma's grandson gave a description of her in an article: 'From evening right up to nine o'clock in the night we had many opportunities of seeing her seated on her asana [prayer carpet], meditating statue-like — straight, erect, externally dead, but obviously in touch with some luminous reality within. She had very big lotus-like, sparkling eyes. Her health was always good, with only minor troubles and ailments. She was of short stature, heavily built, bright-complexioned, very sagacious, well balanced in her judgements, and had a grave composure. She was full of stamina, fortitude, and was a woman of her word'.[29]

Swami Arupananda wrote: 'Even in her old age Yogin-ma had so much inclination for spiritual practices that in the midst of many engrossing occupations and distractions she would not alter the routine of her daily meditation and japam. Every day after her bath in the Ganga she used to spend about two hours, or perhaps more, in meditation, etc. Even terrible cold or rain could not stand in the way of her routine. We would wonder at her steadfastness. From time to time people want some relaxation or they yield to laziness, but Yogin-ma would not miss a single day'....[30] Holy Mother used to tell the women devotees: 'Yogin and Golap have practised so much spiritual discipline. It will do you good to talk about it amongst yourselves'.[31]

An American devotee, Sister Devamata, also gave her reminiscences of Yogin-ma:

> Yogin-ma always seemed to me one of the noblest of Sri Ramakrishna's disciples...She did not abandon her householder life, but no nun in a cloister was more rigid in her spiritual observance than she...Her householder life was lived with her aging mother in a modest home within walking distance of Holy Mother's quarters. She was punctiliously faithful in fulfilling her duty to her mother. No service was ever omitted, no care neglected. Her loving thought was constantly on her. But with

more lingering persistence did it rest in the memory of her blessed association with Sri Ramakrishna. Since her first contact with him, her supreme interest had been centred in her spiritual life. This, as I saw it, was lived at the Udbodhan Office in Mukherjee Lane, where, on the second story, Holy Mother was housed. These two parallel lines of living never crossed or clashed. Each seemed rather to strengthen and sweeten the other.

Her day was too well organized to permit of conflict. She rose before night had lifted and at four went for her bath in the Ganga. She never failed. Sometimes when she was not well, Swami Saradananda would remonstrate with her and beg her to consider her health; but she remained firm. The early bath in the Ganga, with its prayer and sacred chanting, was a religious duty and should not be put aside. The bath over, she returned to her home, gave her mother the necessary care, and at seven o'clock she was climbing the stairs at the Udbodhan Office to carry a morning greeting to Holy Mother. This done, she went below to a room underneath the stairs. Here she decided on the purchases to be made at the bazar and cut the vegetables for the noon meal. She regarded this as her special privilege. At about eleven she returned to the upper room to conduct the puja...The hour of prayer in that upper chamber where the shrine was, counted among the most precious in the day for me. Yogin-ma and I were alone — she before the altar, I beside an inner window opening on the court. Holy Mother came and went. Others entered the room. It was all essentially informal, but Yogin-ma's thought remained fixed on the puja. She was very strict in conforming with all the usages and traditions of worship. She would never speak while she was worshipping, and it seemed at times as if Holy Mother was teasing or testing her, for she would go up to her and ask her a question. Yogin-ma would give a monosyllabic answer behind closed teeth without moving her lips. Mother would smile and walk away...

After the puja Yogin-ma served the noon meal — to the ladies in the front rooms near the shrine, to Swami Saradananda and the Udbodhan staff in a large dining room at the rear of the second story. When the meal was eaten, she went to her mother; but in the late afternoon she was back once more in the room under the stairs conferring with Swami Saradananda. This was the one hour of real recreation in all the day; for when they had disposed of immediate questions, they lived over again and yet again the blessed days with Sri Ramakrishna. They told each other stories of the Master they had heard a hundred times; they talked of Swamiji (Swami Vivekananda) and the other disciples who had gone; they spoke tenderly and devoutly of Holy Mother. It was a cherished hour — that hour spent together in the little room underneath the stairs. Arati [the vesper service] seemed but the culmination of it, and Yogin-ma passed half in dream from the memory of the Master to his worship in the shrine. With her heart aglow she waved the incense and burning camphor before the picture; then with the same warmth of love she turned, when arati was over, to distribute the offered food to his children...

Yogin-ma was most loving to me always. It troubled her apparently that I was born in America instead of India. Often she would say to me: 'Devamata, I wonder why Thakur sent you so far away to be born. You belong here. You are one of us'.[32]

Yogin-ma was always active — never in the least bit lazy. Every afternoon, after returning home from Holy Mother's house, she would cook rice and curries. This food she offered to the Lord in her shrine, and then she and her mother partook of the prasad. After eating she would take a little rest and then study one of the scriptures. She did not know Sanskrit, so she would read a Bengali translation of the original. Sometimes in the afternoon she would attend the Gita class given by Swami Saradananda.

Yogin-ma had two images of Baby Krishna, which she served and worshipped with much love and affection. 'One day', she said, 'while meditating at the time of worship, I saw two incomparably handsome boys. They came, smiling and hugging me and stroking my back, and said, "Do you know who we are?" I replied: "Yes, I know you quite well. You are the heroic Balarama, and you are Sri Krishna". The younger one [Krishna] then said, "You won't remember us". "Why?" "No, you won't on account of them", and he pointed to my grandchildren'. Soon after, his words were fulfilled. Yogin-ma became very much preoccupied with her grandsons after her daughter's death, and her mind came down to the normal plane from that high spiritual mood.[33]

Yogin-ma's daughter, Ganu, passed away in 1909 at Varanasi. Ganu's husband had died three years earlier in 1906, and some of their children died while still young. But with Swami Saradananda's help, Yogin-ma raised three orphan grandsons, one of whom eventually became a monk of the Ramakrishna Order. When Yogin-ma's mother was dying in 1914 after a long, full life, she was taken in her last hour to the bank of the Ganga. Swami Saradananda sat near her, chanting the name of God as she passed away. Yogin-ma cried like a child.

God provides everything to those who are devoted to him. Although Yogin-ma was born in a well-to-do family and was married to a wealthy husband, she had to live on a small pension, which was agreed upon at the time of her separation from her husband. She was frugal, however, and managed all her personal expenses with money left over. This she gave away in charity or used for pilgrimages. She visited almost all of the important holy places of India, from Kedarnath and Badrinath in the north to Kanyakumari in the south, from Dwaraka in the west to Kamakhya in the east. Wherever she went she would give a little money to the poor. She never refused anyone. On Yogin-ma's visits to Jayrambati or Kamarpukur, the birthplaces of Holy Mother and Sri Ramakrishna, she would give some money to their relatives. Even in Calcutta, if any beggars came to the Udbodhan Office, Yogin-ma always gave them something. At this Golap-ma would say: 'Beggars who come to us demand pice and won't go without getting it. Yogin is at the root of all this'.[34]

In 1909 Swami Saradananda started to write *Sri Sri Ramakrishna Lilaprasanga (Sri Ramakrishna, The Great Master)*, and he asked Yogin-ma to give him her reminiscences of the Master. Accordingly, she recounted all the incidents that she knew about. This book was first published in the *Udbodhan*, a Bengali magazine. Every month, before the manuscript was sent to the press, it was read aloud to Yogin-ma, and she gave her valued suggestions. She also greatly helped Sister Nivedita in her *Cradle Tales of Hinduism*, as Nivedita acknowledged in the introduction. Yogin-ma had a wonderful memory and could faithfully relate stories from the Puranas, the Ramayana, the Mahabharata, and the *Sri Sri Chaitanya Charitamrita*.

Holy Mother also had much regard for Yogin-ma's judgement and would consult her not only about domestic matters but about spiritual affairs and even mantras as well. Once an elderly gentleman asked Holy Mother to bless him with initiation. She agreed out of compassion, but when he came for the ceremony, she asked him a few questions and learned that he was sceptical about Sri Ramakrishna's divinity. Holy Mother was disturbed. She anxiously called Yogin-ma, who hurried to the shrine. 'Yogin, what shall I do?' asked Holy Mother. 'This person does not accept the Master'. Yogin-ma immediately replied: 'Well, Mother, it does not matter. The mantram you will give him has the power to change him in time. Don't worry. Initiate him'. Holy Mother followed Yogin-ma's advice, and her prediction came true. After a short time the man became devoted to Sri Ramakrishna.[35]

Doubt is like a disease of the mind. It comes and goes. Although Yogin-ma was an intimate companion of Holy Mother, she at one time doubted her divinity. She said to herself: 'Sri Ramakrishna was the embodiment of renunciation, and Mother is engrossed in the world, preoccupied day and night with the thought of her brothers, sisters-in-law, nephews, and nieces'. Soon after this she was one day seated on the bank of the Ganga, meditating, when Sri Ramakrishna appeared to her in a vision and said, 'Do you see what is being carried by the water of the Ganga?' Yogin-ma looked and saw the corpse of a newborn baby. She also saw many people offering worship to Mother Ganga. The Master then said: 'Can anything make the Ganga impure? Regard her [Holy Mother] in the same way. Never doubt her. Remember, she is not different from this [meaning himself]'. Yogin-ma immediately rushed to Holy Mother and, after telling her the whole story, apologized. Holy Mother smiled and consoled her.[36]

Holy Mother's passing away in 1920 created a tremendous void in Yogin-ma's mind. Yogin-ma longed to join her and the Master. Then in 1922 Swamis Brahmananda and Turiyananda passed away, bringing Yogin-ma more grief. But, in spite of her failing health, she went with Swami Saradananda in 1923 to Jayrambati for the dedication of Holy Mother's temple on the site of her birthplace.

During the last two years of Yogin-ma's life she suffered from diabetes. Although her austere body became weak and fragile, her mind was always alert, and she never forgot her blessed association with Sri Ramakrishna, Holy Mother, and the other direct disciples of the Master. She would often go into bhava samadhi, sweetly uttering the words, 'Ha Gopala! Ha Gopala!' For two or three days before she passed away she lay speechless and refused to take even a little liquid. Swami Saradananda asked the doctor who was attending on her to examine her to see if she was in a coma, as is common when there is diabetes. The doctor checked carefully but could not find any symptoms of coma. The swami was then assured that the Master's words had come true — that Yogin-ma would give up her body in a state of jnana, that is, she would merge into Brahman.[37]

On Wednesday, June 4, 1924, at 10:25 P.M., when all the activities of the monastery were over, Yogin-ma passed away at the Udbodhan house, next to the room where Holy Mother had lived. Swami Saradananda sat near her head at the time of her death and repeated Sri Ramakrishna's name, while a monk recited from the second chapter of the Bhagavad Gita. Yogin-ma's body was then cremated on the bank of the Ganga according to the Hindu custom, with the chanting of Vedic mantras.

12

Gauri-Ma

Three types of people are generally found in this world. The first type is mainly interested in worldly enjoyment; the second type enjoys the world but also keeps his mind on God; and the third type is totally devoted to spiritual pursuits. God created human beings with different temperaments and tendencies so that he could play with them in various ways. Gauri-ma, or Mother Gauri, belonged to the third group of people. She had completely dedicated herself to God.

One day a holy man was on his way to visit the Divine Mother at Kalighat, in South Calcutta, when he was stopped by an old woman who wanted to pay her respects to him. Gauri-ma, who was then nine years old, was playing nearby with some other girls. Seeing that holy man she felt an irresistible attraction and rushed over to him and bowed down. The holy man asked: 'Your friends are playing and you have come to me. Why?' Gauri-ma replied: 'Oh, they love to play that way, but I don't like it. I felt an attraction in my heart, so I came to you'. The holy man touched the little girl's head and blessed her, saying, 'May you attain devotion to Krishna'.[1]

Later, Gauri-ma found out from the old woman, who happened to be their neighbour, that this holy man had an ashrama at Nimta, in Belgharia, ten miles north of Calcutta. Without saying anything to her parents, Gauri-ma left home and through inquiry found the way there. The holy man was meditating inside his cottage when she arrived, so she waited. After some time he received her cordially and arranged for her to stay in a neighbour's house. The next day was *Raspurnima*, the full moon night of autumn when Krishna played with the gopis. The holy man asked Gauri-ma to bathe in the Ganga, and when she returned he initiated her. Meanwhile, her absence from home had been discovered and there was a terrible commotion. Her brother found out from the old neighbour woman that she had gone to Nimta, so he immediately went to bring her back. When he arrived the holy man told him: 'Please don't

Gauri-ma (1857-1938)

scold her. She is just a little girl. It is hard to keep a yellow bird in a cage'. Gauri-ma then returned home with the consent of her guru.[2]

Gauri-ma's original name, given by her family, was Mridani, but she was also called Rudrani. Her monastic name was Gauri Puri. Sri Ramakrishna and Holy Mother used to call her Gaur-dasi (handmaid of Gauranga). To others she was known as Gauri-ma, since her complexion was a gold colour like that of the Divine Mother Gauri, the consort of Shiva. Gauri-ma was born in 1857 and was the fourth child of seven children. She had two brothers and four sisters. Her father, Parvati Charan Chattopadhyay, and mother, Giribala Devi, were both very devoted to God. Parvati Charan was an orthodox brahmin, who would go to his office with religious marks on his forehead, even though he was sometimes ridiculed by his European boss for it. Giribala was very kindhearted and was also quite talented. She composed many devotional songs and hymns, which were published in *Namasara* and *Vairagya-Sangitamala*. Since Giribala had inherited her father's wealth and property, the whole family lived most of the time in his Calcutta residence.

A palmist once prophesied about Gauri-ma, 'This girl will be a yogini'.[3] Even from her very childhood she was fond of decorating the family shrine and would worship the Lord in her own way. She often gave alms to poor, helpless people. Moreover, she was a strict vegetarian and never craved for good food or fancy clothes. One day she went with her older brother somewhere by boat and on the way she thought: 'Why do women wear jewellery? Shall I be unhappy if I do not have any ornaments?' She had a gold bangle on her wrist, which her family had given her. On a whim, she took it off and bit into it. When she found the gold had no taste she threw it into the Ganga. Later, of course, she was scolded by her parents.[4] She loved to hear her uncle Chandi tell stories about the holy places of India, especially those of the Himalayan region. This stirred her imagination and made her long to travel to those places herself.

Even as a child, Gauri-ma was fearless and uncompromising, and no external pressure could make her deviate from a resolution which she considered right. She was first sent to a Christian missionary school in South Calcutta, where her academic talents were recognized and rewarded with a gold medal. But she left the school because she could not tolerate the narrow-minded religious views of the missionaries. Other girls also followed Gauri-ma's example, all of them enrolling in a Hindu school. Gauri-ma had a sharp mind and a good memory. During her early teens she learned Sanskrit grammar and memorized many hymns to gods and goddesses, as well as parts of the Gita, Chandi, Ramayana, and Mahabharata.

Some time after Gauri-ma's initiation, a nun from Vrindaban was a guest in her home. This nun had a Damodar Shila, a stone image of Vishnu, which she worshipped daily. While leaving, the nun gave her beloved Vishnu to Gauri-ma and said: 'This image of God is my all in all and is very living. He fell in love with you, so I hand him over to you. My child, worship him. It will do good to you'.[5] Gauri-ma accepted the precious gift and took that image of the Lord as her husband. For the rest of her life she carried him wherever she went and served him.

Observing her dispassion for the world, her relatives tried to arrange her marriage when she was ten years old. But Gauri-ma boldly rejected the idea, saying, 'I shall marry that person who never dies'. She was happy with her beloved husband, Lord Vishnu. When Gauri-ma became thirteen, however, a bridegroom was selected against her will, and a marriage date was set. Gauri-ma was extremely upset. One day she became so angry that she started throwing away the things which had been collected for the wedding ceremony. Then she entered her room with her image of Vishnu and a picture of Chaitanya and locked the door from inside. Most of her relatives tried to console her and convince her to marry, but she was adamant. That night her mother requested her to open the door and let her in, and Gauri-ma obeyed. Seeing the agony and pain of her daughter, Giribala said: 'My child, since you have real dispassion for the world, I shall not force you to marry. I hereby dedicate you to God. May he protect you from all dangers'.[6]

Giribala knew that her husband and other relatives were so angry with her daughter that they might even beat her, so she secretly sent Gauri-ma to a neighbour's home through the back door. Gauri-ma hid there until her relatives' anger had been assuaged. Thus God saved his devotee from the bondage of marriage.

All people cannot be put in the same category. Some people are meant to lead a householder's life and others are meant for the monastic life. Each is great in his own place. Gauri-ma longed to become an itinerant nun, but it was not easy for a young girl to travel by herself. She waited for an opportunity and prayed to God to show her the way. In 1875, when she was eighteen years old, Gauri-ma left with an uncle, aunt, and some neighbours for a pilgrimage to Gangasagar (the confluence of the Ganga and the Bay of Bengal). Here, on the third day of their stay, she disappeared into the huge crowd of pilgrims. Her relatives and neighbours spent three days searching for her in vain and then returned to Calcutta. Giribala was grief-stricken at the news and fell ill. The family sent messengers to different holy places of India to announce a reward of one thousand rupees to anyone finding the girl.[7]

After running away from her relatives, Gauri-ma had hidden herself in a bush near their tent. From there she could watch their movements. As soon as she saw them leave she joined a group of monks and nuns who came from the Himalayan regions. She dressed like the nuns so that she would not be recognized. The group visited several holy places, travelling by train or on foot, and finally reached Hardwar after three months. Gauri-ma had heard from her uncle Chandi about Hardwar and Rishikesh, where the ascetics of the Himalayas practise austerities. Now, seeing the panoramic view of the Himalayas and the Ganga, her enthusiasm for God-realization was aroused more than ever.

From Rishikesh, Gauri-ma visited Devaprayag, Rudraprayag, Kedarnath, Badrinath, and then returned to Hardwar. Soon after this she visited Jamunotri (the source of the Jamuna river) and Gangotri (the source of the Ganga), Jwalamukhi, and also Amarnath, which is in Kashmir. She did not come down to the plains for fear of being caught by her relatives. In order to disguise herself she cut her hair and wore an ochre cloth, or she sometimes put on a long robe and turban, such as a man would wear. Furthermore, she tried to hide her physical beauty by smearing ashes and dirt on her body, and at times even pretended to be crazy so that no one would bother her. She carried the image of Vishnu around her neck, and in her bundle there were a few articles for daily use, as well as her pictures of Kali and Chaitanya, and two books, the Chandi and the Srimad Bhagavatam. Seldom did she talk, but when pressed for her identity she said that she was married and lived with her husband. Needless to say, she meant that Lord Vishnu was her husband.

During her itinerant days, Gauri-ma practised severe austerities, such as fasting, observing silence, meditating, and studying the scriptures. Sometimes she repeated her mantram from sunrise to sunset. She often begged her food from door to door, but at some places the villagers came forward to provide food and shelter for her. Thus for three years she endured cold, hunger, and other ordeals as she travelled on foot to the holy places of the rugged Himalayan region.

Gauri-ma went next to Vrindaban, the playground of her beloved Krishna. One of Gauri-ma's uncles lived nearby in Mathura. Seeing her in a temple one day, he forced her to come home with him and secretly sent word to her parents in Calcutta that she had been found. Gauri-ma guessed what her uncle was doing and fled to Jaipur. From there she visited Pushkar, Prabhas, Sudamapuri, Dwaraka, and other holy places of western India. Once a local ruler invited Gauri-ma to be his guest in the palace, but she refused. Since this ruler had no children, he asked Gauri-ma for her blessings. Gauri-ma pointed to the deity in the temple and told him: 'You won't get a better child than him. Please love him with all your heart and soul, and you will attain peace'.[8]

There was an epidemic of cholera in a certain village near Sudamapuri, and many people had already died when Gauri-ma heard about it. Immediately she went to the head of the village and offered her services to help nurse the victims. She also organized a committee to care for the patients and engaged twelve brahmins to perform a special ritual for three days. In this way the morale of the people was lifted, and within a few days the epidemic subsided.

From there Gauri-ma went to Dwaraka. One day, while she was repeating her mantram in front of the Krishna temple, she had a vision of Krishna in the form of a boy. A vision is only temporary, however, and instead of satisfying her, it increased her longing all the more. Deeply feeling the pang of separation from her beloved Lord Krishna, she again returned to Vrindaban. There she started vigourous austerities. One night she even tried to take her own life in the Lalita kunja (grove), but at that critical moment she had a vision and lost outward consciousness. The next morning some women found her lying unconscious. They knew who she was so they devotedly took care of her.

The news spread of her return to Vrindaban, however, and when her uncle found out he came and took her to his home. He showed Gauri-ma a letter written by her grief-stricken mother and convinced her to return with him to Calcutta. When Giribala saw her daughter she wept and embraced her. Gauri-ma's family was very happy to have her back.

It is hard for a person to live in one place who has gotten the taste of freedom in a wandering life. Moreover, comforts and an easygoing life are impediments to monastic life. One day Gauri-ma told her mother that she was going to Puri to visit Lord Jagannath and that she would return soon. Thus, Gauri-ma left home again. From Puri she went to Sakshigopal, Alalnath, and Bhubaneswar, and she also visited some monasteries at this time. In 1880 Gauri-ma became acquainted with Radhamohan Basu, a wealthy landlord of northern Calcutta. He had a large estate in Orissa and also a retreat in Vrindaban. Radhamohan, a devotee of Krishna, was greatly impressed with

Gauri-ma's renunciation and devotion. In 1882 Gauri-ma accepted an invitation to visit his Calcutta home, and it was there that she met his son, Balaram Basu, who was a great devotee of Sri Ramakrishna. Balaram also was a friend of Gauri-ma's elder brother.

One day, soon after she arrived, Balaram said to Gauri-ma: 'Sister, let us go to visit Sri Ramakrishna at Dakshineswar. You have never seen such a wonderful holy man. He goes into samadhi every now and then. If you do not see him, you will certainly miss something in your life'. Gauri-ma smiled and replied: 'I have seen many monks in my life, and I have no desire to see another. If your holy man has real power, then let him pull me'.[9]

The pull came at last in a mysterious way. One morning Gauri-ma began her daily ritual to the deity. She first bathed the stone image of Vishnu and then was about to place it on the altar when she saw two live human feet there, without a human body. At first she thought that it was an optical illusion, but observing carefully, again and again, she saw only those two human feet. Gauri-ma was frightened. The hair on her body stood on end, and her hands started trembling so much that she dropped the image. She then lost consciousness and fell to the floor. After a few hours Balaram's wife learned that Gauri-ma was lying unconscious, so she went there. Although she called her repeatedly, she could not get any response. Then Balaram came there and realized that Gauri-ma was in samadhi. Some time later Gauri-ma regained a little outward consciousness and pointed to her heart. She felt that somebody had tied a string to her heart and was pulling it. She passed the whole day and night in a semi-conscious state.[10]

The next morning, without telling anyone, Gauri-ma tried to leave, but the gatekeeper stopped her. Just then Balaram arrived and asked her: 'Where do you want to go? Sister, would you like to meet the Master in Dakshineswar?'[11] Although Gauri-ma did not answer, Balaram understood that her silence meant assent. He immediately ordered the coachman to get the carriage ready, and they left for Dakshineswar with Balaram's wife and some other women. When they arrived, they found Sri Ramakrishna seated in his room, winding thread around a stick and singing:

O Mother, for Yashoda Thou wouldst dance,
    When she called Thee her precious 'Blue Jewel':
Where hast Thou hidden that lovely form,
    O terrible Shyama?
Dance that way once for me, O Mother!...*

*This song signifies the oneness of Krishna and Kali.

Immediately after their arrival, Sri Ramakrishna finished winding the thread and cordially received them. Gauri-ma understood that Sri Ramakrishna had attracted her heart, which he had indicated by the winding of the thread. Then when she bowed down to the Master, she saw the same two human feet that she had seen the previous day on the altar. She was overwhelmed with joy and astonishment. Sri Ramakrishna just smiled. He asked Balaram about Gauri-ma, and then he talked to them about spiritual life. While seeing them off, the Master said to Gauri-ma, 'Come again'.[12]

The next day, after bathing in the Ganga, Gauri-ma went to Dakshineswar with two pieces of cloth and her inseparable companion, Lord Vishnu. As soon as she entered the Master's room he said, 'I was thinking of you'. Gauri-ma told him about herself and about her recent vision of the Master's feet on the altar. 'Father', she said, 'I did not know that you were hidden here'. The Master smiled and said, 'If you had met me earlier, would you have practised so much austerity?'[13]

Sri Ramakrishna then took Gauri-ma to the nahabat and introduced her to Holy Mother, saying: 'Hello, you were looking for a companion. Here is one for you'.[14] After this Gauri-ma lived at Dakshineswar whenever Holy Mother was there. When Holy Mother had to go to her village home, Gauri-ma stayed at Balaram's house. Gauri-ma would sometimes cook for the Master, and once in a while she would sing for him in her melodious voice. Sri Ramakrishna had a very high opinion of her and once said, 'Gauri is a perfect soul — a gopi of Vrindaban'.[15]

One day Kedar Nath Chatterjee introduced his friend, Mr. William, to Sri Ramakrishna. The Master talked to him about God and then requested him to meet Gauri-ma at Balaram's house. When Mr. William first saw Gauri-ma he felt an intense spiritual vibration and addressed her as Mother Mary. He also prayed to her for her blessings. Gauri-ma was impressed with his devotion. She talked to him for a while and offered him some prasad.

Sri Ramakrishna wanted to fulfill a special mission through Gauri-ma. He realized that the women of the society were terribly neglected, especially in the area of education, and it was his wish that Gauri-ma should work among them. One day he said to her: 'The women of Jadu Mallik's family have been wanting to see you. Please visit them'. But Gauri-ma replied: 'That is your business, Father! Why do you praise me so much to others?'[16]

On another occasion Gauri-ma was picking flowers near the nahabat when the Master came there with a pot of water. Holding a branch of the bakul tree with one hand, he began pouring water with the other. Then he said, 'Gauri, let me pour water and you knead the mud'. Surprised, Gauri-ma answered: 'There is no clay here. How can I knead the mud? This place is full of stone chips'. The Master smiled and said: 'My goodness! What I meant and what you have understood! The condition of women in this country is very poor and painful. You will have to work for them'. Gauri-ma did not like the idea, however. 'It is hard for me to get along with worldly people', she told him. 'I don't care for all the hustle and bustle. Give me a few girls, and I shall take them to the Himalayas and mould their character'. But the Master shook his head and said: 'No, no. You will have to work in the city. You have practised enough spiritual disciplines. Now you should serve the women with your spiritual energy'.[17]

Gauri-ma regarded Sri Ramakrishna and Holy Mother as her own parents, and she was very free with them. She recognized the Master to be an avatar and believed that he and Chaitanya were the same. One day Sri Ramakrishna was talking to Holy Mother and Gauri-ma in the nahabat and he started teasing Gauri-ma. He had noticed that Gauri-ma was very fond of Holy Mother, so he asked, 'Whom do you love more? Her or me?' Gauri-ma answered through a song:

O Flute Player, Krishna, you are never greater than Radha;
When people are in trouble, they call for you;
But when you are in trouble, your flute sounds the name of Radha.

Holy Mother was very embarrassed, and she pressed Gauri-ma's hand. The Master laughed and left the place.[18]

Early one morning Holy Mother started down the steps of the bathing ghat to take her bath in the Ganga. Since it was still dark she did not notice that a crocodile was lying on one of the steps. Fortunately, at the sound of her approach, it jumped into the river before she had come down that far. Holy Mother screamed and ran back to the nahabat. Gauri-ma held her, trying to comfort her, and joked: 'It was not a crocodile, Mother. It was Lord Shiva. He came to have the touch of your feet'. 'Set aside your fun', replied Holy Mother. 'I am about to die of fear'. 'You are the embodiment of fearlessness, Mother. How can you have fear?' said Gauri-ma.[19]

Once Sri Ramakrishna stood on the semi-circular verandah and called, 'O maya, please come'.[20] Gauri-ma was astonished and asked the Master why he was calling for maya. Then he explained that the natural tendency of his mind was to soar to a very high realm, and it was hard to bring it down. He was calling for maya so that his mind would stay in a lower plane, making it possible for him to help his disciples. This shows what love the Master had for them. He used to send them to different temples of Dakshineswar or to the Panchavati for meditation. Over each one he kept a watchful eye, and if he observed that a disciple was performing too much austerity or fasting, he would say: 'Please eat your meals regularly and then practise your japam and meditation. The Divine Mother is not a stranger. She is your very own. She will not be angry if you eat first and then call on her. In this Kali yuga the human body cannot bear excessive austerities, and it is hard to practise spiritual disciplines if one's health is not good'.[21] At the Master's behest, Gauri-ma sometimes cooked food for the disciples, whom she regarded as her own children.

One day Rakhal (later, Swami Brahmananda) was very hungry and mentioned it to the Master. At that time there were no restaurants or sweet shops in Dakshineswar, so the Master went to the bank of the Ganga and called loudly: 'Hello, Gaur-dasi! Please come. My Rakhal is hungry'. After a short while a boat became visible, coming from the direction of Calcutta. When it anchored at the temple garden ghat, the Master found that Balaram, Gauri-ma, and others had come with some *rasagollas* (cheese balls soaked in sweet syrup). He immediately called Rakhal: 'Come, Rakhal! They have brought rasagollas. Come and eat! Didn't you say you were hungry?' Rakhal was very embarrassed. He said to the Master, 'Sir, why are you talking about my hunger in front of others?' 'What does it matter?' said the Master. 'Since you are hungry, you should eat. What is the harm in saying so?'[22]

The Master passed his days at Dakshineswar in various kinds of ecstatic moods. One day he was in samadhi in the rose garden, and his cloth became entangled in the thorny bushes. Gauri-ma found him and brought him back to his room. A couple of times she found the Master in ecstasy on the steps of the bathing ghat. Holy Mother and the disciples had to keep constant watch over the Master because he so often lost outward consciousness.

Gauri-ma was happy in Dakshineswar, but she had a desire to practise more austerities in a secluded place. The Master understood her intention so he did not stop her. One day she left for Vrindaban. There she practised japam and meditation from sunrise to sunset for nine months. Meanwhile Sri Ramakrishna was preparing to end his divine play. A few days before he passed away on August 16, 1886, the Master talked about Gauri-ma: 'She was very close to me for such a long time, but now she won't see me anymore. I have a deep feeling for her'.[23] Balaram wrote letters to Vrindaban inquiring about her, but no one knew where she was.

After the Master's passing away, Holy Mother, Lakshmi, M.'s wife, and Golap-ma, along with Swamis Yogananda, Abhedananda, and Adbhutananda went on a pilgrimage. At the birthplace of Radha, near Vrindaban, Swami Yogananda by chance saw Gauri-ma seated in meditation. He did not disturb her but immediately brought the news to Holy Mother. The next day all went to see Gauri-ma. When she heard the sad news about the Master, she wept, holding Holy Mother. Both of them cried profusely then. Holy Mother told her that after the Master had passed away she had started to remove the bracelets from her arms and put on the traditional widow's garb when the Master appeared before her and forbade her to do so. He told her to consult with Gaur-dasi. After listening to the story, Gauri-ma said, 'Mother, the Master is eternal and ever present, and you are the goddess Lakshmi'.[24] Then she further explained by quoting the Vaishnava Tantra that if one's husband is Krishna, one could not be a widow.*[25]

From Vrindaban Gauri-ma again visited Gangotri, Jamunotri, Kedarnath, and Badrinath. She then returned to Calcutta and stayed with Balaram's family, where she had an attack of cholera. After recovering, her mother took her home, but again she became sick with a high fever. Since she was a nun and a wanderer by nature, she was very uncomfortable living with her family. As soon as she was

---

*According to Gauri-ma's Bengali biography this incident happened at Vrindaban, but in At Holy Mother's Feet, Holy Mother says this incident happened at Kamarpukur: 'When I was living at Kamarpukur after returning from Vrindaban [after the Master's passing away], people began to comment about this and that, and I was so afraid of what people would say that I took off my bangles. I used to wonder how I could possibly stay in a place where there was no Ganga; I wanted to bathe in the Ganga; I had always had this weakness. One day I saw the Master walking along the road in front of me, from the direction of Bhutir Khal. Behind him followed Naren, Baburam, Rakhal, and other disciples, crowds of them. A fountain of water gushed forth from near his feet and the waves flowed on ahead of him in a strong current! I said to myself, "Now I see that he is everything and the Ganga rises from his lotus feet". Quickly I broke off handfuls of hibiscus blossoms from the plant beside Raghuvir's house and offered them into the Ganga. Then the Master said to me: "Do not take off your bangles. Do you know the Vaishnava Tantra [scripture]?" I answered, "What is the Vaishnava Tantra? I do not know anything". He said, "Gaur-mani will arrive this evening; she will explain everything". Gaur-dasi really did come in that very afternoon and explained it all to me. From her I heard that one's husband is really pure consciousness'.[26]

partially cured, she left for South India without telling anyone. There she visited Tirupati, Kanchi, Madura, Rameshwar, and Kanya Kumari. At Rameshwar she worshipped Lord Shiva with water she had brought from Gangotri. After visiting some holy places of Central India, she returned to Calcutta.

In 1894 Swami Vivekananda wrote from America to his brother disciples: 'If you want any good to come, just throw your ceremonials overboard and worship the Living God, the Man-God — every being that wears a human form — God in his universal as well as individual aspect... Spread ideas — go from village to village, from door to door — then only there will be real work... We want both men and women. There is no distinction of sex in the soul... Where is Gaur-ma? We want a thousand such mothers with that noble stirring spirit'.[27] In Vrindaban Holy Mother had also reminded Gauri-ma: 'The Master said that your life was meant for serving women — the living goddesses'.[28]

Gauri-ma's twenty years of travel gave her firsthand knowledge of the Indian people, especially of women. At last she felt an inner urge to fulfill the mission which Sri Ramakrishna had designated for her. In 1894 she founded the Sri Sri Saradeshwari Ashrama for women on the bank of the Ganga in Barrackpore, fourteen miles north of Calcutta. There were twenty-five members of the ashrama, and Gauri-ma trained them, following the ancient tradition of India. Everyone rose very early in the morning, bathed, and then practised japam and meditation. After that they did the household chores and studied under Gauri-ma's supervision. The ashrama was designed like a village, with thatched huts surrounded by trees. There was no school building, so Gauri-ma held classes either under a tree or on the verandah of a thatched hut. Holy Mother once visited the ashrama and blessed Gauri-ma's pioneering work.

Once Holy Mother praised Gauri-ma's love and steadfast devotion: 'It is amazing how Gaur-dasi has passed her life holding a stone image of the Lord'.[29] Gauri-ma treated that image as her living husband. One afternoon she was trying to take a little nap, but she was restless. Then she remembered that she had not offered any milk to the Lord for lunch. As a result, his meal was not complete and he was not getting any sleep. Immediately she got up, brought a glass of milk to the shrine, and offered it to the Lord. Then she got some rest. On another occasion Gauri-ma was ill, so she offered some sweets and fruits instead of a regular meal to the Lord and went to bed early. At midnight she got up and went to the kitchen to make some luchis (fried bread) for the Lord. Hearing the sound of noise in the kitchen, a student rushed there. Gauri-ma explained with a smile, 'After a short sleep the Lord told me he was hungry, so I started cooking'.[30]

Although the ashrama was at Barrackpore, Gauri-ma had to depend on the financial help of Calcutta devotees. Because of this, in 1911 she transferred the ashrama to North Calcutta, to a place not far from the Holy Mother's residence. Fifty dedicated women joined the ashrama, and three hundred girls received their education there. Gauri-ma had to raise funds, supervise the building construction, do household chores, and look after the training of the workers. Some of the direct disciples of the Master and some devotees helped her financially, but it was not enough. Once she organized a meeting and invited judges and many distinguished people of Calcutta in order to explain to them the aims and objectives of the Saradeshwari Ashrama. She emphasized that education for women was essential for the revival of the society, and also reminded them of the ideals and contributions of the great women of ancient India. Gradually some generous and noble-minded people came forward to help her with her work. She also travelled to various parts of the country and lectured on the need for more women's education in India. She had a magnanimous personality and the power to convince people. Although she was just a penniless nun, her faith in the Master brought success.

It is a person's actions that make him great, not his name. Great people are few in this world, but truly, Gauri-ma was one of them. Once Holy Mother said to a devotee about her: 'Gaur-dasi takes wonderful care of the girls at her ashrama. If anyone is ill, she does all her personal services herself. She never had to do these things before, but the Master is making her do them this time, this being her last birth'.[31]

One morning in Calcutta, Gauri-ma went with some of her students to bathe in the Ganga. After arriving there she noticed that a girl was being carried away by the current of the river. Some people were watching the girl and lamenting, but they did nothing to rescue her. Gauri-ma scolded them, and then quickly tied her cloth around her waist and jumped into the water, saying, 'Victory to the Divine Mother'. Her students knew that Gauri-ma could not swim, so they screamed. In the meantime two men also jumped into the water, and they rescued the girl. Fortunately Gauri-ma had not gone into deep water.[32]

Gauri-ma would sometimes show a rough exterior, but her heart was full of love and tenderness. Once a wealthy drunkard came to pay his respects to her, but she bluntly told him, 'I don't allow drunkards to touch my feet'. The man was hurt and said, 'You are the mother of everyone, so why are you reluctant to be the mother of a drunkard?' 'All right', answered Gauri-ma, 'if you give up drinking, I shall be your mother'. 'Then bless me, Mother', said the drunkard. He bowed down to her and left. Later, Gauri-ma found out that he had actually given up drinking, changed his life-style, and become a devotee of God.[33]

Even after establishing the school, Gauri-ma continued her pilgrimages to various parts of India. She met many interesting people and gathered much experience. When she was practising austerities at Triveni, in Allahabad, a beautiful woman, wearing expensive clothes and jewellery, came to her one day and began to cry.

'Why are you crying?' asked Gauri-ma.

'Is there any hope for me, Mother?'

'What happened? Why are you so depressed?'

The woman described her sad life and moral lapses to Gauri-ma and then said, 'Please tell me how I can attain peace'.

Gauri-ma told her: 'The path of peace is extremely difficult. No one can tread on that path without shunning the cravings for worldly enjoyments. If you really want peace and bliss in your life, call on God. Don't look back. What has happened has happened. Forget it'.

After receiving some spiritual instructions from Gauri-ma, the woman threw her jewellery into the Jamuna, cut her long hair, put on an ordinary cloth, and left for Rishikesh to practise tapasya. Many years later Gauri-ma met her again and was impressed by her transformation.[34]

While in Gaya, Gauri-ma heard that some women pilgrims were being harassed by some rascal priests for money. The priests had even threatened the women that unless their demands were met they would not let them leave the city. Since Gauri-ma was very much respected there, she was able to meet the priests and convince them to allow her to talk to the pilgrims so that she could find a solution to the problem. Accordingly, the priests took her to the women and let her speak to them privately. One of the women asked Gauri-ma: 'Mother, you are a woman. If they capture you, how can you rescue us?' She replied with a smile: 'Who will capture me? Don't worry. God is with me and he will rescue you'. She then left, giving the priests the impression that she was going to get some money. Within a short time, however, Gauri-ma returned with a police officer whom she knew personally, and he rescued the women.[35]

Gauri-ma was a brave woman herself, and she wanted to see this quality in other women. Some women devotees knew that she sometimes dressed as a wandering monk, in a long robe and turban, so one day, out of fun, they asked to see her in those clothes. Gauri-ma warned them that they would be frightened. Early one afternoon, Gauri-ma put on her robe and turban and, with a bamboo staff in her hand, appeared before those women when the men were away at work. Seeing a stranger in the inner apartment, the women screamed. Gauri-ma then disclosed her identity and scolded them: 'What is this? Why are you so afraid of a man? When you saw a stranger enter the inner apartment, why didn't you throw something at him instead of screaming? Isn't it possible for three women to push out one man? It's not enough for women to be good housewives. They must be strong and learn to protect themselves'.[36]

One day in 1916 Gauri-ma went to visit Belur Math. Swami Brahmananda received her graciously and encouraged the monks to ask her about how she met the Master, and about her itinerant days and tapasya. One monk said: 'We heard that when you left home you were a young girl. Weren't you afraid to travel by yourself — and without any money?' Gauri-ma replied: 'My son, all fear is pertaining to the body. I had something with me so that no one could harm me'. Then she said in a firm tone, 'By the grace of the Master, I regard lustful persons as worms, and their place is always under the feet'.[37]

Once when Mahatma Gandhi came to Calcutta, at the time of the noncooperation movement, Gauri-ma's disciple Raja Rao arranged for her to meet him at the home of Chittaranjan Das. Gandhiji was impressed when Gauri-ma talked to him in fluent Hindi, and he then inquired about her activities. She spoke to him about *nishkama karma* (unselfish action) according to the Bhagavad Gita, and mentioned the ideal of Sri Ramakrishna and Swami Vivekananda for the present age, 'Serve man as God'. She also explained to Gandhiji the importance of women's education in India. Both Gandhiji and Chittaranjan Das were overwhelmed with her personality, and they appreciated her work among women.[38]

During Sri Ramakrishna's birth centenary celebration in 1936, Gauri-ma gave an address in Bengali which was broadcast on All India Radio. The following is a free translation:

Om. Salutations to Sri Ramakrishna.
Man forgets the duty of his life due to his inertia and his involvement with the petty matters of the world. Being infatuated by maya, he forgets God. Sri Ramakrishna was born in this age to

awaken God-consciousness in the minds of people. His centenary celebration is reminding mankind of the eternal truth — his life-giving message.

Whenever I think of Sri Ramakrishna, I picture him in my mind in samadhi at Dakshineswar, and I hear his melodious singing: 'O Mother, make me mad with Thy love! What need have I of knowledge or reason?' On this auspicious occasion, let us give up dry discussion and intellectual reasoning, and enkindle within ourselves burning faith and complete surrender to God. Let us put into practice the immortal message of the Master. And let us pay our homage to that great woman, Sri Sarada Devi, who, through her austerity and self-sacrifice, helped her husband fulfill his mission.

Sri Ramakrishna was not only an ideal monk or a living-free soul, he was a devout follower of Shakti [divine power] — a great source of Shakti. His power is now spreading in all directions, and in his name various philanthropic institutions are coming into existence. His heart melted for the poor and the afflicted. Swami Vivekananda got the idea of worshipping the living gods [God in human form] from his Master, and he spread this idea all over the world.

There is no end to what we can say about the divine life of Sri Ramakrishna. Language and expressions are inadequate to describe his infinite nature. Various faiths and sects and diversified ideas are mingled in him. There is no division, aversion, or friction in his ideal — there is only a great harmony and unity. Let us remember that great soul, Sri Ramakrishna, whose life was a blend of action, knowledge, and devotion, and thereby purify ourselves.

Peace, Peace, Peace.[39]

There is a saying, 'An organization succeeds, not because it is big, or because it is long established, but because there are people in it who live it, sleep it, dream it, and build future plans for it'. Gauri-ma practised this in her life. Following what the Master had asked her to do, she became one of the pioneers of education for women of modern India. She founded a beautiful educational institution according to the ancient ideals of India, and she trained the women of .the ashrama, but all the while she considered herself a 'maidservant of the ashrama'. Because she led such a pure, dedicated, and unostentatious life herself, she was a wonderful exemplar for her students. She used to tell them, 'Remember, the beauty of a woman is not enhanced through clothes and cosmetics, but through physical and mental purity'.[40]

As Gauri-ma grew older, her body began failing, but she passed her days in various kinds of spiritual moods. One day she told two nuns,

'Look, I shall go to Vrindaban, so don't cry for me'.[41] At this time if anyone asked any mundane questions she told them: 'Don't talk to me about the world anymore. Talk only about the Master so that I will get joy and you will attain blessedness'.[42] Neither attachment nor delusion nor fear of death could touch Gauri-ma. She was absorbed in the bliss of the Self.

On Monday, February 28, 1938, the day of Shiva-ratri (the spring festival of Lord Shiva), Gauri-ma announced, 'The Master is pulling the string'.[43] In the afternoon she began to prepare herself for her final departure and asked her students to help her get dressed. She put on a silk sari and shawl, and a flower garland was placed around her neck. She indicated that her chariot was coming. That night she talked to her assistant, Durga Devi, about the forthcoming festival of the Master and advised her to follow the tradition.

The next morning, Tuesday, March 1, Gauri-ma handed over her beloved image of Vishnu to Durga Devi, and then she felt relieved. She was quite cheerful the whole day and talked frequently about the Master. That evening she uttered aloud three times, 'Guru Sri Ramakrishna', and then started repeating her mantram silently. At 8:15 Gauri-ma passed away. Her body was cremated the next day at the Cossipore cremation ground, where the body of her beloved guru, Sri Ramakrishna, had also been cremated.

Cossipore garden house, where Sri Ramakrishna passed away on August 16, 1886.

13

Pratap Chandra Hazra

Religion helps human beings to evolve from a lower to a higher nature. As every saint has his past, so every sinner has his future. The history of religion bears testimony to the fact that the avatar (Divine Incarnation) appears in every age, and holding the light of dharma (religion), he illumines the path for evildoers, hypocrites, and the poor in spirit. An avatar manifests power in two ways: With the help of his pure, eternal companions, he reestablishes religion which has become corrupt or has declined, and he destroys the wickedness of the wicked, and thereby demonstrates his redeeming power.

Pratap Chandra Hazra's role is very important in the divine drama of Sri Ramakrishna. Hazra's character displayed nearly every human flaw. He was egotistical, untruthful, greedy, selfish, jealous, mischievous, shrewd, hypercritical, and hypocritical. Such a character is not uncommon in society. Although close association with a person of this type is very difficult, Sri Ramakrishna lived with Hazra in Dakshineswar for about six years. The Master dealt with this unmanageable person and also protected others from his bad influence.

On July 22, 1883, Sri Ramakrishna said about Hazra in an ecstatic mood: I have found Hazra to be a piece of dry wood. Then why does he live here? This has a meaning too. The play is enlivened by the presence of troublemakers like Jatila and Kutila'.*[1]

Pratap Chandra Hazra was born some time around 1846 in the village of Maragore, a few miles west of Kamarpukur, the birthplace

---

*According to the legend of Krishna, Radha was the main gopi and a great devotee of Krishna. Radha's mother-in-law, Jatila, and sister-in-law, Kutila, gave her a difficult time because of her love for Krishna. These two troublemakers persecuted Radha and spread scandal against her so that she could not visit Krishna. But these impediments only increased Radha's love more and more. Jatila and Kutila made the Radha-Krishna episode more interesting through their meanness, hatred, cruelty, and jealousy.

of Sri Ramakrishna. His father, Narayan Hazra, was a farmer of moderate means. Pratap was educated in the village school and was raised according to the Vaishnava tradition. He did not have much faith or devotion for God. After his father died the responsibility of maintaining the family fell on him, and he had to support a mother, a wife, and several children. Though farming was his vocation, he did not care for it, and as a result his family was in debt for over one thousand rupees. He failed in all his undertakings, and finally as a last resort he started to repeat God's name, hoping that God would provide money for him. His family survived with a meagre income which came from some parental property.

In 1879 Sri Ramakrishna went to visit his parental home in Kamarpukur, and from there he went to Sihar, the home of his nephew Hriday. He heard about the devotees of Pnului-Shyambazar (a village a few miles from Sihar) who passed their days singing kirtan. Natavar Goswami of Belte, a village adjacent to Shyambazar, who had met the Master previously, had invited him to sanctify his home. The Master went there with Hriday and later narrated his experience: 'I had a vision of Gauranga before I entered the village, and I realized that I should meet Gauranga's devotees there. For seven days and nights I was surrounded by a huge crowd of people. Such attraction! Nothing but kirtan and dancing day and night. People stood in rows on the walls and even were in the trees... When God incarnates himself on earth he attracts people through the help of Yogamaya, his divine power. People become spellbound'.[2]

That unceasing religious fervour became a threat to Sri Ramakrishna's health, so Hriday secretly took him to Sihar. It was here that Hazra first met the Master. Hazra had met Hriday before and had also heard about the Master. Hazra's native village was only a few miles from Hriday's, and as soon as he heard that Sri Ramakrishna was staying at Sihar, Hazra went to visit him. Hazra asked the Master: 'Does God have ears? I call him so much, but I don't get any response. Does he really listen to my prayers?' Sri Ramakrishna smiled and said: 'Listen, this is why your prayer does not reach God. You are a son of a farmer. You have seen how the peasants irrigate their sugarcane fields, digging a channel from a reservoir. If there is any leak in the channel, how can one expect the water to reach the field? All the water in the reservoir can be pumped out and still the field will remain dry. Desires are like the holes of the channel. You practise japam and austerities, no doubt, but they all leak out through the holes of your desires. Your prayers will not reach God until your mind is free from worldly desires'.[3]

Although Hazra understood Sri Ramakrishna's words, it was quite certain that they had little effect on his doubting nature. There is no record of Hazra's reaction to his first meeting and conversation with the Master. However, in 1882 Hazra left home in a spirit of pseudo-renunciation and moved to Dakshineswar. Sri Ramakrishna received him cordially and arranged for his room and board in the Kali temple. The Master even provided clothes and other necessities for Hazra, and from time to time he talked to him about God. Hazra felt very happy in these new surroundings and he chose his seat for sadhana (spiritual disciplines) on the southeast verandah of Sri Ramakrishna's room. He used to bathe in the Ganga daily, eat the prasad of the Divine Mother, and repeat his mantram with a rosary.

According to Hazra's way of thinking, religion meant performing rituals, making japam with a rosary, studying the scriptures, putting religious marks on one's forehead, and so on. But after he arrived in Dakshineswar he noticed that Sri Ramakrishna didn't do any of these things. One day Hazra gave the Master some advice: 'Sir, you are not following the religious tradition. If you continue in this way, people will not respect you. At least for the sake of appearance you should make japam with a rosary like me. Those who come to you will consider you religious if they see that you are telling the beads'.[4]

Hearing Hazra's advice, Sri Ramakrishna burst into laughter. He called for Latu, Harish, Gopal, and Ramlal and said: 'Do you know what Hazra says to me? He is advising me to repeat japam with a rosary. But I cannot do that anymore. He says that if I do not do that, people won't respect me. Is it true?'

The devotees became disgusted with Hazra, and Harish furiously said: 'Sir, don't pay any attention to Hazra's words. He is a rustic man with rustic intellect'. 'Don't say that', said the Master. 'The Divine Mother is speaking through him'. Harish scornfully retorted: 'What do you say, Master? Do you mean that the Divine Mother could not find anyone other than Hazra to give you advice?' 'Yes', answered the Master. 'Mother conveys her message like this'.[5]

Sometimes Sri Ramakrishna would tease Hazra. On January 1, 1883, the Master was sitting near Hazra and talking to the devotees. Presently he remarked: 'Hazra is not a man to be trifled with. If one finds the big dargah [Muslim shrine] here [*referring to himself*], then Hazra is a smaller dargah'.[6] This statement of the Master's made the devotees laugh, but it only inflated Hazra's ego.

On October 26, 1884, M. recorded in the *Gospel*:

After the devotees had left the Master, Mahimacharan brought Hazra to the room. M. was present. Mahima said to Sri

Ramakrishna: 'Sir, I have a complaint against you. Why have you asked Hazra to go home? He has no desire to return to his family'.

Master: 'His mother has told Ramlal how much she is suffering on account of his being away from home; so I have asked Hazra to go home, at least for three days, and see her. Can one succeed in spiritual discipline if it causes suffering to his mother?... Besides why should a jnani like Hazra be afraid of going back to the world?'

Mahima (*with a smile*): 'Sir, that would be a pertinent question if Hazra were a jnani'.

Master (*smiling*): 'Oh, Hazra has attained everything. He has just a little attachment to the world because of his children and a small debt'.

Mahima: 'Where, sir, is Hazra's knowledge?'

Master (*smiling*): 'Oh, you don't know! Everybody says Hazra is quite a person. Everybody knows that he lives in the Dakshineswar temple garden. People talk of nothing but Hazra. Who would bother to mention my name?' (*All laugh.*)

Hazra: 'You, sir, are incomparable. You have no peer in the world. Therefore nobody understands you'.

Master: 'There you are! To be sure, no one can have dealings with the incomparable. So why should people mention me at all?'

Mahima: 'What does he know, sir? He will do your bidding'.

Master: 'That is not so. You had better ask him about it. He said to me, "You and I are on even terms" '.

Mahima: 'He argues a great deal'.

Master: 'Now and then he teaches me a lesson. (*All laugh.*) Sometimes I scold him when he argues too much. Later, when I am lying in bed inside the mosquito curtain, I feel unhappy at the idea of having offended him. So I leave the bed, go to Hazra, and salute him. Then I feel peace of mind'.[7]

Spiritual ego is so subtle that it is very difficult to wipe out. Hazra developed a superiority complex by practising a little japam. He did not have the depth of true scriptural knowledge, but he nonetheless pretended that he had the authority of the scriptures. This often created confusion among the devotees. Sri Ramakrishna corrected him on many occasions. Once he said to Hazra: 'Why do you address the Pure Atman as "Ishvara"? The Pure Atman is inactive and is the witness of three states. When I think of the acts of creation, preservation, and destruction, then I call the Pure Atman "Ishvara". What is the Pure Atman like? It is like a magnet lying at a great distance from a needle. The needle moves, but the magnet lies motionless, inactive'.[8]

On another occasion Hazra started to explain *Tattvajnana* (Knowledge of the Reality) to the devotees in front of the Master. He told them: 'The meaning of Tattvajnana is the knowledge of the existence of the twenty-four tattvas, or cosmic principles'. He was wrong, however, about the meaning of the word.

A devotee: 'What are they?'

Hazra: 'The five elements, the six passions, the five organs of perception, the five organs of action, and so forth'.

M. (*to the Master, smiling*): 'He says that the six passions are included in the twenty-four cosmic principles'.

Master (*smiling*): 'Listen to him! Notice how he explains Tattvajnana! The word really means "knowledge of Self". The word "Tat" means the Supreme Self, and the word "Tvam", the embodied soul. One attains Supreme Knowledge, Tattvajnana, by realizing the identity of the embodied soul and the Supreme Self'.

Embarrassed, Hazra left the place, and Sri Ramakrishna said to the devotees: 'He [*meaning Hazra*] only argues. This moment perhaps he understands, but the next moment he is his old self again... Hazra said that a man could not be liberated unless he was born in a brahmin body. "How is that?" I said. "One attains liberation through bhakti alone. Savari was the daughter of a hunter. She, Ruhidas, and others belonged to the sudra caste. They were liberated through bhakti alone". "But still —" Hazra insisted... I said that there was nothing greater than the bhakti that sought no end and had no selfish motive. Hazra contradicted me. I said to him, "A wealthy man is annoyed when a petitioner comes to him. 'There he comes', he says angrily. 'Sit down', he says to him in an indifferent voice, and shows that he is much annoyed. He doesn't allow such a beggar to ride with him in his carriage". But Hazra said that God was not like such wealthy people of the world; did He lack wealth, that He should feel pinched to give it away? Hazra said further: "When rain falls from the sky, the Ganga and all the big rivers and lakes overflow with water. Small tanks, too, are filled. Likewise, God out of His grace grants wealth and riches as well as knowledge and devotion" '.

M.: 'Hazra is a chatterbox. He won't achieve anything unless he becomes silent'.

Master: 'Now and then he comes to me and becomes mellowed. But he is a pest; again he argues. It is very hard to get rid of egotism. You may cut down an aswattha tree, but the next day a sprout will spring up. As long as the roots remain, the tree will grow again'.[9]

Sri Ramakrishna's patience in putting up with Hazra was

superhuman. Even though the Master was actually Hazra's host in Dakshineswar, Hazra criticized him in front of others. But then Hazra's sharp tongue spared nobody. He was also fastidious, with a mania for cleanliness and piety. Still, Sri Ramakrishna was his well-wisher and one day said to him: 'Don't eat too much, and give up this craze for outer cleanliness. People with a craze do not attain Knowledge. Follow conventions only as much as necessary. Don't go to excess...[10] What you are doing is right in principle but the application is not quite correct. Don't find fault with anyone, not even with an insect. As you pray to God for devotion, so also pray that you may not find fault with anyone...[11] It is Narayana Himself who has assumed all these forms. One can worship even a wicked person'.[12]

Hazra: 'Does God listen to our prayer for bhakti?'

Master: 'Surely. I can assure you of that a hundred times. But the prayer must be genuine and earnest. Do worldly-minded people weep for God as they do for wife and children?'[13]

Sri Ramakrishna's advice uplifted Hazra's mind for a moment, and with humility he tried to take the dust of the Master's feet. 'What is this?' Sri Ramakrishna said, and drew his feet back. Disappointed, Hazra said to the Master, 'Why should I not take the dust of his feet who has so kindly kept me with him?' Immediately the Master said: 'Satisfy God and everyone will be satisfied. "If He is pleased, the world is pleased" '.[14]

It finally dawned on Hazra that he was not pure enough to serve the Master or touch his feet. So he decided to make his body and mind pure by swallowing the holy mud of the Ganga and repeating the mantram day and night. Entering his mosquito curtain, he lay down on a blanket and began to count his beads. He kept a lump of holy mud of the Ganga near his head, and after each rotation on the rosary he ate one small globule of the mud. He continued this throughout the whole day and night. The all-knowing, compassionate Master became pleased with Hazra. He went to his room and called him. But Hazra continued his japam without responding to the Master's call. Then Sri Ramakrishna lifted the mosquito curtain and, taking hold of his hand, led him to his room. He then requested Hazra to massage his feet, thus fulfilling Hazra's unspoken desire.[15] (Taking the dust of the feet of a holy man is a symbolic gesture of reverence and humility, still widely practised in India today.)

Swami Adbhutananda mentioned in his reminiscences: 'One day Hazra had a desire to massage the Master's feet, but the Master wouldn't let him. Hazra felt hurt. He left the room and sat outside and was very morose. At last the Master called him back, and on that day only he served the Master'.[16]

Hazra was extremely shrewd and calculating, and he would always try to exploit the wealthy devotees of Sri Ramakrishna. Whenever he would find any opportunity he would call them and talk about high philosophy. His motive was to get money from them so he could pay off his debts. Hypocrisy and spirituality never go together. Referring to Hazra's manipulative behaviour, Sri Ramakrishna said to the devotees: 'Hazra used to practise much japam and austerity here. But in the country he has his wife, children, and land. Therefore along with his spiritual discipline he carried on the business of a broker. Such people cannot be true to their word'.[17]

Hazra used to sit on the southeast verandah, which served as one of the entrances to the Master's room. Sometimes a newcomer would ask Hazra, 'Could you tell me where Sri Ramakrishna Paramahamsa is?' 'Why do you want to see him?' Hazra would reply. 'If you want to hear about God, sit here. I shall tell you about him'.[18] Once Nag Mahashay and Suresh Chandra Datta went to Dakshineswar to meet Sri Ramakrishna. They first met Hazra, a bearded gentleman seated majestically outside the Master's room. When they asked about Sri Ramakrishna, Hazra said: 'Yes, he lives here. But today he has gone to Chandannagore. You had better come another day'. Both were extremely disappointed. When they were about to leave they noticed someone inside the room beckoning to them to enter.[19] It was Sri Ramakrishna. Although Hazra had lied to these devotees, the Master forgave him.

Hazra even dared to slander Sri Ramakrishna to his face. He said to the Master, 'You love a boy if he comes from a wealthy family or if he is handsome'. Sri Ramakrishna answered: 'If that is so, then why do I love Harish, Latu, and Narendra? Narendra hasn't a penny to buy salt to season his rice'.[20] However, Hazra's comment disturbed the Master very much. On another occasion he said to the devotees: 'Now and then Hazra comes forward to teach me. He says to me, "Why do you think so much about the youngsters?" One day, as I was going to Balaram's house in a carriage, I felt greatly troubled about it. I said to the Divine Mother: "Mother, Hazra admonishes me for worrying about Narendra and the other young boys. He asks me why I forget God and think about these youngsters". No sooner did this thought arise in my mind than the Divine Mother revealed to me in a flash that it is She Herself who has become man. But She manifests Herself most clearly through a pure soul. At this vision I went into samadhi. Afterwards I felt angry with Hazra. I said to myself, "That rascal made me miserable". Then I thought: "But why

should I blame the poor man? How is he to know?'' I know these
youngsters to be Narayana Himself'.[21]

In spite of all his shortcomings Hazra had steadfast devotion for his
japam and rosary. He strongly believed that he would get money,
name and fame, and occult power by repeating the mantram. One
day Sri Ramakrishna snatched away Hazra's rosary and told him that
without longing for God he would not attain anything.[22] On another
occasion the Master said to Hazra: 'Love of God, when it is intense
and spontaneous, is called raga-bhakti. Vaidhi-bhakti, formal
devotion, depends on scriptural injunctions. It comes and it goes...
Only an Incarnation of God and his companions attain raga-bhakti'.
These words of the Master penetrated into Hazra's heart, and he
exclaimed, 'Ah me!' Then Sri Ramakrishna continued: 'One day I
was returning from the pine grove when I saw you telling your beads.
I said to the Divine Mother: ''Mother, what a small-minded fellow he
is! He lives here and still he practises japam with a rosary! Whoever
comes here [referring to himself] will have his spiritual consciousness
awakened all at once; he won't have to bother much about japam. Go
to Calcutta and you will find thousands telling their beads — even the
prostitutes'' '.[23]

Sri Ramakrishna's mind was above likes and dislikes. Even-
mindedness is one of the signs of an illumined soul. From time to
time he scolded Hazra, but he never hated him nor did he harbour
any ill-feeling towards him. On the contrary, the Master showed
Hazra respect and demonstrated to his disciples how to cope with
this type of unmanageable person. M. recorded in the Gospel:

Hazra was sitting on the northeast verandah counting the beads of
his rosary. The Master went and sat in front of him, taking the
rosary in his own hands.
    Master (to Hazra): 'You see, I cannot use the rosary. No, perhaps
I can. Yes, I can with my left hand. But I cannot repeat the name of
God with it'.
    With these words Sri Ramakrishna tried to perform a little
japam. But hardly had he begun when he went into samadhi. He
sat in that state a long time, still holding the rosary in his hand.
The devotees looked at him with wonder in their eyes. Hazra also
watched the Master without uttering a word. After a long time Sri
Ramakrishna regained consciousness of the outer world...
    He went across the cement courtyard towards the Kali temple...
and saluted the Mother. Coming back to his room, accompanied
by M. and Bhavanath, he saluted Hazra, who cried out in dismay:
'What are you doing, sir? What is this?' The Master said, 'Why
should you say it is wrong?' Hazra often argued with the Master,

declaring that God dwelt in all beings and that everybody could attain Brahmajnana [knowledge of Brahman] through sadhana.[24]

It was great fun to live with Sri Ramakrishna. Not only was he a spiritual guide to his disciples, but he would also join them in picnics, or go to the theatre with them, or watch their frivolous games. M. mentioned in the *Gospel*:

> The devotees were engaged in a game of golakdham.* Hazra joined them. The Master stood by, watching them play. M. and Kishori reached 'heaven'. Sri Ramakrishna bowed before them and said, 'Blessed are you two brothers'. He said to M., aside, 'Don't play anymore'. Hazra fell into 'hell'. The Master said: 'What is the matter with Hazra? Again!' No sooner had Hazra got out of 'hell' than he fell into it again. All burst into laughter... The Master said: 'This too has a meaning. Hazra is so vain that he thinks he will triumph over all even in this game. This is the law of God, that He never humiliates a righteous person. Such a man is victorious everywhere'.[25]

Hazra would become extremely jealous if he found the Master entertaining someone else and not paying attention to him. Once a Vaishnava priest came to Dakshineswar, intending to spend a couple of days in the temple garden. The Master received him cordially, which upset Hazra. He asked the Master to send the priest to the temple officer, because he was afraid that he might have to give the priest some milk and food from his own share. Sri Ramakrishna sternly scolded Hazra: 'Now, you rogue! Even I prostrate myself before him because he is a goswami [a Vaishnava priest]. And you, after leading a worldly life and indulging a great deal in "woman and gold", have so much pride because of a little japam! Aren't you ashamed of yourself?'[26]

One day in a playful mood, Sri Ramakrishna asked Hazra to evaluate the spiritual progress of the devotees. The Master said: 'Tell me what you think of the people that come here. How much sattva does each one possess?' Without hesitation Hazra replied, 'Narendra has one hundred percent and I have one hundred and ten percent'. 'What about me?' asked the Master. Hazra said: 'You still have a trace of pink [meaning rajas]. You have only seventy-five percent, I should say'. Hearing Hazra's comment, all the devotees burst into laughter.[27]

Hazra was a close friend of Narendra's (Swami Vivekananda).

---

*A game in which the player tries to get to 'heaven' by passing through different 'planes'; but on each false step he falls into a particular 'hell'.

Hazra would prepare smoking tobacco for both of them and they would discuss deep philosophy. Sometimes Narendra teased him, saying: 'Really you are a wonderful *siddhapurusha* [perfect soul]. At last I have found a rare soul who is constantly telling his beads. Your rosary is very nice -- such big and bright beads. There is none like you'. This swelled Hazra's pride, and he said to the disciples of the Master: 'You people cannot understand me — not even Sri Ramakrishna. Only Naren knows me'.[28]

Knowing Narendra's inclination to the path of knowledge, Sri Ramakrishna instructed him in Vedantic nondualism, which asserts that every thing and every being are nothing but Brahman. Unwilling to accept this view, Narendra left the Master's room and went to Hazra. 'Can it be', he asked, 'that the waterpot is God, that the drinking vessel is God, That everything we see and all of us are God?' Narendra laughed scornfully at this idea and Hazra joined him. As they sat laughing, Sri Ramakrishna came up to them and asked, 'What are you two talking about?' Without waiting for an answer, the Master touched Narendra and immediately went into samadhi. This marvellous touch of the Master caused a revolution in Narendra's life and he experienced the knowledge of Oneness.[29]

Despite his sceptical temperament, Hazra was quite intelligent and he could understand a little of Narendra's discussions regarding the doctrines of Western agnostic philosophers. Whenever Narendra visited Dakshineswar he would spend an hour or two with Hazra, who listened with great attention to Narendra's words. Narendra liked Hazra's sharp and witty tongue, and Hazra praised Narendra with flattering respect. Seeing their mutual admiration and appreciation, the devotees would say jokingly, 'Hazra is Narendra's "ferend" [friend]'.[30] When Narendra's father died, his family faced a period of extreme financial difficulty. During this time Narendra entered the Master's room, after spending a long time with Hazra. Sri Ramakrishna affectionately asked Naren: 'Were you with Hazra? Both of you are in the same boat. You know the saying about the two friends: "You are away from your country and he is away from his beloved". Hazra, too, needs fifteen hundred rupees'.[31]

One day Sri Ramakrishna was resting on his bed while Baburam (Swami Premananda) fanned him. Narendra sat smoking with Hazra on the eastern porch of the Master's room. Hazra said to Narendra: 'You are all mere boys! You are visiting Sri Ramakrishna off and on, and he just keeps you satisfied with fruits and sweets. Hold him — press him — and get something [power, wealth, and so on] from him'. As soon as the Master heard this from his room he jumped up from his bed, rushed to the verandah, and shouted: 'Naren, come to my room right now. Don't listen to his calculating advice. The beggar pesters the rich man, saying, "Sir, give me a pice! Give me a pice!" Being disgusted with the beggar, the rich man throws a small coin to him, saying, "Take this and get out of here". You are my very own. You will not have to ask for anything from me. Whatever I have, it is all yours'.[32]

Given the opportunity, Hazra would pollute the minds of the young disciples of Sri Ramakrishna, create confusion in the minds of the devotees, and generally disrupt the spiritual ministry of the Master. Still Sri Ramakrishna tolerated him. Hazra also tried to influence the wealthy visitors of Dakshineswar. He said to them: 'You see Rakhal and the other youngsters. They do not practise any spiritual discipline. They simply wander about merrily...[33] What will you gain by merely sitting in his room? Come and listen to what I have to say'.[34]

Hazra used to chant, 'Soham, soham [I am Brahman]'.[35] The Master told him, 'You indulge in reasoning only; that is why you are so dry'. Hazra retorted, 'No, I am dry because I drink the nectar of the sun'.[36] Sri Ramakrishna protected his young disciples from Hazra's evil influence as the mother bird protects her young from the storm by spreading her wings. He cautioned his disciples: 'Don't associate with Hazra. Yours is the path of devotion. What will you do with that dry knowledge?'[37]

Sri Ramakrishna experienced the Truth of Brahman and that Truth he taught to his disciples. But Hazra argued and contradicted the Master in front of people. M. narrated in the *Gospel* about the mental condition of the Master:

Master (*to Bhavanath*): 'The truth is that ordinary men cannot easily have faith... Hazra can never be persuaded to believe that Brahman and Shakti, that Shakti and the Being endowed with Shakti, are one and the same. When the Reality appears as Creator, Preserver, and Destroyer, we call it Shakti; when it is inactive, we call it Brahman. But really it is one and the same thing — indivisible. Fire naturally brings to mind its power to burn; and the idea of burning naturally brings to mind the idea of fire. It is impossible to think of one without the other.

'So I prayed to the Divine Mother: "O Mother! Hazra is trying to upset the views of this place [*referring to the Master himself*]. Either give him right understanding or take him from here". The next day he came to me and said, "Yes, I agree with you". He said that God exists everywhere as All-pervading Consciousness'.

Bhavanath (*smiling*): 'Did what Hazra said really make you suffer so much?'

Master: 'You see, I am now in a different mood. I can't shout and carry on heated discussions with people. I am not in a mood now to argue and quarrel with Hazra'.[38]

Patience has its limit. Day by day Hazra became so egotistical that it became unbearable for the Master to cope with him. Hazra would treat the cooks and servants of Dakshineswar as menial staff and would not even speak to them. Out of deference to the Master, people refrained from humiliating him. M. recorded in the *Gospel* on April 24, 1885, how Hazra disrupted the peaceful atmosphere of the temple garden of Dakshineswar:

Narendra (*to the Master*): 'Hazra has now become a good man'.

Master: 'You don't know. There are people who repeat Rama's name with their tongues but hide stones under their arms to throw at others'.

Narendra: 'I don't agree with you, sir. I asked him about the things people complain of. He denied them'.

Master: 'He is steadfast in his devotions. He practises japam a little. But he also behaves in a queer way. He doesn't pay the coachman his fare'.

Narendra: 'That isn't true, sir. He said he had paid it'.

Master: 'Where did he get the money?'

Narendra: 'From Ramlal or someone else'.

Master: 'Did you ask him all these things in detail? Once I prayed to the Divine Mother, "O Mother, if Hazra is a hypocrite then please remove him from here". Later on I told him of my prayer. After a few days he came to me and said, "You see, I am still here". (*The Master and the others laugh.*) But soon afterwards he left.

'Hazra's mother begged me through Ramlal to ask Hazra to come home. She was almost blind with weeping. I tried in various ways to persuade him to visit her. I said: "Your mother is old. Go and see her once". I couldn't make him go. Afterwards the poor mother died weeping for him'.

Narendra: 'This time he will go home'.

Master: 'Yes, yes! He will go home! He is a rogue. He is a rascal. You don't understand him. You are a fool. Gopal said that Hazra stayed at Sinthi a few days. People used to supply him with butter, rice, and other food. He had the impudence to tell them he couldn't swallow such coarse rice and bad butter. Ishan of Bhatpara accompanied him there. He ordered Ishan to carry water for him. That made the other brahmins very angry'.

Narendra: 'I asked him about that too. He said that Ishan Babu had himself come forward with the water. Besides, many brahmins of Bhatpara showed him respect'.

Master (*smiling*): 'That was the result of his japam and austerity... Do you know how I look on people like Hazra? I know that just as God takes the form of holy men, so He also takes the form of cheats and rogues'.[39]

M. again recorded about Hazra in the *Gospel* on May 9, 1885:

The conversation drifted to Hazra and his egotism. For some reason he had had to go away from Dakshineswar.

Narendra: 'Hazra now admits he was egotistic'.

Master: 'Don't believe him. He says so in order to come back to Dakshineswar. (*To the devotees*) Narendra always insists that Hazra is a grand person'.

Narendra: 'Even now I say so'.

Master: 'Why? You have heard so much about him, and still you think so?'

Narendra: 'He has slight defects but many virtues'.

Master: 'I admit that he has devotion to his ideal. He said to me, "You don't care for me now, but later you will be seeking my company" '.[40]

Hazra played his part very well in the divine drama of Sri Ramakrishna. The Master needed a religious hypocrite in order to illustrate important spiritual lessons for his disciples. Hazra served that purpose. In addition, he became an object of amusement and laughter for the Master as well as for the devotees. Later, Hazra temporarily moved to the house of Ishan Chandra Mukherjee in Mechuabazar, Calcutta, but he kept in close contact with Narendra. The latter gave Hazra a humourous name: 'Thousand-a'.[41] (In Bengali *hazar* means thousand, so Hazra became 'Hazar-a'. In other words, a man worth a thousand. Of course one of the main motives behind Hazra's religious austerity was to clear his debt of over one thousand rupees.)

On January 1, 1886, Sri Ramakrishna became the kalpataru (wish-fulfilling tree) at the Cossipore garden and blessed many devotees, saying, 'Be illumined'. Hazra was then staying at Cossipore, but on that auspicious day when the Master bestowed his grace on the devotees, Hazra was absent. After returning to Cossipore, he heard what had happened and felt extremely disappointed. Narendra as a friend came forward to help Hazra. Narendra's nature was to uplift the poor, fallen, depressed, and neglected human beings. He took Hazra to Sri Ramakrishna's room. The Master was then resting. Narendra requested him to bless Hazra, but the Master was reluctant to do anything for him. Later, due to Narendra's persistence, the compassionate Master told him: 'His time has not yet come. He will get the blessing at the time of death'.[42] Thus Hazra was assured by the Master that he would attain enlightenment at the end of his life.

On January 6, 1886, Hazra fasted the whole day and then appeared before Sri Ramakrishna for special grace. Knowing his motive, the Master asked his attendant to tell Hazra to leave the room. Immediately Hazra caught hold of the feet of Sri Ramakrishna. This was too much for the Master as he was not well. 'What is this nonsense?' said the Master indignantly. 'Don't hold my feet'. He had to call Latu to make Hazra leave.[43] Later Latu said: 'Hazra escaped the snares of the world by holding onto Naren. It was due to Naren's insistence that the Master blessed Hazra'.[44]

Sometime thereafter, Hazra's eldest son, Yatindranath, came to Calcutta and persuaded his father to come home. Hazra went home but could not adjust himself to family life even though he was a householder. He lived in the parlour of his house for some days and then again returned to Dakshineswar.[45]

After the passing away of Sri Ramakrishna in August of 1886, Hazra's egotism increased even more. When Sarada, a young disciple of the Master, met Hazra at Dakshineswar, the latter said to him, 'What do you think of me?'[46] He even asked Sarada to serve him by preparing tobacco. Latu later recalled, 'After the Master passed away, Hazra began to think of himself as an avatar [Divine Incarnation] — even greater than the Master'.[47] In 1894, during the birth anniversary of Sri Ramakrishna, Hazra met the devotees of the Master and practised his japam as usual, sitting on the northeast verandah of the Master's room.

Gradually a great change came over Hazra's life. He began to tire of his egotistical ways. The association and the teachings of Sri Ramakrishna slowly worked their effect on his mind. He returned home and began to lead a steady householder's life. His wife gave birth to another son, named Sharatchandra, and then a daughter. Although in the beginning Hazra would not admit that Sri Ramakrishna was anything more than a holy man, later he came to understand the Master's greatness and finally took refuge in him.

Naturally many were curious about Hazra's death. Someone asked M. about this, and he replied, 'Hazra passed away chanting the name of Sri Ramakrishna'.[48] According to the author of *Yugavatar Sri Ramakrishna*, Hazra passed away in 1900, holding the picture of Sri Ramakrishna on his chest and looking at him.[49] A detailed death account of Hazra's final days was published in *Tattvamanjari*, a

Bengali monthly:[50]

Hazra had a little fever for three days; except for that, he had no other disease. A village doctor looked after him. In the evening of the third day, Hazra said to his wife: 'Look, you inform the villagers tomorrow morning that they should be present at our house before 9:00 A.M. as I am going to die at that time'. His wife thought her husband was delirious with fever, so he was talking like that. She did not take it seriously at all. However, early the next morning Hazra persuaded his wife to spread his death forecast among the villagers. Some ignored it, thinking Hazra was crazy, and some came to watch the fun.

At 8:30 A.M. Hazra took his rosary and started to practise his japam as usual. People knew that it was his nature to do so. All of a sudden they noticed a change coming over Hazra's face, as if he were intently *seeing* somebody. After a while he burst forth with the words: 'Welcome! Most welcome! Here comes the Master! Master, after such a long time you have remembered me'. He then said to his wife: 'Please bring a seat. Be quick! Don't you see that Paramahamsadeva has come?' His wife stood there idly. But when Hazra repeated his request, she reluctantly spread a carpet there.

Then addresssing Sri Ramakrishna, Hazra said, 'Master, please sit on the asana and wait here till I die. Please be gracious unto me'. Saying so, Hazra began to repeat his mantram again. After a short time he exclaimed: 'Welcome! Welcome, Ramdada [Ram Chandra Datta, a devotee of the Master]! How fortunate I am!' He then requested his wife to give an asana to Ram Chandra, which she did. Hazra with folded hands requested that Ram Chandra too sit near him till death. Then again he started to repeat his mantram. Again he exclaimed: 'Welcome! Yogin Maharaj [Swami Yogananda, a disciple of the Master] has come! Oh, what a joyful day!' He then asked his wife to give an asana to Swami Yogananda and requested that he sit near him till death.

He then addressed Sri Ramakrishna with folded hands, saying: 'Master, you are so gracious unto me. Please do me another' favour. Please come with me to the tulsi grove [an auspicious spot on the courtyard] where I want to give up my body'. With Sri Ramakrishna's consent, Hazra asked his wife to carry those three asanas and his bed to the tulsi grove. Then going there, Hazra requested that they sit on their respective asanas, and he lay down on his bed. He continued his japam and then repeated thrice, 'Hari, Hari, Hari'. In this way Hazra passed away. The villagers were amazed. They moved his body and found that it was devoid of consciousness. They then arranged his funeral and glorified him as a great soul.

The blessed death of Hazra proved that the grace of an avatar can eradicate a soul's evil karma. Hazra had been hypocritical, spiteful, mercenary, untruthful, and egotistical, but Sri Ramakrishna's infallible blessing created a transformation in his life. Furthermore, what happened in Hazra's life will help create faith in the mind of a faithless person. The Hindu scripture says that whether a person thinks of God with love or with enmity, he will reach God, because the thought of God destroys evil propensities. As Sri Ramakrishna glorified and transformed the life of Hazra, Hazra also glorified the greatness of the Master by acting out the role of a 'rascal'. Hazra's character will never be forgotten.

14

M.
(Mahendra Nath Gupta)

Men who have walked with God have walked with their hands free of worldly possessions and their minds emptied of everything except the thought of God. People generally are bound to the world by their desires for wealth, sense pleasures, and name and fame. When these desires are given up, the desire for God can arise in the mind. Thus, for ages spiritual aspirants have practised renunciation in order to turn their minds fully to God.

It is not possible for spiritual aspirants who are householders to give up everything. The householder is the mainstay of the social order, and that role requires family and social responsibilities. He cannot easily answer the call to 'give up and follow me'. In the present age, Sri Ramakrishna has given a new teaching especially for householders: 'Let the boat be in water, but let there be no water in the boat; let an aspirant live in the world, but let there be no worldliness in him'.[1] He moulded the lives of his householder disciples to be models exemplifying this principle. Each disciple played a very different role in the divine drama of Sri Ramakrishna, as can be seen by studying their lives. Yet along with taking care of their families, family problems, household duties, social commitments, and jobs, all of them, at the same time, led God-centred lives. Sri Ramakrishna taught them this technique: 'Do all your duties, but keep your mind on God. Live with all — with wife and children, father and mother — and serve them. Treat them as if they were very dear to you, but know in your heart of hearts that they do not belong to you... If you enter the world without first cultivating love for God, you will be entangled more and more'.[2] Sri Ramakrishna's inspiring teachings uplifted his disciples. His divine love protected them as a mother bird protects her fledglings from rain and wind by spreading her strong wings over them.

M., the recorder of *The Gospel of Sri Ramakrishna*, was one of the householder disciples of Sri Ramakrishna. In later years, people would say: 'If you want to forget the world, go to see M. He knows

189

M. (Mahendra Nath Gupta, the recorder of *The Gospel of Sri Ramakrishna*.)
(1854-1932)

how to remove worldly desires from the mind and instill the thought of God there'. People flocked to him, and he would talk to them only about God. When they would ask, 'Please tell us something about Sri Ramakrishna', he would quote the conversation between the disciple and the teacher in the Kena Upanishad: The disciple said, 'Teach me the Upanishad', and the preceptor replied, 'I have already told you the Upanishad'.[3] By this, M. meant that as he knew only Sri Ramakrishna and nothing else, whatever came through his lips was about him.

Once Sri Ramakrishna asked Subodh, one of his young disciples, to visit M. and talk with him about God. The boy, who was to become one of Sri Ramakrishna's monastic disciples, replied: 'Sir, he lives with his wife and children. What could I learn from him?' Sri Ramakrishna smiled at these words expressing stern renunciation but told Subodh: 'He will not talk about his personal life. He will talk only of what he has learned here'. When Subodh went to see M., he related this conversation to him. M. said humbly: 'It is quite true. I am nobody, but I live beside the ocean, and I keep a few pitchers of that water with me. When a guest comes, I offer that to him. What else am I to talk about?'[4]

M. was the pen name of Mahendra Nath Gupta. He was born in Calcutta on July 14, 1854. His parents were spiritually-minded people, and he was very devoted to his mother. When he was four years old, he went with his mother to attend the Car Festival of Jagannath at Mahesh, and on their way back they stopped at the Dakshineswar temple garden. He later recounted his memory of that day: 'The temple was all white then, new and glistening. While going around the temple, I lost sight of my mother and was crying for her on the temple porch. Immediately a handsome brahmin came out of the temple and, touching my head, consoled me. Then he called out: "Whose child is this? Where has his mother gone?" '[5] M. told the devotees, 'Most probably he was Sri Ramakrishna, because at that time he was the priest in the Kali temple'.[6]

From his childhood M. had religious and mystical inclinations. When he was five years old, he used to climb to the roof of his house to gaze at the vastness of the sky or to stand there during the monsoon and experience the torrential rains. He had read in the Mahabharata that one should love and worship one's teacher, so when the family priest visited their home, M. saluted him and served him personally. On his way to school he would bow down at the temple of the Divine Mother which was on the other side of the College Street Market. When he was in the eighth grade he started to keep a diary, and the following entries show his religious nature: 'I got up in the morning and prostrated before my parents'. 'As usual, on my way to school I saluted Mother Kali and Mother Shitala'.[7] *The Gospel of Sri Ramakrishna* ultimately originated from this habit of keeping a diary, and M. himself commented about his great work, 'I was an apprentice for fifteen years'.[8]

M. was a brilliant student. He received his secondary education at the Hare School in Calcutta, where he was second in his class, and in 1875 he graduated third in his class from the Presidency College. He was a favourite student of C. H. Tawney, a well-known professor of English, who later wrote a brochure on Sri Ramakrishna. While M. was in college he married Nikunja Devi, a cousin of the Brahmo leader Keshab Chandra Sen. At that time Keshab was the hero of modern Bengal, and M. was very much influenced by him.

After graduating from college, M. took up the profession of a teacher. He served as headmaster in several schools in Calcutta. In February 1882, when he met Sri Ramakrishna, M. was the headmaster of the Shyambazar Branch of the Vidyasagar School. He was an excellent teacher, well versed in both Eastern and Western philosophy, as well as in history, literature, astronomy, and science. Moreover, he had studied the New Testament so thoroughly that he could quote many passages from memory. Long after M. had met Sri Ramakrishna, a Christian minister once expressed his amazement at the depth of M.'s knowledge of the Bible. M. told him politely, 'Sir, we lived with Christ [to M., Ramakrishna and Christ were the same], so we understand his teachings a little'.[9]

God's divine play in this world is such that we sometimes find suffering leading to happiness, and again, success leading to a downfall. M.'s mother had died when he was young, and without her, family squabbles gradually disrupted the harmony in the joint family. M. was a peace-loving soul, and he finally could no longer bear the pettiness and selfishness of his family members. He decided to leave home. One night at ten o'clock he left for his sister's house at Baranagore, accompanied by his wife. He hired a horse carriage, but one of the carriage wheels broke near Shyambazar. He approached a friend's house nearby for lodging for the night, but got a cold reception. Luckily, at midnight he found another carriage and was able to reach his sister's house. M. said later that at that time of his life his mental anguish was so great that he was thinking of taking his life.

The next afternoon he went for a walk with his nephew Sidhu, whose father, Ishan Kaviraj, was Sri Ramakrishna's physician. Sidhu took him to the temple garden of Dakshineswar, and there M. met Sri Ramakrishna for the first time. M. put it beautifully: 'I was thinking of killing myself, but instead I found my real Self. My family troubles led me to God'.[10] It is interesting that Sidhu, who took M. to Sri Ramakrishna, never visited Sri Ramakrishna again.

M. writes of that first visit:

They [M. and Sidhu] arrived at the main gate at dusk and went straight to Sri Ramakrishna's room. And there they found him seated on a wooden couch, facing the east. With a smile on his face, he was talking of God. The room was full of people, all seated on the floor, drinking in his words in deep silence. M. stood there speechless and looked on. It was as if he were standing where all the holy places met and as if Shukadeva himself were speaking the word of God, or as if Sri Chaitanya were singing the name and glories of the Lord in Puri... M. looked around him with wonder and said to himself: 'What a beautiful place! What a charming man! How beautiful his words are!'...

As he left the room with Sidhu, he heard the sweet music of the evening service arising in the temple from gong, bell, drum, and cymbal... The sounds travelled over the Ganga, floating away and losing themselves in the distance. A soft spring wind was blowing, laden with the fragrance of flowers; the moon had just appeared. It was as if nature and man together were preparing for the evening worship.[11]

On this first day, M. spoke very little with Sri Ramakrishna. He later said to the devotees: 'After meeting Sri Ramakrishna, I completely forgot my past. His towering personality and spiritual magnetism erased my sad memories'.[12]

On his second visit, M. was scolded by Sri Ramakrishna and, as he described, his ego was crushed. With a humility born of greatness, he immediately perceived the truth in Sri Ramakrishna's words and accepted it. It is as if M.'s belief in intellectual knowledge was overpowered by Sri Ramakrishna's spiritual wisdom once and for all. Generally people prefer to hide their weaknesses, but M. was so sincere that he meticulously recorded all the scoldings he received from the Master, as well as his reactions to them. M.'s record runs: 'Thus rebuked, M. sat speechless. His pride had received a blow. After a few minutes Sri Ramakrishna looked at him kindly and said affectionately: "You see, you have certain good signs. I know them by looking at a person's forehead, his eyes, and so on"'.[13]

On this occasion M. asked Sri Ramakrishna four vital questions of life. For readers of The Gospel of Sri Ramakrishna, it is as though he had asked them on behalf of humanity: (1) 'How may we fix our minds on

God?' (2) 'How ought we to live in the world?' (3) 'Is it possible to see God?' (4) 'Under what conditions does one see God?' Reading Sri Ramakrishna's responses to these questions in the first few pages of the book, one can already see how he incorporated parables, symbols, songs, stories, folklore, myths, scientific reasoning, day-to-day household examples, and examples from nature and from animal and human behaviour in his teachings. He seldom used scriptural testimony. He taught from his personal experience and explained the deep truths of spiritual life in an utterly simple way, and this captivated M. Never before had he met such a man.

On his fourth visit, M. found Sri Ramakrishna in his room surrounded by a group of young men. As soon as M. came in the room, the Master laughed and said to them, 'There! He has come again'. Then he explained the cause of his laughter: 'A man once fed a peacock with a pill of opium at four o'clock in the afternoon. The next day, exactly at that time, the peacock came back. It had felt the intoxication of the drug and returned just in time to have another dose'.[14] For the remaining five years of the Master's lifetime, M. returned for dose after dose of this divine intoxicant — direct association with God Incarnate — and then shared it freely with other seekers of God. At the beginning of each volume of the Bengali Gospel, he has quoted a verse from the Bhagavatam: 'O Lord, your words, like sweet nectar, refresh the afflicted. Your words, which poets have sung in verses, vanquish the sins of the worldly. Blessed are they who hear of you, and blessed indeed are they who speak of you. How great is their reward!'[15]

As other Incarnations of God have had someone to witness or collect their teachings, perhaps M. was this same great soul born again for that purpose. Sri Ramakrishna recognized M.'s value at first sight, and his comments about M. indicate that M. was not an ordinary person: 'I recognized you on hearing you read the Chaitanya Bhagavatam. You are my own. The same substance, like father and son... Before you came here, you didn't know who you were. Now you will know'.[16] 'Once [in a vision] I saw Gauranga and his devotees singing kirtan in the Panchavati. I think I saw Balaram there and you too'.[17] 'Yes, I know everything: what your Ideal is, who you are, your inside and outside, the events of your past lives, and your future'.[18] 'I can see from the signs of your eyes, brows, and face that you are a yogi. You look like a yogi who has just left his seat of meditation'.[19]

At one of their first meetings Sri Ramakrishna wanted to evaluate M.'s understanding of his spiritual state. He asked M.: 'What do you think of me? How many annas of knowledge of God have I?' 'I don't understand what you mean by "annas" ', replied M. 'But of this I am sure: I have never before seen such knowledge, ecstatic love, faith in God, renunciation, and catholicity anywhere'.[20]

On another occasion Sri Ramakrishna asked, 'Have you found anyone else resembling me — any pandit or holy man?' M. replied, 'God has created you with His own hands, whereas He has made others by machine'.[21] This remark made the Master laugh.

On July 28, 1885, Sri Ramakrishna, with M. and others, visited the house of two brahmin sisters, one of whom was grief-stricken because of her daughter's death. One sister was busy with the arrangements for the Master's refreshments, while the other, the grief-stricken one, was so overwhelmed with joy at his presence that she would not leave the room where he was. M. was reminded of the story of Martha and Mary in the Bible, and later he told that story to Sri Ramakrishna. The Master then said:

'Well, after seeing all this, what do you feel?'

M.: 'I feel that Christ, Chaitanyadeva, and yourself — all three are one and the same...'

Master: 'Yes, yes! One! One! It is indeed one. Don't you see that it is He alone who dwells here in this way'...

M.: 'You explained clearly, the other day, how God incarnates Himself on earth'.

Master: 'Tell me what I said'.

M.: 'You told us to imagine a field extending to the horizon and beyond. It extends without any obstruction; but we cannot see it on account of a wall in front of us. In that wall there is a round hole. Through the hole we see a part of that infinite field'.

Master: 'Tell me what that hole is'.

M.: 'You are that hole. Through you can be seen everything — that Infinite Meadow without any end'.[22]

Patting M.'s back, Sri Ramakrishna expressed his pleasure at M.'s understanding.

After he had been visiting the Master for some time, M. felt the urge to renounce family life and become a monk. But Sri Ramakrishna had set out a different path for him and discouraged him from this idea, saying: 'You are well established in God already. Is it good to give up all?'[23] Another day he said: 'God binds the Bhagavata pandit to the world with one tie; otherwise, who would remain to explain the sacred book? He keeps the pandit bound for the good of men. That is why the Divine Mother has kept you in the world'.[24]

Again, one evening when M. was alone with him at Dakshineswar,

Sri Ramakrishna said in an ecstatic mood: 'Let nobody think that if he does not do Mother's work, it would remain undone. The Mother can turn even a straw into a teacher'.[25] This erased any doubts left in M.'s mind. He understood that he should surrender completely to the will of the Master. He remained living as a hidden yogi in his family setting. He practised inner *sannyasa* (renunciation), without being indifferent to his duties and responsibilities. He was successful as a teacher, yet he had the calmness of a yogi. He was very humble and would serve monks and devotees with deep sincerity. Thus he combined the virtues of a householder with the spiritual intensity of a monk.

As a headmaster, M. had much contact with students. Many of Sri Ramakrishna's disciples were his students — Rakhal, Subodh, Sarada, Baburam, Purna, Binod, Bankim, Tejachandra, Khirod, and Narayan. He was teased by the devotees for being a 'kidnapper-teacher', for many of the boys came to Sri Ramakrishna through him.

M. practised spiritual disciplines under Sri Ramakrishna's guidance. Once the Master found him meditating on the verandah of the nahabat at Dakshineswar and said: 'Hello! You are here? You will get results very soon. If you practise a little, then someone will come forward to help you... The time is ripe for you. The mother bird does not break the shell of the egg until the right time arrives'.[26] These words gave M. tremendous encouragement, and he often quoted them in later years. As he visited Sri Ramakrishna more and more, he gradually lost interest in reading Western philosophy and science, and he did not care much about listening to the lectures of Keshab Sen and other scholars. He thought constantly of the sayings of Sri Ramakrishna, such as, 'One can certainly see God through the practice of spiritual discipline', or 'The vision of God is the only goal of human life'.[27]

Sri Ramakrishna's love and affection captivated M.'s mind, and he felt very close to the Master. 'You are my very own, my relative; otherwise, why should you come here so frequently?'[28] said the Master. On another occasion he said to M.: 'You don't want anything from me, but you love to see me and hear my words. My mind also dwells on you. I wonder how you are and why you don't come'.[29]

Another passage in the *Gospel* gives us a glimpse of the deep relationship between Sri Ramakrishna and his disciples:

> It was the day of the Car Festival [July 14, 1885]. Sri Ramakrishna left his bed very early in the morning. He was alone in the room, dancing and chanting the name of God... It was about half past six

in the morning. M. was going to bathe in the Ganga, when suddenly tremors of an earthquake were felt. At once he returned to Sri Ramakrishna's room. The Master stood in the drawing room. The devotees stood around him... The shaking had been rather violent, and many of them were frightened.

M.: 'You should all have gone downstairs'.

Master: 'Such is the fate of the house under whose roof one lives; and still people are so egotistic. [*To M.*] Do you remember the great storm of the month of Aswin [October 5, 1864]?

M.: 'Yes, sir. I was very young at that time — nine or ten years old. I was alone in a room while the storm was raging, and I prayed to God'.

M. was surprised and said to himself: 'Why did the Master suddenly ask me about the great storm of Aswin? Does he know that I was alone at that time earnestly praying to God with tears in my eyes? Does he know all this? Has he been protecting me as my guru since my very birth?'[30]

Undoubtedly M. received many blessings from the Master, but his personal life was full of trials and tribulations. He was worried about his wife, whose mind was a little unbalanced. One day he spoke of this to the Master: 'What should one do if one's wife says: "You are neglecting me. I shall commit suicide."'? Sri Ramakrishna replied: 'Give up such a wife if she proves an obstacle in the way of spiritual life... The wife that hampers her husband's spiritual life is an ungodly wife'. This stern answer put M. into a serious mood. The other devotees who were present remained silent. Sri Ramakrishna understood M.'s predicament, and after a little while he whispered in M.'s ear: 'But if a man has sincere love for God, then all come under his control — the king, wicked persons, and his wife. Sincere love of God on the husband's part may eventually help the wife to lead a spiritual life'.[31] These words of hope soothed M.'s worried mind.

Sri Ramakrishna taught that religion is not a matter of preaching, but of transforming oneself and thus inspiring others. One day towards the end of his life, he compared himself and his blessed group to a troupe of bauls (religious minstrels), who suddenly appeared, danced, and sang the name of God, and then disappeared into the unknown, leaving people amazed and inspired. On M.'s second visit, the Master had scolded him for his criticism of those who worship images. 'That's the one hobby of you Calcutta people — giving lectures and bringing others to the light! Nobody ever stops to consider how to get the light himself. Who are you to teach others? He who is the Lord of the Universe will teach everyone'.[32] On another occasion, the Master said to M., 'The less people know about your thoughts of God, the better for you'.[33]

Sri Ramakrishna used to present religion according to his own experience and in a tangible way. Once M. asked him what meditation on the formless God was like. The Master told him: 'You see, one must practise spiritual discipline to understand this correctly. Suppose there are treasures in a room. If you want to see them and lay hold of them, you must take the trouble to get the key and unlock the door. After that you must take the treasures out. But suppose the room is locked, and standing outside the door you say to yourself: "Here I have opened the door. Now I have broken the lock of the chest. Now I have taken out the treasure". Such brooding near the door will not enable you to achieve anything. You must practise discipline'.[34]

Then one day eight months later, Sri Ramakrishna, accompanied by M. and other devotees, went to visit Mati Seal's garden house at Belgharia. M. recorded: 'For a long time the Master had been asking M. to take him to the reservoir in the garden in order that he might teach him how to meditate on the formless God. There were tame fish in the reservoir. Nobody harmed them. Visitors threw puffed rice and other bits of food into the water, and the big fish came in swarms to eat the food. Fearlessly the fish swam in the water and sported there joyously.

'Coming to the reservoir, the Master said to M: "Look at the fish. Meditating on the formless God is like swimming joyfully like these fish, in the Ocean of Bliss and Consciousness" '.[35]

During Sri Ramakrishna's lifetime, M. visited Kamarpukur, the Master's village home, and bowed down to all the places associated with the Master's boyhood and later life there, regarding them as places of pilgrimage. Sri Ramakrishna was touched by M.'s devotion and remarked, 'His love is like that of Vibhishana, who, when he found a human form, at once dressed it in rich apparel and worshipped it by waving lights, saying, "This is the form of my Ramchandra" '.[36]

The great teachers of the world keep religion alive. They teach with the authority of direct experience and transmit power to their disciples, who in turn spread their teachings among humanity. Sri Ramakrishna commissioned M. to carry his message, just as he commissioned Swami Vivekananda. At the Cossipore garden house, the Master wrote on a piece of paper, 'Naren [Vivekananda] will teach people'. When the young man objected, the Master told him, 'Your very bones will do it'.[37] Regarding M., Sri Ramakrishna once said in an ecstatic mood, addressing the Divine Mother: 'Mother, why have you given him only one kala [a small part] of power? Oh, I see. That will be sufficient for your work'.[38]

Once Sri Ramakrishna remarked about M., 'This man has no ego'.[39] Where there is ego there is no God, and where there is God there is no ego. Sri Ramakrishna had effaced M.'s ego forever, and thus he became a perfect instrument in the hands of the Master.

When one of Sri Ramakrishna's devotees asked M. to show him his diary, M. refused, saying, 'I am writing it for myself, not for others'.[40] Whenever he would get a little extra time during his work as a teacher, he would retire to a solitary room on the roof to read his diary and reflect and meditate on the words of the Master. Once, speaking of the origin of the Gospel, M. said: 'I was involved in worldly activities, bound to my work, and could not visit the Master whenever I wished. Therefore I used to note down his words in order to think about them in the intervals before I met him again, so that the impressions made on my mind might not be overlaid by the stress of worldly work and responsibilities. It was thus for my own benefit that I first made the notes, so that I might realize his teachings more perfectly'.[41]

Like M., Tarak, who later became Swami Shivananda, once started to make notes of the Master's teachings and conversations, but Sri Ramakrishna forbade him to do so, and Tarak threw all of his notes into the Ganga. The job of recorder was earmarked for M. From the Gospel it seems that sometimes the Master would not begin an important discussion without M. being present. And again, the Master sometimes asked M. to repeat to him what he had said, and if M. had not understood it correctly, he would clarify the meaning for him. (See the entry in the Gospel dated November 9, 1884.)

M. was gifted with artistic ability and an accurate memory, which enabled him to faithfully recreate in writing what he had seen and heard. The scenes in the Gospel are so vividly depicted, that it is as if the reader is being transported to the very time and place and is watching and listening to the Master and his devotees. M. had been influenced by the writing of medieval Sanskrit poets such as Kalidasa and Bhavabhuti and had imbibed the contemplative spirit and serene atmosphere of the hermitages of ancient India through them. His own poetic nature can be seen in the descriptive passages in the Gospel, such as the following:

Sri Ramakrishna was going to the pine-grove. A beautiful, dark rain-cloud was to be seen in the northwest... After a few minutes M. and Latu, standing in the Panchavati, saw the Master coming back towards them. Behind him the sky was black with the rain-cloud. Its reflection in the Ganga made the water darker. The disciples felt that the Master was God Incarnate, a Divine Child five years old, radiant with the smile of innocence and purity. Around him were the sacred trees of the Panchavati under which he had practised spiritual discipline and had beheld visions of God. At his feet flowed the sacred river Ganga, the destroyer of man's sins. The presence of this God-man charged the trees, shrubs, flowers, plants, and temples with spiritual fervour and divine joy.[42]

Aldous Huxley wrote in the foreword to the English translation of the *Gospel*, 'Making good use of his natural gifts and of the circumstances in which he found himself, M. produced a book unique, so far as my knowledge goes, in the literature of hagiography'.[43] One can challenge the historicity of Christ, Buddha, or Krishna, but no one can challenge the historicity of Sri Ramakrishna. His conversations are meticulously documented according to place, persons, time, day, month, and year, and have come directly from M.'s diary. He himself said: 'My account is not a collection from other sources. I recorded whatever I heard with my own ears from the Master's lips and whatever I saw of his life with my own eyes'.[44] He wrote at the beginning of each volume of the Bengali edition that there are three kinds of information about Sri Ramakrishna: The first is recorded by the person who observed it on the same day as it happened; the second is recorded by the observer but at a later time; and the third is also recorded at a later time, but by someone who heard it from someone else. The *Gospel* belongs to the first category. M. would struggle to make his account accurate, for he once said: 'Sometimes I meditated on one scene over a thousand times. Sometimes I had to wait for a word of the Master to come to mind as a chataka bird waits for a drop of rainwater to fall'.[45]

Although tautology is a weakness in logic, it is not a weakness in the scriptures. The scriptures will reiterate the same truth in different ways so that it penetrates into us. M. was once asked to remove some of the repetitions from the *Gospel*, but he replied: 'I cannot do that. Sri Ramakrishna told the same parable to different people. If I remove a particular section, the train of the conversation will be broken. Moreover, you won't be able to see the effect of the *Gospel* in a particular person's life. You see, sometimes the brilliance of a diamond is enhanced by changing its setting. Putting it on the dusty ground gives one effect, and putting it on a green lawn will give another. But putting it in a blue velvet casket will give the most brilliant effect of all. The same is true of the words in the *Gospel*'.[46]

M. was reticent about himself even in the *Gospel*. His family name was Mahendra Nath Gupta, but he referred to himself always impersonally, using names such as Mani, Mohinimohan, Master, a devotee, an Englishman (meaning an English-educated person), a servant, or, most often, M. (in Bengali, Sri Ma). Among Sri Ramakrishna's immediate circle of devotees, he was known as Master Mahashay, respected teacher, but since the publishing of the *Gospel*, he has come to be known almost universally as M.

After the passing away of Sri Ramakrishna, the other disciples asked M. to publish his diary, but he was reluctant to do so. However, one day he read some of his notes to Sri Sarada Devi, the spiritual consort of Sri Ramakrishna, and she approved of them. M. regarded this as a divine sanction. In 1897 he published two pamphlets in English under the title *The Gospel of Sri Ramakrishna*. A few years later, the *Gospel* was published in its original Bengali language in five volumes as *Sri Sri Ramakrishna Kathamrita*.* This was then translated into English by Swami Nikhilananda and published in one volume in 1942. Swami Vivekananda wrote to M. in response to the earliest publications: 'You have hit Ramakrishna in the right point. Few, alas, few understand him!'[47] 'The move is quite original and never was the life of a great teacher brought before the public untarnished by the writer's mind, as you are doing. The language also is beyond all praise — so fresh, so pointed and withal so plain and easy... I now understand why none of us attempted his life before. It has been reserved for you — this great work. He is with you evidently... The Socratic dialogues are Plato all over. You are entirely hidden'.[48]

M. regularly visited the Baranagore Monastery and supported the monastic disciples in every possible way. He used to join them in practising spiritual disciplines, and he was never tired of speaking of their spiritual fervour to others. He would idealize the monk's life of renunciation and purity above all. To him the monks were the full-time lovers of God, while the householders were part-time, because of their worldly obligations. M. regarded Sri Ramakrishna as the embodiment of renunciation and purity and the monks of his Order as those continuing to carry that same lofty banner. When a monk would come to visit him, he would give up his work and sit near him like a servant, saying: 'A holy man has come. The Lord himself has come in one form, as it were. Shall I not postpone my eating and bath for him? Absurdity can go no further if I cannot do that'.[49]

Though outwardly M. was a householder, inwardly he himself was

*Volume I was published in 1902, Volume II in 1904, Volume III in 1908, Volume IV in 1910, and Volume V in 1932.

like a monk, full of intense devotion to God and renunciation of things of the world. Sometimes he would get up at night and, taking his bed roll, would leave his home to sleep on the open verandah of the Calcutta University Senate Hall among the homeless people of the city. When asked why, he explained, 'The idea of home and family clings to one and does not leave easily'.[50] He led a simple, unostentatious life. The same plain style of clothing that he wore when he first met Sri Ramakrishna he continued to wear all through his life. He had one change of clothes — an extra shirt and an extra wearing cloth for going out.

Sometimes he would go to the railway station to watch the stream of pilgrims returning from Jagannath at Puri. He liked to see their bright, serene faces, and occasionally he would ask for a little prasad from them. He had heard from the Master that one who eats prasad attains devotion. If anyone brought him prasad, he would even save the containers in which it was carried, thinking that they would remind him of God. He would bow down to the place on Bechu Chatterjee Street where the Master's elder brother had once conducted a school, and also at the house of the Mittra family at Jhamapukur, where the Master had once worked as a priest. Observing his companions' surprise, M. would say, 'Do you know that anyone who walks through this street will become a yogi?'[51] Sometimes when he went to Dakshineswar, after the Master's passing away, he would bring back a wet towel with him, squeeze the water from it, and sprinkle the water on the devotees, saying, 'I brought this water from the ghat on the Ganga where the Master used to bathe'.[52]

In 1905 M. gave up his position as a headmaster and purchased the Morton Institution, a school which was then situated in Jhamapukur Lane but was later moved to 50 Amherst Street. He used to live there in a solitary room on the roof of the school building, and there he would meet the monks and devotees who came to see him in the morning and evening. Swami Raghavananda's record runs: 'In the sweet and warm months of April and May, sitting under the canopy of heaven on the roof garden at 50 Amherst Street, surrounded by shrubs and plants, himself sitting in their midst like a rishi of old, the stars and planets in their courses beckoning us to things infinite and sublime, he would speak to us of the mystery of God and his love, and of the yearning that would rise in the human heart to solve the eternal riddle, as exemplified in the life of his Master'.[53]

M. went on pilgrimage to Varanasi, Vrindaban, Ayodhya, and other holy places. At Varanasi he met Trailanga Swami, an illumined monk observing a vow of silence, whom he fed with sweets. He also met Swami Bhaskarananda, with whom he had a long talk. In 1912 he went on a pilgrimage with Sri Sarada Devi to Varanasi again, and from there travelled to Hardwar, Kankhal, Rishikesh, and Vrindaban in the company of monks. He visited Puri and Bhubaneswar several times. But he was mainly attracted to places connected with Sri Ramakrishna, especially Dakshineswar, where the Master had lived for thirty years. In the eye of a lover, every detail of his beloved's life and activities is important. So it is with the devotee of God. He has intense interest in all things, places, and persons associated with God's manifestation on earth. He takes great pleasure in visiting or hearing about such places, because they make the Lord more real to him. To the devotees of Sri Ramakrishna, every spot at Dakshineswar is sacred. M. would sometimes accompany the devotees to the temple garden and would point out places where special conversations, meetings, or incidents had taken place. He was never tired of narrating those stories.*

Once a devotee told M. that he planned to visit Dakshineswar. M. told him to prepare himself for the visit. Then, suddenly in an inspired mood, M. said: 'When you see Dakshineswar, you will have an idea of what Sri Ramakrishna's surroundings were like. The temple garden was the backdrop for divine scenes. At Dakshineswar you will see the bel tree under which the Master practised great Tantric sadhanas. There is the Panchavati, where he went through many spiritual exercises. You will also see the Master's room. When you enter his room, visualize the Master seated with his disciples and

---

*In the first volume of the Bengali *Gospel* and in the first English edition, *The Gospel of Sri Ramakrishna*, volume I (published by Ramakrishna Math, Madras), M. has left a short description of the Dakshineswar temple garden for future pilgrims, pointing out the places they should see: the bel tala, where the Master practised Tantra; the pine grove; the Panchavati, a sacred grove of five trees (banyan, pepul, neem, amalaki, and bel); the madhavi-lata plant, which was planted by the Master; the meditation room, where the Master practised Vedantic sadhana; the goose tank; the bakultala ghat; the nahabat, where Sri Sarada Devi lived; the chandni-ghat, where the Master used to bathe; the flower garden; the Kali temple; the nat-mandir; or theatre hall; the office rooms and guest rooms; the twelve Shiva temples; the Radha-Krishna temple; the new image of Krishna and also the old one with the broken leg, which was repaired by the Master; the red-tiled courtyard, which was touched by the blessed feet of the Master; the southern, northern, and semi-circular western verandahs around the Master's room; the room itself, where he lived for fourteen years; the kuthi, where he lived in a room on the ground floor for sixteen years; the gazi pond; the gazitala, where the Master practised Islam; the main gate; the back gate; and the orchard.[54]

talking to them on divine subjects. We always found the Master absorbed in spiritual moods. Sometimes he would be in samadhi. Sometimes he would be singing and dancing. At other times he would be talking to the Divine Mother. We were fortunate enough to see a man who actually talked to the Divine Mother. We were fortunate enough to see a man whose experiences form, as it were, a living Veda. It is the revelations of such people that we have to rely upon, not our "ounce of reason". For the intellect cannot go far in spiritual matters; it has been weighed and found wanting. Christ said to his disciples, "I speak of things which I have seen with my own eyes; and yet you believe me not". One has to put one's faith in the words of a man of realization. When you go to the temple, you must purify yourself and strip yourself of all sensuality. Only the pure in heart can see God. You must also open yourself to the Master's presence and influence. This pilgrimage to Dakshineswar will help you a good deal in progressing towards God-realization'.[55]

On another occasion M. advised: 'One should see everything connected with the Master in detail. For example, in the Master's room there are cots, a jar containing Ganga water, pictures of gods and goddesses — Kali, Krishna, Rama, Chaitanya and his kirtan party, Dhruva, Prahlad, Christ extending his hand to the drowning Peter, and a white marble image of Buddha, which was given to him by Queen Katyayani, the wife of Lalababu. There was a picture of the goddess of learning on the western wall. Whenever a new person would come, the Master would look at that picture and pray, "Mother, I am an unlettered person. Please sit on my tongue"', and then he would speak to him. If a person can imprint these divine sights on his mind, he will have deep meditations, and even sitting at home he can live at Dakshineswar with the Master'.[56]

M. made a wonderful comment about Dakshineswar: 'The spiritual fire is blazing intensely there, and whoever goes there will be purified. The body does not burn, but mental impurities are consumed in no time. Then a man can attain immortality. God himself, in a physical form, lived there for thirty years! One can tangibly feel the spirituality at Dakshineswar'.[57]

There is a beautiful verse in the *Sri Sri Chaitanya Charitamrita*: *Adyapiha sei lila kare gora rai, kono kono bhagyavane dekhibare pai.* 'Chaitanya is still performing his divine play; only the fortunate ones can see it'. Sri Ramakrishna's divine presence is still at Dakshineswar, and the temple garden is not much different today than the way it was during his lifetime. But until we are able to see the eternal play of the Master at Dakshineswar, like the fortunate ones who see the play of Chaitanya, we are indebted to M. for his devoted firsthand account of what took place.

Once Miss Josephine MacLeod asked M., 'What was your experience of Sri Ramakrishna?' M. replied: 'He was always conscious of God. He was never separated from that state, and we saw him twenty-four hours a day. This is not possible for an ordinary God-realized man, but only when God incarnates in a human body. He declared that in his body Satchidananda had descended on earth. One day he told me, "Christ, Chaitanyadeva, and I are one and the same entity". When he thus revealed his real nature to us, we would feel bewildered and wonder, "Is this the temple priest or God himself speaking?"'

Miss MacLeod: 'How did he speak to you?'

M.: 'He told us, "The Mother of the Universe speaks through my lips". He spoke from inspiration. On several occasions he said, "I am an illiterate man, but Mother pushes heaps of knowledge to me from behind"'.[58]

Once a devotee said to M.: 'You are very fortunate. You have seen and heard Sri Ramakrishna. You have even touched him and served him'.

M. replied: 'Don't think in that way. The Master said that all his wealth and power will go to his children. Discrimination, renunciation, knowledge, devotion, and love are his wealth. These good qualities will come to the soul who thinks of him'.[59]

On another occasion, M. said to a devotee: 'Do you know what we received from the Master? Burning faith'.[60]

Like Job in the Old Testament, M. took the trials and tribulations of life as a test of his faith in God. He regarded the world as a seething cauldron, but he kept his mind above it. When people would come to him with their difficulties, he would say: 'God created anger, passion, and other troubles in order to mould great souls. An expert boatman can manage his boat in a cyclone. He enjoys navigating in the teeth of tidal waves, but weak people sit inside the boat and cry. There is a kind of bird called the stormy petrel. When a storm begins at sea, the animals on the shore hide in the forest. But the stormy petrel comes out of its nest and flies into the gusty wind with its wings spread. We should follow its example. Be of good cheer. We need strength and should have determination to surmount the troubles and depressions of life. As long as we have human bodies we will have to face these'.[61]

On another occasion, a young man came to visit M. 'Do you have a question?' asked M. The young man answered, 'Sir, I am in turmoil and have no peace'. M. burst into laughter and then said to the others present: 'Do you hear what this young man says? He is in the world and says, "I have no peace". After drinking a bottle of wine, you are asking, "Why should I be drunk?" '[62] M. had heard from the Master again and again: 'Lust and gold alone is the world. It makes one forget God'.[63] 'All seek to enjoy lust and gold. But there is too much misery and worry in that'.[64]

Sri Ramakrishna had asked M. to work for the Divine Mother, and he did so for fifty years. Even though his health was delicate, he never gave up working. Swami Nityatmananda wrote of a touching incident in his memoirs: 'I was responsible for the printing of the Kathamrita [the Bengali Gospel] while it was at the printer's, but I had many things to do and was unable to finish the proofreading in time. At one o'clock at night I saw a light in M.'s room. I entered and found he was reading the proofs of the Gospel by a kerosene lantern. He was not well at all, and moreover, as he was working at an odd hour, his eyes were watering. I was pained at this. I lovingly chastised him and he replied with affection: "People are finding peace by reading this book, the Master's immortal message. It is inevitable that the body will meet its end, so it is better that it is used for spreading peace to others. We are in the world and have utterly experienced how much pain is there, yet I have forgotten that pain through The Gospel of Sri Ramakrishna. I am hurrying so that the book may come out soon". Indeed, M. died while the last portion of the last volume was at the press. He was born to write and teach The Gospel of Sri Ramakrishna'.[65]

On June 4, 1932, M. left his body in full consciousness. He breathed his last saying this prayer, 'Mother — Guru Deva — take me up in thy arms'.[66] The Mother took her child up in her arms and the curtain fell.

When M. would talk about Sri Ramakrishna, he would have no body-consciousness. It seemed as though his soul was trying its utmost to break out of its cage of name and form, trying to encompass the Infinite. His love and devotion for Sri Ramakrishna was so great, it would spread to those who heard him speak. One day in an inspired mood, M. was trying to describe his Master. He said:

'The Master was like a five-year-old boy always running to meet his Mother.

'The Master was like a beautiful flower whose nature was to bloom and spread its fragrance.

'The Master was like a bonfire from which other lamps were lighted.

'The Master was like a celestial vina always absorbed in singing the glory of the Divine Mother.

'The Master was like a big fish joyfully swimming in calm, clear, blue waters, the Ocean of Satchidananda.

'The Master was like a bird which had lost its nest in a storm and then, perched on the threshold of the Infinite, was joyfully moving between the two realms, singing the glory of the Infinite'.

After trying to describe the Master in many ways, he said that all these similies were inadequate. The Infinite cannot be expressed in words.[67]

M. offered his life at the feet of his guru and attained eternal life, and through his great life's work, *The Gospel of Sri Ramakrishna*, he has been immortalized.

Nag Mahashay (Durga Charan Nag)
(1846-1899)

15

Nag Mahashay
(Durga Charan Nag)

There is a saying, 'Gurus are available by the thousands, but real disciples are very few'. A real disciple is one who translates the teachings of his guru into the actions of his life. Durga Charan Nag was one such rare soul. Once he overheard Sri Ramakrishna say, 'It is very difficult for doctors, lawyers, and brokers to advance on the path to God'. Referring to doctors in particular, he said, 'If the mind dwells on tiny drops of medicine, how can it conceive of the Infinite?' Durga Charan was then practising homeopathic medicine. He noticed that most of the time his mind was reflecting on the faces of his patients, and this disturbed his meditation. He therefore thought that the advice was meant for him. Immediately he resolved, 'I will not make my living from that profession which is an obstacle to the realization of God'. He returned home and that very day threw his medicine box and medical books into the Ganga.[1]

How can we harmonize God and the world? How can we live in this world without being worldly? How can we love and not be attached? Is it necessary to renounce the world for God-realization? What is the duty of a householder? What is the goal of human life? These and other vital questions Sri Ramakrishna answered for the modern world. He did so, not only through the use of tales and parables, but also by quietly moulding the lives of perfect exemplars of his teachings. The life of Durga Charan Nag is just such a model of an ideal householder. Sri Ramakrishna demonstrated to the modern world through him that a person can lead a married life and at the same time have the highest spiritual experience.

According to Vedantic tradition, the life of a householder is based on spirituality. He should follow the path of truth and dedicate the results of all his actions to the Supreme Being. It is not an easy path. He is a true hero', said Sri Ramakrishna, 'who can perform all the duties of the world with his mind fixed on God. None but a very strong man could stop to admire a bridal procession moving by while carrying a load of two maunds [164 pounds] on his head'.[2]

It was because of his extraordinary personality that Durga Charan Nag came to be known as Nag Mahashay. (Nag is the surname, and Mahashay is a title meaning a great-souled one.) An illumined soul is ever contented, ever blissful, ever free. He has no craving for heaven or for the world; he transcends the pairs of opposites. The Ashtavakra Samhita describes the signs of such a great soul:

> Those desirous of worldly enjoyment and those desirous of liberation, both are found in this world. But rare indeed is the great-souled one [mahashay] who is not desirous of either enjoyment or liberation.[3]

Swami Vivekananda once said about him, 'I have travelled many places in the world, but nowhere have I come across such a great soul as Nag Mahashay'.[4]

Durga Charan Nag was born on August 21, 1846, at Deobhog, a small village in that part of Bengal which is now Bangladesh. His father, Dindayal Nag, was a pious man who was employed for a modest salary by a large commercial firm in Calcutta. Although two daughters and another son were also born to Dindayal, only Durga Charan and one of the daughters survived childhood. Durga Charan lost his mother when he was eight years old and was then brought up by an affectionate aunt. This aunt used to narrate to the boy at night tales from the Ramayana and the Mahabharata. Sometimes after falling asleep Durga Charan's dreams would vividly reproduce scenes from those tales. Other nights he would see the forms of gods and goddesses in his dreams. In the mornings, when he described these dreams to his aunt, she would be filled with awe.

Durga Charan was a handsome, modest, and sweet-natured boy. He was not very fond of sports, but occasionally, at the urging of his friends, he would join them in their games. His love of truth was so great that, even in play or fun, he would never speak a lie. And if any of his friends did so, he would immediately have nothing to do with that person. He was often drafted as a mediator when a dispute arose among his playmates, and the boys, knowing his fairness, accepted his decision without question. Once some mischievous boys insisted that he tell a lie so they could win a game, but Durga Charan refused and consequently they lost. Enraged, they dragged him through a rice field until his body was covered with cuts and bruises. He returned home in the evening in pain but without a word of complaint against anyone.

There was a grade school near his village that offered classes through the eighth grade. Durga Charan completed the course there and wanted to go to Calcutta to continue his education, but, because of financial difficulties, his father was unable to send him. Durga Charan then decided on his own to attend Dhaka Normal School, which was ten miles from his home. His aunt was opposed to the idea because it meant that he would have to walk twenty miles every day, and she could not bear the thought of his undertaking such a hardship. But as he was determined, she at last relented. Every morning she cooked rice and vegetables together for his breakfast, and, when necessary, he bought puffed rice at school for his lunch. Thus for fifteen months, in chilling rain and scorching heat, he patiently walked back and forth the twenty miles. During this time he missed only two days of school. His thirst for knowledge was so great that he did not mind the physical discomforts.

Once, while returning home, Durga Charan encountered a ghost, but he did not become frightened. He thought to himself, 'I have not done any harm to him, so why should he harm me?'[5] As he hurried on his way he heard the loud laughter of the ghost behind him but did not look back. On another occasion, during the rainy season, he fell into a pond from a slippery road. He tried to climb out several times by holding the grass and bushes of the slope but failed. Finally he stopped and began to chant the name of the Lord. After gaining new strength, he pulled himself out of the pond.

One of the teachers of the school noticed the sincerity and determination of Durga Charan and offered him free board and lodging. Durga Charan humbly declined, saying, 'No, sir, I do not feel any difficulty in coming here'. The teacher was amazed and remarked, 'I know not what this boy will be in the future'.[6]

Although Durga Charan did not study in that school for very long, he was able to master perfectly the Bengali language. During this time he wrote several essays on religion and how to build character which later were published in a pamphlet entitled *Advice to Boys*.[7]

When he was fifteen years old his marriage was arranged to a girl of eleven. At that time child marriage was commonly practised in India, although betrothal might be a more accurate term. After the marriage the bride would return to her parents' home, and later she would come to live with her husband when they were both grown. Five months after his marriage Durga Charan moved to Calcutta with his father. He began studies in the Campbell Medical School but, for some unknown reason, discontinued them after a year and a half. Later he studied homeopathy under Dr. Behari Lal Bhaduri, a renowned physician of Calcutta. His success in his profession was immediate. He had a rare intuition in diagnosis and even as a student performed some remarkable cures. He refused to set any fixed fee for his services. Whatever people offered he accepted, provided it was not more than what he considered just. He treated poor patients free of charge, sometimes even giving money to them for food and medicine. Some unscrupulous people took advantage of his kindness, but he did not mind. He served men as God.

Since Durga Charan lived mostly in Calcutta and his wife lived with her family in Deobhog, he seldom saw her. But even when he did visit his family in the village, it is said that he would spend the nights sitting on the branch of a tree in order to avoid her company. It was not that he had no love for her. He was then in his late teens, and he felt that without chastity one could not realize God. The snares of worldly life could not trap this free soul. His wife died, however, very suddenly and unexpectedly.

Durga Charan was very much shocked at the news of her death. He started to devote more of his time to the study of the scriptures and to meditation. Often in the evenings he would go to the cremation ground of North Calcutta and stay there until late at night. The funeral pyres on the bank of the Ganga reminded him of the impermanence of human life and the unreality of the world, and he would think: 'Vanity, vanity, all is vanity! God alone is the Truth. Unless he is realized, life is truly a burden. How shall I realize him? Who will show me the way?'[8]

About this time he met Suresh Chandra Datta, who was a member of the Brahmo Samaj, a religious and social reform movement of India. They spent much time together in discussions about spiritual life, and although their religious views were poles apart, they developed a close friendship. Suresh was very impressed with Durga Charan's spotless character, faith, and love for God.

Dindayal soon discovered that his son was losing interest in medicine and was practising spiritual disciplines in a cremation ground at night. Naturally this worried him, but he thought that another marriage would cure his son of this religious madness. Consequently, he selected a bride and insisted upon the marriage. Durga Charan pleaded: 'Once before you persuaded me to marry, but that girl died; again you are going to place someone's daughter in the jaws of death!... Father, give up your resolve. I beg you, kindly do not put me in bondage again. As long as you are living I shall serve you heart and soul; I shall serve you a hundred times more devotedly than your would-be daughter-in-law. Please spare me'.[9]

Dindayal wavered. He thought that if the marriage would not make his son happy then it might be better to cancel it. But no sooner had he agreed to the cancellation than the thought struck him that if his son did not marry, his lineage would come to an end. In his grief over his son, Dindayal quit taking food and wept secretly. Seeing the pitiable condition of his father, Durga Charan reluctantly agreed to the marriage. Before he left for his native village with his father, he went to the holy river Ganga and prayed, 'O Mother, I have heard that you are the purifier of all sins; therefore, if I be defiled by the dirt and dust of the world by becoming a householder, wash them off me'.[10]

As married life does not suit everybody, so also monastic life is not meant for all. God created human beings with different temperaments. Although Durga Charan did not want to marry, one should not think that he hated married life. On the contrary, he once said: 'Marriage with the pure desire for progeny does not defile a man. But only saints and sages of yore were fit for such marriages. After observing austere brahmacharya [chastity] for a long time, they would marry and then, having sons like Vyasa, Shukadeva, Sanaka, and Sanatkumara, they would finally retire to the forest to lead the life of a recluse. But it cannot be so in this iron age. Nowadays people do not have sufficient austerity and self-control, so the children born of lust become wicked and immoral'.[11]

After his second marriage Durga Charan again returned to Calcutta with his father, leaving the young bride, Sharatkamini, in Deobhog. He abhorred the idea of taking service under anyone, so he again settled into the practice of medicine. Once he cured a critically ill patient in the house of his father's employer and in gratitude was offered a silver casket filled with rupees as payment. But he courteously declined to accept it and asked for only twenty rupees (less than two dollars) as his legitimate remuneration. His father was infuriated when he heard of it and said, 'You will never succeed in your profession, I tell you, if you go on this way'. But Durga Charan replied: 'I cannot help it. What I believe to be wrong, I cannot do, come what may. God is Truth. Have you not always taught me to walk in the path of righteousness? In all conscience, how could I have demanded more? False conduct brings ruin'.[12]

An easygoing life is the bane of spiritual aspirants. Ordeals, trials, and tribulations help them to grow. It is easy to navigate a ship in a calm sea, but he is the real captain who can save his craft in a storm. Durga Charan's faithfulness to his ideal was tested through marriage and then through money. As a doctor he had a good reputation, but, in spite of it, he remained unattached. Lust and greed, and name and fame are the greatest obstacles to God-realization. He was confronted with these obstacles at every step of his life, but his efforts to overcome them only made him stronger.

When a wild lion is encaged, he roars and tries his utmost to break out of the cage. Similarly, Durga Charan was desperately trying to sever the bonds of maya. His heart was crying for freedom. Once he met a holy man who told him, 'However strong might be your faith, and intense be your love for God, unless you are initiated by a guru and practise sadhana according to his instructions, you cannot have the vision of God'.[13]

The lives of the mystics prove that when intense longing for God dawns in a soul, God responds and makes everything favourable for the devotee. One morning Durga Charan was seated on the bank of the Ganga when his family guru arrived there, unexpectedly, on a boat. When he was asked the reason for his coming to Calcutta, the guru replied, 'I have come at the special command of the Divine Mother to initiate you'.[14] However, the initiation only created in him more hunger for God. He was carried away by divine intoxication and often lost outward consciousness. Once, while he was meditating on the bank of the Ganga, the flood tide rose and swept him into the river. It was several moments before full consciousness returned to him and he was able to swim ashore.

Eventually Durga Charan's young wife, Sharatkamini, came to Calcutta to serve her husband and old father-in-law. Though Dindayal was greatly troubled about his son, his sympathies were more with his daughter-in-law who, it seemed to him, was rejected by her husband. Sharatkamini, however, was not disturbed; she knew that her husband was not an ordinary man. His mind always dwelt in God, and no power of maya could tempt or bind him. One day Durga Charan said to his wife: 'Love on the physical plane never lasts. Blessed is he who can love God heart and soul. Even a little attachment to the body endures for several births, so be not attached to this cage of flesh and bones. Take refuge in the Divine Mother and think of her alone. Thus your life here and hereafter will be ennobled'.[15]

Sharatkamini herself was like a nun — very pure, dedicated, self-effacing, and unselfish. She did not try to possess her husband for her own self-interest; she was simply his co-pilgrim. She was happy to serve her husband and father-in-law and, later, the many devotees that came to their house. Her life shows that when a person comes in close contact with a God-intoxicated soul, that person's mind rises above the physical plane.

After some time Dindayal decided to retire from his job and live in his village home. Handing over the charge of his Calcutta house and his job to his son, he left for Deobhog with his daughter-in-law. Durga Charan remained alone in Calcutta.

People read about God, talk about God, hear about God, but how many really want to experience him directly? This desire completely possessed Durga Charan. One day his friend Suresh came to him with news about Sri Ramakrishna, the saint of Dakshineswar. They both decided to go immediately to Dakshineswar and see him. They arrived there about two in the afternoon and inquired about the Master. Pratap Hazra, a strange devotee, informed them that Sri Ramakrishna had gone to Chandannagore and asked them to come back another day. They were terribly disappointed and about to leave when they noticed someone inside a room beckoning them to enter. It was Sri Ramakrishna.

The Master received them cordially and asked them about themselves. During the course of the conversation he advised: 'Live in the world like a mudfish. The fish lives in the mud but its skin is always bright and shiny. Similarly, remain at home unattached and the stain of worldliness will not touch your mind'. He asked them to meditate in the Panchavati grove for some time, and then he took them to see the different temples. As they were leaving, Sri Ramakrishna said to them: 'Come again. A relationship grows through frequent visits'.[16]

The following week they again went to meet Sri Ramakrishna. Welcoming them he said: 'I am very glad to see you. It is for you that I am here'. He beckoned Durga Charan to sit near him and said: 'Don't fear, my child. You have attained a very exalted state'. The Master then sent him out of the room to do some small tasks. When he had left, the Master turned to Suresh and remarked: 'Did you notice? This man is like a blazing fire!'[17]

The next time, Durga Charan went to Dakshineswar by himself. Sri Ramakrishna asked him, 'What do you think of me?' Durga Charan saluted him with folded hands and replied: 'You cannot hoodwink me any more, Divine Master. Through your grace I have come to know that you are that Supreme One'.[18]

It was a few months after his first meeting with Sri Ramakrishna that Durga Charan gave up his medical practice. Although he had taken over his father's job, he began to devote more time now to meditation and felt a strong urge to renounce the world. With that intention, he one day went to see the Master. As soon as he reached there, the Master said in an ecstatic mood: 'What harm is there in remaining as a householder? Only keep the mind fixed upon God. The householder's life is like fighting from within a fortress. Remain in the world like the ancient king Janaka, unattached. Your life will be an example of how a householder should live'.[19] Durga Charan was speechless. He returned home, obeying the behest of the Master.

It is true that God helps those who help themselves; but it is equally true that God helps those who do not help themselves. According to most theistic religions, self-effort is essential for the beginners, while self-surrender is practised by the advanced spiritual aspirants. Self-surrender is considered to be the highest state in spiritual life. Durga Charan had completely surrendered himself to his Master's will, but it gradually became impossible for him to continue his routine work. However, his employer was very kind to the Nag family. An arrangement was made whereby a faithful man of the company would work on behalf of Durga Charan, who would then get a commission. All through Durga Charan's life, the financial matters of the Nag family were taken care of by this employer.

Such was the employer's faith and trust in Durga Charan that once, during the time of an epidemic, he wanted to leave the plague-stricken city but was worried about leaving his possessions unattended. Durga Charan was not afraid of the plague, so the employer left everything in his care and fled. Durga Charan accepted the responsibility as a sacred trust and later returned the property to the employer just as he had received it.

An interesting incident happened one day when Durga Charan went to his country home to visit his father. A cow, tied near the corner of the house, was straining to reach a pumpkin plant that was growing nearby, but the rope she was tied with was too short. Durga Charan happened to see the cow and out of compassion released her so she could eat the plant. Seeing this, Dindayal flew into a rage and said: 'You yourself do not earn money. Instead of helping the household, why are you causing harm to it? You have given up your medical practice. Now how will you maintain yourself?'

'Please don't worry about that. God will take care of me', replied Durga Charan.

'Yes, I know. Now you will go naked and live on frogs!'

Durga Charan immediately stripped himself, picked up a dead frog from the courtyard and started eating it. He then said to his father: 'Now I have fulfilled both of your commands. Please don't worry about my food and clothing any longer. Chant the name of the Lord, I beg you, and don't think about household affairs in your old age'. Dindayal now thought that his son had indeed become mad and, in order to avert further bizarre behaviour, said to his daughter-in-law, 'Hereafter, let none go against his wishes'.[20]

Durga Charan could not tolerate worldly talk. If anyone started such a conversation, he would skillfully change the subject to spiritual matters. If he happened to become angry with someone, he would mercilessly beat his own body with whatever object he had near at hand as self-punishment. He would not contradict anyone, nor would he indulge in criticizing others. Once he inadvertently made a critical remark about a person and, as soon as he was aware of it, picked up a stone and hit his own head with it until it bled profusely. It took about a month for the wound to heal. He justified this strange action by saying, 'The wicked deserve right punishment'.[21]

His austerity defies description. The Bhagavatam says, 'He who has controlled the tongue has controlled everything'.[22] It is hard to concentrate the mind on God if it is always drawn to good food, and, because of this, Durga Charan was very particular about control of the palate. He would not use any salt or sugar on his food in order to curb his desire for delicacies. Once he lived for two or three days on only rice bran. He often abstained from food and water for days. He gave up using shirts and shoes and wore only a plain cloth and chadar (cotton shawl). Observing his austerity and self-effacement, Girish Chandra Ghosh, a close friend of his, remarked, 'Nag Mahashay has knocked on the head of his rascal ego so severely that it cannot raise its hood anymore'.[23]

When Durga Charan returned to Calcutta, he went to see Sri Ramakrishna and expressed his agony that he had not yet achieved complete self-surrender to the Lord. The Master consoled him, saying, 'If you love "this" [pointing to himself], everything will be all right'.

'Sir, how shall I pass my days at home?'

'You will not have to do anything. Only remain in the company of the holy'.

'I am a simple, uneducated man. How shall I recognize the holy men?'

'Listen, you will not have to look for them. You stay at home, and the real holy people will come to you of their own accord'.[24]

During the last days of Sri Ramakrishna, when he was stricken with throat cancer, Durga Charan rarely went to visit him because he could not bear to see his beloved Master suffer. One day, when he did go to pay his respects to him, Sri Ramakrishna said: 'Oh, you have come. Look, the doctors have failed. Can you do anything to cure me?' Durga Charan reflected for a moment and then resolved to transfer the Master's disease into his own body. He said in an inspired mood: 'Yes sir, I know how to cure you. By your grace I will do it right now'. But as he approached, the Master understood his motive and pushed him away, saying, 'Yes, I know you have that power to cure the disease'.[25]

Just a few days before the Master passed away, Durga Charan went to see him. As he entered the room he heard Sri Ramakrishna express a desire to eat an amalaki fruit, which is soothing for the throat. A devotee replied that none were available as they were out of season. But Durga Charan thought that if the word *amalaki* came from the lips of the Master, then it must be available somewhere, and, without saying anything, he left in search of it. For two days he checked different gardens in the suburbs of Calcutta, and at last on the third day, he appeared before the Master with a few amalaki fruits. The Master was very pleased and asked Holy Mother to cook some rice and hot curry for Durga Charan. But when the food was served he would not touch it. It was his fasting day (Ekadashi, i.e. the eleventh day of the moon). However, when the Master himself touched the food and sanctified it, Durga Charan took it as prasad. And in his exuberant devotion, he not only ate the food, but the leaf-plate as well. From that time on the devotees were careful when serving him prasad on a leaf-plate. As soon as he finished the meal they would snatch away the leaf-plate. They even removed seeds and pits from fruit before offering them to Durga Charan, lest he should swallow them also.[26]

When Sri Ramakrishna passed away on August 16, 1886, Nag Mahashay quit eating and remained in bed. Hearing about this, Swami Vivekananda went to his house along with two of his brother disciples. After repeated requests he got up from bed, and Swami Vivekananda told him that they had come there for lunch. Immediately Durga Charan went to the market, brought back groceries, and cooked for them, but he would not eat anything himself. When they urged him to eat, he said, 'Alas, how can I offer food to this wretched body which has not yet been blessed with God-realization?' It was with great difficulty that Swami Vivekananda finally persuaded him to take some food.[27]

After his Master's death, Nag Mahashay spent most of his time in Deobhog, managing the household and caring for his aged father. There he lived a simple, unassuming life, concealing his glowing spirituality under a veil of great humility. But as fire cannot be hidden, so it is with spirituality. Gradually the name of Nag Mahashay spread far and wide. People came to him for advice and to enjoy his holy company. He served everyone with amazing self-effacement. Once Swami Vivekananda observed that the whole of East Bengal was blessed because of the birth of Nag Mahashay.

Service to man is service to God. Nag Mahashay saw that it is God who appears in various human forms, and therefore he would serve each guest with love and respect. No one could leave his house without having been fed. He even reserved a room for visitors to stay in adjacent to his shrine.

Nag Mahashay suffered from chronic colic pain. Once when he was in pain, some visitors arrived. Since there was no rice or other groceries in the house, he immediately left for the market without another thought about his own condition. He never allowed anyone to carry even large articles for him, and this time, while returning home with the heavy load of rice on his head, he fell on the street, overcome with pain. Plaintively he prayed to Sri Ramakrishna: 'Master, what shall I do? The living gods are at my house and I am delayed in serving them. Wretched indeed is this cage of flesh and bones which has created an obstacle to the service of God today'. After a while when the pain had subsided a little, he returned home and asked Sharatkamini to cook for their guests immediately. He then bowed down to the visitors and apologized for serving them so late.[28]

Another time two guests came at night. It was the rainy season, and all of the thatched huts were leaking except one, which was Nag Mahashay's bedroom. When the guests were fed, he said to his wife: 'We are very fortunate today! Can we not sacrifice a little comfort for these living gods? Let us pass the night sitting under the eaves and chanting the name of the Lord'. That wonderful couple then vacated their room for the guests and spent the night under the eaves in meditation and japam.[29]

Since Nag Mahashay could not bear others serving him in any way, he would not allow anyone to repair the roofs of the thatched huts. Whenever he chanced to be away from home for a few days, Sharatkamini would hire someone to make the repairs in his absence. Once he was home for a long period and, although the roof badly needed repairing, she could not get any chance to have it done. Finally she secretly engaged a roofer, hoping the work could be finished quickly before her husband noticed. But Nag Mahashay saw the man working on the roof. He became very disturbed and started hitting his forehead, saying: 'Master, why did you ask me to stay at home? I am taking service from others for my comfort. Fie on this householder's life!' Seeing his agony, the roofer came down. Nag Mahashay fanned him, served him tobacco, paid him the whole day's wages, and then sent him home.[30]

When it was necessary for him to travel by boat, he would not allow the boatman to row but insisted on plying the oars himself. During the rainy season the whole village became flooded with water, and it was impossible to visit a neighbour or to go shopping without a boat. But since Nag Mahashay did not have one, his wife had to manage the household with the help of neighbours. Moreover, she had to collect firewood for the entire rainy season beforehand.

Once a young devotee of Nag Mahashay came from Dhaka to visit him. It was a rainy day and there was no boat to cross the inundated area, so he decided to swim, although it was quite a distance. When the devotee reached the northern boundary of Nag Mahashay's garden it was 9 o'clock at night, and he was cold and completely exhausted. Much to his surprise, however, Nag Mahashay was waiting there for him.

'Alas! What have you done?' Nag Mahashay asked. 'The fields are infested with venomous snakes at this time. Why did you take such a risk in this dangerous weather?' He hurried the young devotee into the house. Sharatkamini gave him a dry cloth to put on and then rushed to the kitchen to cook food for him, only to find that all the dry firewood was gone. Without a moment's hesitation Nag Mahashay began cutting down a pole in his house. He would not listen to anyone's objections. 'Here is a man who has come to see me', he said, 'even at the risk of drowning and snakebite, and can I not give up the attachment for this ordinary cottage for him? I would be blessed if I could serve such people at the cost of my life'.[31]

Every evening Nag Mahashay waved light and incense before the picture of Sri Ramakrishna, and the devotees sang vesper songs and kirtan. Primarily he was a worshipper of Shakti, the Divine Mother, but he had love and respect for all faiths. Like his Master he believed that all paths lead to the same goal, and whenever he passed a mosque or church, he would bow down with devotion.

The Bhagavad Gita states: 'A man consists of the faith that is in him. Whatever his faith is, he is'.[32] A man of faith is free from fear, worry, and anxiety. Once there was a terrible fire in a neighbour's house which was only fifteen yards from his own. A strong wind was blowing and occasionally sparks fell on Nag Mahashay's roof. While the villagers were fighting to stop the blazing fire, Nag Mahashay stood before it with folded hands, unperturbed. Sharatkamini, however, was frightened and started throwing clothes, bedding, and blankets outside. Seeing her, Nag Mahashay cried out: 'Shame on you! Still you have no faith in God! Brahma, the god of fire, has come. Instead of worshipping him, you are busy protecting these trifling objects! Victory to Sri Ramakrishna!' He started to dance in the courtyard. Then he added, 'If God protects, no one can destroy; and if God destroys, no one can save'. The neighbour's house was burned to the ground, but Nag Mahashay's house remained undamaged.[33]

There is a common belief among the Hindus that those who bathe in the holy river Ganga during *Ardhodaya Yoga* (an auspicious day which comes once every fifty years) become free from impurities and ignorance, and go to heaven. Three or four days before that auspicious occasion Nag Mahashay left Calcutta, which is on the bank of the Ganga, to return to his village. His father was furious and said to him: 'People are selling everything they own to go and bathe in the Ganga on this holy occasion, and you have come back home, leaving the Ganga! I really don't understand your attitude towards religious life! Still a few days are left. Take me to Calcutta'.

But Nag Mahashay humbly said: 'If a man has true devotion, Mother Ganga reveals herself in his house. It is needless for him to go any place'.

On the day of Ardhodaya Yoga, several of Nag Mahashay's devotees came to visit him. Suddenly one of the women noticed a stream of water gushing out of the southeast corner of the courtyard. The devotees gathered around it in amazement and watched as it formed a flowing stream. Nag Mahashay was in his room when he heard the excitement of the devotees. He came out and, seeing the stream, bowed down to it reverently. Then, sprinkling a little water on his head, he prayed: 'Victory to Mother Ganga! Mother, purify us'.

Word of the mysterious water spread throughout the village, and on that auspicious day devotees and villagers alike were blessed by bathing in that miraculous stream. Hearing of this episode some time later, Swami Vivekananda commented: 'The wish of a great soul like Nag Mahashay can make the impossible possible. Their infallible will power can even liberate people'.[34]

Seeing God in everything is the culmination of Vedantic experience. When Nag Mahashay was asked why he remained with his hands folded reverently so much of the time, he replied, 'I perceive God in every being and in everything'.[35]

It is said that nonviolence is the highest virtue, a virtue that Nag Mahashay practised to the letter throughout his life. No one ever saw him kill an insect, and when he walked through the street, he was always vigilant lest he step on any creature. A devotee was one day seated with him on the porch of the shrine when he noticed that the eastern bamboo fence was covered with anthills. Thinking to protect the fence from further damage, the devotee jumped on it and shook it so vigorously that a large section of the anthill fell to the ground. Nag

Mahashay cried out: 'Alas, what have you done? For a long time they lived happily building their homes on the fence, and today you have made them homeless. It is unfair'. Seeing the tears in his eyes, the devotee was overwhelmed. Nag Mahashay then approached the ants and said: 'Please climb up on the fence again and build your comfortable homes. You have nothing more to fear'.[36]

Once a few European officers of the Narayangunj Jute Mill came to Deobhog to hunt birds. As soon as Nag Mahashay heard the gunfire, he ran up to the hunters and with folded hands begged them to stop shooting. The hunters did not understand what he was saying and no doubt thought he was crazy. They reloaded their rifles and were about to shoot again when Nag Mahashay leapt forward and with superhuman strength seized their weapons. He then carried the rifles home. The Europeans were humiliated and angry, and they decided to bring legal charges against him. Meanwhile Nag Mahashay sent the rifles back to the hunters through one of the workers at the jute mill. The worker explained to the Europeans about Nag Mahashay's saintly nature, and they never returned to Deobhog to hunt.[37]

Spirituality is not something that can be measured with a measuring rod. When a person becomes spiritual his heart expands and he feels intensely for others. Nag Mahashay would feel the hunger of the dogs, cats, fish, and birds, and he would feed them accordingly. Once when he met a fisherman with a basket of live fish for sale, Nag Mahashay bought all of the fish and immediately set them free in a neighbouring pond. On another occasion a cobra appeared in his courtyard, and Sharatkamini, fearing it would bite someone, wanted it to be killed. Nag Mahashay said to her, 'It is not the snake of the jungle, but the snake of one's own mind that injures a man'. Then, with folded hands, he addressed the snake: 'O goddess of the snake, your abode is in the jungle. Mother, please go back to your own place and leave this poor man's cottage'. Amazingly, the snake then followed him to the jungle. 'If you do not harm anyone in this world', he commented, 'no one will harm you. The reflection in the mirror shows exactly the same face you make at it'.[38]

It would pain him if anyone even tore a leaf off a tree. There was a cluster of bamboos adjacent to his cottage, and the branches were damaging the wall. They had even penetrated inside the cottage, but he would not cut them back. When someone offered to cut them for him, he said, 'Is it proper to destroy something which you have no power to create?'[39]

People talk about 'cosmic consciousness', 'universal brotherhood', 'oneness of God', 'unity in diversity', and 'God in everything', but are these beautiful concepts mere imagination? Men get strength and inspiration when they find a person who has experienced and demonstrated these sublime truths. A man of God actually knows God's will, and whatever he does is good for all.

Once a devotee came to visit Nag Mahashay. Nag Mahashay and his wife gave their room to him and they slept in the kitchen. In the middle of the night, the devotee was suddenly awakened by a startled outcry. He rushed to the kitchen as Sharatkamini was lighting a candle. They found that a cat had jumped on Nag Mahashay's face and had scratched the white of his left eye. Sharatkamini wept at the sight of the wound, but Nag Mahashay consoled her, saying: 'Don't worry. It is nothing. Why do you think so much about this rubbish body? God came to me in the form of a cat to punish me for my past karma. Truly, this is the grace of God'. Fortunately the scratch was healed in a few days and his sight was not damaged.[40]

Once, when Nag Mahashay went to a pond to wash his hands and feet, a snake bit a toe on his left foot. In spite of the pain, Nag Mahashay did not move, and after a short while the snake left. When Sharatkamini saw the bleeding toe she was very much worried. But Nag Mahashay said to her: 'Don't worry. It was just a water snake. Thinking my toe was food, it bit me'.[41] Indeed, his capacity to endure suffering was remarkable. When he suffered excruciating colic pain he never complained but would sometimes say: 'Victory to Sri Ramakrishna! Master, I could not serve you well with this body so it became diseased as a fitting punishment. Blessed is the colic pain which reminds me of Sri Ramakrishna! Master, it is your grace. Without your boundless grace there is no other way for a man to attain liberation'.[42]

He whom God loves, everyone loves. Although it is true that God loves all, the mystics are very special because they carry the message of God. As Sri Ramakrishna used to say, 'God is in all men, but all men are not in God'. Truly, Nag Mahashay was loved by all. When he went to the market for shopping, the shopkeepers competed with one another to sell their merchandise to him. They believed that if they could sell something to a holy man such as Nag Mahashay, then that day their sales would increase. He never bargained or asked for the change which was due him. But generally the shopkeepers sold to him at a reduced rate, or they gave him some extra quantity free of charge as a token of their love.

Yogis are frequently tested in their spiritual lives through temptations. Although some fail to pass the tests, these fallen yogis are also great teachers. Their lives reveal to us the pitfalls along the spiritual path so that we might avoid them. A real yogi, however, does not take a false step. Nag Mahashay did not wear the ochre cloth of a monk, but he was a true yogi. Once a middle-aged widow was much drawn to him. She visited him quite often and showed much love and respect for him, but Nag Mahashay understood her worldly motive. He said to his wife one day: 'Look, I think even the dogs and the vultures would not relish this rubbish body, and that woman has a craving for it. The Master is testing me in many ways. Victory to Sri Ramakrishna!' His wife forbade the widow to visit their house anymore. Later, however, the woman's life was changed, and she became a sincere devotee of Nag Mahashay.[43]

To him all women were the veritable manifestation of the Divine Mother. 'I have never touched a woman in my life, so I have nothing to do with this world', he said to his father when the latter scolded him about his unmindfulness of the household.[44] His purity was almost tangible. Desire for progeny, wealth, and name and fame simply could not appear in his mind. But as he himself observed: 'A man can overcome the temptation of gold and diamonds through renunciation, but he needs the grace of God to overcome lust. Where there is lust, there God is not; and where God is, there cannot be lust. As long as your body is not burned into ashes, do not be proud of your chastity. No one can escape maya unless the Divine Mother allows one to pass'.[45] Without having taken any monastic vows, he was a true monk. Swami Premananda once said:

> I tell you for a fact, I am not enamoured of the mere ochre cloth. I want renunciation and dispassion. I very much appreciate the life of Nag Mahashay. He did not wear the ochre cloth, and yet what a great soul he was and how great was his renunciation!
>
> When I visited Dhaka the last time, I went to Nag Mahashay's place before I left. One of his friends told me that a brahmin used to come to his house to read the Bhagavata. He would read a verse and Nag Mahashay would expound for a long time. Pandits *read* the Bhagavata, but Nag Mahashay had actually *realized* the truths it contained, and they were, therefore, as vivid to him as any sensible object.[46]

He who seeks Self-knowledge shuns carnality like poison, comfort like a demon, and crowds like a snake. Nag Mahashay, like other mystics, loved obscurity, to be away from the eyes of the public. Normally he chose to visit Sri Ramakrishna on weekdays, when few visitors were present, avoiding Sundays and holidays when crowds would come, so there is no mention of his name in the huge volume of *The Gospel of Sri Ramakrishna*.

Later in his life, when his own reputation as a holy man drew people to Deobhog to seek his company, he frequently left home secretly to visit Calcutta. The first place he went on reaching Calcutta was the Kalighat temple where he would bow down to the Divine Mother. Then he would leave his cloth bundle at his residence and go straight to Girish Chandra Ghosh to salute him. He once said about Girish: 'If one is in the company of Girish Babu for even five minutes, one gets freed from worldly delusion... He has such keen insight that he can see at a glance the innermost recess of a man's heart, and by virtue of this powerful insight he was able to recognize the Master as an avatar'.[47]

Girish also had tremendous love and regard for Nag Mahashay. He knew Nag Mahashay did not accept gifts, but in spite of that he one day presented a blanket to him. Out of his deep respect for Girish, Nag Mahashay accepted the blanket by putting it on his head and went home. Later a devotee went to visit him and found him seated with the blanket on his head. Hearing of this, Girish found a tactful way of taking it back so that Nag Mahashay might not suffer any further discomfort.[48]

Although this type of behaviour seems very strange to ordinary people, it is called in devotional scriptures *urjhita bhakti*, or exuberant devotion. When this type of devotion awakens in the heart of an aspirant his behaviour becomes erratic. For no outwardly discernable reason he may smile, cry, dance, sing, or even remain motionless like a log. The least reminder of the Beloved puts him into ecstasy. Once, for example, when he went to visit Holy Mother, the spiritual consort of Sri Ramakrishna, she gave him a piece of mango. But instead of eating it, Nag Mahashay rubbed it on his head. Holy Mother then fed him herself. She also gave him a cloth, but Nag Mahashay never used it. On special occasions he would tie it around his head. Sometimes he would say, 'Mother is more gracious than father'.[49]

After Swami Vivekananda's return from the West in 1897, Nag Mahashay came to Belur Monastery to see him. Swamiji earnestly requested him to live at the monastery, but Nag Mahashay declined because the Master had asked him to stay at home and lead the life of a householder. In the course of conversation Swamiji said to him: 'It is you who have really appreciated and understood Sri Ramakrishna. We only spend our time and energy in useless wanderings'.[50] When Swamiji heard that he was in debt, he immediately wanted to take care of it; but Nag Mahashay humbly declined to accept the gift of a monk. Swamiji expressed a desire to visit his home in Deobhog, which made him very happy. Unfortunately he could not do so during Nag Mahashay's lifetime.

Years before, when Sri Ramakrishna had introduced Nag Mahashay to Swami Vivekananda, he said: 'This man has genuine humility. There is no hypocrisy in it'.[51] Humility was one of the main traits of his character. 'I and mine' are the warp and woof of maya, which bind the soul, and these were totally obliterated from his personality. Girish once humourously remarked that the great enchantress, Mahamaya, was in trouble when she tried to bind Swami Vivekananda and Nag Mahashay: 'As she tried to trap Vivekananda he became bigger and bigger, and at last he became so big that all her fetters were too short and she had to let him go. And when she attempted to trap Nag Mahashay, he began to make himself smaller and smaller until he had at last reduced himself to such a degree that he could easily slip through the holes of her net'.[52]

One day Nag Mahashay was at Girish Ghosh's house with other disciples and devotees of Sri Ramakrishna. They were speaking about the Master when Swami Niranjanananda turned to Nag Mahashay and said: 'Well, sir, our Master used to say that one who thinks of himself as mean and wretched actually becomes so. Why then do you always think of yourself as so low and degraded?' Nag Mahashay replied: 'Ah, I see with my own eyes that I am low and degraded. How can I think that I am Shiva? You can think like that. Girish Babu can say that he is Shiva. You have such great devotion for the Lord. Where is such devotion in me? If you all help me, if the Master grants me his grace, my life will be blessed'. The utter sincerity and humility of his words silenced Swami Niranjanananda. He could neither contradict him nor could he pursue the subject any further. Girish Ghosh later said, referring to the incident: 'If a man is sincere, and if all idea of egotism has really vanished from his mind, he attains to the state of Nag Mahashay. The earth becomes blessed by the very touch of the feet of such great men'.[53]

Nag Mahashay's humble, guileless, and gentle behaviour easily conquered the hearts of all. Once two monastic disciples of Swami Vivekananda came to visit him at his village. He entertained them with great care and respect, and when it was time for them to leave, he accompanied them to the railway station. But the train was very crowded. When the two swamis tried to get in, the other passengers would not make room for them. Seeing the monks being treated disrespectfully, Nag Mahashay cried out in agony, 'O Lord, forgive these people who have ill-treated the holy men!' At the sight of his intense suffering, the passengers inside the train became ashamed of their behaviour and hurriedly made room for the monks.[54]

It is sometimes assumed that nonviolence and humility arise from weakness and faint-heartedness, but, on the contrary, they actually originate from inner moral and spiritual strength. An ideal character is one that is the combination of the gentleness of a flower and the power of a thunderbolt. Nag Mahashay's life was just such a blend of these two opposite qualities. He was humble but not cowardly. Once a distinguished rich man was criticizing Sri Ramakrishna in Nag Mahashay's presence. With great humility he pleaded with the man to stop, but the man did not pay any attention. At last Nag Mahashay became very angry. He took the man's shoe and started to beat him with it, forcing him to leave the place. That man also lost his temper and threatened Nag Mahashay's life. But after a few days the wealthy man came to Nag Mahashay and begged his forgiveness.[55]

On another occasion Nag Mahashay was going by boat from Calcutta to Belur Math to see Swami Vivekananda. As soon as the monastery came into view he bowed down with reverence. Observing his exceptional devotion towards the monastery, a passenger of the boat started to criticize the monks. Soon other passengers joined him. But Nag Mahashay could not bear it. Immediately he became furious and protested: 'What do you know about monks? You only know how to satisfy your cravings for lust and gold! You are blind, ignorant! Fie upon your tongues that speak ill of the monks!' Seeing Nag Mahashay's wrath, those people became terrified and asked the boatman to put them ashore immediately. When Swami Vivekananda heard of the incident, he remarked, 'At times it is necessary to behave like a lion'.[56]

As a son Nag Mahashay was ideal. He not only served his father with much love and attention in his old age, but he also looked after his father's spiritual life as well. Daily he read from the scriptures to his father, and he carefully protected him from the company of worldly-minded people so that Dindayal could not get any chance to listen to worldly gossip, or 'maya-purana' as he called it. Gradually, due to the spiritual influence of Nag Mahashay, a great change came over Dindayal's life. He began to devote most of his time to prayer, japam, and meditation. Swami Turiyananda once narrated the following story:

> I went to his [Nag Mahashay's] house and saw his father practising japam, sitting in a corner. Nag Mahashay said to me, 'Bless my father that he may have true devotion to God'. 'He has already got it', I replied. 'He is constantly repeating the name of God. What

more do you want?' Nag Mahashay rejoined: 'What is the use of rowing a boat which is at anchor? My father is much attached to me. What good will his japam do?' 'If he is not to love a son like you, whom else should he love?' I asked. 'Don't say so, don't say so', he cried out. 'Only bless him that he may lose all attachment for me'. Oh, what a great man Nag Mahashay was![57]

One morning, after serving his father as usual, Nag Mahashay left for the market. There was no reason for him to be especially concerned about Dindayal at this time. Although his father was aged, he seemed to be in good health. However, in his absence Dindayal was walking in the street when suddenly he fell to the ground unconscious. As soon as Nag Mahashay got the news he rushed to his father and carried him home. A doctor diagnosed the cause as apoplexy. Shortly after, at the age of eighty, Dindayal passed away while repeating the name of the Lord. Nag Mahashay also chanted the Lord's name in his father's ears and prayed for his liberation.

Nag Mahashay performed the rites and rituals as enjoined by the scriptures for his departed father, although he had to borrow money, even mortgaging his own house, for the ceremony. He later related an interesting story about his father's tremendous self-control. Once Dindayal was going by boat from Calcutta to East Bengal on business. Along the way he landed at a place where he discovered by chance a hidden jar of gold coins. Though tempted, he felt it was a sin to covet another's wealth. Immediately he covered the treasure as he had found it and left the place.[58]

Nag Mahashay never initiated anyone, but he was an awakener of souls, and his life was a source of inspiration to many people. Like his Master, he spoke only about God, and he would often remind the devotees: 'God first, and then the world' and 'A man has a right to demand money from his employer in the evening if he worked the whole day; similarly, if a man calls on God all through his life, he can force God to give him a vision or realization'.[59] If anyone addressed him as 'guru', he would knock his head on the ground and say: 'I am an insignificant person. What do I know? All of you come here to bless me with the dust of your holy feet. In this age the monastic disciples of Sri Ramakrishna are the real gurus'.[60]

Sharat Chandra Chakrabarty was a great devotee of Nag Mahashay and later wrote his biography. One day he begged Nag Mahashay to initiate him, but he refused. Seeing Sharat Babu's disappointment, Nag Mahashay said: 'Don't lose heart. Lord Shiva himself will be your guru'.[61] Binodini Mittra, the daughter of Nag Mahashay's cousin and another of his biographers, related in her book how that blessing was fulfilled:

It was May 1897. Swami Vivekananda was staying at the Alambazar monastery after returning from the West. Sharat Babu went to see Swamiji and found him resting in his room. He sat down to wait for Swamiji to get up, but all of a sudden he saw that Lord Shiva was lying where Swamiji had been. He could not believe his own eyes at first, but as he stared at the figure he could not doubt what he saw. He then remembered the boon Nag Mahashay had given him. Swamiji later initiated him.[62]

Three years after the passing away of his father, Nag Mahashay became seriously ill with colic and dysentery. He said to his wife: 'My *prarabdha karma* [action performed in a past life, the fruit of which is being reaped in the present life] has almost come to an end — only a little is left. Don't worry about this cage of flesh and bones'.[63] He refused any medical treatment, but he would take a little juice of the hinche green, a kind of medicinal creeper that grows on the surface of ponds, which Sri Ramakrishna had mentioned as being good for the stomach. He had very little body-consciousness. In spite of the cold winter weather, he left his own room and moved to the porch, using only a torn blanket for his bed.

Sharat Babu hurried to Deobhog as soon as he heard the news of Nag Mahashay's illness, and tended on him the last thirteen days of his life. Nag Mahashay said to him, 'As long as life remains in this cage of flesh and bones, please talk to me about Sri Ramakrishna and the scriptures'.[64] Three days before his passing away, he asked Sharat Babu to consult the almanac and find an auspicious date for a journey. As soon as he heard the date, he said, 'If you permit me, I shall start my journey on that day'.[65] Sharat Babu was dumbfounded. With tearful eyes he reported the conversation to Nag Mahashay's wife.

The last few days Nag Mahashay was in samadhi off and on. Because Sri Ramakrishna had asked him to stay at home and live the life of a householder, he had never gone on a pilgrimage to the holy places, although he had once gone to Gaya to perform the last rites for his father. Two days before he passed away, at 2 o'clock in the morning, he said to Sharat Babu: 'Sri Ramakrishna has come here to show me the holy places. Please tell me the names of holy places you have seen, and I will visit them one after another'. As Sharat Babu mentioned the name of each place — Hardwar, Prayag, Varanasi, and Puri — Nag Mahashay immediately had a vision of it and vividly described what he was seeing.[66] Sharat Babu knew he was witnessing the blessing of Sri Ramakrishna upon his disciple, yet, seeing Nag Mahashay's pain and suffering, he could not help thinking that God was a cruel Master. But Nag Mahashay read his mind and said: 'Please, never doubt the boundless mercy of God. What good will this body be to the world? Look, I am bedridden; I cannot serve you, so Sri Ramakrishna, out of compassion, is taking away this body'. Then he said in a feeble voice, 'Let the body and its suffering know each other; O my mind, you be happy'.[67]

On December 27, 1899, the auspicious time of his final departure came. Nag Mahashay was in bhava samadhi. Sharat Babu began to chant the name of Sri Ramakrishna in his ear and, placing the picture of the Master in front of him, said, 'This is the picture of your Master, in whose name you have renounced everything'. Nag Mahashay opened his eyes and saw the face of his beloved Master. With folded hands he saluted him and murmured, 'Grace, grace — you blessed me out of your boundless mercy'. He then slowly merged into mahasamadhi.[68]

16

Suresh Chandra Datta

The Hindu scriptures say, 'A householder should establish his life in spirituality; he should follow the path of truth; and he should dedicate his actions and their results to the Eternal Being'.[1] Human society is nothing but the sum total of individuals. If the life of an individual householder is weak, worldly, dishonest, and disreputable, then the family life, social life, and national life are also polluted. Therefore, for the betterment of society the character of each individual being must be developed. Of course, there are few ideal citizens in any society, but those who do exist protect the society from various vicissitudes and are a source of inspiration to all.

Suresh Chandra Datta was an ideal householder disciple of Sri Ramakrishna. He was born in 1850 at Hatkhola (in West Calcutta), in an aristocratic family. From boyhood Suresh was honest, humble, simple, and self-reliant. Originally a Brahmo, he first heard about Sri Ramakrishna from Keshab Chandra Sen.

Suresh and Durga Charan Nag, who had moved to Calcutta from Dhaka to study medicine, both lived in the same area. They became close friends, and Suresh used to address Durga Charan as 'Uncle'. Durga Charan was then studying homeopathic medicine, and since it required some knowledge of English he began to study *Hiley's English Grammar*. But his English pronunciation was poor, and Suresh would tease him by saying, 'Your pronunciation has a strong accent peculiar to all people of East Bengal'.[2] However, since Suresh had a good command of the English language, he was able to help Durga Charan.

Every evening Suresh would go to Durga Charan's house to discuss religion. Suresh was a staunch follower of the Brahmo Samaj, which advocated the belief in God without form, while Durga Charan was an orthodox Hindu who obeyed every scriptural injunction. Daily the two men had heated religious discussions, but their different views were never reconciled. One day, in one of their friendly squabbles, Durga Charan said to Suresh: 'The gods and

231

goddesses of the Hindus as well as the formless Brahman are all true. But to attain Brahman is so difficult, I doubt whether one or two in a million can ever reach this stage. Hence arises the necessity to believe in the various gods and goddesses of Hinduism... Do you think that the Vedas, Puranas, Tantras, and mantras are all false?'[3] Suresh retorted: 'Uncle, set aside your scriptures. I have no faith in them'.

From time to time Suresh would take Durga Charan to attend Keshab Sen's lectures. They would also meditate with Brahmo devotees at night on the bank of the Ganga. Durga Charan longed for God and a guru to guide him. Fortunately, Suresh happened to hear at Keshab's Brahmo Samaj about Sri Ramakrishna, the Dakshineswar saint, but he waited for two months before he suggested to Durga Charan that they visit the Master. That very day after lunch they left for Dakshineswar.

It was a hot summer day in April or May, probably in 1883.[4] They arrived at Dakshineswar at two o'clock in the afternoon. Both were delighted to see the panoramic view of the temple garden and to feel its peaceful atmosphere. Slowly they reached the eastern verandah of Sri Ramakrishna's room and asked a bearded gentleman named Pratap Chandra Hazra about the saint who lived there. But Hazra deliberately misinformed them, saying that the saint had gone to Chandannagore that day.[5]

Weary and dejected, they were about to return home when they noticed someone inside the room beckoning them to enter. It was Sri Ramakrishna. He received them graciously, asked them to sit down, and explained that Hazra often told that story in order to keep strangers away. Then he asked them to sit closer and began to chat.

The Master talked to them for some time and in the course of conversation said: 'Live in this world like a mud fish. There is nothing wrong in staying at home. The mud fish lives in the mud but is not soiled by it. Similarly, live in this world but never be contaminated by its evils'.[6] Then Sri Ramakrishna sent them to the Panchavati grove to meditate. After half an hour they returned to the Master's room, and Sri Ramakrishna took them around to the various temples in the Dakshineswar compound. He first walked to the twelve Shiva temples and prostrated before each deity, circumambulating their respective shrines. Durga Charan followed the Master's example, but Suresh merely looked on, for he had no faith in Hindu gods and goddesses.

Sri Ramakrishna took them next to the Krishna and the Kali temples. Both Suresh and Durga Charan were astonished by the ecstatic mood which overpowered the Master when he entered the Kali temple. As a restless child holds the hem of its mother's garment and moves around her, so the Master went around the image of Kali and prostrated before her. At about five o'clock, after returning to the Master's room, Suresh and Durga Charan took their leave of Sri Ramakrishna, who gave them this parting advice: 'Come again. Our acquaintance will grow deeper if you keep on coming regularly for some time'.[7]

The experiences of that first meeting left an indelible impression on their minds, and they could not help but talk about Sri Ramakrishna. The next week they both visited the Master again. On seeing these two sincere seekers, Sri Ramakrishna exclaimed in an ecstatic mood: 'You have done well in coming again. I have been waiting here for you for a long time'.[8] The Master once again asked them to meditate in the Panchavati grove.

Suresh visited the Master eight or nine times in the company of Durga Charan. Undoubtedly he must have visited Sri Ramakrishna many more times alone or with others, otherwise he could not have compiled so many of the Master's teachings, which he later published in a book. Suresh was not the first, however, to record and publish Sri Ramakrishna's teachings, but the second.

The first book of Sri Ramakrishna's teachings was *Paramahamser Ukti*, recorded in Bengali by Keshab Chandra Sen and published on January 24, 1878. Later, Girish Chandra Sen, a follower of Keshab, added more teachings to that work, along with a short life of the Master. This book consisted of one hundred and eighty-four teachings of Sri Ramakrishna.

The second recorder of *Paramahamsa Ramakrishner Ukti* was Suresh Chandra Datta, who published 'Part One' in Bengali on December 23, 1884 (during the Master's lifetime), and 'Part Two', in 1886. Gradually he collected more teachings and in 1894 published a six-part edition of his book, each part containing one hundred teachings. In this edition Suresh included a short biographical sketch of Sri Ramakrishna. In the collection of sayings and in the publication of the book, he was greatly assisted by Haramohan Mittra, another householder disciple of the Master. Later the six parts, along with added material, were published in one Bengali volume, *Sri Sri Ramakrishnadever Upadesh*, containing nine hundred and fifty teachings.[9] In the introduction Suresh stated his heart's realization — that Sri Ramakrishna was an Incarnation of God.

The third recorder was Ram Chandra Datta, who first published *Tattwasara* in 1885, and *Tattwaprakashika* in 1886. This Gospel consisted of three hundred teachings. The fourth recorder was Mahendra Nath Gupta (M.), who published five volumes in Bengali under the title *Sri Sri Ramakrishna Kathamrita* (1902–1932). Finally, the fifth recorder was Swami Brahmananda, who compiled *Sri Sri Ramakrishna Upadesh*. His collection was first published on January 14, 1905, and it consisted of two hundred and forty-eight teachings of the Master. All five *Gospels* of Sri Ramakrishna were first published in Bengali (Sri Ramakrishna's mother tongue), and only the last two have been translated into English.

Suresh played an important part in spreading the ideas of Sri Ramakrishna. He freely distributed his book on the Master's birth anniversary. Moreover, he wrote a number of Bengali booklets (*Ramakrishna Samalochana, Bhagavan Ramakrishna and the Brahmo Samaj, Ramakrishna Lilamrita, Sadhak Sahachar, Narada Sutra*, etc.) to publicize the Master's unique life and message.[10]

In his biography Suresh mentioned a few incidents about the Master which he himself had witnessed. For example, one day the Master assumed a mood of a woman. He put on his dhoti (man's cloth) like a woman, and showed Suresh how a woman charms a man. He acted as a housewife and began to serve food to an imaginary husband. When the husband refused to eat any more, the wife said, 'Please have another piece of sandesh and another piece of jilipi'. As she fed her husband the wife let him know what she wanted: 'My neighbour friend got a seven-string necklace yesterday. I wish I could have one like that'. Suresh was dumbfounded as he watched the Master, perfect to the last detail in the way a wife behaves, moves her hands, glances at her husband, and wheedles a necklace out of him.[11]

On another occasion Suresh went to Dakshineswar and noticed that the Master was talking to a young man. After a while, when the young man had left the room, the Master said to Suresh: 'This person does not believe in God. He regards monks and holy people as thieves and cheats, and he thinks I am a hypocrite and a fraud'. Presently the young man reentered the room. At once the Master smiled and talked to him in a friendly manner. When the man wanted to leave, Sri Ramakrishna said, 'Please come another day'. Suresh was moved, watching the unselfish love of the Master.[12]

In 1885, during the Afghan War, Suresh received a job in the military department earning a monthly salary of two hundred rupees. He was assigned to Quetta, in the northwestern part of India. Before his departure from Calcutta, Durga Charan urged him to receive initiation from the Master. But Suresh had no faith in mantras or in

God with form. After a prolonged discussion with Durga Charan on this point, they agreed that Suresh should abide by the wishes of the Master.

The next day both men went to Dakshineswar, and Durga Charan raised the question of initiation. 'Yes, Durga Charan is right', Sri Ramakrishna said to Suresh. 'A person should practise spiritual disciplines under the direction of a guru. What prevents you from admitting this?' 'Sir, I have no faith in mantras', replied Suresh humbly. 'All right', said the Master. 'Do not worry about it now. Everything will come in time'.[13]

In Quetta it was not long before Suresh began to feel very keenly the need for initiation. He continued his spiritual disciplines as usual. During this time an ugly incident tested his strength of character. At that time the British Government of India was pouring money into the war, and all financial bills submitted by officers were automatically approved in order to expedite war supplies. Taking advantage of this situation, Suresh's superior officer drafted a false bill misappropriating funds. To protect himself from possible detection, the officer offered one third of the amount to Suresh, who not only flatly refused to accept the bribe but also threatened to resign from his post to prevent possible implication. Humiliated, the officer became furious and threatened to take severe military action against Suresh if he resigned from his post. The helpless Suresh was forced to continue working under the officer. Fortunately, however, he knew a kindhearted Englishman who was the medical officer of the department. Having no other solution, Suresh approached him and told him the story. The doctor, who admired Suresh's honesty, certified him as physically unfit for military service. Thus Suresh was discharged from his duties, being detained only long enough for a replacement.

As soon as he was relieved of his job, Suresh headed for Calcutta. He had only twenty rupees in his hand, which he spent during his first few days in Varanasi. Penniless, he continued on foot to Calcutta, five hundred miles away. When the long walk exhausted him, Suresh would chant from the Bhagavad Gita, his only companion. He did not beg for food during the journey, relying instead on whatever the villagers offered him. In this way he travelled as far as Bhagalpur, where a generous person bought him a train ticket to Calcutta.[14]

Arriving in Calcutta, Suresh had to find a job to support his family. His younger brother, who earned only twenty-five rupees a month, should not, Suresh felt, be burdened with the responsibility of his wife and daughter. Being of an independent disposition, he found a temporary solution to the problem. After managing to collect a little money Suresh went to a potato market and bought a forty pound sack of potatoes. He then engaged a porter to carry the sack to the other side of the Ultadingi bridge, to a thinly-populated suburb of Calcutta. Hiding his regular clothing in a bag, he donned a torn cloth, and like a common vegetable vendor, sold the potatoes door-to-door, earning half a rupee a day. In this way he managed to maintain his family, who had no idea of what he was doing. Meanwhile he looked for a good job, and after several weeks he found one at sixty rupees a month. Content with plain food and clothing, he devoted more time to spiritual pursuits. Thus he set the example of an ideal devotee possessing unwavering faith.

Another incident occurred in Calcutta which indicates his uncompromising honesty and faith in God. The Lipton Tea Company had sponsored an English essay competition. The subject was 'Tea', and the winner was to receive a prize of five hundred rupees. Suresh won the competition. The British director of the company in London was so pleased with his writing that he offered Suresh a job with a monthly salary of two hundred and fifty rupees. Suresh took the job, only to give it up shortly thereafter when another English executive directed him to adulterate the tea formula. Thus Suresh changed his jobs many times with the faith that God would always provide for him.

One day in 1886 Suresh went to see Sri Ramakrishna at the Cossipore garden house. The Master was then bedridden because of his illness. He asked Suresh: 'Where is your doctor friend? He is said to be a good physician. Tell him to come here sometime soon'.[15] Seeing the fragile condition of the Master, Suresh could not bring himself to ask for initiation. Instead, he went home and informed Durga Charan that the Master wanted to see him.

Suresh repented for not having followed his friend's advice about asking for initiation. After the Master's passing he lamented and passed the nights in prayer and meditation on the bank of the Ganga. One night while crying to God he fell asleep on the river bank. Before daybreak the next morning he dreamt that Sri Ramakrishna had come out of the water and approached him. The Master uttered a mantram in his ear. As Suresh was about to take the dust of Sri Ramakrishna's feet, the form of the Master disappeared.[16]

Suresh kept in contact with Swami Vivekananda, who visited his home several times, as well as other disciples of Sri Ramakrishna. At one time, when the Ramakrishna monastery was at Alambazar,

Suresh and Durga Charan stayed overnight with the monks. The two friends would also visit Dakshineswar and reminisce about their memorable days with the Master.

After receiving initiation from Swami Vivekananda, Sharat Chandra Chakrabarty wanted to offer a special worship to the Master. Swamiji, however, discouraged him because it would have been difficult for Sharat to collect all the necessary articles and then reach the Alambazar monastery from Calcutta early enough in the morning. Suresh came to know about this and assured Sharat that he would arrange everything for the worship of the Master. The next morning, at four o'clock, Suresh accompanied Sharat to the New Market of Calcutta, bought everything needed, and then sent Sharat to the monastery by carriage. When Sharat requested Suresh to ride in the carriage with him, Suresh said: 'No, I cannot go by carriage. I am carrying a pot of sweet curd for the Master, so I must walk. Otherwise it may spill with the jerking of the carriage. I want to be careful, because it is to be offered to the Master'. Sharat reached the monastery at sunrise, and Swamiji, seeing that his disciple had bought all the Master's favourite things, said in amazement: 'This is definitely not the result of your management. Tell me who did the shopping'. When Sharat mentioned Suresh's name, Swamiji said, 'Why didn't you bring him with you?' Sharat told him the story, and Swamiji, with tears in his eyes, said, 'Look, he whom the Master has touched, has become gold'.[17]

Beyond the gaze of public eyes, Suresh led an intense spiritual life as taught by Sri Ramakrishna. Although he did not take monastic vows, his life was adorned with all the godly qualities — nonattachment, purity, unselfishness, truthfulness, and love for God. Suresh died in Calcutta on November 18, 1912.

Navagopal Ghosh (1832-1909)

17

Navagopal Ghosh and Nistarini Ghosh

'If you find a companion who is good, wise, and loving, walk with him all the way and overcome all dangers', said Buddha in the Dhammapada. 'And if you do not find a good companion, then live alone and walk alone "like an elephant in the forest" '.[1] It is not easy to live alone in this world. Only a person of renunciation who possesses nothing can move about freely and fearlessly. Even when people go on pilgrimage they usually travel with others for safety and convenience. In the spiritual journey it is God's grace when a husband and wife have the same nature, same interest, and same goal. For the seekers of God it is a great boon to have harmony and peace in family life. Spiritual life requires a good environment, mental serenity, and holy association. Therefore, a couple possessing mutual love, respect, and trust progresses faster spiritually.

Navagopal Ghosh and his wife, Nistarini, were blessed with a harmonious marriage. They had several children. Both went to see Sri Ramakrishna with Kishori Mohan Roy, a devotee from Krishnanagar, some time in 1882. On their first visit the Master asked for their names and inquired where they lived. He then advised Navagopal to sing kirtan every day. The couple returned home and did not visit the Master again for three years, but Navagopal, following the instruction of the Master, sang kirtan every day with his family, using a drum and cymbals.

Sri Ramakrishna remembered Navagopal, and one day in 1885, when Kishori arrived at Dakshineswar, the Master asked him: 'Hello, how is that person who came here with you three years ago? He lives in Badur-bagan. He is a big officer, and he gives medicine free to poor people. If you see him, please ask him to visit me at least once'.[2]

Hearing about the Master's inquiry from Kishori, Navagopal was delighted and amazed. He thought: 'Sri Ramakrishna is respected by all and is considered to be an avatar, yet he remembers an insignificant person like me even after such a long time!' The Master's compassion brought tears to his eyes. The following Sunday

Navagopal went to Dakshineswar with his wife and children. The Master asked him why he had not visited sooner. Navagopal replied that his family responsibilities did not allow him much time. Nevertheless, he had followed the Master's instruction and daily glorified the name of God by singing kirtan during the last three years. Sri Ramakrishna assured him that he would not have to be confined to any more preparatory devotion. Then he advised Navagopal to visit him three more times, saying that would be enough for him to attain the higher realm of bhakti (devotion).[3]

Navagopal was born in 1832 in the village of Begampur, Howrah, Bengal. He was a high official of the Henderson Company and earned three hunded rupees a month. His strong body was of dark complexion, and his face radiated joy. He was very simple, generous, and devoted to God. After the death of two wives, Navagopal had married Nistarini. Gradually Sri Ramakrishna and Navagopal's family became very close and Navagopal began to visit Dakshineswar frequently. The Master was very fond of Nistarini's children, especially Suresh, who was a good singer and drum player even at the age of six.

During this period devotees often arranged festivals in their Calcutta homes on Sundays and invited Sri Ramakrishna and other devotees. They would hire a singer and musicians to entertain the Master and would prepare a sumptuous feast. Once Navagopal expressed a desire to arrange such a festival, and the Master agreed to visit his home. Navagopal arranged everything according to the instructions of Ram Chandra Datta, who among the devotees had the most experience in arranging festivals. Navagopal decorated his worship hall and engaged a scholar to read and explain the Bhagavatam. As soon as the Master arrived, the scholar stopped reading and Banoary, a Vaishnava singer stationed in the courtyard, started to sing Krishna kirtan.

The Master had been seated in the worship hall, but suddenly he jumped up and rushed to the courtyard and stood near the singer and the musicians in the pose of Krishna with his flute in his hand. He was in deep samadhi. Navagopal brought a long garland for the Master, which he placed around his neck. The garland had a lovely fragrance and was so long that it touched the Master's feet. Other devotees encircled the Master and sang kirtan in chorus. Some of them experienced ecstasy. When Sri Ramakrishna returned to the normal plane of consciousness he took his seat, but the ecstatic mood continued. At that time Ram told Navagopal to ask the Master for a boon. Navagopal prostrated himself before the Master and said: 'I am drowned in worldliness. Kindly tell me how I may get out of it'. 'Don't worry', replied the Master. 'Remember me once a day if you can do nothing else'.[4]

Navagopal then saw a glowing light on the face of the Master. At first he thought it was an optical illusion, so he went to wash his eyes. But again he saw the same light. Amazed, Navagopal asked his brother Jaygopal whether he saw anything unusual in the Master. 'No, he looks just as usual', replied his brother. At last Navagopal realized that the Master, out of mercy, had shown him his divine, luminous form.

In the meantime Nistarini had prepared dinner for the Master and escorted him to the inner apartments. Many women devotees were present and they took the dust of the Master's feet. The Master sat on a seat on the floor, and Nistarini served one dish after another. She brought the Master's favourite sandesh (sweet). A desire came to her mind to feed the Master sweets with her own hand. Sri Ramakrishna read her thought and said: 'What? You want to feed me with your own hand?' After a pause he smiled and told her: 'All right. Feed me'. Saying so, he opened his mouth. As Nistarini put a sweet into the mouth of the Master, she saw that a mysterious being [Kundalini, or the Serpent Power] gulped it down. Becoming frightened, she stopped feeding the Master. The Master slowly ate by himself and gave the prasad to Nistarini. She felt reluctant to eat anything before feeding her other guests, but when the Master persuaded her to partake of the prasad, she obeyed and sent the remaining prasad downstairs. The news of what Nistarini had seen in Sri Ramakrishna's mouth spread quickly among the devotees, and immediately there arose a loud uproar among them, and they all shared that prasad of the Master. Hearing their noise, the Master told Nistarini that he had asked her to take the prasad first because he knew that after it was offered to the guests there would be none left. Then the Master went downstairs and the singer sang some more songs.[5]

Nistarini felt very free with the Master, a rare trait in spiritual life. This feeling of freedom originates from simplicity, purity, love, and unselfishness. God loves to play with these free souls, because they do not bother him with worldly desires. Sri Ramakrishna said of Nistarini: 'She is a great soul. She is a partial incarnation of one of the ten forms of the Divine Mother'.[6] On another occasion the Master said, 'Through the influence of his wife, Navagopal escaped from maya'.[7]

The Master was very fond of Nistarini and would allow her to touch his feet. Later she related some incidents that occurred during her association with the Master: 'When I would come, he would send all the gentlemen out of the room and talk to me alone. Once he asked me why I came — what I found in him to draw me so often to Dakshineswar. I replied: "It is hard to explain. That which made Prahlada forget his father, Dhruva and others forget their parents, that I find here".

'A friend had told me I should chant *Haribol* [repeat the name of the Lord] and I did so. But it caused great perplexity in my mind. "Here I am calling upon Hari", I said to myself, "and yet I am told that one should seek salvation through the guru alone". I went to Dakshineswar to see Sri Ramakrishna but before I could explain my trouble, he said to me, "Guru and Hari are one" '.[8]

On another occasion Nistarini was amazed to see the Master's power of mimicry. Sri Ramakrishna had dressed himself in a sari (woman's cloth) and put on bangles and jewels. He then acted just like a young wife begging her husband for more jewels. For an hour or more the Master kept up the fun.[9]

Nistarini knew that the Master was omniscient and that he answered the sincere prayers of devotees. She described the following incident to Sister Devamata (Laura Glenn, an American devotee):

> One Sunday we were all at Dakshineswar. A poor woman came bringing four *rasogollas* [sweet, juicy cheese balls] for the Master, but his room was so full of devotees that she dared not enter and offer them to him. She went to Mother's verandah [nahabat] and began to weep bitterly that she had come so far and now she must go away without seeing the Master. We knew too that to bring even these four rasogollas meant a great sacrifice for her. Suddenly while she was thus weeping, Gurumaharaj [Sri Ramakrishna] appeared on the round verandah overlooking the river. He stood for a few minutes gazing at the Ganga, then he came down the steps and walked quickly towards Mother's house. When he entered the verandah, he looked hither and thither as if searching for someone. Then, seeing the poor woman, he went to her and said, 'I am feeling very hungry; can you give me something to eat?' The woman in great joy offered him her rasogollas. He ate all the four with evident relish and returned to his room, while she went home with her heart full of happiness.[10]

One of the characteristics of a Divine Incarnation is that he gives shelter to those who take refuge in him. His all-encompassing love is not confined only to human beings. Even the animals find tender shelter with him. Nistarini witnessed this in Sri Ramakrishna. She told Sister Devamata: 'Once a cat took refuge in Sri Ramakrishna's room at Dakshineswar* with her little kittens. The mother cat would sometimes sleep on his bed near his feet and if he reached down and touched her with his hand, at once she would get up and seem almost to make *pranam* [bow before him]. It troubled the Master much to know what to do with the cat and her kittens, for he felt that they did not get proper food at the temple; so one day when I came to see him, he asked me, "Will you do something for me?" I clasped my hands before him and said, "Whatever it is, that I must do". But again he asked and I replied as before. Then he told me of the cats and asked me to take them. "Remember", he said, "that they have taken refuge with me, so see that they get the best of care".

'I took them home and whenever I went to the temple he would question me in every detail about the cats: Were they getting proper food? Had the kittens grown? What did I mean to do with them? He was much concerned lest I might give them away to someone who would not treat them kindly, and again he would remind me, "Remember, they took refuge with me". The mother cat never had another family. At the end of a year she was suddenly taken ill and died. As she was dying I poured Ganga water into her mouth and repeated Gurumaharaj's name'.[11]

Once on the day of the Ganga worship, Navagopal hired a boat and visited Dakshineswar with Girish and other devotees. On the way they discussed whether or not one should bathe in the Ganga on that auspicious day. Since it was raining and there was a tremendous crowd at the bathing ghat, they were not eager to do so. Above all, they had strong faith that if they could see the Master, they would receive merit comparable to bathing in the Ganga. When they reached the Master, he said to them immediately: 'What is the matter with you? Will you not bathe in the Ganga? Today is *dashahara*, a very auspicious day. One should bathe in the Ganga'. At once all devotees went to the Ganga and bathed.[12]

On September 1, 1885, Navagopal went to visit the Master at Dakshineswar. It was the Janmashtami day, the birthday of Krishna. Many devotees had come, including Girish, who was drunk. When Girish raised the question of guru and Ishta [Chosen Deity], the Master said, 'He who is the Ishta appears in the form of the guru'. And again, 'The guru disappears into the form of the Ishta'.

A Devotee: 'Guru's head and disciple's feet'.

Girish (*joyously*): 'Yes! Yes! It is true'.

*According to another version, this incident happened at Cossipore.

Nistarini Ghosh (Wife of Navagopal Ghosh)
(?-1932)

Navagopal: 'But listen to its meaning. The disciple's head belongs to the guru; and the guru's feet belong to the disciple. Do you understand?'.

Girish: 'No, that is not the meaning. Haven't you seen the child climbing on the head of the father? That is why the disciple's feet are mentioned'.

Navagopal: 'But then the disciple must feel like a young baby'.

The Master settled their argument with an analogy: 'There are two classes of devotees. One class has the nature of a kitten. The kitten depends completely on its mother. It accepts whatever its mother does for it...There is another class of devotees. They have the nature of the young monkey. The young monkey clings to its mother with might and main. The devotees who behave like the young monkey have a slight idea of being the doer... The aspirants of both classes are devotees of God... He alone does everything. He alone is the Guru and He alone is the Ishta. He alone gives us knowledge and devotion'.[13]

Nirode, a son of Navagopal, who later became Swami Ambikananda of the Ramakrishna Order, wrote in his memoirs: 'My parents were devotees of Sri Ramakrishna and often visited him at Dakshineswar. During her pregnancy my mother decided that if a son was born to her she would dedicate him to the service of Sri Ramakrishna. Through the grace of the Lord I was the son born to her. She resolved to keep her promise. One day, when I was a few weeks old, my mother carried me snugly bundled up in a sheet to Dakshineswar. My father accompanied us. Sri Ramakrishna, in an ecstatic mood, was standing alone. As soon as he saw my parents, he said to my mother, "Hello, what have you brought for me?" Mother placed me at the feet of the Master and told him, "I have brought you this offering". Sri Ramakrishna looked at me for a few moments and remarked: "Ah! What a nice child! You offer it to me? Good!" He took me on his lap, put his right palm on my head as a blessing, and then placed me back in my mother's arms, saying: "Take care of this child now, but know that he belongs to me. In due time I will take him back". Years later when I joined the Ramakrishna Monastery, my mother was the happiest of all, for she felt that Sri Ramakrishna had accepted me'.[14]

On January 1, 1886 (Kalpataru Day), Sri Ramakrishna blessed many devotees by his touch at the Cossipore garden house, which lifted them into the higher realms of consciousness. On that auspicious day the Master fulfilled the prayers of most of the devotees. Seeing Navagopal, Ram Chandra Datta said: 'Hello, sir, what are you doing?

The Master has become a kalpataru [wishfulfilling tree] today. Please go to him right now. If you have anything to ask for, this is the right time'. Navagopal rushed to the Master and, bowing down to him, asked, 'Master, what will happen to me?' After a little pause, the Master asked, 'Will you be able to practise a little japam and meditation?' Navagopal replied: 'I am a family man with several children. Moreover, I am very busy with my various household duties and taking care of my family members. Where is the time to practise spiritual disciplines?' The Master kept quiet for a while and then said, 'Can't you even repeat the Lord's name a few times regularly?' 'I don't have time, Master'. 'All right! Will you be able to repeat my name a few times?' 'Yes, that I can do'. Then the Master said: 'That will do. You will not have to do anything else'.[15]

When the Master was ill in Cossipore, Nistarini would visit him quite often carrying some sweets for him. She related the following story to Sister Devamata: 'As I stood hesitatingly before him, he asked, "What do you want?" "I want to give you some sweetmeats", I said. "Very well!" he said, and he let me put some in his mouth. Still I stood before him. "Are you satisfied?" he asked. "No? Then what do you want?" I clasped my hands and answered, "I want to give you more sweetmeats". He let me put a little more in his mouth, and seeing me still unsatisfied, he asked the question a third time. When again I asked to feed him, he said: "No, no more now. Wait. In my *sukshma sharira* [subtle body] I shall take all the sweetmeats you and everyone can offer me" '.[16]

Nistarini told Devamata another significant episode in connection with the picture of Sri Ramakrishna (shrine pose): 'Once I went to Cossipore garden, but I found so many visitors there that I could not go upstairs [where the Master's room was]. I waited for some time and then Gurumaharaj sent down one of his photographs, saying, "Tell her to be content with looking at this today". Later he told me, in referring to the picture, that it would "travel in railway carriages and on ocean steamers and by bearers, and that people would carry it in their pockets and even on their watch chains" '.[17]

After the passing away of the Master in 1886, Navagopal and his wife lived on their memories of Sri Ramakrishna. When Navagopal would return from his office, a servant would wait near the gate with a bag of candies. All the children of that area came to know that they would get candies from Navagopal if they danced and loudly chanted 'Jai Ramakrishna' (Victory to Ramakrishna). This became a daily affair. When Navagopal would pass through the street, the children would call, 'Here comes Jai Ramakrishna!' Thus he became very popular in that area, and the children would rush to him for candies.

Towards the end of his life Navagopal moved from Calcutta to Ramakrishnapur, Howrah (on the west side of the Ganga). He was attracted to that place because of the similarity of its name to that of the Master. Once in his new house he decided to install a porcelain image of Sri Ramakrishna in the shrine. On that occasion he invited Swami Vivekananda and other disciples and devotees of the Master. It was February 6, 1898. Swami Vivekananda arrived at the ghat of Ramakrishnapur by boat from Belur Math. He was dressed in regular ochre cloth with a turban on his head. He was barefoot. Many people stood assembled on both sides of the road to catch a glimpse of Swamiji. He led the procession singing the famous nativity song on Sri Ramakrishna, 'Who art thou laid on the lap of a poor brahmin mother?...' and he himself played the khol (an earthen drum).

Navagopal and Nistarini received Swamiji with reverence and later took him to the shrine. Hearing Swamiji speaking highly of every arrangement, Nistarini said to him: 'What ability do we have to worship and serve the Master? We have only a poor home and little means. Please bless us by installing the Master in our shrine'. Swamiji humorously replied: 'Your Master never had in his fourteen generations such a marble-floored room to live in! He had his birth in that rural thatched cottage and passed his days without caring for comfort. And if he does not live here so excellently served, where else should he live?' Swamiji's comment made everybody laugh. After dedicating the shrine, Swamiji composed extemporaneously the salutation mantram of Sri Ramakrishna: 'I bow down to Ramakrishna, who established religion, embodying in himself the reality of all religions and being thus the foremost of Divine Incarnations'.[18]

In 1903 Navagopal and his family went on a pilgrimage to Vrindaban and stayed at Balaram Basu's retreat house, where Swamis Brahmananda and Turiyananda were then practising austerity. Nirode became very close to Swami Brahmananda and became his disciple. He was an accomplished singer and the swami made him his attendant. On that occasion Navagopal went with Swami Brahmananda to visit Prayag and Vindhyachal.

After retirement Navagopal used to bathe in the Ganga every day, and on his way back home he would chant 'Jai Ramakrishna'. Many people would join with him in the chanting and he would distribute sweets among them. His daily duty was to give medicine from the charitable dispensary; those who were very poor would receive food

from him. He performed kirtan at his house every day and the neighbours would join in. Thus he spread the message of the Master. Through
contact with him many people became devotees of Sri Ramakrishna.
His mind dwelled on the Master, and as a result maya could not over-
whelm him. Everyone else in his family was full of grief when his married
daughter died, but the ever-joyful Navagopal said: Everything
happens according to the will of the Master. It is needless to lament'.[19]

In 1909, at the age of seventy-seven, Navagopal passed away. Before
his death he blessed his wife and other members of his family, saying:
'Please don't grieve for me. The human body is subject to destruction.
I am not the doer. It is the Master who does everything. We are his
children. He will look after you. Giving up lamentation, please chant
the name of Sri Ramakrishna'.[20] Then, while consciously chanting the
name of the Master, Navagopal breathed his last. Those present saw
an expression of radiant joy on his face without any trace of pain.

Nistarini outlived her husband by many years. She was very close
to Holy Mother and other direct disciples of the Master. When the
monks became extremely sick at the monastery, she would take them
to her home and arrange proper diet and medicine for them, serving
them as if they were her own children. Because her son was a monk,
the other monks felt very free with her and respected her. Swami
Brahmananda stayed at her home for some time.

Nistarini took her granddaughter Rani to Belur Math before the
girl's marriage and sought blessings from Swami Brahmananda. The
swami blessed Rani, touching her head. When they had left he said to
Swami Shivananda, 'This girl will marry but family life is not meant
for her'. After her marriage she returned from her husband's home.
An unknown fear possessed her. She would cry to the Master in the
shrine, 'Master, protect my life'. Nistarini again took Rani to Belur
Math and said to Swami Brahmananda, 'Maharaj, Rani is married but
she does not want to go back to her husband'. The swami said, 'Your
health is not good. Who will take care of the shrine? Henceforth, Rani
will serve the Master'. Nistarini then asked him: 'If you knew that
family life was not meant for her, why did you not tell me
beforehand? I would not have spent so much money for her
marriage'. 'It was in her destiny', replied Swami Brahmananda. Later
he initiated Rani, and she lived like a nun. Holy Mother, hearing
Rani's story, told her: 'My child, this world is a hot frying pan. The
Master saved you from it'.[21]

When Nistarini had taken the responsibility of the cat at
Dakshineswar, the Master blessed her, saying: 'May all good attend
you. May you have the vision of your Chosen Deity'. Her Chosen

Deity was Ramachandra. One day in the later part of her life, while repeating her mantram she saw Lord Rama in front of her. As she was about to take the dust of his feet, she saw her beloved guru, Ramakrishna, in place of Ramachandra. Then the Master said to her, smiling, 'Now you know who I am'.[22]

As Nistarini grew old she suffered from dropsy. Still she continued her service to the Master. She would ask her children to sprinkle a little Ganga water on her head and take her to the kitchen. There she would make sandesh for the Master. When somebody tried to dissuade her, she would reply: 'What do you mean? I fed the Master with my own hand. I promised him that I would serve him. Now as long as I am alive, I shall do so'. Others would make luchi (fried bread) and other dishes, but Nistarini always made the Master's favourite sweet.[23]

When Nistarini became bedridden, she could not bear the touch of any impure person. Monks were then sent from Belur Math to serve her. On March 20, 1932, Nistarini hugged the picture of Sri Ramakrishna, repeated his name, and in deep meditation slowly passed away. When news of her death reached Belur Math, Swami Shivananda said to the monks:

'They are not just ordinary mortals; they are the companions of the Master. They come in every age with the avatar to play their respective parts in his divine drama. When Holy Mother was in Vrindaban [1886–87], she went one day to attend the vesper service at the Radharaman temple. There she saw Nirode's mother [Nistarini] fanning Lord Krishna with a *chamara* [yak's tail]. Later the Mother said to her women companions, "During the vesper I saw Navagopal Babu's wife fanning the deity with a *chamara*". Ah, what love and what devotion she had for the Master! She was, as it were, like one of the gopis [cowherd girls of Vrindaban]. Once her sons told her: "Mother, you talk so much about the Master; now look, how your Master has put us into straitened circumstances! Enough of it! Don't talk too much about the Master anymore". To this she replied: "What do you say? I love the Master. I have given my heart once for all to him. How foolishly you boys talk!"...

'They were bought with his love; they dedicated themselves at his feet. Ah! The more I think of her love for the Master, the more I feel a tickling sensation in my heart. Lust is self-centred and love is God-centred. Nirode's mother once told somebody, "You may do all kinds of spiritual practices, but your real success lies in knowing how to die". Well, she proved it in her life. Hugging the Master's picture, and repeating his name, she has gone to the Master'.[24]

Adhar Lal Sen (1855-1885)

18

Adhar Lal Sen

It is said in the Mahabharata: 'Human life is not eternal, and moreover no one knows when the all-devouring death will come. Therefore one should begin to practise religion when one is young'.[1] Sri Ramakrishna knew that Adhar's life would be short, so one day he said to him, 'Do quickly whatever you want to do'.[2] The Master implied that he should associate with holy people and strive to realize God. Adhar understood what the Master meant, and for six months he visited Sri Ramakrishna every evening after working at his office. For this he had to spend two and a half rupees every day for the carriage fare, and the trip took about an hour and a half each way. Sometimes he was so tired that he would fall asleep on the carpet in the Master's room. A few people criticized Adhar for this, but the Master said to them: 'What do you people know? This is the Divine Mother's place. It is the abode of peace. Instead of engaging in worldly talk, he sleeps. That is all right. A little peace still comes to such people'.[3] Before the main gate of the temple garden was closed at 10:00 P.M., the Master would wake Adhar up and send him home.

Adhar's nephew, Bepin Behari Sen, wrote in his reminiscences: 'Almost every day after returning home from his office my uncle would bathe, eat something, and then go to Dakshineswar. At that time there were no automobiles, so he had to go by a hired carriage, returning home about midnight. Sometimes his young daughter and I would accompany him to Dakshineswar, and on those occasions he would return a little earlier.

'One day we were present at the time of the *arati* [vesper service] at Dakshineswar. Sri Ramakrishna stood before the Divine Mother with folded hands, looking at her intently. I noticed that his lips were moving. When the arati was over a conch was blown. The Master then took in his hand that part of his cloth which was draped over his shoulder and touched the Mother's feet with it. Touching the cloth to his head, he returned to his room. In order that the Mother might not suffer any discomfort or pain from his hand he had touched her feet very carefully. His constantly moving lips indicated that as long as he was in the temple, he was chanting hymns to the Mother'.[4]

Adhar Lal Sen was born on March 2, 1855, at Ahiritola, Calcutta, to Ramgopal Sen and his wife. This couple had two daughters and six sons, Adhar being their fifth son. Ramgopal was a wealthy thread merchant, and after some time he built a new house at 97 Beniatola Street in Calcutta to accommodate his large family. In accordance with their family custom, Adhar was married at the age of twelve, in 1867.

Adhar was a precocious boy. His academic record was extraordinary, and he was awarded the Duff Scholarship in English literature. He graduated from the Presidency College in 1877. A poet by nature, he had two books of Bengali poems published in 1874, when he was only nineteen. These were *Lalita Sundari* and *Menaka*. Three years later, just before his graduation, two more were published — *Nalini* and *Kusum-Kanan*. In 1880 he translated *The Wanderer* by Lord Lytton, the then Governor General of India, into Bengali, and it was published under the title *Lyttoniana*. In spite of his youth, Adhar received much praise from the literary circles of Calcutta. In his writings one gets a glimpse of his loving and idealistic nature as well as his religious fervour. Further, his questioning of idol worship and animal sacrifice in *Lalita Sundari* shows the influence which Christian and Brahmo teachings exerted on him. In *Menaka* he doubted the existence of God, but later, in the 'Mahavir' poem of *Kusum-Kanan*, he glorified the ideas of nondualistic Vedanta.[5]

On February 10, 1879, Adhar was appointed deputy magistrate at Chittagong in East Bengal (now Bangladesh). This was a high government post, and Adhar was then only twenty-four. Seeing the beauty of the place — the river, the sea, the mountains, and the forest of evergreens — Adhar was greatly moved. In 1880 he went on an official visit to Sitakunda, a sacred spring, and explored its antiquities. He then wrote a paper, 'The Shrines of Sitakunda', which he read at the March 2, 1881 meeting of the Royal Asiatic Society. His fellow members were impressed with the depth of his learning. Adhar was transferred from Chittagong to Jessore on July 14, 1880, and again on April 26, 1882, to Calcutta.[6]

Through his writings and his position in the government, Adhar became acquainted with the elite of Calcutta society, including Bankim Chandra Chatterjee, Haraprasad Shastri (who had been a classmate of his), Mahesh Chandra Nyayaratna, and Krishnadas Pal. Adhar was younger than most of these writers and scholars, but nevertheless they held him in high regard.

Although Adhar doubted the existence of God for some time in his younger days, he was basically a devotee. His father, Ramgopal, was a devout Hindu and observed various religious festivals in their home. This religious environment naturally made a deep impression on Adhar's mind. Ramgopal died on November 16, 1880.

Through the influence of some Vaishnava friends Adhar began to study the *Sri Sri Chaitanya Charitamrita* and the *Sri Chaitanya Bhagavat*. He also read in the *Indian Mirror* and the *Sulabh Samachar* newspapers about Sri Ramakrishna and cherished a desire to meet him.[7] After he was transferred to Calcutta that opportunity finally came. On Friday, March 9, 1883, M. recorded in *The Gospel of Sri Ramakrishna*:

> The Master enjoyed a nap after his noon meal. Adhar and other devotees gradually gathered. This was Adhar's first visit. He was a deputy magistrate and about thirty years old.
>
> Adhar (*to the Master*): 'Sir, I have a question to ask. Is it good to sacrifice animals before the deity? It certainly involves killing'.
>
> Master: 'The shastra [scripture] prescribes sacrifice on special occasions... I am now in such a state of mind that I cannot watch a sacrifice... Again, in a certain state of mind I see God in all beings, even in an ant. At that time, if I see a living being die, I find consolation in the thought that it is the death of the body, the soul being beyond life and death.
>
> 'One should not reason too much; it is enough if one loves the Lotus Feet of the Mother. Too much reasoning throws the mind into confusion. You get clear water if you drink from the surface of a pool. Put your hand deeper and stir the water, and it becomes muddy. Therefore pray to God for devotion'...
>
> A Devotee: 'Can one see God?'
>
> Master: 'Yes, *surely*. One can see both aspects of God — God with form and without form. One can see God with form, the embodiment of Spirit. Again, God can be directly perceived in a man with a tangible form. Seeing an Incarnation of God is the same as seeing God himself. God is born on earth as man in every age'.[8]

Adhar was deeply impressed with the Master at his very first meeting with him. His doubts about God were completely dispelled. Surrendering himself to the Master, he experienced peace and joy. Sri Ramakrishna in turn recognized Adhar as one belonging to his inner circle of devotees and began to treat him as his own.

On April 8, 1883, Adhar visited Sri Ramakrishna for the second time. He also brought some of his friends, one of whom, Saradacharan, was filled with grief over the death of his eldest son. Saradacharan was a retired deputy inspector of schools and passed his time in meditation and prayer. Because of his depressed state of mind, Adhar had brought him to the Master for consolation. The Master was in samadhi when they arrived. After regaining outer consciousness he gave some valuable advice to the householder devotees and then heard from Adhar about his friend's bereavement. Immediately Sri Ramakrishna began to sing, as if to himself: 'To arms! To arms, O man! Death storms your house in battle array!'... Then he said: 'What can you do? Be ready for Death. Death has entered the house. You must fight him with the weapon of God's holy name. God alone is the Doer... Give your power of attorney to God. One doesn't come to grief through letting a good man assume one's responsibilities. Let his will be done'.[9]

Knowing that Adhar's life would be very short, Sri Ramakrishna took him to the northern verandah of his room and gave him some special advice. Adhar died eighteen months later.

Master (to Adhar): 'You are a deputy magistrate. Remember that you have obtained your position through the grace of God. Do not forget him, but remember that all men must one day walk down the same path. We stay in the world only a couple of days.

'This world is our field of activity. We are born here to perform certain duties. People have their homes in the country but come to Calcutta to work.

'It is necessary to do a certain amount of work. This is a kind of discipline. But one must finish it speedily. While melting gold, the goldsmith uses everything — the bellows, the fan, and the pipe — so that he may have the hot fire he needs to melt the metal. After the melting is over, he relaxes and asks his attendant to prepare a smoke for him. All this time his face has been hot and perspiring; but now he can smoke.

'One must have stern determination; then alone is spiritual practice possible. One must make a firm resolve.

'There is great power in the seed of God's name. It destroys ignorance. A seed is tender, and the sprout soft; still it pierces the hard ground. The ground breaks and makes way for the sprout.

'The mind becomes very much distracted if one lives long in the midst of "woman and gold". Therefore one must be very careful... Always keep your mind fixed on God. In the beginning you must struggle a little; later on you will enjoy your pension'.[10]

It was on this occasion that Adhar first saw the Master in samadhi. He had previously observed his friend Saradacharan go into ecstasy while listening to devotional songs, but he was disturbed by it, for Saradacharan's face at that time seemed to be full of pain and sadness. Seeing the bliss on the Master's face, Adhar was happy and relieved. Later Adhar said to Saradacharan: 'By seeing your trance I conceived a disgust for it. It seemed to suggest a great suffering within you. Can divine ecstasy ever cause pain? The blissful ecstasy of the Master has opened my eyes. I would have found it impossible to come here anymore if his ecstasy had been like yours'.[11]

Adhar had many good tendencies and was eager to follow the Master's advice. Sri Ramakrishna told him that the easiest way for a householder to keep the mind in God was by associating with holy people. Therefore, besides coming himself to Dakshineswar, Adhar would also invite the Master to his house quite often and arrange a festival or a kirtan. On July 14, 1883, Sri Ramakrishna went to Adhar's house to hear a recital by Rajnarayan of the Chandi, a hymn glorifying the Divine Mother. When Rajnarayan sang, 'I have surrendered my soul at the fearless feet of the Mother; am I afraid of Death anymore?'[12] the Master went into deep samadhi.

On July 21 the Master again went to Adhar's house. Adhar had been yearning to see the Master that day, but he had not known definitely whether Sri Ramakrishna was coming or not. Seeing the Master, Adhar earnestly said: 'You haven't been here for a long time. I prayed to God today that you might come. I even shed tears'. The Master was pleased and said with a smile, 'You don't mean that!'[13]

In order to impart spiritual knowledge to people, an Incarnation of God lives in the world in the company of devotees, and wherever he finds genuine spiritual hunger he immediately responds. On August 18, 1883, Sri Ramakrishna again visited Adhar's house. He sang and danced in ecstasy in Adhar's drawing room. While he was still in a divine mood, he said to Adhar, 'My son, meditate on the Deity whose name you chanted'. M. wrote in the *Gospel*: 'With these words he touched Adhar's tongue with his finger and wrote something on it. Did the Master thereby impart spirituality to Adhar?'[14]

In March 1884 the Government of India appointed Adhar a member of the Faculty of Arts of Calcutta University. Adhar was glad to have the opportunity to help spread education among the masses, so he was quite busy attending meetings of different committees in addition to his regular duties. Because of this he could not visit the Master for some time. On March 24, 1884, he went to see Sri Ramakrishna at Dakshineswar.

Master: 'Hello! Why haven't you come all these days?'

Adhar: 'Sir, I have been busy with so many things. I had to attend a conference of the school committee and various other meetings'.

Master: 'So you completely lost yourself in schools and meetings and forgot everything else?'

Adhar: 'Everything else was hidden away in a corner of my mind. How is your arm?'

Master: 'Just look. It is not yet healed'...

After a time the Master suddenly said to Adhar: 'Look here. All these are unreal — meetings, school, office, and everything else. God alone is the Substance, and all else is illusory. One should worship God with one's whole mind'.

Adhar sat without speaking a word.

Master: 'All else is illusory. This moment the body is and the next moment it is not. One must make haste to worship God.

'But you don't have to renounce everything. Live in the world the way the tortoise does. The tortoise roams about in the water but keeps its eggs on land. Its whole mind is on the eggs'.[15]

Adhar was a serious and reserved person, and people seldom saw him show emotion in public. But he did not hesitate to express his inner feelings to the Master. Adhar had read in the *Sri Sri Chaitanya Charitamrita*: As the fragrance of musk or the blue lotus captures the environment, so also does the sweet fragrance of Krishna's body. The nose of a person is useless that does not smell the divine fragrance; it breathes mechanically like a bellows. Krishna's touch, like the philosopher's stone, illumines the devotee's heart. He who is not touched by Krishna is wretched, and his body is like a piece of black iron.[16]

Perhaps with this in mind, Adhar humbly said to the Master: 'Sir, you haven't been to our place for a long time. The drawing room smells worldly and everything else appears to be steeped in darkness'.[17] Sri Ramakrishna was very much moved at Adhar's words. He suddenly stood up and in an ecstatic mood blessed Adhar, touching his head and heart. In a voice choked with love, the Master said: 'I look upon you as Narayana himself. You are indeed my own'.[18]

Once Adhar went to the home of Mahimacharan Chakrabarty, a wealthy and learned but also proud man who often visited Sri Ramakrishna. Mahima was at that time studying Tantra scriptures from a scholar. Adhar listened to the scholar's elucidation for a while but did not approve of his interpretation. The three of them then started debating on the theme. Not being able to come to any conclusion, they at last decided to consult Sri Ramakrishna, who had practised Tantra and knew the subject very well. As soon as they arrived at Dakshineswar the Master, without hearing anything from them, started to talk about that very subject, and his words shed new light on it. Adhar was very much impressed. This incident increased his faith in the Master.[19]

'As long as I live, so long do I learn', Sri Ramakrishna once said. Although he taught his disciples, he also learned many things from them. On August 3, 1884, Adhar told the Master about his visit to the Chandranath Hills and to Sitakunda, sacred places of Chittagong. In the course of conversation Adhar mentioned: 'Near Sitakunda I visited a well where I saw fire in the water. It is always burning on the water with leaping tongues'. The Master was surprised to hear that and he asked, 'How is it possible?' Adhar explained that the water contained phosphorous.[20]

On September 6, 1884, Sri Ramakrishna went to Adhar's house to listen to a kirtan. Both Narendra (Swami Vivekananda) and Vaishnavcharan sang many devotional songs, causing the Master to go into samadhi. Later Sri Ramakrishna himself sang, and he also danced, intoxicated with esctatic love. An intense spiritual atmosphere was created in Adhar's parlour. At the sound of the loud music a large crowd gathered in the street. Adhar had also prepared an elaborate meal for the Master and the devotees. When the feast was over, Sri Ramakrishna returned to Dakshineswar.[21]

The next day Adhar visited the Master. He had previously asked Sri Ramakrishna to pray to the Divine Mother to grant him the job of vice-chairman of the Calcutta Municipality. The salary for this job was one thousand rupees a month. In his efforts to get it, Adhar had talked to many rich and prominent men of Calcutta. But the Master did not like the idea that Adhar had flattered so many people just to get a job. The Master said: 'I said to the Mother: "O Mother, Adhar has been visiting you. May he get the job if it pleases you". But at the same time I said to her: "How small-minded he is! He is praying to you for things like that and not for Knowledge and Devotion." '... The Master then continued: 'Nivritti [inwardness of the mind] alone is good, and not pravritti [the inclination to outer enjoyment]... Be satisfied with the job you have. People hanker after a post paying fifty or a hundred rupees [a month], and you are earning three hundred rupees!'... Adhar replied: 'Well, Narendra can support his family with fifty or with a hundred rupees. Will he not try for a hundred?' Immediately the Master said: 'Worldly people think highly of their wealth. They feel that there is nothing like it... But does God care for money? He wants from his devotees knowledge, devotion, discrimination, and renunciation... Listen. There is no scarcity of moths when the lamp is lighted. When God is realized, he himself provides everything for his devotees'.[22]

Though Sri Ramakrishna asked Adhar to be content with his present position, one day when he met Jadu Mallik, a very wealthy

and influential man of Calcutta, he asked him to help Adhar get the
job. Some time later, however, the Master saw Jadu again and told
him that Adhar had not been accepted for the position. Jadu
comforted the Master, saying that Adhar was still young and could
try for it later.

Sri Ramakrishna never forced his devotees to renounce the world.
He helped people to grow in their own ways. Once he told Adhar,
'You have both — yoga and bhoga [enjoyment]'.[23] But at the same
time the Master did not hesitate to say harsh truths to his beloved
devotees when necessary. On one occasion he said to Adhar: 'You
are a scholar and a deputy magistrate, but with all that you are
henpecked. Go forward. Beyond the forest of sandalwood there are
many more valuable things: silver mines, gold mines, diamonds, and
other gems. The woodcutter was chopping wood in the forest; the
brahmachari said to him, "Go forward" '.[24]

On another occasion, Adhar went with the Master to Jadu Mallik's
house to visit the goddess Simhavahini (another name of Durga), but
he did not give an offering to the goddess as is the custom. When the
Master said something to Adhar about it, Adhar replied, 'Sir, I did
not know that while saluting a god or goddess one is supposed to
offer something'.[25] Sri Ramakrishna came to fulfill and not to destroy.
He wanted his disciples to follow the ancient traditions. At the
Master's behest, Adhar engaged Vaishnavcharan, a famous devotee
and singer, to sing devotional songs for him every day after his office
work.

Adhar used to perform the Durga Puja every year in his home.
Bepin Behari Sen, Adhar's nephew, wrote in his memoirs: 'Once Sri
Ramakrishna came to our house at the time of the Durga Puja to
attend the worship of the Divine Mother. Master Mahashay [M.] and
Rakhal Maharaj [Swami Brahmananda] were with him. Sri
Ramakrishna stood before the image with folded hands and went into
samadhi. After returning to normal consciousness he said, "I have
never before seen such a smiling image". Because of his presence our
house was crowded and overflowing with joy. My uncle was so
absorbed in serving the Master that he could not think of anything
else. After an hour Sri Ramakrishna ate something and then left.
Although the worship was still going on, all of us felt an air of
sadness in the house after his leaving'.[26]

Swami Adbhutananda mentioned Adhar in his reminiscences:

We often went with the Master to Adhar Babu's house in
Shobhabazar. He looked upon Adhar Babu's house as one of his
Calcutta parlours. Sometimes Adhar Babu would arrange a festival

at his house and would feed us well. His mother was a great
devotee. She would buy costly mangoes in the off-season and send
them to the Master, together with bananas and sweets. The Master
took great delight in these things. On one occasion at Adhar
Babu's house the Master told him, 'Please be sure not to give me a
sour mango'. So Adhar Babu brought him the best mango he could
find. The Master relished it greatly and said, 'Most likely this one
was selected by your mother!'

One day we were invited to Adhar Babu's house, but Adhar
Babu had forgotten to invite Ram Babu. Ram Babu was greatly
offended and complained to the Master, 'What wrong have I done
to have been left out like this?' The Master tried to console him and
said: 'Look, Ram, Rakhal was asked to arrange this, and he simply
forgot to invite you. Should you be angry with Rakhal? He is just a
boy'. Later Adhar Babu himself went to Ram Babu's house and
invited him to the gathering...

Many famous kirtan singers would come to Adhar Babu's house.
I remember once hearing a song based on the Chandi that
impressed me very much...

One day Adhar Babu asked the Master, 'What powers do you
have?' The Master laughed and said, 'By the grace of the Mother I
lull to sleep those very deputy magistrates who are feared and
respected by many others'.

The Master visited Kalighat [the famous Kali temple in South
Calcutta] now and then and would rejoice there with the devotees.
Adhar Babu would provide his carriage for the Master on those
occasions.[27]

On December 6, 1884, Adhar arranged a festival and invited several
other deputy magistrates to meet the Master. These men wanted to
judge Sri Ramakrishna's holiness. One of them was Bankim Chandra
Chatterjee, perhaps the greatest literary figure of Bengal during the
later part of the nineteenth century. Adhar introduced Bankim to Sri
Ramakrishna, saying: 'Sir, he is a great scholar and has written many
books. He has come here to see you'.[28] A detailed account of this
meeting is found in The Gospel of Sri Ramakrishna (December 6, 1884).
Swami Adbhutananda mentioned this meeting in his reminiscences:
'It was also at Adhar Babu's that I first saw Bankim Chandra
Chatterjee. Bankim was extremely intelligent. He tried to test the
Master, but he came away outdone'.[29]

Sri Ramakrishna once warned Adhar not to ride horseback, but
Adhar did not take his words seriously. On January 6, 1885, Adhar
went by horse to inspect the Manicktala Distillery. On his way home,
at Shobhabazar Street, he fell from the horse, fracturing his left wrist.
Tetanus quickly developed, and he completely lost his voice.

Bepin Behari Sen wrote: 'My uncle fell from a horse, fracturing his left arm and incurring the fatal injuries from which he passed away eight days later. Once during these last days Sri Ramakrishna came to see him. The Master looked very pale that day. He stroked my uncle's body and wept. By then my uncle had almost lost his voice, but when he saw the Master, tears rolled down his cheeks. The Master talked to him a little, but since I was so young I could not follow what was being said. I did observe, though, that my uncle's face beamed with joy when he saw the Master. After a while the Master ate something and with a heavy heart left'.[30]

Later Sri Ramakrishna told the devotees that the accident had occurred because Adhar had had a vision of his Chosen Deity while riding the horse. Overwhelmed with joy, Adhar had lost control of the horse.[31] He passed away at 6:00 A.M. on Wednesday, January 14, 1885. When the news of Adhar's death reached the Master, he immediately went into samadhi. Regaining normal consciousness, he wept and said to the Divine Mother: 'Mother, you asked me to stay in the world with the devotees, cherishing devotion. Now look, how much pain I have!'[32] It is something to think about — that an Incarnation of God would cry for his devotee. It is said that out of grief Sri Ramakrishna remained in bed for three days, covering himself with a cloth.[33] He also told the devotees: 'One by one my parlours are closing. I see an end coming to my gatherings'.[34]

19

Girish Chandra Ghosh

It is often very difficult for people to understand the actions and behaviour of the great teachers of the world. People judge these great ones according to their own mental make-up and sometimes criticize them without understanding the motive behind their actions. The life story of Buddha tells how the rulers of Vaisali were disappointed when Buddha accepted a dinner invitation from the courtesan Ambapali and refused theirs. Jesus' disciples were surprised when they found their Master talking with the socially scorned Samaritan woman near Jacob's well; and again, Simon could not understand why Jesus would let a fallen woman anoint his feet. Similarly, the charge was levelled against Sri Ramakrishna that he did not show 'sufficient moral abhorrence' towards prostitutes and drunkards. On the contrary, we find that one of the marked characteristics of these great souls is that they love the virtuous and the sinner alike. In fact, just as a mother may show more affection to her handicapped child than to her healthy one, so the great teachers of the world are in some ways more sympathetic towards the wayward children of God than towards the virtuous ones. After all, what glory is there in making a good man good? Buddha, Christ, Sri Ramakrishna, and other God-men paid special attention to the fallen, the downtrodden, and the destitute, and by their redeeming power they lifted the lowly to the highest state. They transformed sinners into saints.

Girish Chandra Ghosh is just such an example of the transforming power of Sri Ramakrishna. Before he met Sri Ramakrishna, Girish Ghosh had led a reckless, hedonistic life. He was a self-proclaimed libertine and a rebel against God. Yet he had a strong mind, and was a man of tremendous heart. The turn that Sri Ramakrishna gave to Girish's life is epitomized in a conversation that took place between them on December 14, 1884:

Master: 'Have faith in the Divine Mother and you will attain everything'.

Girish: 'But I am a sinner'.

261

Girish Chandra Ghosh (1844-1912)

Master: 'The wretch who constantly harps on sin becomes a sinner'.

Girish: 'Sir, the very ground where I used to sit would become unholy'.

Master: 'How can you say that? Suppose a light is brought into a room that has been dark a thousand years; does it illumine the room little by little, or all in a flash?'

A little later Girish asked, 'Tell me what I should do'.

Master: 'Give God your power of attorney. Let him do whatever he likes'.[1]

The life story of Girish is very interesting. It gives hope to the hopeless, faith to the faithless, and inspiration to the seekers of God. Girish was born of pious parents in Calcutta on February 28, 1844, and grew up a lively, carefree soul. He inherited from his father a sharp intellect and a pragmatic approach to life, and from his mother a love for literature and devotion for God. But it was his grandmother who introduced him to the rich heritage of India's epics and mythology. In the evenings she would recount to him some of those ancient stories, and he would listen with rapt attention. Once she was describing the episode of Krishna's departure from Vrindaban, one of the moving scenes of the Bhagavatam. Krishna's uncle, Akrura, was sent to bring Krishna to Mathura, much to the despair of the shepherd boys and girls of Vrindaban. When Krishna sat in the chariot the boys began to cry, and they pleaded with him, 'O Krishna, do not leave us!' The girls held the wheels of the chariot, and some of them grabbed the reins of the horses. But Akrura would not pay any heed to them. He left Vrindaban with Krishna, and thus the days of joy that Krishna's playmates had known in his company came to an end. Girish was listening intently and, with tearful eyes, he asked his grandmother, 'Did Krishna ever return to Vrindaban?' 'No', replied the grandmother. Girish asked the question three times and each time got the same answer. He then burst into tears and ran away. The story upset him so much that for the next several evenings he refused to listen to any more tales.[2]

When he was only eleven years old his mother died. Although his father was very loving and indulgent towards Girish, he wanted the boy to learn to stand on his own feet and depend on none but God. Once Girish went with his father by boat to visit Navadwip, the birthplace of Sri Chaitanya, which is several miles up the river Ganga from Calcutta. On the way their boat was suddenly caught in a crosscurrent. As it whirled around in imminent danger of sinking, Girish clung tightly to his father's hand. Luckily the boatman was able to navigate the boat to safety. When they reached the shore, Girish's father said to him: 'Why did you hold my hand? Don't you know that my life is dearer to me than yours? If the boat had started to sink, I would have snatched my hand from you and tried to save my own life. You would have been forsaken'. Speaking of this incident many years later, Girish said, 'My father's cruel words hurt me terribly, but I learned that there is no one but God to hold to at the time of danger'.[3] Three years after his mother's death, Girish lost his father.

From his boyhood Girish was a voracious reader and a free thinker. With his father's permission he enrolled in one school after another, yet he was not happy in any of them. He found the discipline confining, and their methods of teaching did not satisfy his thirst for knowledge. A year after his father's death he was married, and he then left school completely without having earned a degree.

Girish was born in a transitional period of Indian history. In Calcutta particularly, Western education and culture were thrust upon Indian society, challenging the traditional Indian culture and religions. Consequently, the youth of his generation grew up in an atmosphere of doubt, atheism, and cultural chaos. At the threshold of maturity, with little stability either in his family or in society to guide him, Girish started drifting into drunkenness, debauchery, waywardness, and obstinacy. He became the leader of a group of mischievous youths in his locality. Sometimes he would even desecrate images of Hindu gods and goddesses. Within a few years he became a neighbourhood menace. Yet side by side with his perverse behaviour, Girish would raise money to help the poor secure food and medicine, or arrange for the cremation of those in his community who had died. After studying homeopathic medicine he was able to treat people himself.

Girish would often watch the people on the street through a small opening in his door. One afternoon, when the men of the neighbourhood were at work, he observed a hypocritical astrologer, in the guise of a monk, collecting information from a maidservant about the women of the household where she worked. The man then entered that house as a fortune-teller, and the simple, curious women came to him to have their palms read. Girish could not tolerate it. He grabbed a branch of a flower tree in the courtyard, broke it off, and ran and attacked the astrologer. He did not stop chasing him until the astrologer was out of the locality.[4]

Although Girish was no longer in school, he did not give up his studies. He eventually became a member of the Asiatic Society and other well-known libraries of Calcutta. His reading included the Ramayana, the Mahabharata, the Puranas, and Bengali literature. In this way he gradually became well versed in history, logic, philosophy, zoology, and English literature. He also studied science and medicine. He did not care for superficial knowledge. His capacity for deep penetration into any subject, plus his keen observation of human character and wonderful imagination, are what later made him a natural poet and playwright.

Once a friend of Girish's, who later became a judge of the Calcutta High Court, said to him, 'It is impossible to translate the conversations of the witches of Shakespeare's Macbeth into Bengali'. Immediately Girish decided to translate the whole play.[5] It was his nature to rise to any challenge or to do just what he was told not to do. If anyone would say, 'Don't go there. There is a ghost', he would immediately run to that place to see the ghost. He was fearless, independent, and proud of his strength. No one could make him begin work or quit work through pressure or intimidation. He used to say, 'A beast can be tamed by the whip, but not a human being'. His attitude was: If I do not enjoy my work, why should I do it? What he considered right he did, without caring whether others criticized him or not.[6]

Meanwhile, Girish's recklessness and debauchery continued. His father-in-law finally decided to introduce some kind of discipline into Girish's life and secured for him a job as a bookkeeper in his own office. It was while working there that Girish translated Macbeth into Bengali.[7] Unfortunately, that manuscript was lost when the company went out of business because Girish was then away from the office taking care of his sick wife. However, he later retranslated Macbeth, and it was staged at the Minerva Theatre in Calcutta. Girish worked in various capacities in different businesses during the next fifteen years. He had indomitable energy and was becoming increasingly more involved in the theatre. Thus it was common practice for him to work all day at the office and then go to the theatre in the evening to act in a play, returning home at three or four o'clock in the morning.

That person is indeed unfortunate who loses his mother in childhood, his father in boyhood, and his wife in early manhood. In 1874, when Girish was just thirty, his young wife died, leaving him with one son and one daughter. Shortly thereafter he lost his job. A thick, dark cloud of despair seemed to hover over him. As God created grief to subdue man, so man created wine to subdue grief. Again Girish drifted, trying to forget his sorrows with the help of alcohol. But at the same time, his pent-up emotions found an outlet in a series of exquisite poetical compositions.

During this period he went to Bhagalpur, in Central India, for a short while on some business. One day while he was there he went for a walk with some friends and, in a boisterous mood, jumped into a deep ravine. When he tried to climb out he found he was unable to do so. His friends then attempted to rescue him but they also failed. One of them commented: 'Now we are in real trouble. You are an atheist, and yet no one can save you now but God. Let us all pray together'. Girish found himself joining wholeheartedly in the prayer, and strangely, just then he found a way out of the ravine. After he was safe he said to his friends: 'Today I have called on God out of fear. If I ever call on him again, it will be out of love; otherwise I will not call on him, even at the cost of my life'.[8]

After returning to Calcutta Girish remarried and also found another job. His new supervisor was an Englishman who introduced the practice of summoning his employees by ringing a bell. One day he rang for Girish. Girish heard the bell but did not respond. The supervisor sent an attendant to ask Girish whether he had heard the bell or not. Girish simply replied, 'No, I didn't hear the bell', and continued with his work. The supervisor became angry when he heard the report and went to Girish himself. 'I am calling you. Why don't you respond?' 'I did not hear the bell', answered Girish. 'Even so, how am I to know that the bell is calling me? The bell never said, "Girish, Girish" '. Then more seriously he said: 'Listen, sir. So far I have spoken to you as a gentleman; now I shall be frank. I am not your servant or bearer. I am not accustomed to standing and sitting according to a bell. I feel it is humiliating for a subordinate to be summoned by a bell. And when its employees are humiliated, a company loses its reputation'. The owner of the company came to know of the incident and supported Girish. Later the supervisor apologized to Girish, and they eventually became close friends.[9]

Six months after his second marriage Girish became ill with a virulent type of cholera, and physicians gave up hope for his recovery. Girish was lying on his bed in a semi-conscious state, surrounded by weeping relatives, when he had a vision: A resplendent female form, wearing a red-bordered cloth, appeared before him. Her face was full of compassion and love. She sat near him and, putting something in his mouth, said, 'Please eat this prasad [sanctified food] and you will be cured'. Girish slowly regained consciousness, and from that moment his recovery began.[10] He later recounted this mysterious vision to his brother disciples and added, 'Sixteen years later [in

1891], when I first went to Jayrambati to see Holy Mother, I found to my surprise and delight that the woman who had saved my life with the holy prasad was none other than Holy Mother herself'.[11]

Disease, the death of a loved one, an accident, or untold suffering invariably lead to a turning point in one's life. Girish was experiencing all of these and, in spite of his proclaimed atheism, he began to wonder if in fact a greater Reality did exist. He wrote in his memoirs: 'At such a crisis I thought: "Does God exist? Does he listen to the prayers of man? Does he show him the way from darkness to light?" My mind said, "Yes". Immediately I closed my eyes and prayed: "Oh God, if thou art, carry me across. Give me refuge. I have none". I remembered the words of the Gita, "Those who call on me only in the days of affliction, to them too I bring succour and refuge". These words sank deep in my consciousness and gave me solace in sorrow. I found the words of the Gita to be true. As the sun removes the darkness of the night, so the sun of hope arose and dispelled the gloom that had gathered thick in my mind. In the sea of trouble I found the harbour of repose. But I had nurtured doubt all these years. I had argued long, saying, "There is no God". Where would the impressions of these thoughts go? I began to reason in terms of cause and effect and argued that such and such a cause had produced such and such an effect, which was instrumental in bringing release from this danger. It is said that doubt dies hard. Again I fell victim to doubt. But I had not the courage to say boldly, "God does not exist".

'Desire for inquiry came. Looking into the current of events, sometimes faith, sometimes doubt, emerged. Everybody with whom I discussed my problem said unanimously that without instruction from a guru doubt would not go and nothing could be achieved in spiritual life. But my intellect refused to accept a human being as a guru; for one has to salute the guru with the words, "Guru is Brahma, Guru is Vishnu, Guru is the Lord Maheshwara [Shiva], the God of gods, etc.". How could I say this to a man like me? This was hypocrisy. But the tyranny of doubt was intolerable. Terrible conflicts pierced my heart through and through. That condition can better be imagined than described. Suppose a man, all of a sudden, is forcibly dragged to a dark, solitary room with his eyes covered, and kept confined there with no food and drink. What will be the state of his mind? If you can picture his mental condition, you will be able to understand something of my own. There were moments when I was breathless with emotion. Thoughts of despair bit through me like a saw. At other times the memory of the past was revived and the darkness of my heart knew no bounds'.[12]

Girish had read about Sri Ramakrishna in the *Indian Mirror*. He also came to know how the famous Keshab Chandra Sen and his followers of the Brahmo Samaj, had been influenced by Sri Ramakrishna. He then became curious to know more about this holy man of Dakshineswar. ·Most probably Girish first met Sri Ramakrishna in 1877 at Dinanath Basu's house in Calcutta. In his reminiscences Girish recorded his first several meetings with Sri Ramakrishna. As he described his first meeting: 'It was dusk. Lights were lit and they were placed in front of Sri Ramakrishna. But he began to make repeated inquiries, saying: "Is it evening? Is it evening?" At this I thought to myself: "What pretention! It is dusk. Lights are burning in front of him. Yet he cannot tell whether it is evening or not". Thinking I had seen enough of him, I came away'.[13]

A few years later Girish saw Sri Ramakrishna for the second time at the home of Balaram Basu. Many people had been invited that day to meet the Master. A dancing girl named Bidhu was seated next to Sri Ramakrishna in order to sing a few devotional songs for him. Girish observed Sri Ramakrishna talking to people and receiving them with the utmost humility, bowing down to the ground. Girish wrote in his reminiscences: 'An old friend of mine, pointing at him, said sarcastically: "Bidhu must have had a previous intimacy with him. That's why he is laughing and joking with her". But I did not like his insinuations. Just at this time Sisir Kumar Ghosh, the well-known editor of *Amrita Bazar Patrika*, arrived. He seemed to have very little respect for Sri Ramakrishna. He said: "Let us go. Enough of him!" I wanted to stay and see a little more, but he insisted and made me come with him'.[14]

In August 1884 Girish's drama on the life of Sri Chaitanya was creating a sensation in Calcutta. Sri Ramakrishna heard about the play and wanted to see it, but some devotees objected because several of the roles were played by women of bad reputation. In those days girls from good families did not become actresses in the theatre. Sri Ramakrishna told the devotees: 'I shall look upon them as the Blissful Mother herself. What if one of them acts the part of Chaitanya? An imitation custard-apple reminds one of the real fruit'.[15]

Girish wrote in his memoirs for September 21, 1884: 'My play, *The Life of Chaitanya*, was being enacted in the Star Theatre. I was strolling in the outer compound of the theatre when Mahendra Nath Mukhopadhyay, one of the devotees of Sri Ramakrishna, came and said to me: "Sri Ramakrishna has come to see the play. If you will give him a free pass, well and good. Otherwise we will buy a ticket for him".

'I replied: "He will not have to purchase his ticket. But the others will have to". Saying this, I proceeded to greet him. I found him alighting from the carriage and entering the compound of the theatre. I wanted to salute him. But before I could do so, he saluted me. I returned his salute. He saluted me again. I bowed my head and he did the same to me. I thought this might continue forever, so I greeted him mentally and led him upstairs and offered him a seat in the box. After arranging with an attendant to fan him, I returned home, feeling indisposed'.[16] This was Girish's third meeting.

After the performance a devotee asked Sri Ramakrishna how he had enjoyed the play. He replied with a smile, 'I found the representation the same as the real'.[17] On this occasion he blessed the actress Binodini, who had played the role of Sri Chaitanya, by touching her head and saying, 'Be illumined'.[18] Binodini wrote in her autobiography: 'I don't care if people of the world look down upon my sinful life. I was blessed by Sri Ramakrishna. His loving, hopeful message still sustains me. When I am terribly depressed I see his sweet, compassionate face in my heart and hear his voice, "Say Hari guru, guru Hari [God is your guru, and the guru is your God]" '.[19]

People came from all over Bengal to honour Girish for his excellent presentation of Chaitanya's life. Even orthodox Vaishnavas (followers of Chaitanya) went to see the play in the theatre — a remarkable fact since the theatre was traditionally regarded as an immoral place. Some of them went to Girish's house to meet him personally. Girish, having performed until late the previous night, was not very enthusiastic about receiving effusive visitors during the day, and he was also tired of flattery. Finally he struck upon a plan to get rid of the crowd. Filling his glass from a bottle, he began to drink. The devout Vaishnavas then asked: 'Sir, are you sick? Are you taking medicine?' Girish replied: 'No, it is not medicine. I am drinking wine'. Finding that his life and the ideal expressed in his play were poles apart, the visitors left. Girish smiled to himself and thought: 'I am Girish Ghosh. I am not afraid or ashamed of anything. Why should I care for others' opinions?'[20]

The fourth time that he saw Sri Ramakrishna, Girish felt for the first time the wonderful divine attraction that drew the devotees to the Master. In his own words: 'I was sitting on the porch of a friend's house, which was at the crossroads, when I saw Sri Ramakrishna slowly approaching, accompanied by Narayana and a couple of other devotees. No sooner had I turned my eyes towards him than he saluted me. I returned his salute. Then he went on. For no accountable reason my heart felt drawn towards him by an invisible string. As soon as he had gone a short distance, I felt an urge to follow him. I could not keep calm, for the attraction I felt was not of this earth. It was something for which no former experience had ever prepared me. It was something unique, which no words could describe. Just at that moment a person, whose name I do not recall, brought me a message from him and said, "Sri Ramakrishna is calling you". I went'.[21]

Sri Ramakrishna was on his way to Balaram Basu's house, and Girish followed him there. His account continues: 'After an exchange of a few words with Balaram, Sri Ramakrishna suddenly exclaimed, "I am all right. I am all right". So saying, he went into a state of consciousness which seemed very strange to me. Then he remarked, "No, no, this is not pretense. This is not pretense". He remained in this state for a while and then resumed his normal state. I asked him, "What is a guru?" He answered: "Do you know what the guru is? He is like a matchmaker. A matchmaker arranges for the union of the bride with the bridegroom. Likewise, a guru prepares for the meeting of the individual soul with his Beloved, the Divine Spirit".... Then he said: "You need not worry. Your guru has already been chosen". I asked, "What is the mantram?" He replied, "The name of God" '.

Still describing the same meeting, Girish wrote: 'Then the talk drifted to the theatre, and he said: "I liked your play very much. The sun of knowledge has begun to shine upon you. All the blemishes of your heart will be washed away. Very soon devotion will arise to sweeten your life with profuse joy and peace". I told him that I had none of those qualities, and that I had written the play only with the idea of making some money. He kept quiet. Then he said, "Could you take me to your theatre and show me another play of yours?" I replied, "Very well. Any day you like". He said, "You must charge me something". I said, "All right, you may pay eight annas". Sri Ramakrishna said, "That will allow me a seat in the balcony, which is a very noisy place". I answered: "Oh no, you will not go there. You will sit in the same place where you sat last time". He said, "Then you must take one rupee". I said, "All right, as you please". Our talk ended'.[22]

Girish was a proud man, very much opposed to the idea of bowing down to anyone. But through the influence of Sri Ramakrishna, his haughtiness, rudeness, and pride gradually began to melt. Girish described his thoughts at his fifth meeting: 'I was sitting in the dressing room of the theatre when a devotee came to me in a hurry and said with some concern, "Sri Ramakrishna is here in his carriage". I replied, "Very well. Take him to a box and offer him a seat". But the devotee answered, "Won't you come and greet him personally and take him there yourself?" With some annoyance I said: "Does he need me? Can't he get there himself?" Nevertheless, I went. I found him alighting from the carriage. Seeing his serene and radiant face, my stony heart melted. I rebuked myself in shame, and that shame still haunts my memory. To think that I had refused to greet this sweet and gentle soul! Then I conducted him upstairs. There I saluted him, touching his feet. Even now I do not understand the reason, but at that moment a radical change came over me and I was a different man. I offered him a rose, which he accepted. But he returned it again, saying: "Only a god or a dandy is entitled to flowers. What shall I do with it?" '23

Girish took Sri Ramakrishna and some of his devotees into the hall of the Star Theatre, where the following conversation took place:

Master: 'Ah! You have written nice plays'.

Girish: 'But, sir, how little I assimilate! I just write'.

Master: 'No, you assimilate a great deal. The other day I said to you that no one could sketch a divine character unless he had love of God in his heart'...

Girish: 'I often ask myself, "Why bother about the theatre any more?"'

Master: 'No, no! Let things be as they are. People will learn much from your plays'.

After the drama, which was on the life of the great devotee Prahlada, Girish asked Sri Ramakrishna, 'How did you like the performance?' Sri Ramakrishna replied: 'I found that it was God himself who was acting the different parts. Those who played the female parts seemed to me the direct embodiments of the Blissful Mother'.24

On this occasion Sri Ramakrishna said to Girish, 'There is some crookedness in your heart'. Girish thought to himself, 'Yes, indeed. Plenty of it — of various kinds'. Then he asked the Master, 'How shall I get rid of it?' Sri Ramakrishna replied, 'Have faith'.25

One afternoon Girish went to the theatre and found a note saying that Sri Ramakrishna would be visiting Ram Chandra Datta's house in Calcutta that day. Girish suddenly felt an irresistible desire to see the Master. He left the theatre for Ram Datta's house, even though he did not know him and had not received a formal invitation. He later wrote in his memoirs: 'It was evening. Sri Ramakrishna was dancing in ecstasy in the courtyard. There was singing accompanied by a drum. The devotees were dancing in a circle around Sri Ramakrishna. The words of the song were, "Nadia is shaken by the surging waves of divine love emanating from the heart of Gauranga''. The courtyard seemed a sea of bliss. Tears filled my eyes. Sri Ramakrishna suddenly became still. He was absorbed in samadhi. The devotees began to take the dust of his feet. I wanted to do the same, but I could not, as I was shy. I was thinking of what others might say if I went to Sri Ramakrishna and took the dust of his feet. No sooner had this thought crossed my mind than Sri Ramakrishna, coming down from samadhi, began dancing again. While dancing he came in front of me and stood still, once more absorbed in samadhi. Now there was no longer any hesitation on my part to touch his feet. I took the dust of his feet.

'After the music Sri Ramakrishna came and sat in the drawing room. I followed him. Then he began to talk to me. I asked him, ''Will the crookedness go out of my heart?'' He said, ''Yes, it will go''. Again I asked him the same question, and he gave the same reply. I repeated it once more, and he said the same thing'.[26]

A great change was coming over Girish. He felt as if Sri Ramakrishna was his own close relative. The Master's loving care and concern made Girish understand that he would not condemn him for his shortcomings. Girish wrote: 'I went to Dakshineswar. I found Sri Ramakrishna seated on the southern porch of his room. He was talking with a young devotee named Bhavanath. I prostrated myself before Sri Ramakrishna and mentally recited the verse, ''Guru is Brahma, Guru is Vishnu, Guru is the Lord Maheshwara, the God of gods''. He said: ''I was just talking about you. And if you don't believe me, ask Bhavanath''.

'After a while, he started to give me some spiritual advice. I stopped him, saying: ''I won't listen to any advice. I have written cartloads of it myself. It doesn't help. Do something that will transform my life''. Hearing these words, Sri Ramakrishna was highly pleased. Ramlal, his nephew, was present. Sri Ramakrishna asked him to recite a particular hymn, which ran thus: ''Go into solitude and shut yourself in a cave. Peace is not there. Peace is where faith is, for faith is the root of all''. I saw a smile playing on the lips of Sri Ramakrishna, and I felt at that moment that I was freed from all impurities. And at that moment, my arrogant head bowed low at his feet. In him I found my sanctuary and all my fear was gone. I prostrated myself before him and was about to return home. He followed me as far as the northern porch. There I asked him, ''Now that I have received your grace, am I to continue the same kind of work that I have been doing?'' Sri Ramakrishna replied, ''Yes, why not?'' From his words I understood that my connection with the theatre would not hurt my spiritual life.

'My heart was filled with joy. I felt as if I was born anew. I was a totally changed man. There was no more doubt or conflict in my mind. "God is real. God is my sanctuary; I have found my refuge in this God-man. Now I can easily realize God". Thoughts like these cast their spell on me night and day. In waking or in dreaming, the same mood persisted: "Fearless am I! I have found my very own. The world can no longer bind me, for even the greatest fear, the fear of death, is gone" '.[27]

There is a saying that if a man takes one step towards God, God takes ten steps towards him. It was not just that Girish was seeking Sri Ramakrishna; even more so, it was Sri Ramakrishna who was seeking Girish to play a vital role in his divine drama.

Long before he met Girish, Sri Ramakrishna had had a vision which he described as follows: 'One day, when I was meditating in the Kali temple, I saw a naked boy skipping into the temple. He had a tuft of hair on the crown of his head, and was carrying a flask of wine under his left arm and a vessel of nectar in his right hand. "Who are you?" I asked. "I am Bhairava [the chief of Shiva's host]", he replied. On my asking the reason for him coming, he answered, "To do your work". Years later when Girish came to me, I recognized that Bhairava in him'.[28]

Girish hated hypocrisy from the bottom of his heart. Being bold and strong in character, he did not find it necessary to hide his weaknesses. And indeed, it takes tremendous courage to unite mind and speech, especially to one's discredit. Girish would say, 'I have drunk so many bottles of wine that if you were to place one bottle on top of another they would reach the height of Mount Everest'.[29] It is true that he drank a great deal and he had once been addicted to opium. He also would visit brothels often. But one should not think that he was a seducer, an exploiter, a cheat, or given to actual cruelty. His strength of character kept him above hypocrisy and other such evils.

When Girish was drunk he had little control over his speech and behaviour. Seeing him in this condition, even the girls of the brothels hesitated to open their doors to him. 'One night', said Girish, 'in a euphoric and drunken mood, I was visiting a house of prostitution with two of my friends. But suddenly I felt an urge to visit Sri Ramakrishna. My friends and I hired a carriage and drove out to Dakshineswar. It was late at night, and everyone was asleep. The three of us entered Sri Ramakrishna's room, tipsy and reeling. Sri Ramakrishna grasped both my hands and began to sing and dance in ecstasy. The thought flashed through my mind: "Here is a man whose love embraces all — even a wicked man like me, whose own family would condemn me in this state. Surely this holy man, respected by the righteous, is also the saviour of the fallen'' '.[30]

One day a devotee complained to Sri Ramakrishna about Girish's habit of drinking and begged him to ask Girish to give it up. But Sri Ramakrishna sternly replied: 'Why do you trouble your head about him? He who has taken charge of him will look after him. Girish is a devotee of the heroic type. I tell you, drinking will not affect him'.[31]

On another occasion Sri Ramakrishna asked Aswini Kumar Datta if he knew Girish Ghosh.

'Which Girish Ghosh? The one connected with the theatre?'

'Yes'.

'I have never seen him, but I know him by reputation'.

'A good man'.

'They say he drinks'.

'Let him! Let him! How long will he continue that?'[32]

Sri Ramakrishna never forbade Girish to drink, as he knew that it takes time to change deep-rooted habits. Yet the silent influence of the Master's love worked miracles.

Girish saw his life changing under the influence of Sri Ramakrishna, yet he could not fathom the nature of this great soul. One day he asked the Master, 'Who are you, sir?' Sri Ramakrishna replied: 'Some say I am Ramprasad [a poet-saint of Bengal], others that I am Raja Ramakrishna. I simply live here'.[33]

Gradually Girish became convinced that Sri Ramakrishna was an Incarnation of God, and he started to spread this idea among the devotees. On a certain occasion Sri Ramakrishna asked Girish: 'Hello! What were you saying about me? I eat, drink, and make merry'.

Girish: 'What should we have been saying about you? Are you a holy man?'

Master: 'No, nothing of the sort. Truly I do not feel that I am a holy man'.

Girish: 'I am not your equal even in joking'.[34]

In the same vein, Girish related once that Sri Ramakrishna had asked the future Swami Yogananda what he thought of him. The young man had replied, 'You are neither a householder nor a sannyasin [monk]'. Sri Ramakrishna was greatly pleased and exclaimed, 'What an extraordinary statement you have just made!'[35] Sri Ramakrishna was happy to know that his disciple had recognized his divine nature, which is beyond all limitations and stages of life.

One day Girish surrendered himself completely to the Master. He asked him for instruction as to what he should do from then on. 'Do just what you are doing now', said Sri Ramakrishna. 'Hold on to God with one hand and to the world with the other. Think of God at least in the morning and evening'. This sounded simple to Girish; but then he recalled that his life was so irregular that it would be hard for him to remember God at those stated hours, so he kept quiet. Sri Ramakrishna read his mind and said, 'Well, if you cannot do that, then remember God before you eat and before you sleep'. But now Girish was reluctant to promise anything to Sri Ramakrishna. He knew that, with his instinctive resistance to self-discipline and rules, he might not be able to keep even this simple observance. Then Sri Ramakrishna went into an ecstatic mood and said to him: 'So you are unwilling to agree even to this. All right. Give me your *power of attorney*. Henceforth I will take full responsibility for you. You won't have to do anything at all'.

Girish was relieved. This sounded to his liking, for he understood that Sri Ramakrishna had relieved him of all responsibility for his own spiritual well-being and had made him free. But, in fact, he had made himself Sri Ramakrishna's slave. Complete self-surrender is more binding than the observance of strict disciplines. One day, soon after this, Girish remarked in Sri Ramakrishna's presence, 'I shall do this'. 'No, no', corrected Sri Ramakrishna. 'You can't talk like that anymore. Say, ''I shall do this if God wills'' '.[36] Girish began to understand the mystery of the power of attorney. As time passed he came to realize that he could not perform any action of his own free will. He had to consciously surrender to the Divine Will, and gradually he found that he was forced to think of the Master every moment. In the later part of his life he would say: 'Look at me. I am not even free to breathe'.[37]

To a large extent progress in spiritual life depends on the intensity of one's effort. Yet it still takes time to eradicate past samskaras (impressions of the mind). In Girish's case, however, his faith and love were so intense that a transformation in his life was brought about very quickly. In spite of this, Sri Ramakrishna once made a remark about Girish to another devotee, 'You may wash a thousand times a cup that has held a solution of garlic; but is it ever possible to get rid of the smell altogether?' Girish heard about it and he was hurt. He went to Sri Ramakrishna and asked, 'Will this smell of garlic go?'

'Yes, it will'.

'So you say it will'.

'All smell disappears when a blazing fire is lighted. If you heat a cup smelling of garlic, you get rid of the smell; it becomes a new cup'.[38]

Now and then Sri Ramakrishna would visit Girish's theatre and bring him sweets. Once the Master fed Girish with his own hands. Girish wrote of this in his memoirs: 'One day when I arrived at Dakshineswar, Sri Ramakrishna was just finishing his noonday meal. He offered me his dessert, but as I was about to eat it, he said, "Wait. Let me feed you myself". Then he put the pudding into my mouth with his own fingers, and I ate as hungrily and unself-consciously as a small baby. I forgot that I was an adult. I felt I was a child of the mother, and the mother was feeding me. But now, when I remember how these lips of mine had touched many impure lips, and how Sri Ramakrishna fed me, touching them with his holy hand, I am overwhelmed with emotion and say to myself: "Did this actually happen? Or was it only a dream?"'[39]

One day Sri Ramakrishna asked Girish to massage his feet, allowing him the opportunity to give him loving, personal service as an intimate disciple. Girish wrote later: 'I was unwilling. I thought, "What nonsense! Who is going to sit and massage his feet?!" But now when the memory returns I become overwhelmed with remorse. It is only the thought of his infinite love that gives me solace'.[40]

Gradually, however, Girish began to notice how other devotees were serving the Master with love and respect, and by contrast, what a terrible life he was leading. He felt bad, but because of his dissolute life style he was reluctant to offer his service. Then one day, when Sri Ramakrishna was visiting the theatre, Girish, under the influence of liquor, voiced his desire: 'I have not been able to serve you in this life. But if you are born again as my son I can do so. Please promise me that you will be my son'. 'What are you saying?' said Sri Ramakrishna. 'Why should I be born as your son? I shall be your guru, your Chosen Deity'. Then Girish became angry and abused the Master in coarse language. The devotees who were present were very much shocked and upset and asked the Master not to see Girish again. Sri Ramakrishna quietly returned to Dakshineswar. He prayed: 'O Mother, Girish is an actor. How can he understand your glory? Mother, please forgive him'.

The next day Ram Chandra Datta visited Dakshineswar. He heard the story of Girish's behaviour the previous evening and told the Master: 'Sir, the serpent Kaliya* told Krishna, "Lord, you have given

*Reference to the story of Krishna subduing the venomous snake Kaliya by dancing on the serpent's head. Kaliya began spewing out quantities of poison and told Krishna, 'Lord, it is you who have given me poison, rather than nectar, with which to worship you'.

me only poison; where shall I get nectar to offer you?'' It is the same with Girish. Where will he get nectar? Girish has worshipped you with whatever you have given him'. Sri Ramakrishna smiled and said to the other devotees present: 'Listen to what he is saying. Get a carriage. I shall go to Girish's house right now'.[41]

Meanwhile, Girish was very repentant. He had refused to eat and was weeping piteously. Suddenly he saw the Master at his house and was overwhelmed. He said, 'Master, if you had not come today, I would have concluded that you had not attained that supreme state of knowledge where praise and blame are equal, and that you could not be called a paramahamsa [an illumined soul]'.[42]

Sri Ramakrishna once said to Girish: 'You utter many abusive and vulgar words; but that doesn't matter. It is better for these things to come out. There are some people who fall ill on account of blood poisoning; the more the poisoned blood finds an outlet, the better it is for them... You will be purer day by day. You will improve very much day by day. People will marvel at you'.[43]

One morning Girish went to Balaram Basu's house and found Balaram cleaning rice. Balaram was a rich landlord and had many servants, but nevertheless he was doing this menial work himself. Girish was amazed and asked Balaram the reason for this. Balaram replied: 'The Master is coming today, and he will have his lunch here. So I am cleaning the rice myself'.

Girish was impressed by Balaram's devotion, but again it saddened him that he could not also serve the Master in that way. He returned home and, closing the door, thought: 'Indeed, God comes to the homes of those who have devotion like Balaram. I am a wretched drunkard. There is no one here who can receive the Master properly and feed him'. Girish lay down on his bed. At 1:30 P.M. he heard a knock at his door. Opening it, he found the Master standing there. 'Girish, I am hungry', said the Master. 'Could you give me some food?' And yet Sri Ramakrishna had finished his meal at Balaram's house only a little while earlier! As there was no food in his house, Girish asked the Master to wait. He then hurried to a restaurant where he purchased some fried bread and potato curry and brought it back to the Master. This food was coarse and hard to digest — not at all the kind of food usually served to the Master. But Sri Ramakrishna ate it with great joy.[44]

Swami Brahmananda once commented that among all of the disciples of Sri Ramakrishna, Swami Vivekananda and Girish Ghosh had the greatest intellectual powers. Yet Girish's intellect could not stand up to the power with which the Master conveyed the incomprehensible nature of Brahman. One day the Master told him: 'What do you know about the knowledge of Brahman? The great sage Narada saw the infinite ocean of Satchidananda from a distance and returned; the ever-pure Shukadeva touched that Ocean only three times; and the great god Shiva drank only three handfuls of its water and lost consciousness'. Girish clapped his hand to his forehead and exclaimed: 'Stop, sir! Say no more. My head is reeling'.[45]

Girish one day requested Sri Ramakrishna to give him a spiritual vision. 'Do not desire such visions', was the reply. 'For even if you have them, you may not believe what you see'.[46] Later Girish understood the import of those words, for he realized that his doubting mind would have considered such an experience to be some kind of magic or illusion.

Once Girish heard the Master say: 'If a passionate desire arises and persists during meditation, stop and begin to pray. Earnestly pray to the Lord that this desire be removed, that it not be fulfilled. Any desire coming up in meditation, particularly a repressed one, gradually becomes intensified. And if one or more of our passions are involved, the results can be most disquieting'.[47]

Girish wrote: 'Sri Ramakrishna instructed everyone to abstain from telling lies. I told him: "Sir, I tell numerous lies. How shall I be truthful?" He replied: "Don't worry about that. You are above truth and falsehood". When I feel tempted to tell lies, I at once visualize the Master's form, and lies will not come out. Sri Ramakrishna has full sway over my heart — he has it by the power of his love. Lust, anger, and all the terrible passions vanish if one feels this transcendental love of his — no other spiritual practice is required. This realization is the highest goal of human life'.[48]

Once Girish wanted to test Sri Ramakrishna's grace and spiritual power. With this in mind, he went to a brothel, intending to spend the night there. But at midnight he experienced an unbearable burning sensation all over his body, and he immediately left the place and returned home. The next morning he went to Dakshineswar and told the whole story to Sri Ramakrishna. The Master listened and then told him firmly: 'Rascal, do you think you have been caught by a poisonless water snake and will be able to escape? You have been bitten by a real cobra. After three cries you will be silenced'. Girish's faith in Sri Ramakrishna was strengthened. He was coming to believe that the Master was a saviour of souls like Sri Chaitanya, who redeemed the two villains, Jagai and Madhai.[49] On another occasion, again wanting to test his guru, Girish deliberately tried to think a worldly thought in Sri Ramakrishna's presence, but he found that he could not.[50]

On July 28, 1885, Sri Ramakrishna went to the home of Nanda Bose, a wealthy man of Calcutta, to see his collection of pictures of gods and goddesses. He was very much impressed. He said to Nanda: 'Though you are a householder, still you have kept your mind on God. Is that a small thing? The man who has renounced the world will pray to him as a matter of course. Is there any credit in that? But blessed indeed is he who, while leading a householder's life, prays to God. He is like a man who finds an object after removing a stone weighing twenty maunds'. (A maund is approximately eighty-two pounds.)

On this same occasion, Nanda Bose served sweets to Sri Ramakrishna and then offered him betel-leaf on a tray. But the other guests had already taken some from that tray. It is the custom that something can be offered to God only if no one else has partaken of it beforehand, so the Master would not accept any. Nanda noticed this and questioned him about it. Sri Ramakrishna replied: 'Before I eat anything I offer it to God. It is a notion of mine'. Nanda was a little proud of his knowledge of Vedanta philosophy. Trying to evaluate Sri Ramakrishna's actions intellectually, he said, 'But the betel-leaf would have gone to God all the same'. He said further: 'You are a paramahamsa. Why do you abide by the injunction or prohibition of the scriptures? They are meant for ignorant people'. Sri Ramakrishna smiled and again remarked, 'It is just a notion of mine'.[51]

Nanda concluded from this that Sri Ramakrishna had not attained the highest nondualistic state of realization, beyond the pairs of opposites and the law of causation. Girish came to know of this and felt bad. He was convinced that the Master had not revealed his divine nature to Nanda because of the man's pride of learning. Wanting to test this himself, Girish invited the Master to his house. Without any comment, Girish brought in a tray of betel-leaf, took one himself, and then offered the tray to the Master. The Master immediately understood Girish's intent and, with a smile, took a betel-leaf from the tray. Mad with joy, Girish saluted the Master again and again and then disclosed the whole story to others who were present.[52] He who makes the rules can also change them. Girish's love had set aside all rules of religious observance. Moreover, the great teachers observe scriptural rules in order to set an example for others, and not for their own benefit.

Thus, Girish came to have firm faith in the redeeming power of Sri Ramakrishna. Years later he would say, 'Had I known that there was such a huge pit in which to throw one's sins, I would have committed many more'.[53]

Once Sri Ramakrishna asked Girish to take a bath in the Ganga, but Girish was reluctant to do so. It is common belief that if a person takes a bath in the Ganga he becomes pure. Girish considered this mere superstition. Finally the Master persuaded him, saying, 'If you [being a great devotee] do not abide by these religious customs, who else will follow them?' Girish obeyed. Later he would bathe in the Ganga on auspicious occasions. One day the thought came to his mind that if the Master had taken on all his responsibilities, why should he have to bathe in the Ganga to be purified? And again, he wondered why the Master had asked him to do it. However, his analytical mind soon found an answer: When sinners take a bath in the Ganga, the goddess Ganga absorbs their sin and makes them pure. On the other hand, it is believed that when holy people bathe, she gains virtue by offering peace and delight to them. He concluded that through the Master's grace he had become so pure that by his bathing the redeeming power of Mother Ganga would increase a hundredfold![54]

Where there is love there is faith. Girish's passionate love for Sri Ramakrishna endowed him with what the Master himself described as 'one hundred twenty-five percent faith'. He loved to talk about Sri Ramakrishna to his friends and bring them to the Master to be blessed. Knowing this the Master one day prayed aloud to the Divine Mother: 'Mother, I cannot talk so much. Give a little power to Kedar, Ram, Girish, and Vijay, so that people may go to them first, learn a little, and at last come here [to me] to have their spiritual awakening in a word or two'.[55]

In the spring of 1885 the cancer that was to prove fatal began to develop in Sri Ramakrishna's throat. In September the devotees moved him from Dakshineswar to Calcutta. There he was closer to the doctor and could be better taken care of by the devotees, who served him, supported him, and came to see him during the last months of his life.

November 6 of that year was the day of the worship of the Divine Mother Kali. Sri Ramakrishna said to one of his disciples: 'It is good to make some arrangements for the worship. Please speak to the devotees about it'.[56] The devotees made arrangements accordingly. In the evening nearly thirty people assembled in the Master's room. Girish described that event: 'Sri Ramakrishna sat down to perform the worship, surrounded by flowers, fruits, and all the various articles for worship. Suddenly he turned to me and said: "It is the Divine Mother's day. One should sit and meditate like this". I do not know what took hold of me at that point. I just rushed forward and, chanting ''Jai Sri Ramakrishna [Victory to Sri Ramakrishna]'', offered flowers at his feet. The others in the room did the same. Sri Ramakrishna immediately went into samadhi, his hands assuming gestures symbolizing fearlessness and the bestowal of boons'.[57]

As Sri Ramakrishna's health was steadily deteriorating, the doctor advised him to move outside of the city, where the air would be better. Consequently, a beautiful garden house was found in Cossipore, and the move was made on December 11, 1885. An arrangement was made whereby the householder disciples of the Master would contribute money for his treatment, his food, and for the rent. The young, unmarried disciples, the nucleus of the future monastic order, would then manage the household, including the nursing and shopping. After a while some of the householder disciples noticed that the expenditures were gradually increasing. They accused the young men of carelessness and asked that the account book be strictly maintained. The young disciples, however, were offended by this and decided not to accept any more money from those householders. When the situation became tense and critical, Girish came forward with a solution: He simply set fire to the account book in front of everyone. Then he told the householder disciples to contribute each according to his capacity, and he would make up the deficit. To the monastic disciples he said, 'Don't worry. I shall sell my house if necessary and spend every bit of money for the Master'.[58]

On January 1, 1886, Sri Ramakrishna felt strong enough to take a walk in the garden. It was a holiday, and many devotees had come from Calcutta to visit the Master that afternoon. He began walking slowly through the garden, and the devotees followed him. Suddenly Sri Ramakrishna said to Girish, 'Well, Girish, what have you found in me that you proclaim me before all as an Incarnation?' Falling to his knees before the Master and saluting him with folded hands, Girish responded with great emotion: 'Who am I to speak of him? Even the sages Vyasa and Valmiki could find no words to measure his glory!'

Sri Ramakrishna was deeply moved. He blessed Girish and the assembled devotees, saying: 'What more need I tell you? I bless you all. Be illumined!' Then he went into samadhi and began to bless the devotees, touching them one by one. With each touch he gave spiritual awakening.[59]

One day, not long after this, Gopal Ghosh (who later became known as Swami Advaitananda) expressed to the Master his desire to distribute ochre cloths and rudraksha rosaries to monks. Sri

Ramakrishna pointed to his young disciples and said: 'Why not give them to these boys? They are full of the spirit of renunciation. You won't find better monks anywhere'. Gopal had twelve pieces of cloth and twelve rosaries, which he handed over to the Master. Then Sri Ramakrishna himself distributed them among eleven of his young disciples. Thus, the foundation of the future Ramakrishna Order was laid by the Master. One cloth and one rosary were left, and the Master asked that they be kept for Girish; for, indeed, he was second to none in his spirit of renunciation.[60]

Girish did not visit the Master very often at Cossipore because he could not bear to see the Master ill. One day Girish went there after the Master had eaten some farina pudding. The unwashed cup with the remnant of the pudding, mixed with the discharge from his throat wound, was still on the floor, and some tiny ants were eating it. Pointing to the cup, Sri Ramakrishna said to Girish, 'Look! And still people call me an avatar!' Girish immediately remarked: 'Sir, now even those ants will get liberation. For what other reason should you have this disease?'[61]

Sri Ramakrishna passed away on August 16, 1886. A devotee brought the sad news to Girish, but Girish would not believe it. He said to the man: 'This is a lie. The Master cannot die'.

'Sir, I have come from that place'.

'You had better go back there'.

'But I have seen him with my own eyes'.

Girish covered his eyes with his hands and retorted: 'You say whatever you want. I have not seen with my eyes, so I do not believe it'.[62]

Girish later said: 'I heard of the Master's passing away, but I did not go to Cossipore to see him. I knew it would be hard for my weak mind to maintain faith in the Master's immortal nature if I were to see his dead body. Moreover, my eyes would stand against my faith and would tell me: "Sri Ramakrishna is dead. Did you not see it with your own eyes?" For this reason I intentionally kept a conflict between my eyes and my ears about the Master's passing away. If my ears tell me, "Sri Ramakrishna is dead", I shall tell them: "You have heard so many rumours about the Master. Are you going to believe everything you hear?" Let people say whatever they want. I did not witness the Master's death, so I do not believe it'.[63]

Girish had the firm conviction that the Master was God himself, and that his body was eternal and full of pure consciousness. Disease or death could not touch his body. Because he was born as a human being, he acted as a human being, and death was also a part of his acting.

Soon after the Master's passing, misfortune again hovered over Girish. He lost his two daughters. His second wife died in 1887, and a few years later a young son, who had been very devoted to Holy Mother, also passed away. In the words of one of his dramas, Girish summed up his feelings: 'Life is painful. The world is empty. A beautiful flower garden has withered away'.[64]

A blazing fire of renunciation was growing in Girish's mind, burning up all his attachments, desires, and impurities. The garlic cup was being heated and the odour was disappearing. One day Swami Niranjanananda, a monastic disciple of the Master, said to him: 'The Master made you a monk. There is no need for you to stay at home'. Girish took the advice of his brother disciple as an order from the Master. He left home barefoot, wearing only a single cloth, and went to the Baranagore monastery. However, his other brother disciples sent him home again because they knew his body would not be able to bear the austerities of a monk's life. Girish then went to visit Holy Mother in Jayrambati, her village home. He loved the spiritual atmosphere of Jayrambati and also nearby Kamarpukur, Sri Ramakrishna's birthplace. The charming beauty of the meadows, the quiet evening sunsets over the open fields, the touching simplicity of the villagers, and especially the affection and grace of Holy Mother, all conspired to console his bereaved heart. Girish asked her permission to embrace the monastic life, but Holy Mother persuaded him to remain a householder, devoting himself to writing plays depicting the Master's life and teachings. After some time Girish returned to Calcutta with new hope and inspiration. Later, when Holy Mother was staying in Calcutta, she went to see his acting a few times and she enjoyed it immensely.[65]

Girish's hedonistic spirit had been subdued by the spiritual touch of Sri Ramakrishna. His life style was now changed. He completely gave up drinking the last twenty years of his life.[66] And yet his previous life style no doubt contributed greatly to his success as an actor and a dramatist. The intensity with which his gigantic heart had felt grief, joy, despair, and hope made it possible for him to portray the characters of his dramas vividly. He used to say that the poet and the playwright could imbue their writings with life and feeling only if they had had firsthand experience of all facets of life themselves. He once said: 'Who can criticize the portrayal of characters in my plays? I have studied the lives of all types of people, from the prostitute to the paramahamsa [illumined soul]'.[67] His power of imagination was so strong that he could actually visualize the characters of his dramas. Once he asked Swami Saradananda to visit him every day so that he

could talk with him about the Master. He said: 'I need a little
diversion. I am now writing a drama on Mirkasim [a Muslim ruler of
Bengal who was betrayed by his own people]. Oh, what a conspiracy!
I cannot bear it any more. I see Mirkasim even in my dreams — his
bearded face moves before my eyes'.[68]

There have been many books and articles written about Sri
Ramakrishna's influence on Girish's plays. Girish himself
acknowledged the fact: 'When I wrote the play *Vilwamangal*, several
of his [the Master's] devotees questioned me about it. I told them I
had learned the art of playwriting from Sri Ramakrishna'.[69] Swami
Vivekananda read Girish's *Vilwamangal** many times and said that
each time he got new light from it.[70]

In one drama, *Rupa-Sanatan*, Girish portrayed Sri Chaitanya
touching the feet of the devotees in salutation. This shocked some
followers of Sri Chaitanya, and they challenged Girish on its
authenticity. Girish replied: 'I saw with my own eyes that Sri
Ramakrishna touched the feet of the devotees. I do not write about
anything I have not experienced. Once there was a religious meeting
with devotional singing in the house of a devotee,' and Sri
Ramakrishna took the dust of that place and smeared it on his body.
When the devotees tried to stop him he said: "Look! Don't you know
this place has been sanctified by the presence of the devotees, by
spiritual talk and devotional singing? God comes to listen where his
devotees glorify his name. The very dust of this place has become
pure by the footprints of the devotees" '.[71]

Girish's writing career began when he was thirty-five and
continued for thirty years. He was a prodigious writer and produced
during that time seventy-nine works, including dramas, satires, and
musicals. In addition, he wrote many short stories, articles, poems,
and songs. His dramas dealt primarily with religious, social,

*The plot of *Vilwamangal* is adapted from a short story of the *Bhaktamala*, a
collection of stories about devotees and saints. Vilwamangal, a rich libertine,
fell in love with a courtesan named Chintamani, who lived on the other side
of the river. Vilwamangal was so infatuated with her that he would visit her
every night. One stormy night, no boatman dared to ferry him across the
river, so he jumped into the rapid current. Holding to a floating corpse,
which he mistook for a log, he crossed the river. It was late and Chintamani's
gate was closed, so he grabbed the tail of a poisonous snake, thinking it to be
a rope, and scaled the wall. Chintamani was dumbfounded when she came
to know of everything. She said to him: 'We do not know what love is. But,
my friend, why do you give your heart to a woman like me? Why do you not
give it to God? You would be illumined'. This was the turning point of
Vilwamangal's life. He later became a saint.

historical, mythological, and patriotic subjects. His innovative spirit
had a lasting effect on theatre in Bengal — in fact, he became known
as the father of the Bengali theatre.[72] He avoided the traditional
flowery language of the theatre because of its heaviness and
artificiality, and introduced irregular blank verse in the conversations
of his dramas. This eventually became known as *Gairish Chhanda*,
that is, Girish's metre.[73] The language of his plays is natural, forceful,
colloquial, and poetic. He felt that action and interaction create the
life force of the drama, and the spirit of the drama is carried along in
its language.[74]

Girish's mind worked so fast and prodigiously that he required
secretaries to take down his words; he could not write them fast
enough himself. Absorbed in the flow of ideas, he would pace back
and forth in his room and dictate all the dialogues of the drama in a
loud voice, as if he was acting each role himself. His secretary always
kept three pencils ready at hand. He could not use a pen and inkpot
because there was never enough time to dip the pen into the pot.
Once the secretary could not keep up with the speed of the dictation
and requested Girish to repeat what he had just said. Girish became
angry and asked him not to break his mood. He told the secretary to
put dots where he had missed words, and he would fill them in
later.[75]

There are many stories about his writing talent. It is said that he
could write one drama in a couple of days. *Sitar Vanabash* (The
Banishment of Sita) was written in one night.[76] He also wrote twenty-
six songs for *Sadhavar Ekadashi* in just one night.[77] Sister Devamata
mentioned in *Days In An Indian Monastery*, 'One of the greatest, a six-
act drama entitled *Vilwamangal the Saint*, was written in twenty-eight
hours of uninterrupted labour'.[78] Swami Subodhananda said, 'We
have seen Girish dictating three different dramas to three secretaries,
one after another'.[79] On another occasion Girish dramatized
Kapalkundala, a famous fictional work by Bankim Chandra Chatterjee,
in one night by dictating it to four secretaries.[80]

Girish was his own greatest competitor. When one of his dramas
was particularly well received, he felt that he had to work harder on
the next in order to surpass the previous one. He was fond of
defeating himself.[81]

Sometimes the monastic disciples of Sri Ramakrishna, in order to
bring a response out of Girish, would tease him: 'You are writing and
acting prompted by your own desires, and yet you say that the
Master gave you the task of saving the fallen people of the world.
Don't you feel ashamed to talk like that?' But Girish would boldly

reply: 'Wait, brother! When I meet Sri Ramakrishna again I shall tell him that I won't act in the role of a villain any more. The next time let his monastic disciples play the villains and I shall act the part of a noble character'. Truly, Girish believed that it was the Master who brought these devotees to the world to act in different roles in his divine drama.[82]

In the early days of his career Girish had very little money and, because of his reputation, it was difficult for him to find financial backing for his ventures. However, in 1869 he founded the Baghbazar Amateur Theatre, and shortly thereafter a rich man invited the theatre company to enact *Sadhavar Ekadashi*, a social drama, in his house on the occasion of the worship of the Divine Mother Durga.[83] In this drama Girish played the role of a drunkard. His portrayal was so realistic that through this role he first made a name for himself in the theatre. This is not surprising when one learns that he said to the stage manager before the performance: 'I cannot portray a drunkard if I have to drink coloured water from a bottle on stage. I want genuine wine'. The result was that even the writer of the drama, who was present, was overwhelmed by Girish's acting. He told Girish, 'This role seems to have been written for you, and without you the play would not be a success'.[84]

Girish soon moved to the Star Theatre and became its manager. His brilliant and creative mind always found ways to overcome the inevitable managerial problems. There was not sufficient money to buy expensive costumes, so he wrote *Chaitanya Lila*, the drama on the life of Chaitanya which Sri Ramakrishna saw, because it required only a few ochre robes and rosaries as costumes.[85]

Girish was actually the moving force behind the establishing of several theatres in Calcutta, including the Baghbazar Amateur Theatre, the National Theatre, and the Star, the Emerald, the Classic, and the Minerva Theatres. He was himself a superb and versatile actor, and wherever he performed, crowds would come to see him. Once he played five different roles in the same play, *Kapalkundala*, and proved by his performance the importance of each of the five characters.[86]

In *Days In An Indian Monastery* Sister Devamata wrote:

> I enjoyed meeting the noted Bengali dramatist, Girish Chandra Ghosh... A gifted actor also, he is called the Garrick of the Bengali stage, as well as the Shakespeare of the Bengali drama.
> The measure of his gift as an actor is given in this incident. Vidyasagar, the scholar and philanthropist, was at Girish Babu's theatre one night when the actor was depicting a profligate. In a

scene where he was abusing a woman, Vidyasagar became so stirred by the vividness of the portrayal that he took off his slipper and threw it at the actor. It struck him and rebounded on the stage. Girish Babu picked it up, placed it on his head, and with a bow to the audience, declared he had never received a more gratifying tribute.[87]

As would be expected, Girish's innovations in the theatre were met with some opposition. His irregular blank verse was criticized by traditional writers. He was also vehemently attacked by puritans for engaging prostitutes to play women's roles in his dramas. Before this, men had enacted women's roles. Often these women proved to be dedicated and talented actresses. They were poorly educated, but Girish trained them and wrote his dramas in simple language so that they could portray the characters with naturalness. The famous star Tinkari said: 'I was an unlettered girl. It was his [Girish's] grace that I am now an actress'.[88]

Girish had a great feeling for art. He knew that the artistic faculty does not manifest itself properly if there is fear, uncertainty, pressure, or exploitation. He later donated sixteen thousand rupees to the authorities of the New Star Theatre to complete its construction and said to them: 'Please do not humiliate or exploit the actors and actresses. Let them act freely'.[89]

Contrary to his reputation, Girish was actually very serious-minded and steady, and because of this he was able to overcome obstacles and criticisms and eventually gain the respect and attention of the public. In fact, Girish's waywardness has been somewhat overemphasized by some. Dhan Gopal Mukerji revealed another side of him in *The Face of Silence*:

Not only was he our greatest modern playwright, he was also a great actor and producer. It was he who revealed to the women of the underworld that they could change their lives for the better by taking up acting as a trade. Many wretched souls he saved by training them to act. Not only that, he also lifted up and revealed to the eyes of the public at least half a dozen actresses of the highest rank, who had hitherto been condemned to a life of vice while boys played the parts of women on the stage. Since Girish, all that has been changed.

The other day in India when one of his star actresses, now an old woman, called on my wife and myself, she told us how 'Father' — that is what she called Girish — worked. 'He brought about a revolution in the life of womanhood in general. Women in terrible penury, instead of being forced down into the abyss of vice, were now rescued by the stage. But Father did not stop there. He brought us all in touch with the teachings of Ramakrishna.

'He wanted us to come to the monastery during the hours of worship and pray to God. Some of us were afraid lest we soil the sacred grounds. Father answered: ''If Ramakrishna were living, he would teach you and me himself. He loves us. Didn't he come to earth for the fallen like ourselves?'' '

Our talks with many other old actors and actresses convinced us that Girish, by staying with his old Bohemian companions, did more spiritual good than if he had left them. After his soul's second birth, he did not act like a moral parvenue; he repudiated nothing of his past. Instead, he slowly permeated his friends and his writings with the spirit of Ramakrishna. And as for the Power of Attorney that he gave his guru, Turiyananda and others testify that he never violated it. All of them affirm, 'Girish was the most religious of us all; he lived, as he said he would, by the promptings of the Indweller'.[90]

Girish introduced among the performers a custom which is practised even today. Before making an appearance on the stage, each actor and actress bows down to a picture of Sri Ramakrishna. Thus, Sri Ramakrishna has become, in a sense, the patron saint of the Bengali theatre, and his photograph can be found hanging backstage in nearly every theatre of Calcutta.[91]

Girish's self-surrender was truly unique and phenomenal. Swami Vivekananda once remarked: 'In G.C. [Girish] alone I have seen that true resignation — that true spirit of a servant of the Lord... I have not met his parallel. From him have I learnt the lesson of self-surrender'.[92]

During the later part of his life, many monks and devotees would visit Girish to learn more about Sri Ramakrishna from him. When he spoke about the Master, his face would flush with emotional fervour. Even Swami Vivekananda, while he was in Calcutta, would say to the devotees, 'Let us go to G.C. and have some ''false talk'' '.[93] What the swami meant was that he would intentionally criticize Sri Ramakrishna so that they could listen to Girish defend the Master with all his faith, vigour, and sincerity. This would create a tremendous spiritual atmosphere. Girish was highly respected by the devotees. Durga Charan Nag remarked: 'If a person sits near Girish for five minutes, he will be uplifted from worldly pain and suffering. He is a great hero — the guardian angel of Shiva'.[94]

Once Swami Vivekananda was giving a class on the Rig Veda and was in the process of explaining how creation evolved from sound when Girish arrived. Turning to him, the swami said: 'Well, G.C., you do not care to study all this. You pass your days with your adoration of this and that god, eh?'

Girish said: 'What shall I study, brother? I have neither time nor understanding enough to pry into all that. But this time, with Sri Ramakrishna's grace, I shall cross the ocean of maya, bidding farewell to your Vedas and Vedanta. The Master takes you through all these studies because he wants to teach many things through you. I don't need them'. Saying this, Girish touched the volume of the Rig Veda with his head and exclaimed, 'Victory to Ramakrishna in the form of the Veda!'

Then Girish said to Swami Vivekananda: 'Brother, you have read enough of the Vedas and Vedanta. Did you find anywhere in them a way for us out of these profound miseries in this country — all these wailings of grief, all this starvation, all these crimes of adultery, and other horrible sins?'

Girish continued narrating graphically the painful picture of Indian society while Swami Vivekananda remained silent. Tears began to flow from his eyes. He rose and left the room.

Then Girish said to the disciple: 'Did you see? What a great, loving heart! I respect your Swamiji, not as a Vedic scholar, but for that great heart of his which made him retire weeping just now at the thought of the sorrows of his fellow beings'.[95]

Even when he was elderly, Girish would fast as a religious observance during the Shiva-ratri celebration (a yearly festival in honour of Lord Shiva). Once someone asked him: 'You are old and not well. Why should you fast?' Girish replied, 'I get something'. 'What?' 'A vision'. 'A vision of whom — Lord Shiva or Sri Ramakrishna?' 'I get a vision of the Master'. 'Does he talk to you?' 'No'. And then Girish added, 'That is the last wish of my life'.[96]

During the last few years of his life, Girish suffered terribly from asthma. Yet he had attained such a state of mind that disease, pain, and grief could not subdue his spirit. Even during his asthma attacks he would say with a smile: 'Look, I have no sympathy for this ungrateful body. I have given it good food for its nourishment, taken care of it with comforts and all sorts of things — yet this very body has courted this terrible asthma! Truly speaking, I don't want this disease to be cured. Every attack of asthma reminds me of the impermanence of the body'. Then he prayed, 'Lord, you are gracious. May I have this faith until death'.[97]

Once, while he was pondering his own death, he thought: 'Well, death is slowly approaching. What will happen after death? I do not know where I shall go'. Girish was thinking in this way when M. (Mahendra Nath Gupta, the recorder of The Gospel of Sri Ramakrishna) came to visit him. M. started to talk with Girish about the Master.

Suddenly, in an inspired mood, Girish said to M.: 'Brother, could you beat me with your shoes? I am not joking. I am serious'. M. smiled and asked the reason for such a request. Girish replied: 'To tell you the truth, I deserve a shoe-beating. Sri Ramakrishna is sitting within my heart and is always protecting me. Yet I wonder what will happen to me after death!'[98]

Another time Girish said to his brother disciples, with his usual vigour: 'Do you think I cannot get rid of this ordinary disease? I can. I can prove it to you. If I roll on the ground of the Panchavati at Dakshineswar and forcefully pray to the Master, this disease will go away. But I know the Master is all-merciful. It is his will that I am undergoing this disease, grief, pain, and suffering. Everything is for my good. This feeling, by his grace, is so strong in my mind that I have no inclination to pray that my disease be cured. Sri Ramakrishna is a wish-fulfilling tree. Whenever I have prayed for anything, I have gotten it'.[99]

Sri Ramakrishna's touch gradually awakened the God-consciousness in Girish, and Girish's great faith and devotion made it even stronger. Once he said, referring to the Master: 'I find that it is not difficult to obey him, love him, or worship him. But indeed it is *difficult to forget him*'.[100]

When people would lament their ill luck at not having been given the chance to meet Sri Ramakrishna, Girish would reply, 'As Mother Ganga flowed in a hundred streams in order to redeem the Sagara dynasty,* so the exuberant love of Sri Ramakrishna is flowing through hundreds of devotees in order to eventually redeem the world'.[101]

Sri Ramakrishna had asked Girish to continue acting and writing dramas, and he did so until the end of his life. On July 15, 1911, he gave his last performance at the Minerva Theatre in Calcutta. It was a cold, rainy day. He was suffering with asthma, and his role required that he come on stage several times bare-chested. People were concerned about his health and asked him not to perform, but he

---

*In ancient times, King Sagara wanted to perform a horse sacrifice in order to attain supremacy and merit. This involved setting a horse free, but heavily guarded, to wander around at will for a year. If in that time no one had defeated the soldiers and stolen the horse, all the lands that it had wandered in would belong to the king performing the sacrifice. King Sagara's sons were guarding the horse, but it got away from them. They later found the horse at the hermitage of a sage. Sagara's sons accused the innocent sage of stealing the horse, and that accusation brought about their ruin. Bhagirath, the great-great-grandson of Sagara, brought the Ganga down from heaven to earth in order to save his departed ancestors.

argued that he should not disobey the Master, who had asked him to act. Moreover, he knew many people would be disappointed if he did not appear. The strain and the weather combined to aggravate his disease. Thereafter his health declined rapidly. To those who were anxious about him he would say: 'This body does not belong to me. It is the Master's. It will remain as long as he keeps it'.[102] He breathed his last on February 8, 1912. His last words were: 'Master, you have come. Please destroy my worldly intoxication. Victory to Sri Ramakrishna! Let us go'.[103]

Girish left the stage of the world as he had left the stage of the theatre — with the flourish and heroism of a seasoned actor. Like a drama in itself, the story of his miraculous transformation has travelled from person to person, place to place, and country to country. His acting, writing, love for art, feeling for the poor and the fallen, and above all, his faith in his guru, have made him immortal.

Kalipada Ghosh (1849-1905)

20
Kalipada Ghosh

How does God, who is infinite, embody himself in a finite human form and act as a man? This is truly a mystery. On different occasions and in many ways Sri Ramakrishna tried to unravel this mystery for his disciples: 'He who liberates others is an Incarnation of God'.[1] 'The Incarnations of God accept the help of maya to fulfill their mission on earth'.[2] 'One can taste devotion and love of God only through his Incarnations. Infinite are the ways of God's play, but what I need is love and devotion. I want only the milk. The milk comes through the udder of the cow. The Incarnation is the udder'.[3] 'When God himself is born as a man, as an Incarnation, holding in his hand the key to others' liberation, then for the welfare of humanity the Incarnation returns from samadhi to consciousness of the world'.[4]

People cannot understand an avatar, or Incarnation of God, because he is different. His birth, life-style, actions, and behaviour are divine and therefore impossible to judge from the human standpoint. An avatar's love and compassion for all — the good, the bad, the pious, the sinful, the destitute, and the drunk — keeps his mind down from the absolute plane of existence and turns it to the relative existence of the world. In this way he brings good to mankind, like the coming of spring. Without any selfish motive he helps people to cross the turbulent ocean of maya. Needless to say, Sri Ramakrishna helped the drunkards and the fallen of society. Because he did so, some narrow, bigoted religious leaders criticized him for not showing 'sufficient moral abhorrence'[5] towards these people.

Kalipada was one of those wayward souls who were saved by the Master. Like Girish, he was an out-and-out bohemian, a debauchee, and a drunkard. Swami Adbhutananda related in his reminiscences how Sri Ramakrishna transformed Kalipada's life:

Girish Babu arrived one night with Kalipada Ghosh. Kalipada was a terrible drunkard. He refused to give money to his family, spending it for wine instead. But his wife was very pure. I heard that many years earlier she had come to the Master, seeking some kind of medicine that would change her husband's tendencies. The Master sent her to Holy Mother. Holy Mother sent her back to the Master. He again sent her to Holy Mother, and this exchange went on three times. At last, Holy Mother wrote the Master's name on a bel leaf that had been offered to the Lord and gave it to Kalipada's wife, telling her to chant the Lord's name.

Kalipada's wife chanted the Lord's name for twelve years. When the Master first met Kalipada, he remarked, 'This man has come here after tormenting his wife for twelve years'. Kalipada was startled but said nothing.

Then the Master asked him, 'What do you want?'

Kalipada asked shamelessly, 'Can you give me a little wine?'

The Master smiled. 'Yes, I can. But the wine I have is so intoxicating that you will not be able to bear it'.

Kalipada took him literally and said: 'Is it real British wine? Please give me a little to soak my throat'.

'No, it is not British wine', said the Master, still smiling. 'It is completely homemade. This wine cannot be given to just anyone, for not everyone can stand it. If a person tastes this wine even once, British wine will seem insipid to him ever after. Are you ready to drink my wine instead of the other?'

For a moment Kalipada was thoughtful, and then I heard him say, 'Please give me that wine which will make me intoxicated my entire life'. The Master touched him, and Kalipada started to weep. We tried to calm him, but he went on weeping in spite of our attempts.[6]

Kalipada Ghosh was born in 1849 at Shyampukur, Calcutta. His father, Guruprasad Ghosh, was very religious-minded and devoted to the Divine Mother Kali. Although Guruprasad owned a small jute business, it apparently did not bring in sufficient money to keep his family out of financial difficulties. Therefore Guruprasad took Kalipada out of school when the boy was in the eighth grade and got him a job with Messrs. John Dickinson & Company, a British paper firm in Calcutta. Kalipada thus had very little education, but he was intelligent and efficient and was gradually promoted until he held an important position in the company.

Kalipada was tall and husky. He had a dark complexion, large eyes, and a bright, cheerful face. He and Girish Ghosh were close friends and often drank together. It was Girish who first took Kalipada to Sri Ramakrishna in 1884. Some of the Master's devotees called them 'Jagai and Madhai', after two ruffians whose lives had been transformed by Chaitanya.

After Kalipada's first meeting with Sri Ramakrishna he returned

home, overwhelmed by the Master's words and personality. He felt
an irresistible desire to see Sri Ramakrishna again. Shortly thereafter,
in November 1884, he went by boat from Calcutta to Dakshineswar.
When the Master saw Kalipada he said that he had just been thinking
of going to Calcutta. Kalipada told him that his boat was at the
landing ghat and that he would be glad to take him there. Sri
Ramakrishna immediately got ready and left with Latu (Swami
Adbhutananda) and Kalipada. As they got in the boat, however,
Kalipada privately instructed the boatman to steer the boat to the
middle of the river. Then Kalipada knelt down and clasped the
Master's feet, saying: 'Sir, you are a saviour. Please save my life'.
'Oh, no, no!' said Sri Ramakrishna. 'Chant the name of the Lord.
You will get liberation'. Kalipada then said: 'Sir, I am a wicked man
and a drunkard. I do not even have time to chant the Lord's name.
You are an ocean of mercy. Kindly save a ruffian such as I, who is
devoid of disciplines and righteousness'.

Meanwhile, Kalipada firmly held on to the Master's feet. Sri
Ramakrishna could not find any way out of this predicament, so he
asked Kalipada to stick out his tongue and then wrote a mantram on
it. The Master said, 'Henceforth your tongue will automatically
repeat this mantram'. But Kalipada was not happy. He said to the
Master, 'I don't want this'. 'Then what do you want?' asked Sri
Ramakrishna. 'When I leave this world', replied Kalipada, 'I shall see
darkness all around, and that terrible darkness will fill me with
horror. My wife, children, and other relatives won't be able to help
me then. At that terrible time you will be my only saviour. You will
have to take me, holding a light with your left hand and me with your
right hand. I shall always be with you then. You will have to fulfill this
prayer of mine'. With his heart full of compassion, the Master said:
'All right, all right. Your prayer will be fulfilled. My goodness! You
have brought me to the middle of the Ganga and have created such a
scene!'[7]

When the boat reached Calcutta Kalipada asked the Master where
he would like to go. To Kalipada's delight, Sri Ramakrishna
expressed a wish to visit his home. Kalipada immediately hired a
carriage and took the Master there. It is said that there were some oil
paintings of gods and goddesses in the room where Sri Ramakrishna
sat. Seeing those holy pictures, the Master was very happy and sang
some songs in ecstasy, creating a wonderful spiritual atmosphere in
the house.[8]

A few months prior to the Master's visit an interesting incident had
occurred. One evening Kalipada's sister, Mahamaya, looked out their

Vishnu-priyangini Devi (Kalipada Ghosh's wife)

second-floor window and saw a horse carriage passing down Shyampukur Street, where their house was located. Inside the carriage was a remarkable-looking person. All of a sudden this person stuck his head out of the window and called to the driver: 'Stop! Stop! Please stop the carriage here. It seems this is the place'. Mahamaya was awed when she saw his radiant face. Immediately she called the people of the household to see this divine person, but before they could come he had put his head back inside. The carriage slowly turned down Ramdhan Mittra Lane and disappeared. Mahamaya never forgot that divine sight. When Sri Ramakrishna visited Kalipada's house, Mahamaya immediately recognized him as the person she had seen that day.[9]

Kalipada began to visit the Master regularly at Dakshineswar and gradually became one of his close devotees. He was a good singer and sometimes sang for the Master. He could also play the violin and flute. One day Sri Ramakrishna heard him playing a flute and went into samadhi. Since Kalipada was an expert cook, the devotees sometimes, out of fun, called him 'housewife'.[10]

Once when Kalipada was at Dakshineswar he went to the Kali temple and started to rebuke the Divine Mother, using abusive words. His chest turned red and tears rolled down his cheeks. Sri Ramakrishna was also there at the time, and hearing Kalipada's scolding he left the temple. He did not approve of that attitude. To his disciples who were present, the Master said: 'Our attitude towards the Divine Mother should be that of a child towards its mother. The other attitude [the heroic attitude] is extremely diffcult'.[11]

When the doctors advised the devotees to move Sri Ramakrishna to Calcutta for his cancer treatment, a house was rented for him in the Baghbazar district. Sri Ramakrishna did not like this house, however, and immediately walked to Balaram's house. He stayed there for a week until another house could be found. Meanwhile, the devotees were happy to have him in Calcutta and flocked to see him. Swami Saradananda described the following scene:

> We came to Balaram's house one afternoon and found the hall on the first floor packed to capacity with people, when Girish and Kalipada commenced singing with great zeal:
>
> O Nitai, hold me!
> Today my heart feels an unknown
> sensation, as it were.
> Hold me, O Nitai!
> I am now being carried away by
> the waves

That rose in the river of love,
As Nitai distributes the name of
Hari.

Entering the room with great difficulty, we saw the Master, who
was in ecstasy, seated in the western extremity of the room facing
the east. We saw his lips adorned with a wonderful smile of bliss
and graciousness...[12]

After a few days Kalipada found a house in Shyampukur, near his
own, for the Master to stay in. He also furnished the house and
decorated the Master's room with pictures of gods and goddesses,
and he bought kitchen utensils and groceries. Again, when he heard
that the Master had expressed a wish to worship Mother Kali on the
night of the Kali Puja, he helped make arrangements for the worship.
As an offering to the Divine Mother, Kalipada's wife prepared farina
pudding, which Sri Ramakrishna later ate as prasad.[13] Sri
Ramakrishna was pleased with Kalipada's generous nature and
called him 'Manager'. Swami Vivekananda sometimes called him
'Dana Kali', or 'the generous Kali'. (*Dana* also means 'demon'.)

On October 24, 1885, while staying at the Shyampukur house, Sri
Ramakrishna explained the mystery of japam to the devotees: 'Japam
means silently repeating God's name in solitude. When you chant his
name with single-minded devotion you can see God's form and
realize him. Suppose there is a piece of timber sunk in the water of
the Ganga and fastened with a chain to the bank. You proceed link by
link, holding to the chain, and you dive into the water and follow the
chain. Finally you are able to reach the timber. In the same way, by
repeating God's name you become absorbed in him and finally
realize him'.[14]

Kalipada listened to the Master, but he had already received the
boon that his tongue would repeat the mantram effortlessly. He
smiled and said to the devotees: 'Ours is a grand teacher! We are not
asked to practise meditation, austerity, and other disciplines'.[15]

When Sri Ramakrishna went in 1884 to see Girish Ghosh's drama,
Chaitanya Lila, he had been extremely pleased with Binodini, the
actress who had played the part of Chaitanya, and had blessed her.
She in turn had become very devoted to the Master but could not find
another opportunity to meet him. Now, hearing of his illness, she
longed to see him again. But the Master's disciples were very strict
about visitors. They feared that if Sri Ramakrishna talked too much or
if he were touched by impure people his disease would be
aggravated. In order to see the Master, Binodini sought help from
Kalipada, whom she knew through Girish. One evening, acting on

Binodini, an actress

Sri Ramarkishna went to the Star Theatre to see the play, *Chaitanya Lila* on September 21, 1884. In this play Binodini acted in the role of Chaitanya, and Sri Ramakrishna blessed her, saying, 'Mother, be illumined'.

his advice, she dressed herself as a European gentleman and went with Kalipada to the Shyampukur house. Introducing her to the disciples as a friend of his, Kalipada took her to the Master, who was alone in his room at that time. Sri Ramakrishna laughed when Kalipada told him who this 'European gentleman' really was. After praising Binodini's faith, devotion, and courage, the Master gave her some spiritual instructions and allowed her to touch his feet with her forehead. When Binodini and Kalipada had left, Sri Ramakrishna told the disciples about the trick that had been played on them. The Master enjoyed it so much that the disciples could not be angry.[16]

Sri Ramakrishna moved from the smoggy Calcutta environment to the garden house at Cossipore on December 11, 1885. On December 23 he touched Kalipada's chest and said, 'May your inner spirit be awakened'. Then, stroking Kalipada's chin, he said with great affection, 'Whoever has sincerely called on God or performed his daily religious devotions will certainly come here'.[17] The Master's blessing and unrestrained love that day made Kalipada a new person. He gave up his bad drinking habit and lost all interest in worldly things.

After the Master's passing away Girish and Kalipada often sat together silently for long periods of time in front of the Master's picture. With tearful eyes they would pray, 'Master, please reveal yourself to us'. When Navagopal Ghosh celebrated the annual festival to Sri Ramakrishna at his house, Girish and Kalipada sang kirtan and danced. Later, as they sat with closed eyes and motionless bodies, Navagopal garlanded them and they uttered in ecstasy, 'Ramakrishna, Ramakrishna'. The devotees were impressed at the transformation in their lives.[18] After Kalipada's passing away Girish dedicated his drama *Shankaracharya* to him. In the dedication he wrote: 'Brother, we saw the embodiment of Vedanta together many times in Dakshineswar. You are now in the abode of bliss, but I am sorry that you could not have seen my drama *Shankaracharya* while you were alive. I dedicate this work to you. Please accept it'.[19]

Though Kalipada was not a writer and playwright like Girish, he composed many songs. These were published in 1893 in a booklet entitled *Ramakrishna Sangit* by the Kankurgachi Yogodyana, a retreat house owned by Ram Chandra Datta. Kalipada visited the Yogodyana quite often, because some relics of Sri Ramakrishna had been installed there and regular worship of the Master was performed. One day Kalipada came with a lot of flowers for the worship. He did not know that if the flowers were carried while wearing shoes they could not be used in ritualistic worship. When

Manomohan told Kalipada of this, Kalipada immediately left those flowers there for use as decoration and went back to the flower market barefooted and bought more flowers for offering.[20]

It has already been mentioned that Kalipada was very successful in his career. It was due primarily to his efforts that John Dickinson Company opened many branch offices in the main cities of India. Although it was a British firm, Kalipada took the liberty of hanging a picture of Sri Ramakrishna in each of the branch offices. [21] He utterly believed that it was the Master's blessings that had transformed his character and brought him prosperity. If there was any vacancy in the office where he worked, he would appoint a devotee of the Master to fill that position. When he moved temporarily to Bombay, Swamis Vivekananda, Brahmananda, Turiyananda, Abhedananda, and Akhandananda each stayed at his house at different times while on pilgrimage. It gave him great pleasure to serve the Master's monastic disciples.

During Kalipada's last illness Swami Adbhutananda went to see him at his Calcutta home. Kalipada had been giving him some money every month for milk and other necessities. Swami Adbhutananda asked him to discontinue that help, but Kalipada replied: 'Brother, by the grace of the Master I have no wants. The Master will be angry with me if you deprive me of serving you with a few rupees'.[22] Since the swami did not like to hurt Kalipada's feelings, he accepted the gift until Kalipada's passing away on June 28, 1905.

Sri Ramakrishna had promised thrice in Swami Adbhutananda's presence that at the time of Kalipada's death he would take him, holding him by his right hand. Just as Kalipada breathed his last he raised his right hand. Swami Premananda was present then. Hearing the news of Kalipada's death from Swami Premananda, Swami Adbhutananda said to some devotees: 'Look, the Master came to Kalipada at his last moment. Holding Kalipada's hand, the Master guided him away. Brother Baburam saw it clearly. Whatever the Master said to anyone is bound to be fulfilled'.[23]

Devendra Nath Majumdar (1844-1911)

21
Devendra Nath Majumdar

Doubt is truly painful. It disturbs one's mental peace, upsets one's nervous system, and ruins one's physical health. Doubt is a formidable enemy in spiritual life. As a caged bird remains idle in the cage and leads a bound, miserable life, so a doubting soul is confined in his own confusion, and lives without peace and happiness in the world. Doubt contracts the heart and causes stagnation in life, whereas faith expands the heart and creates motion. Faith brings joy, without which it is hard to live in this world. And faith lights the path for a soul, guiding it to its destination. Like many other people, Devendra Nath Majumdar doubted the existence of God. He once described to someone the joy he felt when his doubt was finally transformed into faith and how this eventually took him to Sri Ramakrishna.

One day Devendra went to his uncle's home in Manicktala, Calcutta. Since the uncle was not there at the time, Devendra waited in his living room, where he found a copy of a Bengali book, *The Life of Sadhu Aghorenath*. Aghorenath was a follower of Keshab Chandra Sen and a preacher of the Brahmo Samaj, specializing in lectures on Buddhism. Devendra opened the book at random and read the following story: Aghorenath had once gone to preach in the northwestern part of India. On his way through Bihar, about nine miles from the town of Chapra, he took shelter for the night in an empty inn. At midnight a band of robbers entered the building to assault him. When the robber chieftain gave the order to rob and kill him, Aghorenath was frightened. 'Look', he said, 'I'm not a rich man. I don't earn money. I travel and preach the name of God. Please take everything but don't kill me'. Saying this, Aghorenath burst into tears, and asked for a little time to pray to God. After that he sang two Hindi devotional songs. The first song began 'O Lord, you are kind but I am wretched; you are the giver and I am a beggar', and the second, 'Blessed is your name, O Lord'. After singing, Aghorenath lost consciousness. Just as he regained consciousness, he heard one of the robbers say to another: 'This man is a devotee of God. Don't kill him'. Without robbing him, the robbers left.[1]

After reading this story Devendra shouted in great excitement: 'Who says that God does not exist? Here is proof that he exists! Who else could have saved Aghorenath's life?'[2] Devendra returned home, went to his room, and closed the door. Bumping his head against the wall, he wept, praying to God for his vision. Three days and nights he spent in his closed room without food or sleep. Early in the morning of the fourth day he came out of his room and paced back and forth on the roof of the house. As he watched the sun rise he cried out: 'Who says that God does not exist? That is the sign of God'. Then he thought to himself: 'It is true that God is everywhere, but who will help me realize God? I need a guru'.[3]

Devendra Nath Majumdar was born in the village of Jagannathpur in the Jessore district of East Bengal (now Bangladesh) on January 7, 1844. His father, Prasanna Nath, died two months before Devendra was born, but his mother lived a long life. Well-to-do at one time, the family had a Krishna temple adjacent to their house. Devendra had a sister, and a brother named Surendra Nath Majumdar, who was five years older than he. An uncle was their guardian. Like most village boys, Devendra was very lively. His rowdiness once resulted in a broken left hand which, not having been properly set, remained slightly bent the rest of his life.

Devendra attended school but could not keep his mind on his studies. Even then his nature was poetic, and his handwriting was both beautiful and rapid. Playing with the cowherd boys in the meadow was his favourite pastime. Once a boy asked him if he could catch space. Guileless, Devendra really believed that he could. But no matter how much he ran, he could not catch it. Some of these childhood memories he later narrated in his songs.

From boyhood Devendra told the truth. Once a relative complained about his naughtiness to Surendra, his elder brother. Surendra replied: 'Devi [Devendra's nickname] may be naughty now, but one day he will be great, because he never tells a lie'.[4] Knowing Devendra's trustworthiness, a neighbour once asked him to watch his grocery shop while he went on an errand. The neighbour was late in returning, and Devendra, having grown hungry, ate a handful of puffed rice from the shop. Immediately he was overwhelmed by fear and guilt. As soon as the grocer came back, Devendra confessed, but the man merely laughed and told him it was all right. The painful memory of this incident convinced Devendra that the path of untruth causes much suffering. Many years later he recounted this story to his followers.

When Devendra was fifteen his uncle died, and his brother, Surendra, became his guardian. Moving to Calcutta where his brother lived, Devendra continued his studies for another five years. During this period Surendra won fame as a renowned poet. Two of his many books of verse were *Mahila* and *Savita Sudarshan*. His literary work brought him in touch with other writers, and he became a close friend of Girish Chandra Ghosh. Surendra was also a tutor to Adhar Lal Sen. Both Girish and Adhar later became disciples of Sri Ramakrishna. Devendra used to listen to Surendra and Girish discussing literature, history, and philosophy, which strengthened his imagination and increased his knowledge. About this time Surendra taught Devendra sixty-four postures of hatha yoga. Devendra also began sitar lessons with a teacher, and in time he became an expert player.

Although Devendra had no desire to get involved in family life, in 1870 his mother forced him to marry Meghambari, the nine-year-old daughter of Harish Chandra Chatterjee. This young wife was very pure, simple, and devoted to her husband. Since Surendra was supporting the whole family, Devendra led a carefree life. In 1878, however, Surendra died from cholera at the age of forty-one. The entire responsibility of the family fell on Devendra, now thirty-four, who did not have a job. The family suffered terribly from poverty. Indeed, Devendra's mother, wife, and sister-in-law were often close to starvation. Devendra moved to an inexpensive apartment on Nimu Goswami Lane in the western part of Calcutta, and finally got a clerical job in the Tagore family's estate in Jorasanko, Calcutta. The job paid very little, but it was easy to make extra money by cheating and exploiting the poor peasants. Devendra was upright, however, and would not accept an extra penny from anyone, even though he was living in debt. One day he mentioned his condition to his employer, who was so impressed with Devendra's honesty that he cleared up all his debts.

After reading the story about Aghorenath, Devendra began desperately to search for a guru. Neither hatha yoga nor the sermons of Keshab Chandra Sen could give him peace of mind. Having heard about Bhagavandas Babaji, a Vaishnava saint living in Kalna, he decided to go to him for initiation. One day in the early part of 1884, he went to the Ahiritola dock to board a steamer for Kalna, but missed it. Returning home, he stopped at a friend's house and saw on his desk a book entitled *Bhakti Chaitanya Chandrika* (The Life and Teachings of Chaitanya). On page sixty-three of this book he came across Ramakrishna's name. The author mentioned that

Paramahamsa Ramakrishna compared the Nitya (the Absolute) and the lila (the manifestation), or, God without form and God with form, to water and ice. Devendra knew that the word *paramahamsa* was a title for a person who had attained God-realization. He thought to himself, 'Would Ramakrishna be my guide?'[5]

Leaving his friend's house, Devendra met another friend on the street and asked him if he knew anything about Sri Ramakrishna. The friend said, 'Sri Ramakrishna lives in the temple garden of Dakshineswar'. Devendra was so excited that he could not wait to meet Sri Ramakrishna. No sooner did he arrive home than he left again, going by boat to Dakshineswar. He was greatly agitated. As the boat approached the temple garden Devendra saw a man with one arm in a sling standing in the garden.

When the boat was anchored Devendra asked a man who was sitting on the bank of the river where Sri Ramakrishna lived. The man pointed to Sri Ramakrishna's room. Devendra went to the semi-circular verandah on the western side of the Master's room and looked inside. Seeing no one in the room, he waited on the porch. Soon a plainly dressed man with one arm in a sling entered the room through another door. He was wearing slippers, and one part of his lower cloth was pulled up and thrown across his shoulder. Devendra recognized him as the man he had seen from the boat and concluded that he must be the paramahamsa. He bowed down to him, and the Master told him to enter by the northern door. Noticing that Devendra left his shoes at a distance before entering the room, Sri Ramakrishna advised him to keep them on the verandah, for otherwise they might be stolen.

Devendra sat down on a mat on the floor, and the Master asked him, 'Where do you come from?' 'Calcutta'. 'To see the deity in this form, maybe?' The Master posed as Sri Krishna with his flute. 'No, sir', said Devendra, 'I have come to see you'. 'To see me!' exclaimed the Master. 'Ah, what is there to see in me? Look, I have broken my arm. Oh, what pain!' Asking Devendra to feel his injured arm, he said: 'Can you tell if the bone has been fractured? It is so painful! What shall I do?' Devendra examined the arm and asked the Master how the accident had occurred. Sri Ramakrishna replied: 'Sometimes I fall into a peculiar state. The arm was broken on one of those occasions. The pain increases when any medicine is used. Adhar Sen sent some medicine which also increased the swelling, so I have stopped using any medicine. Do you think I shall recover?' 'Yes, certainly'. In a moment all trace of pain seemed to disappear from the Master's face. Like a boy, he called out to some people outside, 'Look here, this gentleman from Calcutta says that my arm will get better!' [6]

Devendra noticed that Sri Ramakrishna's body was delicate like a woman's and his mind frank like a child's. Never before had he seen such an open, artless person. He thought: 'Is this a show? I have come to see a saint, whereas he has made me out to be a saint. He takes me for a prophet. Is it possible for a man to be so artless? Or is it just a pretence?'[7] But gradually the Master's childlike behaviour dispelled all his doubts. In the meantime Sri Ramakrishna asked a devotee named Harish to give Devendra some refreshments. When Devendra finished eating, the Master began to talk about divine love. He said: 'Do you know what *prema* [ecstatic love of God] is? When one has prema, one forgets the world. One even forgets one's own body, which is so dear to a person. As in a dust storm one cannot distinguish the trees and the houses — all look alike, so at the dawn of divine love all ideas of distinction vanish'.[8] Devendra had never before heard such a thing. He sat enchanted, absorbing every word the Master said.

When it was time for the midday meal, Sri Ramakrishna said to Devendra: 'Look, many respectable brahmins eat here. It is a temple, and there can be no objection to your taking prasad with us. The day is already advanced. Don't leave now'. Calling his nephew Ramlal, Sri Ramakrishna said: 'Look here, he is a good man. He will take his food here. Please give him the prasad from the Vishnu temple'. Devendra again wondered: 'How does the Master know that I am a vegetarian? Can he read minds?' While eating his meal Devendra questioned Ramlal about the Master's life. His mind was filled with wonder.[9]

After lunch Devendra rested a little and then visited the temples. When he came back to see Sri Ramakrishna, the Master noticed that he did not look well. He asked Devendra: 'Why do you look so pale? Are you ill?'[10] Devendra had had a relapse of his old malarial fever. The Master was extremely worried about him. Just then Baburam, a young disciple (later, Swami Premananda), arrived. The Master asked him to accompany Devendra on the boat to Calcutta. As they were leaving the Master invited Devendra to come again when he felt better.

When their boat reached the Baghbazar ghat, Devendra told Baburam that he would be able to go home by himself. Baburam wanted to go with him, but Devendra refused to be helped anymore. Somehow he managed to reach a relative's house nearby, where he fell unconscious. For forty-one days he lay in a state of torpor and delirium. Often he uttered Sri Ramakrishna's name, thinking that he was at Dakshineswar. Curiously, whenever extreme pain made him open his eyes, he would see Sri Ramakrishna sitting by his bed. When he recovered, however, he was filled with doubt, and he decided that his visions had been mere hallucinations. As a consequence, the attraction he had felt for the Master gradually diminished. He thought to himself: 'A visit to a holy man is supposed to bring one peace and blessings, but what happened to me? It almost cost me my life. I salute him, but I don't want to go there again'.[11]

As the months passed Devendra's desire to realize God abated somewhat, but did not disappear altogether. Whenever the thought of visiting Dakshineswar came into his mind, he would remember his terrible fever. After a while he decided to repeat the Gayatri mantram, and this practice kept him going. Then one afternoon he called on a friend. Not finding his friend at home, he passed the time until his friend's return reading the *Sulabh Samachar*, a Brahmo Samaj newspaper. In it he saw the following announcement: 'Sri Ramakrishna Paramahamsa will meet his devotees today at 5:00 P.M., at the house of Balaram Basu in Baghbazar'.[12] Devendra's heart leapt. All his reasons for not seeing the Master vanished, and immediately he left for Baghbazar.

At Balaram's house, which was crowded with people, Devendra saw Sri Ramakrishna dancing in ecstasy. Some people were dancing around him while others were singing. Devendra watched it all but did not dare approach the Master because he had stayed away so long. When the kirtan was over the Master stood motionless, deep in samadhi. The devotees gathered around him to take the dust of his feet. Seizing this opportunity to salute the Master without being noticed by him, he pushed his way through the crowd and touched Sri Ramakrishna's feet. Much to his surprise, he felt a gentle tap on the back and heard someone asking: 'Hello, how are you? Why haven't you come to Dakshineswar? I often think of you'. 'Sir', replied Devendra apologetically, 'I was bedridden for a long time, so I couldn't visit you'. Then the Master said in a sweet voice: 'You must come again to Dakshineswar. Won't you?' Devendra's heart had been thoroughly melted by this time. 'Yes, sir', he said, 'I will'.[13]

Soon after this Devendra began to visit the Master regularly. He received instructions from the Master and practised spiritual disciplines under his direction. Eventually Devendra understood that Sri Ramakrishna was not an ordinary holy man. A gracious glance from Sri Ramakrishna was enough to liberate a person. Mentally Devendra accepted him as his guru. One day the Master asked him if he had been formally initiated. Devendra said, 'No, sir, but it is my heartfelt desire that you give me a mantram'. 'I don't give mantras', replied the Master. Devendra was hurt by this answer, but did not lose hope. A few days later, on an auspicious day, Devendra came to Dakshineswar with flowers and a garland, hoping that the Master would initiate him. Pleased to see the flowers, Sri Ramakrishna told Devendra to offer them to the deities in the temples. Devendra said, 'But sir, I brought this garland for you'. Gravely the Master said to him: 'Only gods and dandies accept flowers. Which do you think I am?' By now truly exasperated, Devendra replied, 'You must be in between the two'.[14] Just to please him, however, the Master accepted a few flowers and then told him to take the rest to the Mother's temple. Although Devendra did not receive a mantram then, he began to have visions of the Master everywhere, even as he walked along the streets. He felt that the Master was with him all the time and watching over him.

As Devendra watched the young disciples serving the Master, he too wanted to render him some personal service. One day the Master noticed Devendra carrying his towel and water jug for him. Immediately he said to Devendra: 'Oh, no! Why are you carrying these things for me? My relationship with you is different'.[15] But Devendra did not understand what the Master meant. He thought to himself, 'Am I so lowly that I am unfit even to carry a towel and water for the Master?' He laid the things under the Panchavati trees and sat down while Sri Ramakrishna walked to the pine grove. Devendra began to brood over the Master's behaviour. Gradually his thoughts turned into deep meditation, and he lost outward consciousness. He did not know how long he was in that state, but when he opened his eyes the Master was standing in front of him, smiling. Sri Ramakrishna said to him in a sweet voice: 'Look, you will not have to practise austerities. It will be enough if, in the morning and evening, you chant the name of Hari [a name of Krishna] while clapping your hands. Chaitanya taught this path, and one can attain perfection by chanting Hari's name. Visit this place whenever possible. Your life will be fulfilled in this way'.[16]

Another day Sri Ramakrishna said to Devendra: 'You are visiting this place [meaning himself] frequently. What have you understood? Have you achieved anything?' Devendra answered: 'No, sir, I don't know anything special, but I don't care to go anywhere else to know about God and religion. Moreover, I do not have that restlessness in my mind anymore'. 'You have tried many things, no doubt', the Master said. Then, entwining his fingers, he continued: 'But they were not properly set. You know, every person has his own place'.[17]

Devendra returned home, greatly reassured. Resigning his job, he took up the spiritual practice of chanting Lord Hari's name. Night and day he repeated the mantram alone in his room, which no one was allowed to enter. Outside the door his wife kept a tray of food from which he ate when he was hungry. During this period he enjoyed many wonderful visions as he meditated. Once he saw a group of women in white clothes, with marks on their foreheads, standing before him. One after another they bowed down to him and left. Unable to understand the meaning of this vision, he went to the Master and asked about it. Sri Ramakrishna said: 'They [the women] were the companions of avidya [ignorance]. They have left you'.[18] Another day Devendra felt that he had become separated from his body and was watching it. After some time he thought he was dead. This frightened him, but he soon grew normal again.

As a result of his intense sadhana Devendra experienced ecstatic moods. During this time he was said to have become a bit unbalanced. He could not bear the touch of a worldly person, and he regarded his relatives as poisonous cobras. The world seemed to him a dark, deep well. He was extremely happy when any of the Master's disciples visited him, but when they left he felt unbearable pain. Sri Ramakrishna found out from the devotees about Devendra's condition, and he prayed to the Divine Mother: 'Mother, please don't give him so many experiences. He is a family man, and several people depend on him'.[19] Shortly after this Devendra's mind became normal, and he began to visit the Master again. He then got another job and put his mind on his household duties.

Before Devendra met the Master, he had already known Ram Chandra Datta, Narendra (Swami Vivekananda), and Rakhal (Swami Brahmananda), but now he became very close to them as well as to other disciples. He himself brought several people to Sri Ramakrishna. One of these was a young man of the Tagore family, who went with Devendra to visit the Master at Dakshineswar. Later on this young man left home to become a mendicant. It was partly due to Devendra's urging that Girish Ghosh began to visit Sri Ramakrishna. Devendra also introduced his uncle, Harish Chandra Mustafi, as well as Akshay Kumar Sen and several others, to the Master.

Sri Ramakrishna was the embodiment of purity and renunciation. His own life was a demonstration of how to overcome lust and greed, two great obstacles in spiritual life. Devendra had heard that the Master could not touch metallic objects, but he wanted to witness this for himself. One day, while Sri Ramakrishna was visiting the

Mother's temple, Devendra slipped a silver coin under his mattress. When the Master returned shortly after and tried to sit on his bed, he found that he could not touch it. After trying several times he looked at Devendra and said: 'What is the matter? Why can't I sit on the bed?' Embarrassed, Devendra confessed to the Master what he had done and took back his coin. Sri Ramakrishna said with a smile: 'Oh, you are testing me? Very well'.[20]

On another occasion Devendra visited Dakshineswar, and in the course of conversation the Master said to him: 'You see, I am thinking deeply of a woman whom I have not seen for a long time'. This immediately created a doubt in Devendra's mind. Then the Master told his nephew Ramlal to give Devendra some rasagollas (sweet cheese balls), saying that they had been sent to him by the woman who loved him so much. Devendra's doubt deepened as he ate the rasagollas. After a while Sri Ramakrishna, wishing to go to Jadu Mallik's house in Calcutta to see that woman, not only asked Devendra to lend him a rupee for the carriage fare, but invited him to come along. Devendra readily assented. Young Latu (Swami Adbhutananda) went with them. As they rode in the carriage, the Master saluted temples, mosques, the women in the street, and even a tavern. To the Master all women were forms of the Divine Mother, and again it was she who gave joy to the barroom drinkers. Tapping Devendra's knee, the Master said, 'Look, I don't disturb anyone's faith'.

As soon as the carriage reached Jadu's house, Sri Ramakrishna went directly to the women's section by himself. This strengthened the doubt in Devendra's mind still more. A little while later Devendra and Latu were invited into the women's section for some refreshments. There Devendra saw an old lady seated on a carpet in front of the Master, who was eating a plateful of assorted sweets. The Master was behaving just like a five-year-old boy. Devendra realized then that this woman had a motherly attitude towards the Master, as Mother Yashoda had for her baby Gopala (Krishna). The old lady said to the Master: 'My son, many years ago I read in the Sri Sri Chaitanya Charitamrita about how Chaitanya's mother used to feed her son. Since then I would think that if I could be Chaitanya's mother I could feed him. What great fortune I have today! My son, I never dreamed that you would come today and fulfill my cherished desire!' Saying this, the woman wept as she fed the Master with her own hand.[21]

The Master was all-knowing, and he took this means to remove the doubt in Devendra's mind. But Devendra was conscience-stricken because he had doubted the Master. Later he learned that the old lady was Jadu Mallik's mother.

As part of his job Devendra sometimes had to go to court to
supervise litigations. On those days he followed the custom of
wearing Western clothes to the courtroom. Once, coming back by
boat from the Hooghly court, he stopped at Dakshineswar. But
because he knew that the Master could not bear worldly things such
as the legal documents and newspapers he was carrying, he greeted
the Master from the verandah. When Sri Ramakrishna asked him to
come inside, Devendra told him what he was carrying. 'It does not
matter', said Sri Ramakrishna. 'It will not do any harm to you. Please
come in'.[22] The compassionate Master saw the longing in Devendra's
heart and disregarded everything else.

Another time when Devendra was going by boat to Dakshineswar
with some *mihidana* (a sweet) for the Master, he sat in front of a
Mohammedan who was a great talker. Devendra noticed that as the
man talked his spittle flew in all directions. He could not tell whether
any of it fell on his package of sweets. But if the package had been
defiled in this way, he thought he ought to throw it into the Ganga.
Otherwise, he would be greatly embarrassed in front of other
devotees if Sri Ramakrishna was unable to touch it. By the time he
landed at Dakshineswar he had had a change of heart. Sprinkling a
little Ganga water on the package, he took it to the Master's empty
room and put it in the corner on a shelf. When the Master came back
to his room, he was hungry and began to look for something to eat.
When he found the warm mihidana on the shelf, he ate some of it and
distributed the rest to the devotees. Devendra was moved by the
Master's grace. He left the room, weeping with joy, and told the story
to a devotee.[23]

Devendra and Girish were friends and had known each other long
before either met Sri Ramakrishna. Once the Master went to see
one of Girish's plays at the Star Theatre, where Girish had arranged
a special seat for him. Devendra and Latu accompanied the
Master. After the performance, Girish, who was drunk, humiliated
the Master, using abusive language. Latu became furious and was
about to hit Girish, but Devendra stopped him. The next day
Devendra went to Girish's house and said to him: 'When you drink
you lose control of yourself and talk nonsense. You should go to
Dakshineswar and apologize to the Master'. But Girish replied: 'No, I
shall not go to Dakshineswar. And I shall not apologize either.
Whatever qualities he gave to me I offered back to him. I've been
fasting and crying all day. Doesn't he know it? If he is an avatar,
doesn't he realize what I am suffering? He will have to come here.
Otherwise I shall not eat any food. I shall starve to death'. It was

raining. At four o'clock in the afternoon Sri Ramakrishna arrived at Girish's house with Ram Chandra Datta. Girish fell at the Master's feet, and Sri Ramakrishna blessed him.[24]

One day Devendra came to Dakshineswar and noticed a picture of Sri Ramakrishna hanging on the wall in his room. He had never seen it before. The Master was not there then, and Devendra was looking at it intently. Meanwhile Sri Ramakrishna entered the room and asked, 'What are you looking at?' Devendra saluted the Master and said: 'I was looking at your picture. It is beautiful'. Devendra wanted the picture but was hesitant to ask the Master for it. At last he expressed his desire to Sri Ramakrishna. The Master replied: 'Oh no, you can't have that picture. The boys [the young disciples] hung it there with great care. You had better ask Abinash, who took the picture. He will make a print for you, but he will charge you for it'. The Master told Devendra that, since Abinash was a hemp smoker and forgetful, he should ask Bhavanath, Abinash's neighbour, to remind him to make the print.[25]

Devendra noticed that well-to-do devotees of the Master would often invite Sri Ramakrishna to their houses and arrange festivals. He too wanted to invite the Master, but did not have enough money. Despondent, he talked it over with Girish, who willingly offered financial help. This gave Devendra the encouragement that he needed, and later he decided to bear the cost of it by himself without anyone's help. A few days later he went to Dakshineswar. He was extremely hesitant to invite the Master, but Sri Ramakrishna himself said to Devendra, 'I have been thinking of visiting your house one day'. Devendra replied: 'The same idea came to my mind today, and I have come here to ask that favour of you. You must grace my house this Sunday'. 'But', the Master said, 'you have a small income. Don't invite many people. The carriage hire will also run to a big amount'. Devendra answered with a laugh: 'What if it is small? "One can run into debt to eat butter!"'[26] Sri Ramakrishna laughed a long time at Devendra's words. When Ram Chandra Datta heard from Devendra about the Master's forthcoming visit, he arranged to have Sri Ramakrishna's favourite singer and musician come for the festival.

On April 6, 1885, Sri Ramakrishna came to Devendra's house, along with several devotees. They were entertained with a kirtan and a feast. In the course of conversation the Master said to the devotees: 'If the mind is free from "woman and gold", then what else can obstruct a man? He enjoys then only the Bliss of Brahman'. As the Master listened to the devotional singing, he went into samadhi. Later he talked to the devotees in a joyful mood. Devendra served ice

cream, a favourite treat of the Master's, to Sri Ramakrishna and the
devotees. Since the day was very hot it was greatly appreciated.

When it was time for Sri Ramakrishna to leave, Devendra and the
other devotees escorted him to his carriage. One of the neighbours
was sound asleep on a bench in the courtyard of Devendra's house.
The man had come to see the Master hours before, but being addicted
to opium, he had fallen asleep and missed the festival. When
Devendra woke him up, he rubbed his eyes and asked, 'Has the
paramahamsa come?' Everyone laughed.[27]

A few days later Devendra took the women of his family to
Dakshineswar. Sri Ramakrishna received them warmly and asked the
women to rest for a while at the nahabat, since they had come
through the scorching sun. Holy Mother entertained them. Later they
went to the temples and talked to the Master. After the women had
returned home, they talked together again and again about the
Master and Holy Mother.

One day Devendra expressed to Sri Ramakrishna his desire to
become a monk. The Master did not approve of it. He said to him:
'You do not have to renounce your family. I ask you to stay at
home'.[28] The Master knew that Devendra was the only earning
member of his family, and moreover his mother had earlier lost her
elder son. Sri Ramakrishna sang a song describing the grief of
Shachimata, Chaitanya's mother:

> Why, golden Gaur, should you leave Nadia to become a
>   mendicant?
> Oh, what will happen to your wife, Vishnupriya?
> Vishwarup's loss still I do harbour;
> Do you too want to hurt your unfortunate mother?[29]

This song persuaded Devendra that the Master did not want him to
become a monk.

Once the Master wrote something on Devendra's tongue with his
finger.[30] Devendra knew in his heart that Sri Ramakrishna had
transmitted power to him. After this incident he had various spiritual
visions and could talk about God for long hours at a time.

When Sri Ramakrishna moved to the Cossipore garden house,
Devendra visited him frequently. On January 1, 1886, the Master
called Devendra to his room and said to him: 'Ram has declared me to
be an avatar. Can all of you verify Ram's statement?'[31] That same
afternoon Sri Ramakrishna went for a walk in the garden and in an
ecstatic mood blessed the devotees, saying, 'Be illumined'. Devendra
was one of those so blessed. A few days before the Master passed
away, he said to Devendra: 'Nowadays I always feel that I am

merging into the infinite Brahman'.[32] Devendra understood that the Master was hinting that he would soon enter into mahasamadhi.

After the Master's death Devendra visited from time to time the Baranagore monastery and the Kankurgachi Yogodyana. Once when Devendra was at the monastery with his uncle, Swami Vivekananda asked him to become a monk. Devendra replied that Sri Ramakrishna had told him to lead the life of a householder. Swamiji himself then dressed Devendra in the ochre cloth of a monk, and a group photo was taken at the monastery. Devendra felt such intense renunciation that day that he told his uncle he would not return home. Only after much persuasion did Devendra finally consent to go back with his uncle, but his dispassionate mood continued for a month.[33] Devendra later acknowledged that it was because of Swamiji's power that he had felt that way.

One evening when Swami Vivekananda was returning from Dakshineswar with Devendra, he said to him: 'Look at the Milky Way. It is just like a stream of milk. Do you know that every moment millions of suns and moons are being formed within it? That is the source of the stars. Just imagine what an inconceivable Being is the ruler of this vast universe! And a tiny man with his limited intellect is trying to fathom and comprehend him! Is he so easily obtainable?' After listening to Swamiji, Devendra was absorbed in the thought of the Infinite. He then concluded that it was not possible for a man to realize God. This greatly troubled him, and he could not sleep for three days. At last he went to Girish and told him the cause of his anxiety. Girish said to him: 'But it is also true that the ruler of this universe, from whom this cosmic creation evolves, incarnates himself in a human body and gives liberation to sinners like us'. Devendra was relieved to hear this, and his mind became calm again.[34]

In 1893 Girish became the director of the Minerva Theatre and appointed Devendra as a cashier and supervisor. Devendra was a faithful worker. Seeing that his handwriting was good and that he could write fast, Girish also engaged him to write down his dictation. Several of Girish's dramas were thus taken down by Devendra. Unfortunately, though, part of Devendra's job brought him in contact with the actors and actresses of the theatre, and gradually he drifted, becoming involved with some of the actresses who worked at houses of ill fame. When he finally realized what he was doing, he was filled with self-reproach. In 1895 he cut off all connection with the theatre forever.[35]

Longing for the return of his mental peace and spiritual life, Devendra went to M., the recorder of *The Gospel of Sri Ramakrishna*, and said: 'The Master said that if a person touches the philosopher's stone, he turns to gold. I received the Master's blessings, but why have I fallen to such a degraded state? Does this mean that I did not really touch the philosopher's stone?' M. answered: 'It is true that you became gold by touching the philosopher's stone, but still that gold has fallen in a dustbin'. Devendra was not consoled with M.'s answer. Just as a person becomes restless when a foreign object enters his eye, in the same way Devendra was extremely disturbed. A pure, sincere soul suffers pain and agony when he comes in contact with evil company or has impure thoughts. Devendra next went to Durga Charan Nag, a great devotee of Sri Ramakrishna, for consolation. Hearing his story, Durga Charan said: 'If you work in a room full of soot, you are sure to soil your body, be it ever so little, no matter how clever you may be. But why are you so afraid? You have a guru, and there is the Ganga. They will cleanse you. They will purify you'. Durga Charan said this last sentence with such faith and conviction that all Devendra's guilt and anxiety were removed in a moment.[36]

Devendra was very frank and truthful. He was willing to share his experiences with others and to point out to them the pitfalls in spiritual life. In later years he told his followers: 'If people know the dark period of my life, they will realize that if a person does something wrong in his life once, that does not mean that he has forever fallen from the path of God. At that time I did so many wrong things, yet still the Master did not give me up. If a person has sincere love for God, God will do good to him. If, out of an uncontrolled desire, a person commits a sinful act, he should not be depressed and carry the guilt ever after. He should take refuge in God. Then God will protect him. One good thing happened by those mistakes — the Master has crushed my ego completely'.[37] Then Devendra quoted a saying of Swami Vivekananda's: 'True greatness consists not in rising, but in rising every time we fall'.

After resigning from his job at the theatre Devendra was without a job for a year and suffered terribly from financial troubles. During this same time his mother died. In 1896 he got a job as a manager for the Devnarayan Estate, in Entally, Calcutta. He then led a very solitary life. He would spend some time in meditation in the landlord's garden; at other times he would go to the Keoratala cremation ground in South Calcutta, to practise spiritual disciplines. In 1899 his wife died from smallpox while holding a picture of the Master on her chest.

Gradually, as people came to know that Devendra was a disciple of

Sri Ramakrishna, a small group of devotees gathered around him. On Sunday, May 6, 1900, Devendra and his followers installed a picture of Sri Ramakrishna in a house at 43 Dev Lane, where they would perform kirtan. Thus the 'Sri Sri Ramakrishna Archanalaya' (the worship place of Sri Ramakrishna) came into existence. Devendra composed many devotional songs for the group to sing, which later were published in a book entitled *Devagiti* (The Songs Divine). Every evening Devendra and the devotees would sing devotional songs and talk about Sri Ramakrishna. In a short time this group became known among the followers of Sri Ramakrishna. Swami Vivekananda visited the Archanalaya on February 16, 1901, and Swami Saradananda conducted a scriptural class every Saturday for two months. Swamis Brahmananda, Premananda, Shivananda, and Akhandananda, as well as Girish Ghosh, M., and other devotees also visited the centre quite often.

Swami Vivekananda was a good friend of Devendra's. Knowing that Devendra practised spiritual disciplines with the attitude of a gopi (a shepherd girl of Vrindaban), Swamiji affectionately called him *sakhi*, or 'woman friend'. Once Swamiji sang a song about Radha, and hearing it Devendra began to dance in ecstasy. Swamiji liked his dancing, but not his emotionalism. While singing songs, for example, Devendra would often lose control over himself. Because of this Swamiji suggested that he eat meat and fish, since such food tends to make the nerves strong. Although Devendra had been a vegetarian all his life, he took Swamiji's words as an order of his guru and started to eat fish. It was not possible for him to eat meat, however.

Devendra noticed that the members of his group were enthusiastic about singing devotional songs but they did not practise japam and meditation. One day he told them: 'Look, it is not enough to sing kirtan. One should also regularly practise meditation in solitude. Please rent a house so that you can have a place to practise spiritual disciplines'.[38] In February 1902 the devotees rented a house at 39 Dev Lane, which later became the permanent home of the Sri Sri Ramakrishna Archanalaya. Devendra installed a shrine to the Master and inaugurated daily worship, food offering, and a vesper service. In 1904, at the time of the Jagannath Car Festival, Holy Mother visited the Archanalaya. Devendra composed a song for the occasion: 'O Mother, we are your naughty children. Please take us on your lap'.[39] This song was sung to the Mother by some little boys. She was moved and gave two rupees to Devendra to buy some sweets for the boys. Normally Holy Mother would remain veiled in front of the

Master's men devotees, but that day she removed her veil and blessed Devendra.

Devendra continued as manager of the Devnarayan Estate until 1907, but after that he spent his whole time in spreading the message of the Master. He had quite a few disciples, who greatly loved and respected him. He also inspired many young people to follow Swamiji's teaching to 'serve man as God'. One of Devendra's followers, Nafar Chandra Kundu, used to come to the Archanalaya every evening from his work in order to be in Devendra's holy company. One day Devendra asked him, 'If you saw that a boy was about to drown in a pond, what would you do?' 'I would immediately jump into the pond and try to save him', replied Nafar. Devendra then explained to him that unselfish action is the same as worshipping God. It so happened that on May 12, 1907, when Nafar was on his way to work in South Calcutta, he came across a large crowd gathered in the street. On inquiry he learned that two Mohammedans had fallen unconscious while cleaning in a manhole. He was shocked. He scolded the crowd, 'Two men are dying and you people are watching the fun!' Nafar then jumped into the manhole to rescue the men, saying, 'Victory to the guru!' Unfortunately the poisonous gas inside the manhole killed Nafar.[40]

Devendra was stunned when he heard the news of Nafar's death. He praised his bravery and unselfishness. The government of India, the Calcutta Corporation, the Oxford Mission, and many other philanthropic organizations and prominent people of Calcutta organized a commitee to set up a monument where Nafar had died and to create a permanent fund which would provide a pension for Nafar's family. Devendra was the chief planner and worker on the committee. One day at that time Girish Ghosh said to Devendra, 'If Swamiji were alive, he would appreciate your contribution'.

During the later part of Devendra's life he suffered from various ailments, and in 1906, in order to recover his health, he went to live for some time in Puri. In 1907 he went to Meerut, in North India, where he initiated some devotees. After visiting Hardwar and Rishikesh he came back to Meerut and established a branch of the Sri Sri Ramakrishna Archanalaya. Returning to Calcutta in January 1908 for a short time, he again went back to Meerut. On this trip he had an attack of pneumonia and had to return to Calcutta. After recovering he travelled to Hetampur, Dhaka, Madhupur, and other places at the request of the devotees.

One of Swami Vivekananda's brothers, Mahendra Nath Datta, once wrote about Devendra: 'He [Devendra] was not an original thinker, but he was the best expounder to the masses. In his sweet, homely language, with his poetical effusion, he could make a wonderful impression on the minds of his listeners'.[41] Devendra's magnetic personality drew people wherever he went. With songs and discourses he inspired the devotees, and when he answered their spiritual questions, his humble manner impressed them. Once he talked to them about despondency in spiritual life. He said: 'Struggle is the beauty of life. This beauty vanishes as soon as our struggle ends. In spiritual life one moves backwards and forwards, but in this way one gradually makes progress. No line is perfectly straight in this world. The mind fluctuates like the waves of the ocean. Don't be upset when the mind goes down. It will rise again. There is nothing more harmful than to be despondent. Trials and tribulations make our minds strong, but despondency does not do us any good. Rather, it takes away our strength'.[42]

On another occasion, when he was talking about meditation, he said: 'Just as a man loves to live near his beloved and derives much joy from constantly seeing her, in the same way, in our meditation we try to live near the Chosen Deity and see him clearly. Meditation increases the power of concentration, and without concentration no great work can be performed'.[43]

Near the end of his life Devendra composed a beautiful hymn of eight stanzas to Sri Ramakrishna as the guru. The first stanza runs:

Bhava-sagara tarana karana he
Ravi nandana bandhana khandana he;
Saranagata kinkara bhita mane
Gurudeva daya-kara dina jane.

O thou the means to cross the ocean of worldliness!
O destroyer of the bondage of death!
O guru divine, please show compassion to thy lowly servant,
Who has come to thee for refuge with a mind stricken with fear.

This is one of the popular hymns on Sri Ramakrishna. Once while listening to it, Swami Brahmananda said, 'Devendra composed that hymn while absorbed in a higher plane of consciousness, a state beyond the reach of ordinary people'.[44]

In April 1911 Devendra arranged, the Archanalaya's annual Sri Ramakrishna festival, which was attended by Gauri-ma, Swami Premananda, Girish Ghosh, M., and many people of different religions. Devendra sang and danced the whole day in ecstasy and in many ways gladdened the hearts of the guests. Once he said to a devotee: 'People think that God-vision means seeing God with four arms. It is not like that. If you have a little love in your heart, you will taste the bliss of God. *Love is God'.*[45]

On October 8, 1911, Devendra gave some spiritual instructions to the devotees, and after the vesper service he went to bed. His attendant noticed that he had a little fever, which he still had the next day. On the morning of the tenth, after going to the shrine and bowing to the Master, he drank a glass of water and felt a severe chill. He said to a devotee: 'You can't detain me any longer. I am very close to my end'. Then he said to his attendant, 'Can you find out how much money I owe?' Learning from the attendant that he had a debt of twenty-five rupees, he asked a devotee to pay it for him. The devotee gladly agreed.[46]

That evening, after the vesper service, the devotee saw that Devendra was shivering, and that the hair on his body was standing on end. Sometimes he smiled and sometimes tears flowed from his eyes. He thus passed twenty-two hours. Off and on he chanted, 'Om guru, Om guru'.

The news of Devendra's critical condition reached Belur Math and spread among the devotees of Sri Ramakrishna. Swami Subodhananda, M., Mahendra Nath Datta, and many monks and devotees came to see him. Some sanctified water was put in his mouth, and the devotees in his room chanted 'Om Namo Bhagavate Ramakrishnaya' (Salutations to Bhagavan Ramakrishna). Devendra passed away at the Archanalaya at 1:55 P.M. on Saturday, October 14, 1911, and his body was cremated at Keoratala, South Calcutta, on the bank of the Kali-Ganga.

22

Upendra Nath Mukhopadhyay

According to the Bhagavad Gita, four kinds of people worship God: those who are afflicted, those who seek knowledge, those who crave wealth, and those endowed with wisdom.[1] All four kinds are worthy because their actions and thoughts are in some way connected with God, even though some of them seek worldly prosperity. No doubt God is the kalpataru (wish-fulfilling tree), but this does not mean that he automatically fulfills all desires. As the wise doctor will not prescribe poison to alleviate a patient's pain, similarly the omniscient God answers only those prayers which will ultimately benefit the devotee.

Once a poor but beautiful woman fell in love with a man for his money. After she married him and found herself the recipient of all his wealth, however, the object of her love gradually shifted from money to husband. She realized that any joy in life comes from Spirit, not from matter. This is exactly what happened in the life of Upendra Nath Mukhopadhyay. He went to Sri Ramakrishna seeking wealth and material prosperity.

In *Sri Ramakrishna and His Disciples*, Sister Devamata quoted Swami Ramakrishnananda referring to Upendra: 'At one time there was a very poor boy who used to come almost daily to Sri Ramakrishna, but the Master would never take any of the food he brought. We did not know why. Finally one day Sri Ramakrishna said: "This poor fellow comes here because he has a great desire to be rich. Very well, let me taste a little of what he has brought", and he took a small quantity of the food. The boy's condition began to improve immediately, and today he is one of the most prosperous men in Calcutta'.[2]

Upendra Nath Mukhopadhyay was born in Ahiritola, West Calcutta, at the home of his maternal uncle on February 28, 1868. He lived there with his mother, even though his parental home was at Balagar, Hooghly. Very little is known about his father, Purna Chandra Mukhopadhyay, except that he was a high-class brahmin and had been married several times. Upendra's uncle, Jagabandhu

321

Upendra Nath Mukhopadhyay (1868-1919)

Bandyopadhyay, worked in a watch shop at Radhabazar, and his financial condition was not good. Having no children himself, Jagabandhu brought up his nephew as his own son.

Upendra went to primary school for a time but then discontinued his studies. His uncle scolded him for this and advised him to find a job. Though Upendra was only a boy, within a few days he found a job in a drugstore washing bottles and labelling them. Later, when he realized that the pharmacist was not an honest man, he quit his job and found another in a bookshop at Brindaban Basak, Battala (Upper Chitpore Road). Upendra's monthly salary was five rupees (about 50 cents), and his duties included cleaning the shop, arranging bookshelves, and selling books.

After some time the owner wanted to sell the business for seventy-five rupees. Upendra decided to buy it and asked his uncle for the money. Jagabandhu refused, but his aunt secretly gave him the money. Upendra bought the shop and reimbursed his aunt within three months.

As owner of the bookstore, Upendra collected some small comic books and successfully published them in one volume. After some time he became an agent for other publishers as well as the sole distributor of the works of Surendra Nath Majumdar, the brother of Devendra Nath Majumdar, who was a devotee of Sri Ramakrishna. Upendra lived on the same street as Devendra, so they were acquainted with each other. Adhar Lal Sen also lived in Ahiritola, and Sri Ramakrishna visited his house several times.

In 1884, probably at Adhar's house, Upendra first met Sri Ramakrishna and then began to visit Dakshineswar regularly. Observing some auspicious signs in Upendra, the Master inquired about his background. When Upendra stated his name Sri Ramakrishna said: 'Oh, you are a brahmin! Is there any regular worship at your house?' 'Yes, sir. There is daily worship of Narayana [Lord Krishna] in our house'. Then the Master asked, 'Some day could you bring me some prasad [sanctified food] of Lord Narayana?' Upendra agreed.

Returning home he wondered whether or not his aunt would misunderstand the Master. After long deliberation he finally told her that a brahmin of the Dakshineswar Kali temple had asked for some of Narayana's prasad. Hearing this the devout woman immediately agreed to send prasad to Dakshineswar through her nephew. That day Narendra, Rakhal, and some young devotees were taking their meal at Dakshineswar. When Upendra arrived he offered the prasad to Sri Ramakrishna, who was very pleased. The Master took a little and asked Upendra to distribute the rest among the others.

Some of Upendra's young friends began to visit Dakshineswar with him. This irritated their parents, who complained to his uncle. As a result Jagabandhu grounded Upendra, confining him to the house. But Upendra's compassionate aunt released him. On another day she, being an excellent cook, sent prasad to Dakshineswar on her own.

Upendra was upset because he could not afford to bring the Master a gift as other devotees did. Understanding the cause of his grief, Sri Ramakrishna asked him to buy two-pice worth of jilipis (a sweet). Much later, when Upendra celebrated the Ramakrishna festival at his house, he would always offer the Master jilipis.

Gradually Upendra became known among the devotees of Sri Ramakrishna and attended festivals arranged for the Master in their Calcutta homes. On April 6, 1885, Sri Ramakrishna visited Devendra's house, where Upendra had the great privilege of massaging the Master's feet. When Surendra, Ram, and other devotees started to celebrate the birthday of the Master at Dakshineswar, Upendra also took an active part.

Upendra was a handsome young man with a fair complexion, bright eyes, and beautiful curly hair. He was also industrious and ambitious, and the pain of poverty tormented him. Upendra had no desire to marry, but Sri Ramakrishna knew a couple who had a dark-complexioned daughter named Habi. The Master did not like her name and suggested to her parents that they call her Bhavatarini, which is also the name of the Dakshineswar Kali. From that time on she was known as Bhavatarini.

Once when Upendra's mother was visiting the Master at Dakshineswar, Sri Ramakrishna suggested that she arrange her son's marriage to Bhavatarini. She agreed. Swami Vivekananda, who was present at the time, objected to the marriage proposal, saying that the girl was not pretty and her skin was too dark. But the Master remarked that the girl had some good signs and that this marriage would bring good fortune to Upendra. In 1885 Upendra married her with the consent of the Master. Later, when Swamiji visited the couple, Bhavatarini was reluctant to offer refreshments to him, knowing his objections to the marriage. But Swamiji mollified her and said humourously: 'Since you have wrapped yourself around Upendra's neck, I will have to eat your cooking'.[3]

Upendra's uncle would sometimes remind him that he had neither education nor money, so his life was worthless. It was hard for this sincere teenager to digest such humiliation day after day. He first tried to help himself and then sought divine grace from Sri Ramakrishna.

One day at Dakshineswar Upendra was seated with other devotees near the Master. Pointing to him, Sri Ramakrishna said, 'This boy visits this place desiring money'.[4] On another occasion in a gathering, a devotee said to the Master, 'Sir, you did not bless Upendra'. Sri Ramakrishna replied with a smile: 'He did not express to me what he wants. But I know his wish — that his small door should be big — and it will be'.[5]

On January 1, 1886, at Cossipore, Sri Ramakrishna became a wish-fulfilling tree and blessed many devotees. That day he asked Upendra, 'What do you want?' 'Money'. 'You will get plenty of money', said the Master.[6] It would be an injustice to Upendra, however, if the reader thought that he was only money-hungry. His life indicates that he had true devotion for the Master along with the ambition to acquire wealth.

Sri Ramakrishna passed away on August 16, 1886, and his body was cremated at the Cossipore cremation ground. Upendra was present. After extinguishing the funeral fire, the devotees bathed in the Ganga. However, when Upendra went to bathe, he was bitten by a poisonous snake. Immediately he sat down on dry land while the devotees tied his upper leg tightly so that the poison would not spread, and then they cauterized the wound. By the grace of the Master his life was saved. It took nearly five months for the wound to heal, but the blue mark on his skin remained throughout the rest of his life.[7]

When Upendra started his book business there were no notable Bengali publishers in Calcutta. Battala, in West Calcutta, was just a local book market. Gradually Upendra bought a small printing press and founded the Bengali magazine *Jnanankur* (*The Blossom of Knowledge*). Swami Vivekananda's translation of *The Imitation of Christ* was published serially in this magazine. Later Upendra published the book *Rajbhasha* (*King's Language*), which outlined an easy way to learn the English language. This book sold so well that Upendra amassed a tremendous fortune from it.

Later, in 1889, he published *Sahitya Kalpadruma*, a monthly magazine. He renamed it *Sahitya* in 1891 and transferred the entire rights to Suresh Samajpati. In this same year, a son was born, Satish Chandra, who later successfully took over his father's business.

Gradually Upendra became well established in the publishing profession. He rented a two-storied building and expanded his work in 1896 by publishing the *Basumati*, a weekly Bengali newspaper.

When Swami Vivekananda returned to Calcutta from the West in February 1897, the official reception committee sent nothing more than a news release about his arrival to the Calcutta newspapers. But Upendra freely donated much more publicity. Among other things he printed thousands of handbills and distributed them throughout the city. He also placed, in prominent locations, placards announcing Swamiji's arrival time and the reception site. Furthermore, Upendra published a decorative picture of Swami Vivekananda in his newspaper. Below the picture he printed a new song written by Girish Chandra Ghosh in honour of Swamiji's return. Upendra distributed thousands of free copies of this special issue.

The evening before Swamiji's arrival, Swamis Brahmananda and Yogananda, Girish, Purna, and other devotees were discussing the arrangements. The train was scheduled to arrive at Sealdah Station from Budge Budge port early in the morning, and they were concerned whether many people would attend the reception on such a cold morning. When Upendra arrived and heard of their anxiety he assured them: 'Tomorrow thousands of people will go to see Swamiji. I posted placards all over Calcutta, Baranagore, Cossipore, Bhawanipur, and Alipur, and freely distributed fifty thousand handbills and ten thousand copies of the *Basumati*. I strongly believe that tomorrow before daybreak, by the grace of the Master, the Sealdah Station will be overflowing'. Girish was overjoyed and exclaimed, 'Brother, you have performed a great service through this publicity'.[8] Upendra's forecast was accurate. Twenty thousand people came to receive Swamiji at Sealdah Station, creating a sensation all over Calcutta.

Very soon Upendra became a successful publisher in Calcutta. He moved his business to a more commodious building on Gray Street and expanded production by enlarging his press. The number of subscribers to the *Basumati* increased enormously, and some notable writers such as Panchkari Bandyopadhyay, Jaladhar Sen, and Suresh Samajpati became its editors. The Basumati Sahitya Mandir, Upendra's publication department, published cheap editions of the *Mahabharata* of Kaliprasanna Sinha as well as the works of such esteemed writers as Madhusudan, Bankim Chandra, Tekchand, Girish Chandra, Rangalal, Dinabandhu, Hemchandra, Navin Chandra, and Sharat Chandra. It was Upendra who made this great Bengali literature widely available. Moreover, he published the Bengali translation of many Sanskrit scriptures and other literature such as the Mimamsa, Samkhya, Yoga, and Vedanta philosophies, the Upanishads, the Bhagavatam, and the works of Shankaracharya, Kalidasa, and many others.

The Basumati publication house was a temple of learning. When in

1914, during the First World War, subscribers were anxious to receive the latest news, Upendra started publishing an evening edition called the *Daily Basumati*. It was very popular and later became a regular daily Bengali newspaper.

It is a fact that for most people the desire for money takes one's mind away from God. But this was not true in Upendra's case. The more wealth he acquired, the more his devotion to the Master increased. His magazine spread the message of Sri Ramakrishna and Swami Vivekananda. Swamiji chose 'Namo Narayanaya' (Salutations to God) as the permanent caption for the front page of the *Basumati*, and Upendra gladly agreed. Once Swamiji remarked, 'Upendra has a wonderful business sense'.[9] Upendra, in turn, often consulted Swamis Vivekananda and Yogananda on business matters.

Every November in his Ahiritola house Upendra observed the Ramakrishna festival for a day with a kirtan and a grand feast. He would decorate the picture of the Master with flowers and garlands, and many monks would participate in the festivities.

Upendra, always eager to serve the monks and the devotees of Sri Ramakrishna, kept his place of work open to them. In fact, his workers often referred to the Basumati Sahitya Mandir as 'Ramakrishna Sadavrata' (Sri Ramakrishna's Inn). Swami Akhandananda wrote in his memoirs that whenever he and his brother monks would visit Upendra's bookshop, Upendra would feed them with various kinds of sweets and other delicacies. Then he would send them by share-carriage back to the Baranagore monastery.

Swami Adbhutananda stayed for some time at Upendra's Basumati press and everything was provided for him. At one time Upendra even sent him by boat to Puri for a pilgrimage. When, after his return from the West in 1900, Swami Vivekananda heard from Swami Adbhutananda that Upendra had graciously provided food and shelter for him for some time, Swamiji, touched by Upendra's generosity, prayed to Sri Ramakrishna, 'Master, please bless Upendra'.[10]

Because Upendra had experienced crippling poverty, he had tremendous love and compassion for the poor. He used to help his workers whenever they were in need of financial assistance. Once two young boys from a reformatory were sent by the government to the Basumati Publishing House for training. One of them stole some books and was caught by the police. The kindhearted Upendra went to court and informed the judge that he had given the books to the boy. Hearing this, the judge released him.

On another occasion Upendra arrived at his office and found a young worker encircled by others. He was told that the young man had stolen some type and that the police were there to arrest him. But Upendra told the police he had given the type to the young man. After the police left Upendra said to the youth, 'My boy, go away immediately and never commit such a heinous act again'.[11] Though it may seem that Upendra deviated from the truth, the scriptures say, 'One may tell a lie in order to save another's life'.

There are countless stories about Upendra's generosity. Once the paper merchant who supplied the paper for Upendra's press sent a reminder to him that a large invoice had not been paid. Upendra immediately informed the merchant that he had already paid the paper company's representative. A high official of the company came to the Basumati office to check their account book and discovered that Upendra was right — the bill collector had misappropriated the money. Upendra, knowing that the collector had now and then visited Sri Ramakrishna, stepped forward to assume entire responsibility for the money and requested the official not to take any action against the collector.

One day on his way to the press, Upendra was stopped by a man who needed financial help for his daughter's marriage. Upendra promised to pay him the entire income of that particular day and asked him to come to his Basumati office in the evening. At the end of the day he kept his promise and paid the man three hundred rupees.

Upendra was a self-made man. He earned money by the sweat of his brow and encouraged others to earn money honestly. Tarapada Haldar, a staff worker, recorded his memoirs in Upendra's Centenary Number: 'Upen Babu used to put on a dhoti and a loose fitting shirt, over which he wore a black silk coat. He would carry a silver stick in his hand, and I don't remember whether or not I ever saw him without a Burmese cigar in his mouth. Upendranath had a sweet relationship with his workers. It was not an employer-employee relationship; it was a father-son relationship... He was a true disciple of Sri Ramakrishna. In every step of the prosperous journey of the *Basumati*, Upendra saluted Narayana and sought the blessings of the Master. Sri Ramakrishna was the presiding deity of the Basumati Sahitya Mandir. Upendra did not show his devotion publicly, so we never saw him salute the Master, but he practised his spiritual life beyond the gaze of others'.[12]

Gradually Upendra realized that his Gray Street office was insufficient, so he bought a new building and adjacent land on Bow

Bazar Street (now Bepin Behari Ganguli Street), in Central Calcutta. Because he did not have sufficient funds at the time to buy the property, he had to borrow the money. But by the grace of the Master, he soon paid off the loan.

Upendra was a jolly, loving soul. At the same time he was honest and spiritual. Although he had no formal education, he was known and respected by the great writers and thinkers of Bengal. He had tremendous love and respect for writers and scholars, and it would pain him whenever he found the talent of a writer stifled from lack of money.

Upendra's son, Satish, had the same principles as his father, and achieved similar success. He also imbibed from Upendra a deep love for God. Once he went to Belur Math and asked to become a monk, but the swamis reasoned with him and sent him back home to take care of his father's business.

Upendra believed wholeheartedly that his success was due to the blessings of Sri Ramakrishna. He knew that the beloved Master would guide him in the right direction and protect him from worldly attachment. Throughout his life Upendra experienced his guru's grace, which made him truly wealthy. He passed away on Monday, March 31, 1919, in his uncle's home in Ahiritola, Calcutta.

Front row: Tarak Datta, Akshay Sen, Girish Ghosh, Swami Adbhutananda, and M
Middle row: Kalipada Ghosh, Devendra Majumdar, Swami Advaitananda
Back row: Devendra Chakrabarty, Unknown, Unknown, Abinash Mukhopadhyay,
Mahendra Kaviraj, Vijay Majumdar

23

Haramohan Mittra

According to Hindu scriptures, it is a blessing to be the recipient of the Lord's anger. If an unmotivated, all-loving, all-compassionate God shows displeasure towards anyone, it is for his own good. If a loving mother disciplines her unruly child by force, it does not mean that she is cruel. Caring for her child and thinking of his future, she chastises him, even though it pains her to do so. At the time, the immature, rebellious child may resent his mother, but later, as an adult, he can only be grateful to her.

Haramohan Mittra was born in a poor family and raised by his uncle, Ramgopal Basu, who lived near Swami Vivekananda's house in Simla, Calcutta. Haramohan's mother was a devotee, and, having herself met Sri Ramakrishna several times, she encouraged her son to visit Dakshineswar.

Haramohan was a handsome young man and a classmate of Swami Vivekananda. The Master was very fond of him. In course of time, however, Sri Ramakrishna became indifferent towards him because of his worldly tendencies. On July 3, 1884, the Master said: 'This attachment to "woman and gold" makes a man small-minded. When I first saw Haramohan he had many good traits. I longed to see him. He was then seventeen or eighteen years old. I used to send for him every now and then, but he wouldn't come. He is now living away from the family with his wife. He had been living with his uncle before. That was very good. He had no worldly troubles. Now he has a separate home and does the marketing for his wife daily. The other day he came to Dakshineswar. I said to him: "Go away. Leave this place. I don't even feel like touching you" '.[1]

Haramohan was present on Kalpataru Day (January 1, 1886) when Sri Ramakrishna blessed the devotees at Cossipore. For some reason, however, the Master, approaching Haramohan, simply touched his chest and said: 'Let it be postponed today'.[2]

Sri Ramakrishna's divine touch transformed the life of Haramohan. He later had numerous spiritual experiences, including visions of

331

gods and goddesses. Haramohan was well known among the devotees for his devotion and his sweet, catholic nature. He mixed freely with the disciples of the Master, and Swami Vivekananda, in particular, was very fond of him.

One summer evening in 1887, Swamiji was conversing with Haramohan in his home about the deep meaning of Sri Ramakrishna's message. Inspired, the swami said: 'Look, all philosophical thoughts are at my beck and call; and Western philosophy is also on the tip of my tongue'. Then he continued: 'One can write shelves of philosophical books based on a single teaching of Sri Ramakrishna'. Surprised, Haramohan replied: 'Is that so? But we don't find any such profundity in his teachings. Could you explain one of his sayings in that manner?' 'Do you have the brains', asked Swamiji, 'to understand the Master? Well, take any saying of his, and I shall explain it to you'. 'All right', Haramohan said, 'please explain his story of the elephant-god and the mahout-god, which illustrated his instruction to see God in all beings'.[3]

At once Swami Vivekananda launched into the controversial doctrines of free will versus predestination and self-effort versus the will of God — a perpetual, unresolved conflict among scholars of both the East and West. For three continuous days Swamiji explained to Haramohan in simple language that the Master's story was a solution to that age-old controversy.

Haramohan took an active part in spreading the Ramakrishna-Vivekananda literature. At his own expense he reprinted Swami Vivekananda's *Chicago Addresses* and distributed free copies. He also published the *Teachings of Sri Ramakrishna*, compiled by Suresh Chandra Datta; *Paramahamsa Ramakrishna*, written by the Brahmo leader, Pratap Chandra Majumdar; *Ramakrishna and His Sayings*, by Max Müller, and several pamphlets expounding the life and teachings of Sri Ramakrishna.

While he was in America, Swami Vivekananda gave permission to Haramohan to publish his lectures. He did so to ease the poverty of his old friend. But later, in a letter written on October 28, 1896, Swamiji expressed his irritation at the cheap quality of materials used for the publication. He wrote: 'That Haramohan is a fool,... and his printing is diabolical. There is no use in publishing books that way; it is cheating the public and should not be done'.[4]

In the beginning of the Ramakrishna movement, very few people took the risk of publishing books about Sri Ramakrishna and Swami Vivekananda. Haramohan was a striking exception. His devotion, boldness, and zeal impelled him to undertake this pioneering work.

He not only took the responsibility of publishing these works, but he also defended the Ramakrishna-Vivekananda movement through his writings and lectures. Haramohan had a good command of English, and among his writings are some critical notes on Pratap Majumdar's book, *Paramahamsa Ramakrishna*.

In 1898, when Sister Nivedita (Miss Margaret Noble) read her paper, *Kali the Mother*, at Albert Hall in Calcutta, Dr. Mahendra Lal Sarkar made some disparaging remarks about image worship. In response to his criticism, Haramohan rose and delivered a profound lecture, quoting Sri Ramakrishna in defense of image worship. Another incident occurred after Swami Vivekananda's return to India from the West. Haramohan was present at a meeting in which Christian missionaries were attacking Hinduism, whereupon he protested vehemently. Such instances show that in spite of all his personal shortcomings, Haramohan was a lover of truth and fought to uphold it whenever necessary.

Although he was poor, Haramohan did not covet money. He considered the publications of the Ramakrishna-Vivekananda literature, which were his only source of income, to be his service to the Master. Many people, especially young students, became acquainted with the life and message of Sri Ramakrishna through Haramohan. Once a young boy went to his bookshop to buy a lithoprint of Sri Ramakrishna which, at the time, was not available anywhere else. When the boy asked for the price of the picture, Haramohan said, 'It costs six pice', even though the actual cost was eight annas (fifty pice).

After the boy bought the picture, Haramohan asked out of curiosity, 'How did you come to know about this bookstore?' 'Swami Yogananda gave me your address and asked me to buy the picture', replied the boy. Haramohan was delighted to meet a new devotee of the Master and immediately offered him some fruits and sweets. After that he told him many stories about the Master and remained in touch with him.

Haramohan used to spend part of his income for the service of Holy Mother. Once, when he heard that her bracelet had broken from constant wear, he borrowed money from friends and bought a new pair of bracelets for her. Moreover, he gave jewellery to Radhu (Holy Mother's niece) at the time of her marriage.

Benevolent by nature, Haramohan never hesitated to borrow money to help others. Even if a dog or cat followed him in the street, he would buy some food from a nearby shop to feed it. With the desire to spread religion by publishing religious books at a low price, he gave away more copies than he sold. As a result of his generosity, he suffered financially later in life.

Haramohan thrived on the sweet memories of Sri Ramakrishna. Whenever people came to visit him, he talked only of the Master and forgot all else. Blessed was Haramohan, who received the touch of Sri Ramakrishna on the Kalpataru Day! Although the Master withheld his blessing on that day, he bestowed it in the later part of his life.

24

Gopaler-Ma
(Aghoremani Devi)

It is hard to believe how the infinite God actually assumes a finite human form and plays with human beings. But this play was actually enacted in the life of a woman devotee of Sri Ramakrishna. She was known as Gopaler-ma, or 'Gopala's mother'. Gopala, or cowherd boy, is an epithet of the child Krishna. Gopaler-ma's given name was Aghoremani Devi, but she came to be called Gopaler-ma because of her fervent devotion to the infant Krishna, which culminated in Lord Krishna appearing before her as a child of seemingly solid physical form. Aghoremani attained this high mystic experience by living a life of austerity and renunciation, and through her steadfast love for her Chosen Deity, Gopala.

One way to approach God, according to traditional Hinduism, is by practising any one of five dualistic attitudes, or moods. These attitudes, or moods, are manifested in the relationship between the devotee and God, and they are: *shanta bhava*, the peace and stillness felt in the presence of God; *dasya bhava*, the attitude of a servant towards his Master; *sakhya bhava*, the attitude of a friend towards a Friend; *vatsalya bhava*, the attitude of a parent towards a Child; *madhura bhava*, the attitude of a lover towards the Beloved. The idea behind this classification is to help the spiritual aspirant intensify his relationship with God according to his own inner nature. This is a natural path to God-realization. Gopaler-ma attained her vision of God through the practice of *vatsalya bhava*, the attitude of a mother towards her Child.

Aghoremani Devi was born of a brahmin family about the year 1822 at Kamarhati, a northern suburb of Calcutta. Following the social custom of child marriage, she was married at the age of nine. Her wedding was the first and last time she saw her husband, for he died before the marriage was consummated, leaving her a widow of fourteen years of age. However, she was initiated into spiritual life by her husband's family guru and, with the child Krishna as her Chosen Deity, she was given the 'Gopala mantram'. Since a Hindu brahmin

Gopaler-ma (Aghoremani Devi)
(1822-1906)

widow does not remarry, the love and energy that Aghoremani would have given her husband and children were diverted towards her beloved Gopala. It was Divine Providence that her one-pointed devotion was to make her a saint instead of a faithful housewife.

After the death of her parents she went to live at the temple garden of Govinda Datta at Kamarhati, where her brother was the priest of the Radha-Krishna temple. It was a large estate, located on the bank of the Ganga. Govinda's widow, the owner and manager of the temple, was a very pious woman who lived like a nun. She practised severe austerities, such as sleeping on the floor, bathing three times and eating one meal a day, and observing religious vows, daily worship, japam, and meditation. She was looking for a companion, and through her priest she found Aghoremani, who had a similar nature and spiritual inclination. Aghoremani was also very happy to have the opportunity to live in a solitary, holy place on the bank of the Ganga.

Aghoremani was short but well built, with a tawny complexion and a face that shone with the glow of purity. It is an ancient custom in India for monastics and orthodox widows to shave their heads because they do not care for external beauty, and, following their example, Aghoremani shaved her head. In later years she donned the ochre cloth, the traditional garb of the renunciant.

By selling her jewellery and husband's property Aghoremani received about five hundred rupees, which she invested in securities and left in her landlady's care. With the three or four rupees a month interest earned on the investment, she had to manage her living. Sometimes the landlady helped her, but from time to time Aghoremani was forced to draw on her capital.

Spiritual life is not a matter of show. The more hidden it is, the stronger and more fruitful it becomes; the more it is expressed, the weaker and more superficial it becomes. For this reason mystics like to remain hidden. Aghoremani, like other mystics, was a person of few words, and she led a quiet, contemplative life in the temple garden of Kamarhati. Many years later Sister Nivedita described her surroundings:

> How beautiful was the Ganga, as the little boat crept on and on! And how beautiful seemed the long flight of steps rising out of the water, and leading up, through its lofty bathing-ghat, past the terraced lawn, to the cloister-like verandah on the right, where, in a little room, built probably in the first place for some servant of the great house at its side, Gopaler-ma had lived and told her beads for many a year... Her own little room was absolutely without

comforts. Her bed was of stone, and her floor of stone, and the piece of matting she offered her guests to sit on, had to be taken down from a shelf and unrolled. The handful of parched rice and sugar candy that formed her only store, and were all that she could give in hospitality, were taken from an earthen pot that hung from the roof by a few cords. But the place was spotlessly clean, washed constantly by Ganga-water of her own sturdy carrying. And in a niche near her hand lay an old copy of the Ramayana, and her great horn spectacles, and the little white bag containing her beads. On those beads, Gopaler-ma had become a saint! Hour after hour, day after day, for how many years, had she sat day and night absorbed in them![1]

The tiny room, where Gopaler-ma spent the greater portion of her life, was at the southwest corner of the building. It had three windows on the southern side through which she could see the Ganga. Inside the room were large earthen pots containing rice, lentils, spices, and other things, which she purchased in quantities to last for six months. Fresh vegetables were bought once a week at the local market. She kept her few articles of clothing in a tin trunk, and her cooking pots and pans were neatly stacked in one corner. Both her inner life and her outer life were well organized. This is a sign of a yogi.

The scriptures say that the practices of an illumined soul are meant for spiritual aspirants to emulate. Gopaler-ma's life, devoid of comfort and luxury, and filled with intense longing for Gopala, demonstrates how essential austerity and concentration are to realization. Thus it is both important and helpful for seekers of God to know such details as the daily routine, behaviour, habits, and mode of life of an illumined soul.

Gopaler-ma arose at two o'clock in the morning, washed her face and hands, then started her japam, which continued until eight o'clock. Next, she cleaned the Radha-Krishna temple, washed the worship vessels, picked flowers, and made garlands and sandal paste. She was neat, clean, and meticulous. She would bathe twice a day, mornings in the Ganga and evenings in the pond. After bathing in the Ganga, she meditated for some time under a vilwa tree in the temple garden. Next, she collected dry wood and leaves for her cooking fire. She usually cooked rice, dal, bitter squash, and potato. Her food offering to Baby Gopala was worth seeing. She would place a wooden seat on the floor for Gopala and offer cooked food on a banana leaf-plate, which she set before him. Afterwards she would partake of the prasad and then rest for a while. She practised japam again hen until evening, when she would attend the vesper service of Radha-Krishna and listen to devotional singing. Her supper was always very simple, usually consisting of a few offered coconut balls and a little milk. Again she would start her japam, which continued until midnight. With rare exception, she followed this routine daily for over thirty years — from 1852 to 1883. Perhaps the only break of any consequence in her routine came when she went on a pilgrimage with her landlady to Gaya, Varanasi, Allahabad, Mathura, and Vrindaban.[2]

Swami Ramakrishnananda mentioned an incident which happened shortly before Gopaler-ma met Sri Ramakrishna:

One day she was cooking as usual, but the fire would not burn, the wood was heavy with moisture, and there was an adverse wind which blew the smoke into her eyes. Finally when the bit of rice and curry was done and she was about to pour it out on the leaf, the same adverse wind blew away the leaf. Then she began to scold God for making everything so bad for Gopala. As she was talking, a little boy brought back the leaf, held it out flat on the ground until she had put the food on it and then disappeared. She began to feed her Gopala; but suddenly she began to ask herself who that little boy was and she realized that it was Gopala himself. From that moment she became mad. All day and night she kept crying, 'Where is my Gopala? Where is my Gopala?' She could not sleep or eat. Only at night would she prepare a little food for Gopala, and everyone thought that she had really become mad.[3]

By the 1880s Sri Ramakrishna's name had begun to spread, and it was in the fall of 1884 that Gopaler-ma first went to Dakshineswar, along with her landlady and another woman, to seek an audience with the holy man. As Kamarhati and Dakshineswar are both on the Ganga, they went the three miles by boat. Sri Ramakrishna received them cordially, gave them some advice on devotion, and sang a few songs. He asked them to come again, and graciously, in turn, the landlady invited Sri Ramakrishna to visit her temple garden at Kamarhati. He accepted the invitation.

Only a jeweller understands the value of a jewel. Sri Ramakrishna recognized the spiritual magnitude of both Gopaler-ma and the landlady, and, praising them in his sweet manner, he said: 'Ah! What a beautiful expression on their faces! They are floating in the ocean of bliss and devotion. Their eyes are soaked with divine love'.[4] On another occasion Sri Ramakrishna commented about Gopaler-ma, 'During Krishna's incarnation she was a fruit-seller of Vrindaban, and she would feed Gopala the sweet fruits'.[5]

After her first visit Gopaler-ma felt an irresistible attraction for Sri Ramakrishna, and she noticed a change in her life. Off and on she would think about Sri Ramakrishna, 'He is a nice man and a real devotee'.[6] She decided to see him again soon.

A few days later, while she was practising japam, her desire to see him became so intense that she immediately left for Dakshineswar by herself. It is an ancient custom that one should not visit God or a holy person empty-handed, so on her way she bought two pennies' worth of stale sweets, which was all that she could afford. She was confident that he would not eat them, since so many people brought better offerings every day. But no sooner had she arrived at Dakshineswar than Sri Ramakrishna said: 'Oh, you have come! Give me what you have brought for me'. She was embarrassed, but she reluctantly handed over the stale sweets to him. Like a hungry boy he started to eat them with great relish and said to her: 'Why do you spend money for sweets? Prepare some sweet coconut balls, and when you visit this place bring one or two of them with you. Or you may bring a little of the ordinary dishes which you cook yourself. I want to eat your cooking'.[7]

That day Sri Ramakrishna did not talk about God or religion. He only inquired about this food or that food. As Gopaler-ma later related:

I thought: 'What a strange monk. He talks only about food. I am a poor widow. Where shall I get so many delicacies for him? Enough! I shall not come back again'. But as soon as I crossed the gate of Dakshineswar garden, I felt he was, as it were, pulling me back. I could not proceed further. I had a hard time persuading the mind, and at last I returned to Kamarhati.[8]

A few days later she came to Dakshineswar on foot, carrying some ordinary curry that she had cooked for Sri Ramakrishna. He relished it and said: 'What a delicacy! It is like nectar'. Tears rolled down Gopaler-ma's cheeks. She thought the Master appreciated her humble offering only because she was poor.

During the next three or four months Gopaler-ma visited Dakshineswar several times, always carrying some plain food for the Master. Invariably he asked her to bring some new food on her next visit. Sometimes she would think in disgust: 'O Gopala, is this the outcome of my prayer? You have brought me to a holy man who only asks for food. I shall not come back again'. But as soon as she returned to Kamarhati, she would again feel that irresistible attraction, and her mind would long to see the Master.[9]

At the invitation of Govinda Datta's widow, Sri Ramakrishna went to visit the temple garden of Kamarhati. He attended the worship service of Radha-Krishna and sang many devotional songs. The land-lady and others there were very much impressed, seeing the Master's ecstasy during the kirtan. After taking some prasad he returned to Dakshineswar.

It was the spring of 1885. One morning at three o'clock Gopaler-ma, as usual, started to practise her japam. After finishing the japam she began pranayama and was about to offer the result of the japam to her Chosen Deity when she noticed that Sri Ramakrishna was seated at her left with his right fist clenched. Startled, she wondered: 'What is this? How did he come here at this odd hour?' As she later described:

I looked at him in amazement and thought, 'How did he come here?' Meanwhile Gopala [as she called Sri Ramakrishna] kept on smiling sweetly. As I took courage and grasped his left hand, Sri Ramakrishna's form disappeared and in place of it appeared the real Gopala — a big child of ten months old. His beauty and look beggar description! He crawled towards me and, raising one hand, said, 'Mother, give me butter'. This overwhelming experience bewildered me. I cried out so loudly that if there had been men around they would have assembled there. With tearful eyes I said, 'My son, I am a poor, helpless widow. What shall I feed you? Where shall I get butter and cream, my child?' But Gopala did not listen to me. 'Give me something to eat', he kept on saying. What could I do? Sobbing, I got up and brought some dry coconut balls from the hanging basket. Placing them in his hand, I said, 'Gopala, my darling, I offer you this wretched thing, but don't give me such a poor thing in return'.

I could not perform japam at all that day. Gopala sat on my lap, snatched away my rosary, jumped on my shoulders, and moved around the room. At daybreak I rushed to Dakshineswar like a crazy woman. Gopala also accompanied me, resting his head on my shoulder. I distinctly saw Gopala's two tiny, rosy feet hanging over my bosom.[10]

When Gopaler-ma arrived at Dakshineswar, a woman devotee was present. Her words vividly describe that meeting with the Master:

I was then cleaning the Master's room. It was seven or half past seven in the morning. In the meantime I heard somebody calling, 'Gopala, Gopala' from outside. The voice was familiar to me. I looked and it was Gopaler-ma. She entered through the eastern door like an intoxicated person, with dishevelled hair, staring eyes, and the end of her cloth trailing on the ground. She was completely oblivious of her surroundings. Sri Ramakrishna was then seated on his small cot.

I was dumbfounded seeing Gopaler-ma in that condition. The Master, in the meantime, entered into an ecstatic mood. Gopaler-ma sat beside him and he, like a child, sat on her lap. Tears were flowing profusely from her eyes. She fed the Master with cream, butter, and sweets which she had brought with her. I was astounded, for never before had I seen the Master touching a woman in a state of ecstasy... After some time the Master regained his normal consciousness and went back to his cot. But Gopaler-ma could not control her exuberant emotion. In a rapturous mood she began to dance around the room, repeating, 'Brahma is dancing and Vishnu is dancing'. Watching her ecstasy the Master said to me with a smile, 'Look, she is engulfed in bliss. Her mind is now in the abode of Gopala'.[11]

Gopaler-ma's ecstasy was boundless. Her vision, conversation, and play with her beloved Gopala continued: 'Here is Gopala in my arms... Now he enters into you [pointing to Sri Ramakrishna]... There, he comes out again... Come, my child, come to your wretched mother'.[12] Thus she became convinced that Sri Ramakrishna was none other than her Gopala.

Only a mystic understands the language and behaviour of another mystic. Sri Ramakrishna was happy to see her ecstasy, but then, in order to calm her, he began to stroke her chest and feed her with delicacies. Even while eating, Gopaler-ma said in an ecstatic mood: 'Gopala, my darling, your wretched mother has led a life of dire poverty. She had to make her living by spinning and selling sacred thread. Is that why you are taking special care of her today?'[13] From this time on Aghoremani Devi was known as Gopaler-ma.

Gopaler-ma stayed the whole day at Dakshineswar, and then, before evening, Sri Ramakrishna sent her back to Kamarhati. The same baby Gopala went with her, nestled in her arms. When she reached her room, she started to tell her beads as before, but it became impossible. Her Chosen Deity, for whom she had practised japam and meditation all her life, was now pestering her, demanding this and that, as he played in front of her. When she went to bed, Gopala was by her side. She had a hard bed without a pillow and he began to grumble. At last she cradled his head on her left arm and said: 'My child, sleep tonight in this way. Tomorrow I shall go to Calcutta and ask the daughter of the landlady to make a soft pillow for you'.[14]

The next morning she went to the garden to collect dry wood for cooking. Gopala also accompanied her and helped her. Then, as she was cooking, the naughty child began to play tricks on her. She tried to control him, sometimes with sweet words, and sometimes through scoldings.

Modern man, inclined to be sceptical and scientific, has great difficulty in accepting as real such experiences as Gopaler-ma's. However, from the traditional Hindu point of view, there are much finer states of consciousness than the one in which we experience the sense world, and this has been substantiated again and again by the experiences of saints and seers. When the mind is pure and saturated with Spirit, such high states of consciousness are possible. Gopaler-ma meditated on her beloved Gopala so much that her mind became very pure. As a result, she entered the superconscious realm, and wherever her eyes fell, she saw Gopala. In this realm of mystical experience, verbal expression, mental cognition, and intellectual reasoning do not function. The only consciousness is the direct consciousness of God.

A few days later Gopaler-ma went to Dakshineswar to visit the Master. After greeting him she went to the nahabat, or concert room, where Sri Ramakrishna's spiritual consort, known as Holy Mother, lived. It was Gopaler-ma's habit to practise japam whenever she had time and opportunity. While she was doing japam in the concert room, Sri Ramakrishna came there and said: 'Why do you practise so much japam now? You have plenty of visions!'

Gopaler-ma replied: 'Shall I not practise japam any more? Have I attained everything?'

'Yes, you have attained everything'.

'Everything?'

'Yes, everything'.

'What do you say? Have I really accomplished everything?'

'Yes, you have. It is no longer necessary for you to practise japam and austerity for yourself, but if you wish, you may continue those disciplines [pointing to himself] for the welfare of this body'.

Thus assured by Sri Ramakrishna three times, she said: 'All right. Whatever I do henceforth will be for you'.[15]

Her visions and play with Gopala continued for two months. During this time she was always in an ecstatic mood. She had to force herself to continue her daily routine of bathing, cooking, eating, japam, and meditation. Gradually her divine intoxication subsided; yet she continued to have several visions of Gopala a day. Since she had become convinced that Sri Ramakrishna and Gopala were one and the same, she had fewer visions of the form of Gopala and more of Sri Ramakrishna while meditating, with the voice of Gopala instructing her through him. She went to Sri Ramakrishna one day and said to him, crying: 'Gopala, what have you done to me? Did I do anything wrong? Why do I not see you in the form of Gopala as before?'[16]

Sri Ramakrishna consoled her, saying: 'In this Kali yuga if one has such visions continuously, one's body does not last long. It survives only twenty-one days and then drops off like a dry leaf'.[17] Since Gopaler-ma had experienced the bliss of constant divine inebriation, it was difficult for her to live without it. She had no interest in mundane things. Just as a worldly person is always restless for worldly objects, in the same way her heart was restless for the continuous vision of Gopala. She felt a pain in her chest and thought it was due to the pressure of gas. But Sri Ramakrishna told her: 'It is not gas. It is caused by your spiritual energy. How will you pass your time if it goes away? Let it be with you. When you feel too much pain, please eat something'.[18]

Sri Ramakrishna used to receive gifts of sweets, fruits, and rock candy from various people, but he could not eat all of it. There were some business people who would offer gifts to him believing that such offerings to a holy man would bring them prosperity. This type of food invariably contaminates the mind of the eater. Consequently, the only devotees Sri Ramakrishna would give these things to were Swami Vivekananda and Gopaler-ma. He knew that the minds of these two great souls were in such a high realm that they could never be affected by eating such food.

One day Gopaler-ma came to see the Master with some women devotees. Pointing to her, he said to those present: 'Ah, there is nothing inside this body but God. He fills it through and through'. Then the Master fed Gopaler-ma with various delicacies and gave her some food which he had received from several Calcutta business people. At this, Gopaler-ma said, 'Why are you so fond of feeding me?'

Sri Ramakrishna replied, 'You have also fed me with so many things in the past'.

'In the past? When?' she asked.

'In your previous life', he said.[19]

During the Car Festival of Lord Jagannath in 1885, Sri Ramakrishna went to Balaram Basu's house in Calcutta. Balaram had invited many devotees for the celebration. While he was there the Master spoke highly of the God-intoxicated state and visions of Gopaler-ma, and at his behest, Balaram sent a man to bring her. Just before her arrival the Master was talking to the devotees when suddenly he went into ecstasy. His body assumed the pose of Gopala, crawling on both knees, one hand resting on the ground, the other raised, and the face turned up as if he were expecting someone. Gopaler-ma arrived then and found Sri Ramakrishna in the posture of her Chosen Deity. The devotees were amazed, seeing that divine sight.

'Truly speaking, I don't care for this stiff posture', she said. 'My Gopala should laugh and play, walk and run. But what is this? He has become stiff like a log. I don't like to see this sort of Gopala!'[20]

It was a striking feature in Sri Ramakrishna's life that whenever any mood would come over him he would be fully identified with it. Even in his later years, when he would sing, dance, or make gestures like a woman or a child, people were amazed, seeing their precision and spontaneity. His voice was sweet and melodious, and his movements were natural, simple, and beautiful. There was not an iota of insincerity or display in his behaviour and action.

Sri Ramakrishna stayed in Calcutta for a few days and then left for Dakshineswar by boat. Some of the devotees, including Gopaler-ma, accompanied him. Balaram's family had lovingly given Gopaler-ma some necessary items of clothing and utensils in a bundle which she was carrying on the boat. The Master came to know from other devotees what was in the bundle. Immediately he became grave, and without directly referring to the items, he began to speak about renunciation. He said: 'Only a man of renunciation realizes God. The devotee who is simply satisfied with another man's hospitality and returns empty-handed, sits very close to God'.[21] He did not say a single word to her, but he kept looking at her bundle. Gopaler-ma understood.

The Master always watched over his devotees so that they might not deviate from the path of nonattachment. He could be as soft as a flower, and again as strong as a thunderbolt. His superhuman love conquered the hearts of the devotees, so a little indifference from him would give them unbearable pain. Gopaler-ma was stung with remorse and thought of throwing the bundle away. But she kept it, and when she reached Dakshineswar she related everything to Holy Mother. She was ready to give all the items away, but Holy Mother stopped her and said: 'Let the Master say what he wants. There is no one to give you gifts, and moreover, you have been given some things which you need'. Nevertheless Gopaler-ma gave some of the things away. Then she cooked some curries for the Master and carried the tray of food to him. Seeing her repentance, he behaved with her in his usual manner. She returned to Kamarhati feeling much relieved.[22]

After God-realization the illumined soul is carried along by the momentum of his past karma, but he ceases to be affected by it. He behaves like a witness, completely unattached to the world. He continues his daily routine, and he helps other people towards realization. Gopaler-ma also followed her old routine. But from time to time she would visit the Master, and whatever visions she had during meditation she would relate to him. Once he said to her, 'One should not disclose one's visions to others, because it stops further visions'.[23]

One day, however, Gopaler-ma and Swami Vivekananda (then called Narendranath) chanced to be present at Dakshineswar at the same time. Gopaler-ma was uneducated, unsophisticated, simple, and a devout worshipper of God with form; Narendranath, on the other hand, was learned, sophisticated, intelligent, and a staunch believer in the formless God. As a member of the Brahmo Samaj, he looked down on worship of God with form. Sri Ramakrishna had a tremendous sense of humour, so he engaged these two devotees, with their opposing points of view, in a discussion by requesting Gopaler-ma to relate her visions to Narendranath.

'But will there not be harm in telling them?' she asked. Assured by him that it would be all right, she related all her visions in detail to Narendranath with overwhelming joy and tears.

Devotion is contagious. Narendranath, in spite of his manly exterior and faith in rationalism, could not control his tears. His heart was filled with love and religious fervour. The old lady now and then interrupted her story to say: 'My son, you are learned and intelligent, and I am a poor, illiterate widow. I don't understand anything. Please tell me, are these visions true?'

'Yes, Mother, whatever you have seen is all true', Narendranath assured her.[24]

On another day Gopaler-ma invited Sri Ramakrishna for lunch at Kamarhati. This time the Master went by boat with Rakhal, a young disciple who later became Swami Brahmananda. She received them cordially, and after they had enjoyed the delicacies she had cooked for them, they went to a room upstairs which had been arranged for their rest. Rakhal fell asleep immediately, but the Master was wide awake. Presently a foul odour permeated the room, and he saw two hideous looking ghosts with skeletal-like forms. They said to him humbly: 'Why are you here? Please go away from this place. Seeing you, we are in unbearable pain'. The Divine Presence was no doubt the cause of their pain, either because it reminded them of their own pitiable condition, or because evil spirits cannot bear that Presence.

Sri Ramakrishna immediately arose and gathered up his small spice bag and towel. In the meantime Rakhal woke up and asked, 'Master, where are you going?' 'I shall tell you later', said Sri Ramakrishna. They both went downstairs to Gopaler-ma and, saying good-bye to her, left on the boat. The Master then told the whole story to Rakhal, explaining that he did not say anything to Gopaler-ma because she was staying there alone. At any rate, she knew that ghosts frequented the area, and Sri Ramakrishna knew that her spirituality protected her from their presence.[25]

'One who has steadfast devotion to truthfulness realizes the God of Truth', said Sri Ramakrishna. His own life was based on truth, and whatever he said invariably came true. One day Gopaler-ma cooked for the Master at Dakshineswar. When he found that the rice was not properly boiled, he indignantly said: 'Can I eat this rice? I shall not take rice out of her hand anymore'.[26] People thought that the Master had only warned her to be careful in the future. But shortly afterwards it so happened that cancer developed in his throat, and from then on he could only eat thin porridge and liquids.

As the illness grew worse, Sri Ramakrishna was moved from Dakshineswar to Calcutta, and then to Cossipore (a northern suburb of Calcutta) for treatment. Gopaler-ma now and then would come to serve him. One day the Master expressed a desire to eat a special kind of thick milk pudding. Yogindra, a young disciple, was sent to Calcutta to buy the pudding from the market. On the way, however, he stopped at the house of Balaram Basu, and when the women devotees heard about his errand, they asked him to wait and let them cook it. They meant well, reasoning that the homemade food would be of a better quality than the market food. Yogindra agreed. But when he returned with the pudding and told the Master the reason for his delay, the Master scolded him: 'I wanted to eat the market pudding, and you were told to buy it. Why did you go to the devotee's house and give them trouble over it? Besides, this pudding is very rich and hard to digest. I will not eat it'. Indeed, he did not touch it, but he asked Holy Mother to give the pudding to Gopaler-ma. As he explained: 'This is given by the devotees. Gopala dwells in her heart. Her eating it will be the same as my eating it'.[27]

After the passing away of Sri Ramakrishna, Gopaler-ma was grief-stricken and for a long time lived in seclusion. After a while, however, repeated visions of the Master consoled her bereaved heart. Once she went to attend the Car Festival of Jagannath in Mahesh, on the other side of the Ganga. There she had the cosmic vision of the Lord. She saw her beloved Gopala not only in the image of Jagannath in the chariot, but also in the pilgrims who were pulling the chariot. 'I was then not myself', she said. 'I danced and laughed and created a commotion there'.[28]

Occasionally she would visit Sri Ramakrishna's monastic disciples at the Baranagore monastery. At their request she would cook a couple of dishes and offer them to the Master.

The human mind is a mysterious phenomenon. In general, people are not happy because their minds are always craving worldly comforts and luxuries. The mind becomes impure when it is involved with mundane things, and it becomes pure when it becomes desireless. The impure mind suffers, and the pure mind enjoys bliss. It is very difficult to give the mind to God if it is preoccupied with many worldly possessions. Gopaler-ma's mind, however, was always God-centred. Just as the needle of the compass always points to the north, so also her mind was always directed towards God. Mercilessly she would drive away all distracting thoughts. Swami Ramakrishnananda related the following incident:

One day, after Sri Ramakrishna had passed away, some of his disciples went to see her and found her room full of mosquitoes and other troublesome creatures. Although she did not appear to mind them and kept on repeating the Name of the Lord, it distressed them to see her in such discomfort, so the next day one of the disciples brought her a mosquito curtain. That night when she sat down to repeat the Name, she found her mind constantly wandering to the curtain, thinking whether a cockroach or a rat might not be eating off a corner of it. Seeing this she said, 'What! This wretched curtain thus to take my mind away from my Gopala!' and without ado she made it up into a bundle and sat down again to her devotions with the mosquitoes all about her.

The next morning we were just getting up at the Math when Gopaler-ma appeared. She had walked all the way [at least five miles] and must have started at three o'clock. She laid the bundle down. 'What is it?' someone asked.

'It is the curtain you gave me yesterday. It takes my mind away from God. I don't want it', was her answer; and nothing could persuade her to take it back.[29]

One day in 1887 Gopaler-ma came to Balaram's house in Calcutta. A number of devotees were also there who were aware of her high spiritual experiences, and they began to ask her some questions. She said to them: 'Look, I am an old, illiterate woman. What do I know about the scriptures? Why don't you ask Sharat, Yogin, and Tarak?' But they persisted, so finally she said: 'Wait, let me ask Gopala. O Gopala, I don't understand what they are talking about. Why don't you answer their questions? Hello, Gopala says this...' In this way Gopaler-ma answered the abstruse questions of the devotees. They were amazed. That remarkable question and answer session ended abruptly, however, when Gopaler-ma suddenly said: 'O Gopala, why are you going away? Will you not answer their questions anymore?' But Gopala had left.[30]

In 1897 Swami Vivekananda returned to India from his first visit to the West. Later he sent three of his Western disciples, Sister Nivedita, Mrs. Ole Bull, and Miss Josephine MacLeod, to Kamarhati to meet Gopaler-ma. She received them cordially and kissed them. As she had no other furniture in her room, they sat on her bed. She then served them some puffed rice and sweet coconut balls and shared some of her spiritual experiences with them. When they returned to Calcutta, Swami Vivekananda said: 'Ah! This is the old India that you have seen, the India of prayers and tears, of vigils and fasts, that is passing away'.[31]

Once two women devotees came to Swami Vivekananda at Balaram's house requesting initiation, but he sent them to Gopaler-ma. She was reluctant, however, and said to Swamiji: 'My son, what do I know about initiation? I am a poor widow'.

Swamiji replied with a smile: 'Are you an ordinary person? You have attained perfection through japam. If you cannot give initiation then who can? Let me tell you, why don't you give your own Ishta-mantram to them? It will serve their purpose. Moreover, what will you do with your mantram anymore?'[32]

Gopaler-ma initiated the women but was unwilling to accept any gift or offering from them. When she was persuaded, she followed the custom and accepted two rupees from them so that the disciples might not be hurt. She had no greed or desire for worldly objects. Her simple instruction was:

Listen, offer your body and mind to God. Initiation is not an insignificant thing. Do not leave your seat without repeating ten thousand japam in each sitting. While practising spiritual discipline disconnect yourself from the thoughts of the world. Start your japam at 3 o'clock in the morning so that nobody is aware of it; and again practise in the evening.[33]

She had immense love for the disciples of Sri Ramakrishna. When the news of Swami Vivekananda's passing away reached Kamarhati, she was in her room. She cried out in pain, 'Ah, Naren is gone?' She felt dizzy, saw darkness all around, and fell to the floor, fracturing her right elbow.[34]

Gopaler-ma was then living there by herself, although the place was known for being haunted. During the time that the landlady lived there, a guard looked after the place, but since no one was there now to help her, Swami Saradananda appointed a gardener and sent a woman to take care of her broken arm. Seeing the attendant, Gopaler-ma said: 'Why have you come here? You will have to face a lot of hardship. My Gopala takes care of me. Where will you sleep? You must find a room. They are all under lock and key, so you will have to ask the priest to open one for you. Let me tell you frankly at the outset that there are some evil spirits around. Whenever you hear any strange noise, repeat your mantram wholeheartedly'. At night the attendant slept opposite Gopaler-ma's room, and she heard the sound of heavy, hurried footsteps coming from the roof and a rapping noise through the window. It was quite a test for her.[35]

Gopaler-ma had to face many such ordeals during her long stay in that garden house by herself. She never felt lonely, however, for her beloved Gopala was with her day and night. Moreover, she did not care for a companion because it might interfere with her visions. As she had very little body-consciousness, she was reluctant to take personal service from others. Independence is happiness and dependence is misery. She practised this Vedantic teaching in her life.

In 1903 Gopaler-ma became seriously ill. Swami Brahmananda then sent one of his young disciples to nurse her. The boy brought fruits and vegetables for her and slept in the corner of her room. He awoke very early in the morning, however, when he heard Gopaler-ma talking with someone: 'Wait, wait! Even the birds have not yet sung. Let the morning come, my sweet darling, and then I shall take you for a bath in the Ganga'.

Later the young disciple said: 'No one else lives in your room. With whom were you talking this morning?'

'Don't you know that Gopala lives with me? I was trying to control his naughtiness', she replied.[36]

As her health grew worse, the disciples of Sri Ramakrishna arranged for her to be moved to Balaram's house in Calcutta. But Sister Nivedita expressed a desire to serve this saintly woman, so Gopaler-ma was taken to her residence. A cook was appointed, and Kusum, one of Gopaler-ma's disciples, attended to her personal needs. In return Gopaler-ma gave Nivedita maternal affection and support. Her presence in the house created an atmosphere of spiritual serenity.

'I feel thrilled', Nivedita wrote in a letter at that time, 'when I am with Gopaler-ma. The words of Saint Elizabeth sound in my ears, "What is this to me that the Mother of my Lord should visit me?" For I believe that in Gopaler-ma is sainthood as great as that of a paramahamsa — a soul fully free. I feel that if I can only worship her enough, blessings will descend on all whom I love, through her. Could more be said?'[37]

To see God in everything is the culmination of Vedantic experience. Gopaler-ma had a pet cat in whom she used to see Gopala. One day it was lying peacefully on Nivedita's lap when Kusum came and pushed it away. Immediately Gopaler-ma cried out: 'What have you done? What have you done? Gopala is going away — he is gone'.[38]

Those who carry the Lord in their hearts always enjoy festivity. They never get bored or pass a single dull moment. The body of Gopaler-ma was deteriorating day by day, but her mind was floating in bliss. When Holy Mother went to see her, Gopaler-ma sighed: 'Gopala, you have come. Look, you have sat on my lap all these days; now you take me on your lap'. Holy Mother took Gopaler-ma's head on her lap and caressed her affectionately.[39]

The end came on July 8, 1906. Gopaler-ma was carried to the Ganga, where she breathed her last at dawn, touching the holy water of the river. A monk bent over her and whispered in her ear the words that the Hindu loves to hear in his last hour: 'Om Ganga Narayana! Om Ganga Narayana Brahma!'[40]

Thus the curtain fell on the divine drama of Gopaler-ma. The monks went to her room and found her two most precious possessions, the rosary, which had passed through her fingers millions and millions of times, and a picture of Sri Ramakrishna, who had appeared before her as Gopala. Nivedita took the rosary, and the picture was sent to Belur Math, where it still rests on the altar of Holy Mother's temple.[41]

Once, being asked for some advice from a disciple, Gopaler-ma said: 'Ask advice from Gopala. He is within you. No one can give better advice than he. This is the truth. Cry with a longing heart and you will reach him'.[42]

Golap-ma (Golap Sundari Devi)
(?-1924)

25
Golap-Ma
(Golap Sundari Devi)

Invariably the death of a loved one becomes a turning point in a
person's life. At that time, seeing only darkness and hopelessness all
around, a person begins to think deeply about life. He realizes its
emptiness and transitoriness — that life ends in death and union ends
in separation. Still, the tears flow as grief consumes the heart. Yet,
such is the law of nature that eventually the heart becomes filled by
another loved one and the tears stop. Golap-ma's unbearable grief
was actually God's grace, for in her affliction she turned to Sri
Ramakrishna and her life was transformed.

Golap Sundari Devi, known as Golap-ma, was born in a brahmin
family of North Calcutta, probably in the late 1840s. Her parents
arranged her marriage when she was young to a poor brahmin, but
he died after a few years, leaving her with two small children, a son
and a daughter. When Golap-ma's son was still very young, he also
died, and her mainstay in life then became her daughter, Chandi.
Chandi was a charming, well-mannered girl. When she grew up,
Golap-ma arranged her marriage with Saurindra Mohan Tagore, an
eminent and wealthy landlord of Calcutta. But again fate was cruel to
Golap-ma. Chandi died prematurely, creating a tremendous void in
her mother's life.

Golap-ma cried and cursed herself but could not find any cure for
her grief. Just then Yogin-ma, a neighbour, came to her help. Seeing
Golap-ma's terrible suffering, Yogin-ma had compassion on her and
one day in 1885 took her to Sri Ramakrishna at Dakshineswar. Golap-
ma later described her first meeting with the Master: 'When I first
went to the Master I was tormented with grief for my daughter,
Chandi. Yogin took me to him. He touched my head and removed all
grief from my heart. It was amazing. In a moment my mind became
calm and serene. I immediately laughed like a jnani [a person
endowed with spiritual knowledge]. I felt that I had come to this
world to act in a play. Who is whose mother and who is whose
daughter? In my childhood I had played with cloth dolls, and after

that I played with flesh and blood dolls. This world is nothing but a play with dolls, so why should I cry for my daughter? It is a glorious thing to cry for God. Such was the power of the Master!'[1]

After Golap-ma had unburdened her heart to Sri Ramakrishna by narrating the sad story of her life, he said in an ecstatic mood: 'You are fortunate. God helps those who have no one to call their own'.[2] Then he sang a song:

Dwell, O mind, within yourself;
Enter no other's home.
If you but seek there, you will find
All you are searching for.

God, the true Philosopher's Stone,
Who answers every prayer
Lies hidden deep within your heart,
The richest gem of all.

It is said that the Master's touch, his words, and his singing soothed her grieving heart and brought new hope and happiness to her life.[3]

Greatly moved by her first meeting with the Master, Golap-ma visited him frequently thereafter. On June 13, 1885, she arrived at Dakshineswar while the Master was talking with some devotees. She stood quietly by the north door and listened. The Master noticed her and started talking about human grief. Narrating the bereavement of his boyhood friend, Ram Mallik, he said: 'Ram said he had no children; he brought up his nephew, but the boy died. He told me this with a sigh; his eyes filled with tears; he was grief-stricken for his nephew'. Then the Master said: 'A man came here the other day. He sat a few minutes and then said, "Let me go and see the 'moon-face' of my child". I couldn't control myself and said: "So you prefer your son's 'moon-face' to God's 'moon-face!' Get out, you fool!" The truth is that God alone is real and all else unreal. Men, universe, house, children — all these are like the magic of the magician... The magician alone is real and his magic unreal... God is like an ocean, and living beings are its bubbles. They are born there and they die there. Children are like the few small bubbles around a big one. God alone is real. Make an effort to cultivate love for him and find out the means to realize him. What will you gain by grieving?' Golap-ma understood. She wanted to return home then in the hot sun, but the Master said to her tenderly: It is very hot. Why now? You can go later in a carriage with the devotees'.[4]

After a few visits Sri Ramakrishna introduced Golap-ma to Holy Mother, saying: 'You should feed this brahmin girl well. Sorrow is assuaged when the stomach is full'.[5] Sri Ramakrishna knew that when he was gone Holy Mother would need a companion, so one day he said to her about Golap-ma: 'Keep your eyes on this brahmin woman. She will live with you permanently'.[6] Holy Mother gave shelter to Golap-ma, who thenceforth began to stay with her off and on in the nahabat. During one of Golap-ma's visits Sri Ramakrishna asked her to bring his food, which Holy Mother had cooked at the nahabat. After that she carried it to his room every day. This meant that Holy Mother could no longer see the Master at mealtime as she used to. Golap-ma also spent long hours in the evening in the Master's room, and Holy Mother had to wait with Golap-ma's supper, sometimes until ten o'clock at night. Knowing Holy Mother's inconvenience, Sri Ramakrishna one day asked Golap-ma not to stay in his room so long. But Golap-ma did not understand. She said: 'No, no. Mother loves me very much and regards me as her own daughter. She calls me by my first name'.[7]

One night in Dakshineswar Sri Ramakrishna got up at midnight and said to his nephew Ramlal, 'I am very hungry'. Ramlal searched the room but could not find any sweets or fruits, so he went to the nahabat and informed Holy Mother. She immediately made a fire with some hay and wood and began to cook farina pudding. Golap-ma carried the bowl, containing two pounds of pudding, to the Master. Swami Saradananda wrote: 'She just stepped into the room, dimly lighted by a lamp in a corner, where Ramlal was sitting quietly nearby. She was startled to notice the Master pacing back and forth at that dead of night, calm and silent, with an extraordinary spiritual mood overwhelming him... It seemed to her that the Master's body had become much bigger in both height and bulk, as if he was not a mortal of this earth, but some god from heaven come in the guise of a human being to this earthly sphere so full of misery, wailing, and death... Ramlal had already placed a seat for the Master to sit on. Awe-struck and hesitating, the woman devotee [Golap-ma] went near and placed the bowl of farina pudding in front of the seat. The Master sat down to eat and gradually ate all of it under the influence of that spiritual intoxication'.[8]

Golap-ma later described her vision of the kundalini power accepting oblations in the Master's body: 'It seemed to me that as soon as the Master put food in his mouth the snake-shaped Kundalini Shakti within him was aroused and snatched at the food and devoured it. The Master asked me, "Well, can you tell me who is eating — myself — or someone else?" I told the Master what I had seen. He was pleased to hear it and said: "You are right! You are

right! You are fortunate that you have seen it and understood it''.
Then he smiled'.[9]

Golap-ma was one of Sri Ramakrishna's main women disciples,
and she often got the opportunity to render personal service to him.
Not only did she carry his food to him, but she also cleaned his room.
Besides this she sometimes helped Holy Mother with the cooking and
other household work. Since Golap-ma was a little older than some of
the other women she was very free with the Master and the young
boy disciples. Her relationship with Sri Ramakrishna was through the
heart and not through the brain. Many years later she said: 'By the
Master's grace I saw the living form of my Chosen Deity. After my
first meeting with the Master I used to see for a while a little boy
resembling the Master moving with me'.[10] On another occasion
Golap-ma saw the Master pacing back and forth at midnight in an
ecstatic mood at Dakshineswar. All of a sudden, though, she saw the
Divine Mother in his place, and this frightened her.[11]

Since Golap-ma visited Dakshineswar frequently, the Calcutta
devotees often sent fruit, food, or other things with her for the
Master. Once Balaram's daughter Bhuvan bought some *jamrul* (a
juicy fruit) for the Master and asked Golap-ma to carry them to
Dakshineswar. At first Golap-ma declined, because she doubted the
purity of the fruit. She knew that the Master could not eat any
unclean food, or food that had been touched by an impure person.
Bhuvan persuaded her, however, and Golap-ma took the fruit to
Dakshineswar. Strangely enough, as soon as she arrived the Master
asked for it and ate it with joy. Another time Swami Premananda's
mother made *chandrapuli* (a cake) and asked Golap-ma to take it to the
Master. But Golap-ma noticed that the cake was a little dark, so she
did not bring it with her. When she met the Master this time, he again
asked for some food, and she deeply regretted going there empty-
handed.[12]

Because of Sri Ramakrishna's great affection and kindness towards
her, Golap-ma somehow summoned up the courage to invite him to
her poor dilapidated house in North Calcutta, where she lived with
her brothers. M. beautifully described this memorable visit on July 28,
1885:

The Master arrived at the house of the brahmin lady who was
grief-stricken on account of her daughter's death. It was an old
brick house. Entering the house, the Master passed the cow shed
on his left. He and the devotees went to the roof, where they took
seats. People were standing there in rows. Others were seated.
They were all eager to get a glimpse of Sri Ramakrishna.

The brahmani had a sister; both of them were widows. Their brothers also lived in the house with their families. The brahmani had been busy all day making arrangements to receive Sri Ramakrishna. While the Master was at Nanda Bose's house she had been extremely restless, going out of the house every few minutes to see if he was coming. He had promised to come to her house from Nanda's. Because of his delay she had thought perhaps he would not come at all.

Sri Ramakrishna was seated on a carpet... The brahmani's sister came to the Master and saluted him. She said: 'Sister has just gone to Nanda Bose's house to inquire the reason for your delay in coming here. She will return presently'...

The brahmani's sister exclaimed, 'Here comes sister!'

The brahmani came and saluted the Master. She was beside herself with joy. She did not know what to say. In a half-choked voice she said: 'This joy is too much for me. Perhaps I shall die of it. Tell me, friends, how shall I be able to live? I did not feel such a thrill even when Chandi, my daughter, used to visit the house accompanied by liveried footmen, with armed guards lining both sides of the street. Oh! Now I have no trace of my grief at her death. I was afraid he [Sri Ramakrishna] would not come. Then I thought that, if that happened, I should throw into the Ganga all the things I had arranged for his reception and entertainment. I should not speak to him any more. If he visited a place, I should go there, look at him from a distance, and then come away'...

M. was amazed to see the brahmani's sincere joy and her ecstatic mood. He was about to take the dust of her feet. 'What are you doing?' she exclaimed and saluted M... She said, 'I am so happy to see you all here'...

She was talking like this when her sister came up and said: 'Come down, sister! How can I manage things if you stay here? Can I do it all by myself?'

But the brahmani was overwhelmed with joy. She could not take her eyes from the Master and the devotees.

After a while she very respectfully took Sri Ramakrishna to another room and offered him sweets and other refreshments.

At eight o'clock in the evening Sri Ramakrishna went from Golap-ma's house to that of Yogin-ma. Golap-ma followed him there and then went with him to Balaram's house. After supper M. was alone with Sri Ramakrishna massaging his feet. Referring to Golap-ma and her sister, M. said to the Master: 'How amazing! A similar thing happened with two women at the time of Jesus. They too were sisters, and devoted to Christ. Martha and Mary'.

Master (eagerly): 'Tell me the story'.

M.: 'Jesus Christ, like you, went to their house with his devotees.

At the sight of him one of the sisters was filled with ecstatic happiness... The other sister, all by herself, was arranging the food to entertain Jesus. She complained to the Master, saying: "Lord, please judge for yourself — how wrong my sister is! She is sitting in your room and I am doing all these things by myself". Jesus said: "Your sister indeed is blessed. She has developed the only thing needful in human life: love of God" '.

Master: 'Well, after seeing all this, what do you feel?'

M.: 'I feel that Christ, Chaitanyadeva, and yourself — all three are one and the same'...

Master: 'Yes, yes! One! One! It is indeed one'.[13]

In the middle of 1885 Sri Ramakrishna started to feel some discomfort in his throat. It was the beginning of cancer. Holy Mother was very much concerned about his health. Every day Sri Ramakrishna drank a measured quantity of milk in a cup, but unknown to him, Holy Mother would boil the milk for a long time in order to make it thick. That way he would get more nutrition. One day the Master became suspicious about the quantity of the milk and asked Golap-ma about it. Not realizing Holy Mother's intention, Golap-ma told the truth. Sri Ramakrishna became alarmed, and this made his stomach upset. Finally, Holy Mother straightened out the situation, but she cautioned Golap-ma not to say everything to the Master. Golap-ma apologized.[14]

Once Golap-ma said to Holy Mother, 'Manomohan's mother remarked the other day that since the Master is such a perfect example of renunciation, it does not look well that you adorn yourself with so many ornaments'.[15] Holy Mother at once removed all her jewellery except for two bracelets. Yogin-ma came the next day and persuaded Holy Mother to put on a few more ornaments, but Holy Mother never put on more, for the Master fell ill soon after that. When Sri Ramakrishna heard about the fuss he said: 'What is this? She did not adorn herself with those ornaments. It is I who arranged that jewellery for her. Her name is Sarada. She is Saraswati [the goddess of wisdom]. That is why she loves to adorn herself'.[16] He once told Golap-ma about Holy Mother's nature: 'She is Sarada — Saraswati. She has assumed a human body to impart wisdom to people. But she has hidden her celestial beauty, lest men, by looking at her, should befoul their minds with sinful thoughts'.[17]

Some of the devotees, including Golap-ma, were fortunate enough to be able to accompany the Master to the Car Festival at Mahesh and the Vaishnava festival at Panihati in the middle of 1885. After the Panihati festival the Master's throat pain increased, and the devotees were very worried about him. An interesting incident in this connection is mentioned in the *Life of Sri Ramakrishna*:

> One day Golap-ma told the Master that she knew of an expert physician who might treat his case successfully. Sri Ramakrishna, like a boy, jumped at the idea and proposed to see the doctor the next morning. He set out for Calcutta from Dakshineswar by boat, accompanied by Golap-ma, Latu, and Kali. Reaching Calcutta, they consulted the doctor, who prescribed certain medicines.
>
> On their way back to Dakshineswar they felt very hungry. The Master inquired if any of the devotees had any money. None but Golap-ma had any, and that was but four pice. The Master asked Kali to take it and buy something at the nearest market. Kali purchased an anna worth of sweets from Baranagore. The Master, much to the surprise of the others, ate them all. He then drank water from the Ganga and said, 'Ah, I am satisfied'. As the Master declared his satisfaction, the hunger of the three, who were mutely watching, vanished.[18]

When Sri Ramakrishna moved to Shyampukur, Calcutta, for treatment, Golap-ma temporarily took the responsibility of cooking his food. Holy Mother stayed behind at Dakshineswar. One day Golap-ma, who was simple but not very tactful, made a remark to Yogin-ma that the Master had probably left Dakshineswar because he was annoyed with Holy Mother. When Holy Mother heard about it she was stunned. She went at once to Shyampukur with tears in her eyes and asked the Master if she had really offended him. Sri Ramakrishna denied the whole thing and after consoling her sent her back to Dakshineswar. Later he scolded Golap-ma severely for her thoughtlessness and told her to beg Holy Mother's forgiveness. Golap-ma immediately walked all the way to Dakshineswar. Bursting into tears, she implored Holy Mother to forgive her. It was impossible for Holy Mother to harbour ill feelings against anyone. She just laughed and patted Golap-ma on the back three times. Within a few days the devotees arranged a room at the Shyampukur house for Holy Mother, and she once again devoted herself to the Master's service.

One important trait of Golap-ma's character was that she did not have a sensitive ego. Because of her outspokenness she was often misunderstood, criticized, and humiliated by other devotees, but she never left the Master or Holy Mother. When the Master was at Shyampukur a few devotees sometimes complained about her to Sri Ramakrishna. He would not say anything to her about it directly, but he would caution her through a dream. Golap-ma later said: 'What a wonder! At that time if anybody would complain against me to the

Master, he would tell me in a dream: "This person said this against you. You said that woman [mentioning her name] loves you very much, but she also said this about you". The whole night I would see the Master in my dream, so the criticisms of people would not enter my ears'.[19]

The Master moved from Shyampukur to Cossipore in December 1885, and Golap-ma went there along with Holy Mother. After Sri Ramakrishna passed away on August 16, 1886, Balaram handed over a white, borderless sari to Golap-ma to give to Holy Mother, since orthodox widows do not wear coloured saris or saris with borders. Golap-ma shuddered at the thought and said: 'Good God! Who can give her this white cloth?'[20] But when she went to Holy Mother's room, she found that Holy Mother had torn off the wide red border on her sari. A few days later there arose a dispute between the monastic disciples and the householder disciples about the installation of the Master's relics. Holy Mother said to Golap-ma with a sigh, 'Such a golden person has left us, and now, Golap, they are quarrelling over his ashes!'[21]

Towards the end of August 1886, Balaram arranged for Holy Mother to go on a pilgrimage along with Golap-ma, Lakshmi, M.'s wife, Yogen (Swami Yogananda), Latu (Swami Adbhutananda), and Kali (Swami Abhedananda). They first went to Varanasi and then to Vrindaban, where they stayed for a year. Holy Mother later related an incident concerning Golap-ma that happened when they were in Vrindaban:

> Our Golap's mind is perfectly pure. In Madhavji's [Krishna's] temple at Vrindaban somebody's baby had soiled the floor. Everyone remarked about it, but no one made a move to clean up the place. When Golap noticed this, she tore a strip from her fine cloth and cleaned the spot with it. The other women said, 'Since she is cleaning it up, it must have been her baby'. I said to myself, 'Listen to what they say, O Madhavji!' Some others said: 'No, these are holy women. They are doing it for the convenience of others'.[22]

After returning from the pilgrimage, Holy Mother went to Kamarpukur along with Golap-ma and Swami Yogananda. They went by train as far as Burdwan, but then they had to walk the rest of the way. After walking about sixteen miles Holy Mother was exhausted and hungry. Golap-ma somehow cooked by the roadside some khichuri (rice and lentils) and served it to Holy Mother and Swami Yogananda. Holy Mother exclaimed with joy, 'O Golap, what nectar you have prepared!'[23] After staying with Holy Mother in

Kamarpukur for a few days, Golap-ma and Swami Yogananda returned to Calcutta. Holy Mother spent about a year there (1887–1888) under most trying circumstances, suffering from poverty, loneliness, and people's criticisms. Golap-ma finally found out about it and asked the devotees to bring her to Calcutta. Holy Mother stayed a few days at Balaram's house and then moved to Nilambar Mukherjee's garden house in Belur, which was rented for her by the devotees.

Golap-ma was Holy Mother's Vijaya (a companion of Goddess Durga) and followed her like a shadow for thirty-six years. She went on several pilgrimages with Holy Mother to different holy places of India, such as Deoghar, Puri, Prayag, Hardwar, Rameshwar in the south, as well as Kailoar, Kothar, and other places. She also accompanied her to Jayrambati and Kamarpukur many times. Holy Mother used to say: 'I cannot go anywhere without Golap. I feel secure when she is with me'.[24] While going somewhere by carriage, Golap-ma would hold Holy Mother's hand as they got in and out. And when they walked anywhere, Holy Mother would walk behind Golap-ma like a new bashful bride. In the Mother's household in Calcutta, Golap-ma acted as a supervisor and also guarded Holy Mother from emotional, temperamental devotees. One day a devotee began to worship Holy Mother, who was seated in front of him completely covered with a chadar [shawl]. Golap-ma noticed it, but since it was not unusual she went on with her own work. After quite some time she returned to the Mother and saw that the man was still at it, and she realized that he was going to extremes. Pulling the man up, she said to him in her loud voice: 'Is this a wooden image that you should infuse consciousness into it with all your gesticulations and pranayama? Don't you have any sense that the Mother is perspiring and feeling uncomfortable?'[25]

Holy Mother was very shy and even covered her face with a veil in front of the Master's monastic disciples. Once Swami Vivekananda came to visit her. She covered her face as usual and talked to him through Golap-ma. When Swamiji asked her for her blessings, Golap-ma said: 'Mother says that the Master is always with you. You have many more things to accomplish for the welfare of the world'.[26] When elderly men devotees would ask questions to the Mother, she would whisper her answer to Golap-ma, who would then repeat the Mother's answer aloud to the devotee.

Golap-ma was extremely outspoken. Without caring about others' feelings, she freely expressed her opinions, not even sparing Holy Mother. Holy Mother did not mind, however, because she knew that

Golap-ma was her well-wisher and that her words were spoken from her heart and not from malice. But from time to time the Mother warned her not to hurt the devotees with harsh words, even if they were true, as ·the results would return to her and make her life miserable.

On one occasion when Holy Mother was coming from Jayrambati to Calcutta by train, Swamis Brahmananda and Premananda, along with a few other devotees, went to the railway station to receive her. As Yogin-ma and Golap-ma were helping the Mother from the train, the two swamis rushed to take the dust of her feet. Golap-ma stopped them, however, saying to Swami Brahmananda in her high-pitched voice: 'Maharaj, have you no sense whatsoever? The Mother has just got off the train, tired and worn out by the burning sun. If you make such a fuss about prostrating, how can I restrain the others?' The swamis were abashed and stepped back. In spite of the scolding, though, they followed Holy Mother's carriage to her residence, where Girish Ghosh was waiting to meet her. Seeing him, Golap-ma said: 'My words beat a retreat, Girish Babu, before your grotesque devotion. You have come here to see the Mother, and she is so tired. Without giving her a chance to rest you are here to torture her!' But Girish was equally outspoken. He immediately retorted: 'You are surely a boisterous woman! I thought that the Mother's heart would be soothed by seeing her children's faces after such a long time, and this woman is teaching me devotion to the Mother! Phew!' Girish then motioned for Swami Brahmananda and Swami Premananda to come with him, and the three of them paid their homage to the Mother. Later, Golap-ma complained to Holy Mother about Girish's rude words, but the Mother replied, 'I have warned you many times about criticizing my children'.[27]

Sister Devamata wrote about Golap-ma in *Days In An Indian Monastery*:

> My chief companionship was with the devotees surrounding Holy Mother. Golap-ma — tall and powerful in build, conservative, orthodox, and uncompromising — acted as gendarme to Mother, protecting her against intrusion, guarding her safety, even scolding her when she thought Mother was growing careless in caste observance and too indulgent towards her foreign children... She showed me always the greatest kindness.[28]

It is very important for spiritual aspirants to know the daily routines of illumined souls. Holy Mother once said, 'Golap has attained perfection through japam'. Golap-ma's routine at the Udbodhan house was as follows: She would get up before 4:00 A.M. and after washing would sit for three hours in her room for japam and meditation. Then she would go to the shrine to salute the Master and Holy Mother. After that she would go to the kitchen storeroom and pick out the vegetables to give to the cook. She then started to cut some vegetables so that the cook could begin his work. Later in the morning she would accompany Holy Mother to the Ganga for a bath, bringing back with her a brass jar of Ganga water for the worship. Again she would go to the kitchen and, along with Yogin-ma, cut more vegetables. She also used to make about a hundred betel rolls every day. When the worship was over and the food had been offered, she would set aside some prasad for the Mother and then distribute the rest to the monks, devotees, and workers of the household. After lunch Golap-ma would take a little rest and then read the Mahabharata, the Gita, or a book on Sri Ramakrishna or Swami Vivekananda. She spent her afternoons either cutting more vegetables for supper or sewing torn pillow cases or mosquito curtains for the monks. Later she would talk to Holy Mother or visit Balaram's house, which was nearby. When the vesper service was over she would again salute the Master and Holy Mother and then sit in her room for spiritual practices till 9:00 P.M. During supper she would distribute the offered sweets and fruits to everyone. If anyone was out, Golap-ma would save his food. Her eyes were everywhere in Holy Mother's household.[29]

Golap-ma loved orderliness and cleanliness. If any of the members of the household left any used cloth where it did not belong, she would have it cleaned and put in its proper place. She also kept track of the utensils and worship vessels. She could not stand waste. Holy Mother also disapproved of it. If there were any old, unusable utensils, Golap-ma exchanged them for new ones. Vegetable peelings and leftovers from the plates were fed to the cows. Even the stems from the betel leaves she saved for the guinea pigs in the house, since they were fond of them. She also dried the orange peels and sugarcane peels for use as fuel in the kitchen.

Besides being very frugal, Golap-ma was also kindhearted and charitable. She received ten rupees (less than a dollar) a month from her grandson as an allowance. Half of this she gave to the Udbodhan Office for her food, and the other half she gave away in charity. No beggar would go away empty-handed from the Udbodhan. Golap-ma always responded to their calls, even late at night. Sometimes she would ask those devotees who were doctors to give free treatment to the poor, sick neighbours. She got joy in serving others, but she would not accept any service herself unless she was in great difficulty.[30]

Once a blind beggar stood outside the Udbodhan, calling: 'Radha-Govinda! Mother Nandarani [a name of Krishna's foster-mother], have pity on the blind!' Hearing his call, Holy Mother said to a devotee: 'That beggar passes this way almost every night. Formerly he would say, "Have pity on the blind, Mother". One day Golap said to him: "Look here, along with your prayer for help, why don't you take the name of Radha and Krishna? It will be good for those who hear the Lord's name and for you who chant it. What a pity that you are only harping on your blindness!" Since then he comes here with the name of Radha-Govinda on his lips. Golap gave him a cloth, and he gets money from time to time'.[31]

One day Golap-ma cleaned Holy Mother's bathroom at the Udbodhan, and then, changing her clothes, she started to prepare the fruits for the worship. Nalini, one of Holy Mother's nieces, was very fastidious, and when she saw what Golap-ma had done she was shocked. She told Golap-ma to take a bath in the Ganga to purify herself and then cut the fruits. Golap-ma said, 'Go yourself if you want!' Holy Mother explained to Nalini: 'Golap's mind is pure and noble. That is why she has no obsession about what is pure and what is not. This will be her last incarnation'.[32]

But this does not mean that Golap-ma did not have any regard for the Ganga. On the contrary, her devotion for the Ganga was such that even when she was very old, she would walk with the help of a stick to the river every day for her bath. And if there was any filth on the bathing ghat, she would clean it with a piece of torn cloth and then wash the place with water. Selflessly she served people, practising the ideal of karma yoga.

Although Golap-ma was Holy Mother's companion and guide, the following incident shows how highly the Mother regarded her:

> During her last visit to Varanasi Holy Mother was one day seated with Golap-ma and several other companions, when a woman who had never before seen her came in and wanted to show her respect. Her eyes first fell upon the dignified figure of Golap-ma. As she moved towards her to take the dust of her feet, Golap-ma at once pointed out Holy Mother. Now she approached the Mother, but the latter, out of innocent mischief, indicated by her finger that Golap-ma was the one she was looking for. Golap-ma again directed her attention to Holy Mother, but the Mother again pointed at Golap-ma. This teasing game continued for some time. Then Golap-ma said to the stranger, rather sharply, 'Can't you distinguish a divine face from a human one?' The woman at last discovered the elusive grace and charm of the Mother's face.[33]

Holy Mother passed away on July 21, 1920, and Golap-ma lived for four years after that. She continued her service as usual, but she missed the Mother. She had a little heart trouble and some minor complications and gradually her health began to fail. One day Golap-ma told some women devotees, 'Yogin died in the bright fortnight, and I shall go in the dark one'. A few days before her death she said to a monk: 'It seems to me that this body will not last long. Quite often I see a girl, wearing an ochre cloth and a rudraksha garland and carrying a trident, come out of my body. Then I look at this body and it seems to be dead'.[34] She died at Udbodhan, Holy Mother's house, at 4:08 P.M. on December 19, 1924. Her body was cremated on the bank of the Ganga.

Soon after her death Doctor Bipin came to see her, not knowing that she had passed away. Swami Saradananda said to him, 'The bird has flown away'. 'Could you tell me where the soul has gone?' the doctor asked. 'To the Master', replied Swami Saradananda.[35] During her last visit to Varanasi with Holy Mother, Golap-ma had said to the Mother: 'I do not want liberation. I want you'. Holy Mother had then replied: 'You are foolish! Don't you know that liberation is the Master's real nature?'[36] Golap-ma was a rare soul — full of love, devotion, purity, simplicity, unselfishness, and nonattachment. It is truly amazing how Sri Ramakrishna's touch transformed a poor, grief-stricken widow into a dedicated saint.

Akshay Kumar Sen (1854-1923)

26

Akshay Kumar Sen

The advent of an avatar signalizes a renaissance, a juncture in history when a new age of civilization is ushered in by a great cultural revival. The life of the Divine Incarnation is a force, and his ideas are new and inspiring. In particular, his mysterious charm and sublimity hold a special attraction for writers, poets, dramatists, painters, sculptors, and musicians, energizing their talents. One of the artists to feel the avatar's attraction was the poet Akshay Kumar Sen, whose masterpiece was *Sri Sri Ramakrishna Punthi*, a long narrative poem on Sri Ramakrishna's life.

Akshay was born in 1854 at Maynapur, a small village in the Bankura district of Bengal. Because his father, Haladhar Sen, and mother, Bidhumukhi, were too poor to afford a good education for him, Akshay was brought up in the countryside and educated in a village school. Little is known about his early life beyond the facts that he was devoted to Lord Krishna and lived humbly. In the course of time he married, was widowed, married again, and had two sons and one daughter.

To escape poverty in his native village Akshay moved to Calcutta and found a job as private tutor to the children of the Tagore family of Jorasanko. It so happened that Devendra Nath Majumdar, a devotee of Sri Ramakrishna, was working in the office of the Tagore estate and lived under the same roof as Akshay. But Akshay did not dare introduce himself to Devendra because of his inferiority complex — he felt himself to be unattractive, unlearned, and poor. He felt even further removed from his aristocratic employer.

As a humble devotee of Krishna, Akshay took formal initiation from his family guru a year before he met Sri Ramakrishna, and practised japam and meditation at night on the bank of the Ganga. In time, however, he became discouraged because, in spite of all his spiritual practices, he still had not received the vision of God.

One day Akshay was enjoying a smoke on the verandah when he overheard Devendra and Dhirendra, a young man of the Tagore family, talking about a paramahamsa (a man who has realized Brahman and renounced the world). Akshay was intrigued and wanted to know more about this paramahamsa. He knew that such a high soul was a knower of God — one who could help others to see God.

Later, when Devendra was alone, Akshay approached him, saying: 'Sir, you were talking about a paramahamsa. Could you tell me where he is?' Brushing the question aside, Devendra asked him, 'What good could it possibly do you?'[1] Akshay was hurt, but his curiosity increased. Later he came to know from Dhirendra that Sri Ramakrishna was the paramahamsa, and that he lived in Dakshineswar.

Six months passed. Akshay's mind was possessed by Sri Ramakrishna. Coming from a village, he had no idea where Dakshineswar was located, and without the help of Devendra he would never have the opportunity to meet Sri Ramakrishna. Summoning his resourcefulness, Akshay decided to serve Devendra anonymously. Knowing that he smoked early in the morning, Akshay, before Devendra arose from his bed, prepared perfumed tobacco with burning charcoal and left his hubble-bubble in front of the door to Devendra's room. Devendra, of course, was delighted to have his favourite smoke but wondered who was serving him. Within a few days he found out that it was Akshay who was preparing the tobacco for him. When he asked why, Akshay said, 'Sir, would you please take me to meet the paramahamsa?'[2] Seeing his sincerity and humility, Devendra agreed.

On a Saturday, probably in the early part of 1885, Mahimacharan Chakrabarty arranged a festival and invited Sri Ramakrishna and the devotees to his house at 100 Cossipore Road, in North Calcutta. Akshay heard that Devendra was planning to attend the function and that Dhirendra was going with him. His heart was pounding, for it was unbearable to wait any longer to see this paramahamsa. As the two men were getting into their hired carriage, Akshay rushed to Devendra and holding his feet with both hands, pleaded with him, saying, 'Sir, please allow me to accompany you to the place you are about to visit'. Devendra consented.[3]

The carriage arrived at Mahima's house at five o'clock in the afternoon. Ram, Manomohan, Surendra, M., Vijay Krishna Goswami, and other devotees were present. Devendra and others took the dust of the Master's feet, and Akshay did likewise. Akshay noticed that the Master smiled a little and cast a gracious glance towards him. Then he sat in a corner and looked intently at the

Master. Forgetting his body and surroundings, he was captivated by Sri Ramakrishna's charm and conversation. He felt as though he was being carried away on a current of bliss. After a while the devotees began to sing kirtan in the courtyard. As soon as the Master heard the sound of the drum and cymbals he hurriedly joined the kirtan party and started to sing the following song:

Behold, the two brothers* have come,
who weep while chanting Hari's name,
The brothers who dance in ecstasy and
make the world dance in His name!
Behold them, both weeping, and making
the whole world weep with them,
The brothers who, in return for blows,
offer to sinners Hari's love.[4]

Intoxicated with divine joy, Sri Ramakrishna began to dance with the kirtan group. At times he went into samadhi and remained motionless like a statue; at other times, in partial consciousness, he danced slowly and rhythmically. The Master created such a tangible spiritual atmosphere that Akshay felt as though he were in heaven. Vijay Krishna Goswami, a Brahmo leader, was dancing next to the Master. Suddenly he pointed to Sri Ramakrishna and exclaimed: 'This is our Krishna!'[5] These words were a revelation to Akshay, and he directly experienced their truth — that the Master was none other than Sri Krishna for whom he had been yearning since his youth. The Master appeared to him as the veritable incarnation of love.

The kirtan ended at nine o'clock in the evening, and the devotees began to tend the Master. One fanned him and another brought ice water for him to drink. Meanwhile Mahima arranged a dinner with various delicacies for Sri Ramakrishna and the devotees. After dinner Sri Ramakrishna was taken to a room where he talked with the devotees. Akshay thought to himself: 'The Master has revealed his divine nature to his close devotees. Without his grace and without devotion, none can understand him'. Suddenly Sri Ramakrishna began to sing Lord Krishna's words in his melodious voice:

Though I am never loath to grant salvation,
I hesitate indeed to grant pure love.
Whoever wins pure love surpasses all;
He is adored by men;
He triumphs over the three worlds.

---

*Gauranga and Nityananda

Listen, Chandravali! I shall tell you of love:
Mukti a man may gain, but rare is bhakti.
Solely for pure love's sake did I become
King Vali's doorkeeper
Down in his realm in the nether world.

Alone in Vrindaban can pure love be found;
Its secret none but the gopas and gopis know.
For pure love's sake I dwelt in Nanda's house;
Taking him as My father,
I carried his burdens on My head.[6]

When the festival was over the Master left for Dakshineswar. Akshay got into Devendra and Dhirendra's carriage along with Ram, a householder disciple of Sri Ramakrishna. Ram had befriended him that evening, telling him many wonderful things about the Master. Thus, when Ram got out of the carriage in Simulia, where he lived, Akshay got out with him. In Ram's house he listened to many more stories about Sri Ramakrishna. At two o'clock in the morning he finally went home.

After that first meeting Akshay longed to see the Master again, and his mind was absorbed in thoughts of him. A couple of days later Akshay had the opportunity to go to Dakshineswar with a friend. This time Sri Ramakrishna asked Akshay many things about his life, including whether or not he was a Brahmo.

Generally the Master did not allow Akshay to touch his feet, a refusal which hurt him greatly. Instead, Sri Ramakrishna would say: 'Let your mind be purified. Then you may do so'.[7] Nonetheless, after three visits Akshay was convinced that if anyone could give him the vision of Krishna, it was Sri Ramakrishna. Later he realized that Krishna and Ramakrishna were one and the same. He wrote in his *Sri Sri Ramakrishna Mahima*:

I neither talked with Sri Ramakrishna nor asked any questions, but this I knew: that whosoever received the touch of the Master on his chest, would lose outer consciousness and in that state would see Krishna. Expecting this, I continued to visit him. Not only that, whenever I would see him I would feel myself to be a different person. I used to think how it would be when the Master, out of mercy, touched my chest. Many days passed, but he did not fulfill my desire. I used to go to him with great hope and return home with tearful eyes and disappointment.

I only talked to him twice in my whole life. One day, seeing him alone, I said: 'Master, I am blind [i.e., ignorant]'. To this the Master replied: 'God exists'. [What Sri Ramakrishna meant was: 'You might be blind, but God has eyes to see you'.] Another day I carried an ice cream cone for the Master, but he did not touch it. I asked: 'Master, why did you not eat the ice cream? I feel terrible!' He answered with a smile: 'If you had brought the ice cream at noontime, I would have eaten it. I would have been sick if I ate that cold thing at night, so I did not'.

The way the Master treated me! If he had treated any other person in that way, he never would have returned. So many devotees touched his feet, and yet whenever I would try to touch them, he would withdraw his feet and sometimes even move back, saying: 'All right! All right!' The Master used to speak about abstruse spiritual matters and I could not follow what he meant, so I would sit silently in a corner, my eyes always on him.[8]

It is difficult for an ordinary person to understand the actions and behaviour of an avatar. He may eradicate the bad karma of a devotee through harshness, or he may crush the ego through indifference. If a devotee can endure such ordeals, he achieves something. Akshay tried to wipe away the impurities of his heart through tears and prayers, and gradually he felt the Master's silent benediction. Later he wrote in his book: 'What Sri Ramakrishna demonstrated and explained to me led me to the firm conviction that he is God himself. He is an avatar, Lord of the universe, the Almighty. He is that Rama, that Krishna, that Kali, indeed, that Satchidananda. He is beyond mind and intellect, but again, he is known only through the pure mind and intellect'.[9]

During that trial period Akshay lived in fear and agony. He was afraid of the Master, and yet he felt that the Master was like his father. He was irresistibly attracted to Sri Ramakrishna and yet did not know how to express his love. On one occasion Akshay begged Devendra to ask the Master to bless him. Devendra went to Dakshineswar and delivered Akshay's request to the Master. Sri Ramakrishna said: 'What shall I say? You give him some advice'.[10] Accordingly Devendra told Akshay to chant the name of Hari (Krishna). Akshay took this advice and began to practise japam with longing.

On April 6, 1885, Devendra arranged a festival at his house in Sri Ramakrishna's honour. Akshay was included among the crowd of devotees. Because Devendra was busy supervising the dinner, he asked Akshay to fan the Master. Sri Ramakrishna was sitting in the parlour surrounded by devotees. To Akshay's great delight, he and Upendra sat near the Master and massaged his feet.[11]

On January 1, 1886, Sri Ramakrishna became the kalpataru (wish-fulfilling tree) and blessed many devotees, saying: 'Be illumined'. The occasion was the Master's afternoon walk in the Cossipore

garden. As the Master entered the garden, the devotees followed
him. Akshay, who was seated with a few others on the low bough of
a tree, saw him. He rushed to where Sri Ramakrishna was standing
and found the Master, absorbed in samadhi, in the middle of his
devotees. Akshay picked two champaka (Michelia Champaka)
flowers and offered them at the feet of Sri Ramakrishna.

After a while the Master came down to the normal plane of
consciousness and touched the devotees one by one. This act created
great emotional fervour and excitement among the devotees. Some
received the vision of their Chosen Deity; some experienced the
awakening of the kundalini; some felt unspeakable bliss; and others,
out of ecstasy, began to laugh, cry, and shout. Akshay watched the
entire scene from a distance. Then suddenly the Master's eyes fell on
him, and he called to Akshay: 'Hello!' Akshay ran to the Master, who
touched his chest with his hand and whispered a mantram in his
ear.[12] At once Akshay experienced the effect of the Master's blessing.
He could not contain the onrush of bliss, and unable to withstand
such an upsurge of emotion, he fell to the ground. His limbs twisted
as if he were deformed, and he burst into tears.[13]

On August 15, 1886, Sri Ramakrishna's physical condition became
critical. Swami Vivekananda had arranged for Akshay to fan the
Master that night. When evening came, Sri Ramakrishna tried to eat a
little farina pudding, but could not swallow it. Exhausted, he again
lay down on his bed and went into samadhi. Shashi (later, Swami
Ramakrishnananda) cried out and asked Akshay to call Girish and
Ram, two of the Master's close devotees, from Calcutta. Akshay
immediately rushed to Calcutta, reported the Master's critical
condition to them, and then hurriedly returned to Cossipore.[14]

After his samadhi the Master was extremely hungry and asked for
food. This time he ate a full bowl of pudding without any difficulty,
which greatly relieved the devotees. Then in a clear voice the Master
repeated thrice: 'Kali, Kali, Kali',[15] and slowly lay back on his bed.
After some time he again went into samadhi. His eyes were fixed on
his nose, his face covered with a sweet smile. Sri Ramakrishna passed
away on August 16, 1886, at 1:02 A.M.

After the Master's passing Akshay used to decorate Sri
Ramakrishna's photograph with sandal paste and sing his glory to
the accompaniment of a one-stringed instrument.[16] Although he had
no literary skills, Akshay felt a compelling urge to write something
about Sri Ramakrishna. The scriptures say: 'By the grace of God, the
dumb become eloquent and the lame scale mountains'.[17] Devendra
Nath Majumdar, who had first taken Akshay to meet Sri

Ramakrishna, now suggested that he write about the Master's life. (Akshay acknowledged this encouragement in his book.)

Still, Akshay had doubts about his ability, which he expressed to Swami Vivekananda. Though something was urging him from within to write about the Master, he felt that he did not have the literary skill to do so. Seeing his sincerity, Swami Vivekananda told him the story of the English poet, Caedmon. Caedmon was an illiterate herdsman, who did not even know the alphabet. One night he had a vision of an angel, and by that angel's grace his poetic faculty came to life. Caedmon composed extemporaneously and even recited his hymns and poems in public.[18]

Inspired by this story, Akshay began to write Bengali verse in 1887. After he had finished the early life of Sri Ramakrishna, he read it to Swami Vivekananda at the Baranagore monastery. Swamiji was deeply moved and took him to Holy Mother, who was then staying at Belur. Holy Mother, after listening to the manuscript, blessed Akshay. Later, while she was at Kamarpukur and Akshay was also there, the Mother invited the village women, who had known the Master personally, to come so Akshay could read his book to them. On this occasion the Mother, in an ecstatic mood, again blessed Akshay and asked him to write more about the Master. Akshay gratefully acknowledged that Girish and Swamis Yogananda, Niranjanananda, and Ramakrishnananda had given him the materials for his book.

Akshay wrote the life of Sri Ramakrishna in the style of Krittivasa's *Ramayana* and Kashiram Das' *Mahabharata*. The book was first published in four parts between 1894 and 1901 under the title *Bhagavan Sri Sri Ramakrishna Paramahamsadever Charitamrita*. Later, on November 25, 1901, all four parts were published in one volume under the title *Sri Sri Ramakrishna Punthi*.[19] His Bengali poem of the Master's life has not yet been translated into any other language.

On one occasion Swami Shivananda explained how *Sri Sri Ramakrishna Punthi* came into being:

Akshay Sen, the author of *Sri Sri Ramakrishna Punthi*, helped many people of the world. He was a good man and a great devotee, but extremely poor. The facts which he presented in the *Punthi* are really beautiful. We did not know many of those stories. Akshay collected all the material from contemporaries of the Master at Kamarpukur, Sihar, and other places. He then wrote the life of the Master in the poetic style of the *Ramayana* and the *Mahabharata* in simple village language. Now, even the learned appreciate the *Punthi*. Akshay was not a scholar, but he had tremendous sincerity. We heard that when he started to write this book he held an ordinary job in Ahiritola and used to write at night. We further heard that at night he would go to the bank of the Ganga and call to the Master with a longing heart: 'Master, please give me strength so that I can write something about your precious life'. Immediately he would feel inspiration from within and, returning to his apartment, would start to write. This *Punthi* is well written.[20]

In 1895, during the birthday celebration of Sri Ramakrishna, Akshay publicly read for the first time *Sri Sri Ramakrishna Punthi* on the northern verandah of the Master's room at Dakshineswar. Swami Adbhutananda was present. Impressed, the swami said: 'Akshay Babu, you have performed a great service for the people. You have written the life story of the Master in such a beautiful way that even the women [the majority of whom were not educated at the time] will be able to understand him'.[21]

Akshay sent a copy of his book to Swami Vivekananda, who was then preaching Vedanta in America. In the beginning of 1895 Swamiji sent a letter to Swami Ramakrishnananda from the U.S.A., in which he wrote:

Just now I read Akshay's book. Give him a hundred thousand hearty embraces from me. Through his pen Sri Ramakrishna is manifesting himself. Blessed is Akshay! Let him recite that *Punthi* before all. He must recite it before all in the Festival. If the work be too large, let him read extracts from it. Well, I do not find a single irrelevant word in it. I cannot tell in words the joy I have experienced by reading his book. Try, all of you, to give the book an extensive sale. Then ask Akshay to go from village to village to preach. Well done, Akshay! He is doing his work. Go from village to village and proclaim to all Sri Ramakrishna's teachings. Can there be a more blessed lot than this? Akshay's book and Akshay himself must electrify the masses. Dear, dear Akshay, I bless you with all my heart, my dear brother. May the Lord sit on your tongue! Go and spread his teachings from door to door. There is no need whatever of your becoming a sannyasin [monk]... Akshay is the future apostle for the masses of Bengal. Take great care of Akshay; his faith and devotion have borne fruit.[22]

In this letter Swamiji wrote out a few ideas which he wanted Akshay to include and expand in the next edition of the book.

In the *Punthi*, Akshay divulged that he had received the humourous title of 'Shankcunni Master' from Swami Vivekananda in 1885. 'Cunni' literally means 'a female ghost wearing bangles'; and because he was a schoolteacher, he was called 'Master'. Swamiji called him 'Shankcunni Master' because of his appearance — small eyes, thick lips, a flat nose, a thin body, and a dark complexion. In later years Akshay grew a long grey beard and moustache, wore thick glasses, and often donned a turban. All this contributed to his rather strange-looking appearance.

Akshay's poetic talent did not end with the writing of Sri Ramakrishna's biography. He also put the Master's teachings into simple, melodious verse. This book included 141 teachings of Sri Ramakrishna and was published in 1896 under the title *Padye Sri Sri Ramakrishna Paramahamsadever Upadesh*, or The Teachings of Sri Ramakrishna Paramahamsa in Verse.[23] Fourteen years later, in 1910, Akshay wrote *Sri Sri Ramakrishna Mahima* (The Glory of Sri Ramakrishna) in question-and-answer form.[24] In this book, the reader will marvel at Akshay's literary craftsmanship, rational outlook, and deep understanding of Sri Ramakrishna's life and philosophy.

Akshay worked for some time at the Basumati publication office, which was owned by Upendra Nath Mukhopadhyay, a lay disciple of Sri Ramakrishna. After retiring from that job Akshay left Calcutta for his village home and there passed the remainder of his life. Once, however, Doctor Umesh Babu and other devotees took him to Mymensingh (now in Bangladesh), where he lived for several months, reminiscing about the Master. He was helped financially by devotees from Mymensingh, Dhaka, Madras, and Lucknow.

Once, when Akshay was visiting Udbodhan, Swami Saradananda presented him with a set of *Sri Sri Ramakrishna Lila Prasanga* (*Sri Ramakrishna, The Great Master*) and requested him to read it. Akshay later said to a young monk:

> Brother, I took those books and put them in my room. I was a little conceited, thinking that M. and I had written about the Master, so what else could Swami Saradananda write about him? Then one day it suddenly flashed in my mind that my monastic brother had given me all those volumes free, and I, out of ego, had not even opened them! Brother, I was dumbfounded after reading them. I realized that in the *Punthi* I had made some mistakes because I had received the information second-hand, whereas he had based his stories on direct evidence. Then, though I was old, I corrected my book as much as I could. This is my last corrected edition of *Punthi*. I hand it over to you. I shall not live long. I entrust you to give this volume to Swami Saradananda. Let him publish it in the future if he wishes. My request to Swami Saradananda is to please send a certain percentage of the profit from the book sales for the worship of the Master here.[25]

In spite of his poverty and other family problems, Akshay passed his days in recollectedness of the Master. Every morning before his worship he would pick flowers and clean the vessels. Then in a sweet voice despite his age, he would sing the name of God, accompanied by his one-stringed instrument. After bathing and performing the worship he would either read *Sri Ramakrishna, The Great Master* or write something. In the summer months at noontime Akshay would go to the shrine and fan the Master. During the last three years of his life, when he could not perform worship because of asthma and other physical disabilities, his daughter-in-law, to Akshay's great relief, took the responsibility of the Master's worship.

Akshay was sincerely devoted to Holy Mother. His home and the Mother's parental home were in the same district, so whenever the Mother was in Jayrambati, Akshay would go barefooted with a staff in his hand to meet her. He would always carry something on his head for Holy Mother. Bowing down to her, he would pray for liberation. Once in Jayrambati Akshay called, 'Mother', and the Mother answered, 'Yes, my son'. Akshay then boldly said: 'Mother, I called you "Mother" and you answered "yes", so I have no fear anymore'. To this Holy Mother said: 'My son, do not talk like that. "Success comes only to a careful person" '.[26]

Emotional and oversensitive by nature, Akshay expected love and affection from all, especially from the Master and Mother. At one time he wrote to Holy Mother in Jayrambati complaining that she was paying more attention to her Calcutta devotees than she was to him. The Mother replied in a letter:'... I understand the contents of your letter. You have written about your visit to Jayrambati, but I did not know about it. As long as I am alive you are welcome to visit me. I have no like or dislike for anybody; I consider everyone as my own. There is no division in my mind. When you took refuge in God you became my own. Please do not lament. Whenever you have the opportunity you are free to come here. Your letter surprised me. Keep your mind free from all impurities'.[27]

Holy Mother had told Akshay, 'There will be a little suffering towards the end of your life'.[28] Four days before his death he had a fever and suffered from blood dysentery. When Akshay's end came near, his young brother started to chant the name of Sri Ramakrishna. All of a sudden Akshay said to those around him: 'Please keep quiet now. I see the Master and the Mother'.[29] Everyone present noticed that his face was luminous and his eyes were half-closed. Then he breathed his last. Akshay died at 9:00 A.M. on Friday, December 7, 1923, at the age of seventy-three.

In the divine drama of Sri Ramakrishna, Akshay played the role of minstrel, and his ballads are still spreading the immortal life and message of the Master.

27

Manindra Krishna Gupta

A man prays to God for what he loves most. A lover of wealth prays for money; a lover of name and fame prays for recognition; a lover of pleasure prays for enjoyments; a lover of aesthetics prays for beauty; a lover of the body prays for good health; a lover of knowledge prays for intellectual pursuits. Most people love God's powers, but few love God. We do not realize that if we seek God, we will attain God as well as the wisdom and strength to handle worldly success. If, however, we seek only success and power, we may get them, but eventually they become a bondage.

Once Sri Ramakrishna asked Manindra Krishna Gupta: 'What do you want?' 'I want to express my ideas about the beauty of the world and human nature — that is my desire', replied the young Manindra. 'That is fine', said Sri Ramakrishna with a smile. 'But if you realize God, you will achieve everything'.[1]

In 1870 Manindra Krishna Gupta was born in Calcutta. His grandfather, Ishwar Chandra Gupta, was a famous poet. Manindra's family was related not only to M., the recorder of *The Gospel of Sri Ramakrishna*, but also to Keshab Chandra Sen, the famous Brahmo leader. After Sri Ramakrishna and Keshab met, the Master's name quickly spread among the followers of the Brahmo Samaj as well as the younger generation of Bengal. Upendra Krishna Gupta (Manindra's older brother), Karunamay Sen (Keshab's son), Brahmabandhav Upadhyay (Bhavani Charan Bandyopadhyay), and other young Brahmos rented a house and formed a group called 'Young Men's Nest'. These leaders used to teach young boys religion, morality, ethics, literature, and social work.

During summer vacation or any holiday, Brahmabandhav would visit Sri Ramakrishna at Dakshineswar with his friends. Since Brahmabandhav had great affection for the young boys, he never missed an opportunity to invite them. Thus Manindra met Sri Ramakrishna at Dakshineswar, probably in 1882. In his own words, he reminisced:

Manindra Krishna Gupta (1870-1939)

I was then about eleven or twelve years old. I remember that we used to go on a big boat and that the trip on the Ganga was very pleasant. When we had landed at Dakshineswar, we would bathe either in the Ganga or in the pond — swimming, splashing, and having lots of fun.

Afterwards we would assemble on the northern verandah of Sri Ramakrishna's room. The Master would put out an assortment of offered sweets, fruits, sugar candy syrup, and other delicacies, and he himself would invite us to partake of them. Thus I saw him several times, but all I remember is his sweet and affectionate manner.

After partaking of the *prasad*, our senior members would listen to the teachings of the Master while we youngsters would play in the temple garden or sometimes just rest in the Panchavati.

One day, out of curiosity, I peeped through the eastern door of the Master's room. He was seated on his small cot and I can still remember that he had a small bag containing cinnamon, cloves, and other spices. Now and then as he talked he would take a few of them and put them in his mouth. I don't remember what he was talking about, but one thing I do remember: Pointing to the young audience in his room, he said, 'Look, here is a gathering of bright jewels'. I was so impressed seeing his beautiful, loving face, that I could not turn to look in any other direction. I stood there for some time, forgetting everything. When my companions left his room and moved towards the boat, I followed them.[2]

Because of his father's work, Manindra's family moved to Bhagalpur, so he was not able to see the Master for three years. Then he returned to Calcutta where he enrolled in school. Caring very little for the school curriculum, he used to study art and literature at home. Soon his guardians discovered that Manindra, instead of going to school, was visiting the eastern part of Calcutta to enjoy the natural beauty of the meadow and canal. They scolded him, but could not change his attitude.

In September 1885 Sri Ramakrishna moved to Shyampukur, Calcutta, for his cancer treatment. One afternoon Sarada Babu, an acquaintance of Manindra, asked him: 'Would you like to go with me on a visit?' Manindra had previously accompanied him on walks through the countryside, so he agreed. Seeing that Manindra had misunderstood, Sarada explained further: 'But today I am not going for a walk. Sri Ramakrishna is now living in a house at Shyampukur. Let us go and see him'.[3] Immediately Manindra dressed properly and the two left for Shyampukur.

When they arrived there, Sri Ramakrishna was in his room with M. and Swami Vivekananda. The Master was reclining on his bed, facing north. As soon as Manindra and Sarada entered, the Master rose, and they saluted him. Sri Ramakrishna looked intently at Manindra, then beckoned him to come closer. He smiled a little and whispered: 'Come alone tomorrow. Don't come with him'. Sarada could not hear what the Master had said.

Later, on their way home, Sarada, out of curiosity, asked Manindra, 'What did he say to you?' Manindra was a little hesitant to tell him what the Master had actually said, so he gave a passing answer, 'Well, the Master asked me to visit him another day'. 'My boy, your luck is good', said Sarada. 'He did not talk to me at all'.[4]

On his way home Manindra felt an irresistible attraction for the Master. It was hard for him to sleep that night, and a strange thing happened. He continually saw the smiling face of Sri Ramakrishna all around him and heard his voice saying, 'Come alone tomorrow'. Manindra wrote in his memoirs:

Some may think that because I was then a teenage boy, my description is somewhat exaggerated. But please remember that truth never changes with the passing of time, nor does one's experience. The joy of seeing the moon when one is young is the same as the joy of seeing it when one is old. At any rate, I remember vividly that I had struggled to sleep the whole night and that it was not until the early hours of the morning that I finally fell asleep.

The next afternoon I started again for Shyampukur. I saw M. and some other devotees in the Master's room... It appeared to me that the Master knew of my coming and was waiting to receive me. Before I could sit down, he asked everyone to leave the room and for me to come sit near him.

'Where have you been for so long?' he asked. Saying this, the Master burst into tears. He addressed me as though I were a near and dear relative. He touched me, and I noticed a slight smile on his face. Then all of a sudden, his body became stiff like a corpse. I remained motionless. What was this? Never having seen samadhi before, I knew nothing about it and was quite at a loss. I checked his breath, but could detect no sign of it. His eyes were half-closed and his eyelids were motionless.

After fifteen minutes I saw that he was gradually returning to normal consciousness. Then, touching my chest, he muttered something and asked me in a deep voice, 'What do you want?'[5]

Manindra had the feeling that the Master would give him anything he wanted. But there is a saying: 'If a husking machine goes to heaven, it continues to husk there'. Manindra was a boy of poetry and imagination; he loved the beauty of nature. Without considering the pros and cons, he spontaneously voiced his desire to express his feelings about beauty.

Manindra then began to cry. The Master asked the devotees to take him to the next room. It took them half an hour to stop him from crying and to bring him down from that emotional experience. After that, Manindra became a frequent visitor of the Master and began to serve him under the direction of Swami Vivekananda, who was then the leader of the Master's young disciples.

As Manindra was one of the youngest in the group, the disciples and devotees called him 'Khoka' (young boy). There were not sufficient accommodations for several attendants in the small Shyampukur house, so Manindra would serve Sri Ramakrishna during the day and stay the night at Ram Chandra Datta's house. Gradually he became well known among the devotees of the Master.

One night, during the fall of 1885, there was a meteor shower in Calcutta. The next evening Dr. Mahendra Lal Sarkar visited Sri Ramakrishna as usual. While there, Dr. Sarkar and other devotees talked about the meteor shower in English. Manindra was present. The Master could not understand what they were talking about, since he did not know English. Sri Ramakrishna looked at them blankly, then slowly went into samadhi.

Gradually the Master returned to the normal plane and said: 'Hello, what are you talking about? I saw a meteor shower in this vast universe which is pervaded by Brahman. Are you talking about that?'[6] The devotees, especially Dr. Sarkar, were amazed to hear these words of the Master. But Sri Ramakrishna was very much against miracle-mongering. Once he said: 'Look, if you see that a monk is trying to show his miraculous powers, know for certain that he does not have one iota of spirituality. He is a hypocrite'.[7]

Manindra also recorded another interesting incident which occurred at the Shyampukur house:

> One day the Master was returning from the bathroom to his room, which was across the verandah. I was waiting for him on the northern verandah, and I also followed him. I noticed that Ram Chandra Datta and some other devotees entered the Master's room. Seeing Ram, the Master said: 'Hello, Ram. Just now I had a vision of a monk with a well-built body who was wearing an ochre loin cloth. I have never seen him before'.
>
> Ram replied with a smile: 'Sir, what do we know? You see so many things in heaven and earth — how can we comprehend them all?' 'Really I have seen a monk', said the Master. 'But I don't know who he is'. My memory of that simple, childlike statement is

still vivid. Then the subject was dropped. Slowly the Master sat down on his bed. Ram and other devotees sat in front of him. I sat in the room adjacent to the Master's, which was near the steps. About an hour later I saw a man come upstairs. He wore a black shirt and a black cap. It seemed to me that he was a native of Bihar. He asked me: 'Sir, does Ramakrishna Paramahamsa live here? I have come to see him. Could I see him right away?' 'Of course', I replied. 'Please follow me'. I took him to the Master's room.

After sitting there quietly for a while, he said to the Master: 'Sir, I am a Christian, and for a long time I have meditated in solitude on Christ. Though I am a Christian and my Chosen Deity is Christ, my mode of worship is like the Hindus, and I believe in their yoga scriptures. Once I had a desire to find someone who had attained the highest spiritual realization while still in the world. One day in meditation, I saw two persons. I had the strong feeling that one of them had attained the highest, and that the other one, seated at his feet, though he had not yet reached the highest, was not an ordinary person.

'After this vision, I felt certain that such great souls must exist, but where were they, and how could I find them? I travelled to many places, especially in the western part of India, seeking the two I had seen in my vision. At last I heard of Pavhari Baba of Ghazipur, and I went to see him. But when I met him, I was greatly disappointed, because he bore no resemblance whatsoever to either of the two men I was seeking. But to my astonishment, I saw a picture of one of them hanging on the wall in his room. When I asked Pavhari Baba about it, he said it was a picture of Ramakrishna Paramahamsa. Eagerly I asked, "Where can I find him?" Then Pavhari Baba told me that for many years he had lived at Dakshineswar, but was now very ill and had been moved to Calcutta for treatment by his devotees. So I am here, having come to Calcutta at Pavhari Baba's suggestion'.

Then the man went on to say: 'These clothes in which you see me are not my usual dress'. And as he spoke he stood up and removed his outer garments, revealing an ochre cloth. Instantly the Master also stood up and went into samadhi, raising his hand, as it is seen in the picture of Christ. At this, the monk knelt down before him with folded hands and looked intently at Sri Ramakrishna. The monk was shedding tears and was shivering.

We were all amazed to see the spiritual moods of both. And as my gaze again fell on his ochre cloth, I wondered, 'Is this the holy man in ochre dress whom the Master had seen in his vision?'

After some time the Master came back to normal consciousness and sat on his bed. The monk looked at us, his face beaming with joy, and exclaimed, 'Today I am blessed'. Then he continued more calmly: 'As you see, this inner cloth is my regular dress, and it is also my favourite dress because it is worn by the yogis of India. I was born in a brahmin family, and even though I am a Christian, why should I give up the traditions of my ancestors? I have great faith in our Indian manners and customs'.

Then we took him to an adjacent room, where Swami Vivekananda offered him prasad and food. Finally, we asked the monk* to tell us the cause of his ecstasy. 'Well', he replied, 'today I saw the one on whom I have meditated for so many years. I saw Lord Jesus in him'.[8]

At Shyampukur, though the Master's illness was growing more serious every day, people flocked to him in greater numbers in order to satisfy their spiritual longing. Manindra, Sarada (later, Swami Trigunatitananda), and other newcomers received special instruction from the Master during this time. Because Manindra's nature was soft and emotional, he used to dance in ecstasy upon hearing the Lord's name. On October 30, 1885, Sri Ramakrishna said to M.: 'Manindra has an element of prakriti, of womanliness. He has read the life of Chaitanya and has understood the attitude of the gopis. He has also realized that God is Purusha and man is prakriti, and that man should worship God as his handmaid. How remarkable!'[9]

On November 6, 1885, the devotees made the arrangements for Kali Puja according to the direction of the Master. Doctor Sarkar and several other devotees visited the Master, and the doctor asked to hear some songs. M., Girish, and Kalipada sang, and while listening to their songs, Manindra and Latu entered into ecstasy.

When Sri Ramakrishna moved again to Cossipore, following the advice of his doctors, Manindra took an active part in serving him. Holy Mother once mentioned an incident which happened there: 'When the Master was sick, Manindra and Patu [two teenage devotees of the Master] were fanning him. It was the day of the *Holi* festival [an auspicious day when Krishna played with the gopis with coloured dyes], and all were playing with the colours outside. The Master repeatedly asked the two boys to join in the festival, but they continued to stay and serve the Master. Seeing their love and devotion, the Master exclaimed: "Look, these boys are my Ramlala [the child Rama]" '.[10]

Manindra was well aware that Sri Ramakrishna was his guru and Chosen Deity. But when Kumud Bandhu Sen once asked Manindra about his initiation, he was told: 'One day I was seated near the

---

*The monk's name was Prabhudayal Mishra. His birthplace was in the western part of India, and he belonged to the Quaker sect of Christianity.

Master. Mahim Chakrabarty was present at that time, and he said to the Master, "Last night I saw in a dream that I was giving a mantram to Manindra according to your direction". The Master asked him to repeat the mantram. As soon as Mahim Chakrabarty did so, the Master went into samadhi. Afterwards, when he came down to the normal plane, he asked Mahim to give me that mantram'.[11]

After the passing away of Sri Ramakrishna, Manindra put on the ochre cloth at the behest of Mahim Chakrabarty and lived with him. He always kept in close contact with the monastic disciples of the Master, who were then at the Baranagore monastery. Later he returned home, married, and had several children.

Though Manindra did not finish his schooling, he continued his studies under the supervision of a private tutor until the time of his marriage. His tutor was a brilliant man, and it was through his efforts that Manindra became proficient in literature. Manindra's grandfather, Ishwar Chandra Gupta, had founded a daily newspaper, *Sambad Prabhakar*, which was later inherited by Manindra's father. Since Manindra was reluctant to accept outside work for a living, his guardians encouraged him to edit and manage the newspaper. Through this work he became acquainted with the famous writers of Bengal — Suresh Chandra Samajpati, Akshay Kumar Baral, and others.

Gradually Manindra became involved in the theatre, and he began to write dramas. As a result, the newspaper was neglected. Unfortunately he did not appear to have any significant talent in playwriting, so his financial condition soon became critical. In 1897, when Swami Vivekananda returned to India from the West, he heard about Manindra's pecuniary condition and asked Swami Brahmananda to give Manindra twelve hundred rupees so that his family would not starve. Upon accepting the gift, Manindra burst into tears at the thought of Swamiji's generosity and love for him.

Manindra would visit Alambazar Math, Belur Math, Dakshineswar, and Yogodyana regularly. On auspicious occasions he would arrange a festival of Sri Ramakrishna at his house and invite devotees. He kept in close touch with the monastic and householder disciples of the Master. Holy Mother was very fond of Manindra, and it was due to his influence that several members of his family received initiation from her.

During the later part of his life, when his sons became capable of earning money themselves, Manindra's financial condition improved. Quite often he would visit M. and Swamis Saradananda and Shivananda. At Swami Saradananda's request, Manindra wrote his reminiscences of the Master, and it was published serially in the *Udbodhan* (Vol. 38 to Vol. 41).

After retirement, he spent most of his time thinking and talking about Sri Ramakrishna. Although his outer life had not been very successful, his inner life blossomed through the grace of the Master. Whenever Manindra would speak of Sri Ramakrishna and his devotees, his eyes would fill with tears of joy.

Manindra passed away in 1939 at the age of sixty-nine, at his Calcutta residence. He was a simple, sincere, and humble soul.

his reminiscences of the Master, and it was published serially in the Udbodhan (Vol. 38 to Vol. 41).

Purna Chandra Ghosh (1871-1913)

28

Purna Chandra Ghosh

Most people do not realize how difficult it is for an avatar or for an illumined soul to hear or talk about mundane things. Some even experience a painful sensation in their bodies when they have to listen to worldly talk. Because of this, these great souls long for spiritually-minded companions with whom they can communicate and share their feelings and experiences. Sri Ramakrishna had to wait nearly twenty-three years after his realization for his close disciples to come. He later described his agony to some of the disciples: 'I then felt an indescribable yearning to see all of you. The soul was being wrung like a piece of wet towel, so to speak, and I felt restless with pain. I felt like weeping, but I could not do so lest that should create a scene. I controlled myself somehow. But when the day came to an end and night approached and the vesper music began in the Mother's and Vishnu's temples, I could not control myself. I thought, "One more day has passed away and they have not come". I then got up on the roof of the "mansion", and cried out, calling you loudly: "O my children! Where are you? Come". I felt I might go mad. Then, after long waiting, you at last started coming one by one. Only then was I pacified. And as I had seen you all earlier, I could recognize you as you came, one after another. When Purna came, Mother said: "With this the coming of those of whom you had visions is complete. No one else of this class will come in the future" '.[1] (The name *Purna* literally means 'complete' or 'full'.)

Purna Chandra Ghosh was one of the six direct disciples of Sri Ramakrishna who were designated by the Master as *Ishvarakotis*, that is, great souls who are eternally free from the bonds of karma and who take birth of their own will to do good to mankind. The other five Ishvarakotis were Swamis Vivekananda, Brahmananda, Premananda, Yogananda, and Niranjanananda. Although Purna did not become a monk, he commanded much respect from the Master's devotees for his spirituality. On a number of occasions Sri Ramakrishna talked about Purna's real nature: 'Purna is a part of

Narayana and a spiritual aspirant possessing a high degree of sattva. In this respect he may be said to occupy a place just below Narendra [Vivekananda]'.[2] 'Purna was born with an element of Vishnu. I worshipped him mentally with bel leaves, but the offering was not accepted. Then I worshipped him with tulsi leaves and sandal paste. That proved to be all right'.[3] (The leaves of the bel tree are offered to Shiva, whereas tulsi leaves and sandal paste are offered to Vishnu.)

Purna was born either in the later part of 1871 or the early part of 1872 in a wealthy family of North Calcutta. His father, Rai Bahadur Dinanath Ghosh, was a high official in the Finance Department of the Government of India. His mother, Krishnamanini, was related to Balaram Basu, a devotee of Sri Ramakrishna. Purna was a student at the Shyambazar branch of the Metropolitan Institution, a school founded by Ishwar Chandra Vidyasagar. The headmaster of this school was M., the recorder of *The Gospel of Sri Ramakrishna*. Seeing Purna's bright, prominent eyes, fair complexion, well-built body, and sweet, graceful countenance, M. sensed that he might have some spiritual aptitude. Out of affection he gave him some spiritual instructions and also lent him a copy of the *Sri Sri Chaitanya Charitamrita*, a Bengali biography of Sri Chaitanya. The boy read the book with great interest and was deeply inspired by Chaitanya's life and teachings.

One day in March 1885, M. said to Purna, 'Would you like to see a saint like Sri Chaitanya?'[4] Purna immediately said yes. He was then just thirteen years old and in the eighth grade. Purna's relatives were a problem, however. Since they were rich aristocrats, Purna knew that they would consider it beneath their dignity for him to visit or associate with an ordinary temple priest. They were also very strict disciplinarians. For this reason M. devised a plan to take Purna to the Master secretly, during the school hours. One day he hired a carriage, and they both left school for Dakshineswar.

The Master immediately recognized Purna's divine nature and treated him as one belonging to his own inner circle. At that first meeting he fed Purna with his own hands like an affectionate mother and gave him some spiritual instructions. Purna was so overwhelmed that he was reluctant to leave, but M. reminded him that they would have to return before school was over. The Master said to Purna: 'Come here whenever you find an opportunity. You will get your carriage fare from here'.[5]

There are many obstacles and pitfalls in spiritual life. But even these can be turned to a spiritual aspirant's advantage by increasing his longing and determination, and strengthening his relationship with God. There is a saying, 'Love becomes intensified by troublemakers'.

Such was the case with Purna. Purna wanted to visit the Master again, but he was afraid that his parents would find out about it. Meanwhile, Sri Ramakrishna's heart was also crying for Purna. The Master secretly began to send sweets, fruits, and other things to Purna through some devotees. One day he cried bitterly for Purna in front of the devotees and said to them: 'You are amazed to see me thus attracted towards Purna. I don't know how you would have felt had you seen the longing that arose in my heart when I first saw Narendra and how very restless I was on that occasion'.[6]

Whenever Sri Ramakrishna was eager to see Purna, he would come to Calcutta at midday and would wait at Balaram's or someone else's house near Purna's school. He would then send somebody to bring Purna to him. Thus Purna's second meeting with the Master took place at Balaram's house. On that occasion the Master asked him, 'What do you think of me?' Filled with devotion, Purna replied without hesitation, 'You are God himself, come to earth in flesh and blood'. Sri Ramakrishna was delighted with his answer. He blessed Purna wholeheartedly and gave him some secret spiritual instructions along with a mantram.[7] After returning to Dakshineswar, Sri Ramakrishna said to his disciples: 'Well, Purna is a mere boy and his intellect has not yet matured. How then could he recognize me as an Incarnation of God? Under the impulse of divine impressions some other people also answered that question like Purna. It is definitely due to the good impressions accumulated during previous lives that the picture of untarnished truth spontaneously appears to their pure sattvic minds'.[8]

Purna had a relative who lived near Dakshineswar, and once while visiting that family he had an opportunity to see the Master. Sri Ramakrishna invited him for lunch that day and instructed Holy Mother to cook some delicacies. Taking Purna to the nahabat, the Master introduced him to Holy Mother. Purna did not understand who she was, however. He thought that she was just a woman devotee of the Master. Holy Mother fed him with great care and gave him a rupee according to the Master's direction. Purna accepted the money reluctantly. Only later did he find out that she was Sri Ramakrishna's wife.

Sri Ramakrishna once related a vision that he had just had about Purna:

Do you know what I saw just now in my ecstatic state? There was a meadow covering an area of seven or eight miles, through which lay the road to Sihar. I was alone in that meadow. I saw a sixteen-year-old paramahamsa boy exactly like the one I had seen in the

Panchavati. A mist of bliss lay all around. Out of it emerged a boy
thirteen or fourteen years old. I saw his face. He looked like Purna.
Both of us were naked. Then we began to run around joyfully in
the meadow. Purna felt thirsty. He drank some water from a
tumbler and offered me what was left. I said to him, 'Brother, I
cannot take your leavings'. Thereupon he laughed, washed the
glass, and brought me fresh water.[9]

On another occasion he said:

I want to tell you something very secret. Why do I love boys like
Purna and Narendra so much? Once, in a spiritual mood, I felt
intense love for Jagannath, love such as a woman feels for her
sweetheart. In that mood I was about to embrace Him, when I
broke my arm. It was then revealed to me: 'You have assumed this
human body. Therefore establish with human beings the
relationship of friend, father, mother, or son'. I now feel for Purna
and the other young boys as I once felt for Ramlala [a metal image
of the boy Rama]... Purna belongs to the realm of the Personal
God... Ah, what yearning he has![10]

As a mother bird protects her babies by spreading her wings, so Sri
Ramakrishna protected his young disciples and devotees from the
temptations, trials, and tribulations of life. At three o'clock in the
afternoon of April 6, 1885, the Master reached Balaram's house. It
was terribly hot that day, and the Master was exhausted from the
trip. Seeing M., he asked, 'Why haven't you brought Purna?'

M.: 'He doesn't like to come to a gathering of people. He is afraid
you might praise him before others and his relatives might then hear
about it'.

Master: 'Yes, that's true. I won't do it in the future... Well, how do
you find Purna? Does he go into ecstatic moods?'

M.: 'No, I haven't noticed in him any outer sign of such emotion'...

Master: 'Purna will not show his emotion outwardly; he hasn't that
kind of temperament. His other signs are good... Did you ask him
what he felt after meeting me?'

M.: 'Yes, sir, we talked about that. He has been telling me for the
last four or five days that whenever he thinks of God or repeats his
name, tears flow from his eyes and the hair on his body stands on end
— such is his joy'.

Master: 'Indeed! That's all he needs'.[11]

It is very reassuring and encouraging to hear from the Master
himself about his concern and love for his disciples. He said to M.
about Purna: 'A great soul! Or how could he make me do japam for
his welfare? But Purna doesn't know anything about it'.[12]

Purna's father soon learned about his son's association with Sri

Ramakrishna and forbade the boy to see him anymore. But in spite of increased restrictions at home, Purna continued to meet the Master secretly whenever Sri Ramakrishna came to Calcutta. M. was the go-between and would convey the news to Purna of the Master's visits to Calcutta when he saw the boy at school. On April 12, 1885, Purna met the Master at Balaram's house. The Master was delighted to see Purna and he asked him, 'Do you practise what I asked you to?'

Purna: 'Yes, sir'.

Master: 'Do you dream? Do you dream of a flame? A lighted torch? A married woman? A cremation ground? It is good to dream of these things'.

Purna: 'I dreamt of you. You were seated and were telling me something'.

Master: 'What? Some instructions? Tell me some of it'.

Purna: 'I don't remember now'.

Master: 'Never mind. But it is very good. You will make progress. You feel attracted to me, don't you?'[13]

The matter went too far, however. When Purna's relatives learned of his disobedience they became furious and said to him, 'If you go to him [Sri Ramakrishna] we will smash his carriage with stones and brickbats when he comes to Calcutta'.[14] They also took him out of M.'s school and sent him to another school. The news of Purna's transfer reached the Master and he began to worry about M. On June 13, 1885, the Master said to M.:

Master: 'If I see Purna once more, then my longing for him will diminish. How intelligent he is! His mind is much drawn to me. He says, "I too feel a strange sensation in my heart for you". They have taken him away from your school. Will that harm you?'

M.: 'If Vidyasagar tells me that Purna's relatives have taken him away from the school on my account, I have an explanation to give him'.

Master: 'What will you say?'

M.: 'I shall say that one thinks of God in holy company. That is by no means bad. Further, I shall tell him that the textbooks prescribed by the school authorities say that one should love God with all one's soul'.[15]

One night Purna was studying alone in his room when he suddenly noticed M. standing outside near his window. He immediately came out and M. whispered to him: 'The Master is waiting for you at the junction of Shyampukur Street and Cornwallis Street [now Bidhan Sarani]. Please come with me'. The Master was extremely pleased to see Purna. He said: 'I have brought sandesh [a sweet] for you. Please eat it'. The Master fed Purna with his own hands. Overwhelmed with emotion, Purna began to cry. The three of them then went to M.'s house, where the Master gave Purna some instructions on spiritual disciplines.[16]

In connection with this incident, Kumud Bandhu Sen wrote an interesting reminiscence:

> One evening I was talking to Purna about Girish's love and devotion for the Master. In the course of conversation I said, 'Last night Girish mentioned something wonderful'. Purna asked curiously, 'What did he say?' I replied: 'Girish said: "Who could understand Sri Ramakrishna? Do you think the Master's disciples have understood him? But those who have tasted a drop of his love have realized that the Master's pure divine love was above the world and even beyond any paternal love. God can hide everything except his unbounded love. The disciples and the devotees get intoxicated tasting a little of that love. Otherwise, who, however great he may be, can comprehend the infinite nature of God?" '
>
> As soon as I told him what Girish had said, Purna's face became red and his eyes filled with tears. Grabbing my hand, he took me from his room to the junction of Shyampukur Street and Cornwallis Street and said to me in a choked voice, 'Here — here [I experienced that love of the Master]'. I had never before seen Purna so emotional. Outwardly he had always been very calm and serious by nature. That night, when I saw his radiant face in the street light, I was speechless. He then said, his voice still choked with emotion: 'It is true. Girish is right. Who can understand the Master? Who can measure his unmotivated, unconditional love? I was a mere boy. What did I know about him? His superhuman love made me convinced that he was God incarnate'.[17]

On July 15, 1885, Balaram asked the Master, 'Sir, how was it possible for Purna to know all of a sudden that the world is illusory?' Sri Ramakrishna replied: 'He has inherited that knowledge from his previous births. In his past lives he practised many disciplines. It is the body alone that is small or grows big, and not the Atman. Do you know what these youngsters are like? They are like certain plants that grow fruit first and then flowers. These devotees first of all have the vision of God; next they hear about his glories and attributes; and at last they are united with him'.[18]

Practising spiritual disciplines without having love and longing for God is like eating curries that are without salt. Yearning is the only thing needful in spiritual life, and Purna got this precious trait in the beginning of his life. On July 13, 1885, M. told the Master: 'One day I was riding on a tram. He [Purna] saw me from the roof of his house and ran down to the street. With great fervour he saluted me from the street'. Sri Ramakrishna was overwhelmed to hear that. With tearful eyes he said: 'Ah! Ah! It is because you have helped him make the contact through which he will find out the supreme ideal of his life. One doesn't act like that unless one longs for God'.[19]

How can one live in the world and at the same time keep one's mind in God? The scriptures answered this vital question thus: 'A woman who is attached to a paramour will constantly have her mind on him, even though she is engaged in her household duties'.[20] Likewise, one should establish a relationship with God and constantly think of him. This is exactly what happened in Purna's life. His parents confined him to the house, but his mind dwelt in the Master. On August 29, 1885, the Master received a letter from Purna, in which he had written: 'I am feeling extremely happy. Now and then I cannot sleep at night for joy'. After hearing the letter the Master had said: 'I feel thrilled to hear this. Even later on he will be able to keep this bliss. Let me see the letter'. He pressed the letter in the palm of his hand and said: 'Generally I cannot touch letters. But this is a good letter'.[21]

Swami Abhedananda wrote an incident about Purna in his autobiography:

> One day a young man named Purna Chandra Ghosh came to Dakshineswar. Seeing him, the mood of Gopala [the child Krishna] arose in Sri Ramakrishna's mind. The Master experienced great delight in feeding him. Purna was then a student of the Oriental Seminary. Knowing that the school was close to my house, the Master one day said to me: 'Purna is a good boy. He reminds me of Gopala and I wish to feed him. When his school is over, invite him to your house and feed him sandesh [a sweet] which I shall give you'. I said, 'Yes, I will do that'. This made the Master very happy. He smiled and said, 'You will act as my messenger, just as Vrinda [a gopi] acted as Radha's messenger to Krishna'. Then he handed me a big mango and some sandesh. I carried them home according to the Master's instruction.
>
> After school hours were over I met Purna and brought him to our home at Nimu Goswami Lane. With my own hands I fed him the mango and sandesh which the Master had given me for him. Purna ate them heartily and said with tearful eyes: 'Ah! How kind and affectionate the Master is! His love and affection surpasses even that of our parents. The Master gave you so much trouble just to feed me!' From that time on Purna and I were very close. The next day I went to Dakshineswar and told the Master about Purna. He was delighted to hear my story.[22]

In September 1885 Sri Ramakrishna had to move from Dakshineswar to Calcutta for his cancer treatment. Early in the

morning of October 30, 1885, Purna visited the Master secretly. When
M. arrived the Master said to him, smiling: 'Purna came this
morning. He has such a nice nature!'[23] So far as the records show, the
last time Purna saw Sri Ramakrishna was at the Cossipore garden
house in April 1886, a few months before the Master's death. Purna
came in a hired carriage paid for by M.

After Sri Ramakrishna's passing away Purna became more
withdrawn and indifferent towards the world. He sometimes visited
the monastic disciples of Sri Ramakrishna, but this alarmed his
parents. Fearing that Purna might also become a monk, they forced
him to marry against his will. He was then only sixteen. His father
was a high official in the Finance Department, and he was able to
arrange a good job for Purna in the same department. Purna later
held a high position there. Although he was thus engaged in his
duties as a householder, whenever the devotees would come to visit
him he would talk only about the Master, or he would remain silent, a
reverent listener to their conversation.

In Sri Ramakrishna's divine drama Purna's role was in the
background. He simply led the life according to the Master's
instructions. The other devotees and disciples of Sri Ramakrishna
had much love and respect for him because of his extraordinary faith,
reliance on God, devotion, humility, and selflessness. M. often sent
some of his young students to Purna to get inspiration from his holy
company. When Purna would hear that someone was going to
renounce the world and join the monastery, he would be delighted.

In 1893 the news of Swami Vivekananda's success in the Parliament
of Religions of Chicago reached India. Purna would collect all the
newspaper clippings he could find about him and bring them to
Balaram Basu's house, where Swami Brahmananda and other direct
disciples would meet together. After Purna read them aloud to the
gathering, the monastic disciples would share Swamiji's letters with
him. When Swami Vivekananda returned to Calcutta in 1897, Purna
went to to meet him at the Sealdah Railway Station. He saw Swamiji
from a distance, but the crowd was so big that he could not go near
him. Returning home, he went to take a bath before leaving for his
office. Just then Swami Vivekananda's carriage stopped in front of his
house and Swami Trigunatitananda went inside to call Purna. Purna
was overwhelmed. He immediately came out in wet clothes to bow
down to Swamiji. 'Brother Purna, how are you?' asked Swamiji.
Purna replied: 'Swamiji, by the grace of the Master I am fine. I saw
you at the Sealdah Station from a distance. I came back and was
taking a bath since I will have to go to the office'. 'Very well', said

Swamiji affectionately, 'don't be in wet clothes long. Go to work and later see me at the monastery'. Purna joyfully agreed and bowed down to Swamiji again.[24]

When Purna was thirty-five he became seriously ill and the doctors gave up hope for his life. One day during this critical period Swami Premananda came to see him. Sitting on Purna's bed, he became absorbed in a divine mood. Shortly after this Purna recovered. Swami Premananda later said that the Master had extended Purna's life another seven years because his children were quite young.[25]

Purna was an ideal father to his children, and he performed all the duties of a householder faithfully. He educated his children well and married his daughters in good families. He was kind and generous to his younger brothers and friends. Yet, in spite of his many family responsibilities and social commitments, he maintained a high spiritual mood.

In 1907 Purna was elected secretary of the Vivekananda Society of Calcutta, which had been founded in 1902, just after Swamiji's passing away. The Society was then located on Shankar Ghosh Lane. Purna visited the Society regularly and meditated in the shrine along with the other members. He was a great inspiration to the younger members and gave them advice like a friend. In 1911 Madame Calvé, the famous French opera singer and devotee of Swamiji, visited Calcutta. The members of the Vivekananda Society, led by Purna, received her at the Grand Hotel and presented her with pictures of Sri Ramakrishna and Swami Vivekananda. Purna also arranged her visit to Belur Math. He could not continue his secretaryship of the Vivekananda Society for long, however, because his office was transferred from Calcutta to Delhi.

Although Purna's main office was in Delhi, he had to spend several months a year in Simla for official work. While there, he would go in the evening after office hours to a solitary place on a hill and spend some time in meditation.[26] People seldom saw his spiritual emotion, as he had tremendous power to hold it within. But one day a devotee was singing devotional songs at Purna's Simla home. A friend noticed that tears were flowing from Purna's eyes and that they remained red for a long time. On another occasion, when Purna was walking with a friend, he seemed to be absent-minded. The friend asked him if he had any body-consciousness or not. Touching his throat, Purna replied that he had consciousness above that point, but not below. This indicates that Purna was a *sthitaprajna*, a 'man of steady wisdom'.

Purna was calm, quiet, and unostentatious by nature, but when necessary he could be outspoken and spirited. Once two English soldiers ill-treated some local people of Simla. Purna immediately protested and challenged the soldiers.[27] He was very patriotic and had great appreciation for the freedom fighters of India. He strongly believed that Swamiji's life and message would inspire India's new generation.

Purna always maintained close contact with his brother disciples, even when he was living at Delhi or Simla. Once Swami Turiyananda, after visiting Kashmir, stayed for a while as Purna's guest in his Simla home. Whenever Purna was in Calcutta he would always visit Belur Math regularly. Once Swami Brahmananda, along with many monks and devotees, came to his Calcutta home when Purna arranged a festival. Some of his brother disciples were helped by him financially, and he also sent worship vessels and many other articles to Swami Trigunatitananda for the Vedanta temple in San Francisco. A lifelong habit of study enabled Purna to write well in English, and he used his talents to contribute some valuable articles for the *Brahmavadin*, an English monthly started by Swami Vivekananda.

During Girish Ghosh's last illness in 1911, Purna visited him. Seeing Purna, a beloved disciple of the Master, Girish forgot his pain and suffering. Both talked about Sri Ramakrishna for some time, and when Purna was about to leave, Girish said to him: 'Brother, bless me so that I may remember the Master with every breath. Glory to Sri Ramakrishna!' Purna humbly replied: 'The Master is always looking after you. Please bless us'. The next day Purna told a devotee that the Master would not keep Girish in this world much longer — Girish would very soon return to the Master.[28] Purna's words came true.

Purna had a wealthy friend named Shyam Basu, who was related to Balaram Basu. Shyam Basu used to visit Purna quite often and would call him 'Guruji'. Although he was a sincere gentleman, his moral character was not good. One day a person mentioned Shyam Basu's shortcomings to Purna. At this Purna replied: 'It is true Shyam Basu has some defects like other ordinary people, but whatever he does, he does privately without dragging others into it. Yet he possesses a noble quality that is very rare, and that is his veracity. He keeps his word, remaining ever steadfast like the Himalayas. And if he sees anyone in difficulty, he comes forward to help without passing any judgement'. By the grace of the Master, Purna was free from the disease of faultfinding. Later, through Purna's influence, Shyam Basu's life was changed, and he became very devoted to Sri Ramakrishna and Swami Vivekananda.[29]

Each soul, like a tree, grows in its own way. It is often seen that a person who still has some desires feels unhappy living in a monastery. Similarly, a person whose mind is inclined towards the path of renunciation, and yet is forced to become a householder, cannot derive any happiness from married life. By the mysterious will of God, Purna had had to marry. For the rest of his life he felt uncomfortable and out of place in the company of the worldly, because he had not been able to dedicate himself wholly to God. But though he had not taken any formal vows, the spirit of renunciation was truly there.

Once Swami Shuddhananda, a disciple of Swami Vivekananda, told a young man the following incident about Purna:

> Please study *The Gospel of Sri Ramakrishna* thoroughly. Those words came directly from the Master's lips. It is a wonderfully inspiring book. Listen to a story. Once Purna was passing through a very unhappy time and one day decided to commit suicide. He first took a bath and made himself ready. Then he thought: 'Let me read a page from *The Gospel of Sri Ramakrishna*. Taking the beautiful message of the Master I shall depart from this world'. He opened the book at random, and his eyes fell on these sentences: '*Purna balak bhakta. Thakur Purner mangal chinta karitechen*. [Purna is a young devotee. The Master was thinking of his welfare.]' These words from the *Gospel* changed his suicidal plan. He felt great assurance that the Master was thinking of his welfare.[30]

On July 13, 1885, Sri Ramakrishna had prophesied about Purna: 'Purna is in such an exalted state that either he will very soon give up his body — the body is useless after the realization of God — or his inner nature will within a few days burst forth. He has a divine nature — the traits of a god. It makes a person less fearful of men. If you put a garland of flowers round his neck or smear his body with sandal paste or burn incense before him, he will go into samadhi; for then he will know beyond the shadow of a doubt that Narayana himself dwells in his body, that it is Narayana who has assumed the body. I have come to know about it'.[31]

While he was living at Delhi, Purna contracted a fever which would not abate. Even a change to the exhilarating climate of the Simla hills did not help, but aggravated the disease all the more. However, Purna never lost his equanimity of mind. He knew that the Master was protecting him, and felt no fear, worry, or anxiety. One day, seeing his wife lamenting, he said to her: 'Are we like ordinary mortals? We belong to the Master eternally and in every way. He who fed you before my birth will maintain you and protect you after my death'.[32]

In order to receive better treatment Purna was brought from Simla to Calcutta, where he remained bedridden for about six months before passing away. He endured all physical pain and suffering calmly, without any complaint. If anyone came to comfort him, he would cheerfully say: 'My Master, Sri Ramakrishna, is always seated at my bedside. I have no fear or worry'.[33]

Purna's mother was extremely anxious for her son's life, so she repeatedly went to Holy Mother for her blessings. Holy Mother knew that Purna would not live long, but she could not tell that harsh truth to Purna's mother. One day when Purna's mother came Holy Mother said to her: 'What can I do, my dear? Ask the Master. He will make him well'. 'You can do it if you like, Mother'. 'No, I can only let him know'. After Purna's mother left, Holy Mother remarked: 'The Master told them [Purna's parents] that Purna would not live long if he were married, but she did not listen to him. She hurriedly arranged his marriage so that he could not be a monk'.[34]

As the days passed Purna's body became more emaciated, and he was not allowed to leave his bed because of his extreme weakness. One night, finding that all were fast asleep, he went to the bathroom alone without disturbing anyone. It was his nature not to trouble anyone about himself. While returning to bed he became dizzy and nearly fell. The next day he told a close devotee: 'Who says that the Master does not exist? He is still living and I perceive him clearly. Last night, while returning from the bathroom, I was about to fall unconscious. The Master caught me in his arms and carried me to bed. He is there, just as he was before, and I can see him'.*[35]

The death of an earthbound soul is like a tug of war. His prana (life-force) wants to leave the body, but his unfulfilled desires want the prana to stay. Thus the struggle goes on. In Purna's case, however, it was clearly seen he did not feel any pain at the time of his death and that his mind was soaring high during his last hours. About 10:00 P.M. the physician examined him and reported to his relatives that his last hour was at hand. After the physician had left, the relatives thought that Purna was sleeping peacefully. Without disturbing him they waited for some time. The doctor came again about an hour and a half later, examined the body, and declared that Purna's vital breath had left the body quite some time before. It was November 16, 1913.

---

*There is another account of this incident: Purna actually fell down. His attendant heard the noise, got up, and carried him to the bed. When Purna was asked whether he was hurt or not, he replied: 'No, I am not hurt. I fell on the Master's lap'.[36]

Kanti Ghosh, Purna's younger brother, described Purna's passing away in a letter: 'We could not believe that he was dead. On his final day he was very calm and seemed to be immersed in samadhi. We were surprised when the doctor told us that he had died a couple of hours before. Even at that time the crown of his head was warm. I felt an atmosphere like that of a temple in his room. Another striking thing happened when his body was brought out from his room to the courtyard. At that time some large raindrops fell on his body, but not anywhere else. Moreover, it was a moonlit night'.[37]

Purna Chandra justified his name (*Purna* means 'full'; *Chandra* means 'moon'). He was a stainless full moon, shedding beautiful, soothing light to all, imperceptibly. He was an unattached yogi, endowed with all divine qualities. Through Purna's life, Sri Ramakrishna demonstrated the synthesis of an ideal yogi and an ideal householder.

Kankurgachi Yogodyana (East Calcutta). Sri Ramakrishna visited this place on December 26, 1883. Ram Chandra Datta later installed a portion of the Master's relics here.

References

SRI RAMAKRISHNA (A BIOGRAPHICAL INTRODUCTION)

1. *Bhagavad Gita*, 4.7-8.
2. Christopher Isherwood, *Ramakrishna and His Disciples*, Methuen & Co. (London, 1965), p. 20.
3. Advaita Ashrama, *Life of Sri Ramakrishna*, (Calcutta, 1943), p. 11.
4. Isherwood, *Ramakrishna*, p. 20.
5. *Ibid.*, p. 21.
6. *Ibid.*, p. 28-29.
7. Advaita Ashrama, *Ramakrishna*, p. 69.
8. Isherwood, *Ramakrishna*, p. 65.
9. *Ibid.*, p. 85.
10. *Ibid.*, p. 124.
11. *Ibid.*, p. 148.
12. Swami Saradananda, *Sri Ramakrishna, The Great Master*, trans. by Swami Jagadananda, Ramakrishna Math (Madras, 1956), p. 299.
13. M., *Sri Sri Ramakrishna Kathamrita*, (Calcutta, 1961), Volume 1, p. 5.
14. Isherwood, *Ramakrishna*, p. 167.
15. His Eastern and Western Disciples, *The Life of Swami Vivekananda*, Advaita Ashrama (Calcutta, 1979), Volume 1, p. 77.
16. *The Complete Works of Swami Vivekananda*, Advaita Ashrama (Calcutta, 1966), Volume IV, p. 187.
17. *Ibid.*, p. 185.
18. Eastern and Western Disciples, *Life of Vivekananda*, Volume 1, p. 183.

RANI RASMANI

1. Swami Saradananda, *Sri Ramakrishna, The Great Master*, trans. by Swami Jagadananda, Ramakrishna Math (Madras, 1978), Volume 1, p. 484.
2. *The Complete Works of Sister Nivedita*, Nivedita Girls' School (Calcutta, 1967), Volume 1, p. 191.
3. Prabodh Chandra Santra, *Rani Rasmani* (Calcutta, 1913), p. 4-5.
4. Swami Gambhirananda, *Sri Ramakrishna Bhaktamalika*, Udbodhan (Calcutta, 1964), Volume 2, p. 422.
5. *Rani Rasmani*, p. 19-21.
6. *Ibid.*, p. 21-22.
7. *Ibid.*, p. 31.
8. *Ibid.*, p. 28-32.
9. *Ibid.*, p. 34-35.
10. *Ibid.*, p. 38-41.
11. *Ibid.*, p. 42-44.

12.   *Ibid.*, p. 58-59.
13.   *Ibid.*, p. 63-66.
14.   *Ibid.*, p. 49-50.
15.   *Ibid.*, p. 50-51.
16.   *Ibid.*, p. 71-72.
17.   *The Great Master*, p. 133.
18.   *Rani Rasmani*, p. 73.
19.   *The Great Master*, p. 134.
20.   *Ibid.*, p. 139.
21.   *Bhaktamalika*, p. 432-33.
22.   *The Great Master*, p. 162.
23.   *Ibid.*, p. 480-81.
24.   Advaita Ashrama, *Life of Sri Ramakrishna* (Calcutta, 1943), p. 85.
25.   *The Great Master*, p. 211.
26.   Udbodhan, *Sri Sri Mayer Katha* (Calcutta, 1965), Volume 2, p. 134.

MATHUR NATH BISWAS

1.   Swami Saradananda, *Sri Ramakrishna, The Great Master*, trans. by Swami Jagadananda, Ramakrishna Math (Madras, 1978), Volume 1, p. 497.
2.   *Ibid.*, p. 496-97.
3.   M., *The Gospel of Sri Ramakrishna*, trans. by Swami Nikhilananda, Ramakrishna-Vivekananda Center (New York, 1969), p. 332.
4.   *Shiva Mahimnah-stotra*, Verse 32.
5.   *The Great Master*, p. 494-95.
6.   *The Gospel*, p. 894-95.
7.   *The Great Master*, p. 493.
8.   Christopher Isherwood, *Ramakrishna and His Disciples*, Methuen & Co. (London, 1965), p. 96.
9.   *Ibid.*, p. 98.
10.   *Udbodhan*, Volume 9, p. 17-18.
11.   *The Gospel*, p. 152.
12.   *The Great Master*, p. 531.
13.   *Ibid.*, p. 501.
14.   *Ibid.*, p. 501.
15.   *Ibid.*, p. 532.
16.   *The Gospel*, p. 534.
17.   *The Great Master*, p. 281-82.
18.   *Ibid.*, p. 292-93.
19.   Advaita Ashrama, *Life of Sri Ramakrishna* (Calcutta, 1943), p. 216.
20.   *The Great Master*, p. 530.
21.   Shankaracharya, *Vivekachudamani*, Verse 542.
22.   *The Great Master*, p. 528.
23.   *Ibid.*, p. 528-29.
24.   *The Gospel*, p. 650-51.
25.   *Ibid.*, p. 236.
26.   *Udbodhan*, Volume 49, p. 530.
27.   Akshây Kumar Sen, *Sri Sri Ramakrishna Punthi*, Udbodhan (Calcutta, 1949), p. 141.
28.   *The Great Master*, p. 512-13.
29.   *Ibid.*, p. 514-16.

30. *Ibid.*, p. 518-20.
31. *Ibid.*, p. 500, 502-03.
32. Isherwood, *Ramakrishna*, p. 132.
33. *The Great Master*, p. 651.
34. *Ibid.*, p. 324.
35. *Ibid.*, p. 325.
36. *Life of Sri Ramakrishna*, p. 245.
37. *Ibid.*, p. 245.
38. *The Gospel*, p. 359.

HRIDAYRAM MUKHOPADHYAY

1.   Swami Saradananda, *Sri Ramakrishna, The Great Master*, trans. by
     Swami Jagadananda, Ramakrishna Math (Madras, 1978), Volume 1, p.
     147.
2.   *Ibid.*, p. 147-48.
3.   *Ibid.*, p. 148.
4.   *Ibid.*, p. 150.
5.   *Ibid.*, p. 152.
6.   *Ibid.*, p. 157.
7.   Advaita Ashrama, *Life of Sri Ramakrishna* (Calcutta, 1943), p. 68.
8.   Christopher Isherwood, *Ramakrishna and His Disciples*, Methuen & Co.
     (London, 1965), p. 67.
9.   *Life of Sri Ramakrishna*, p. 77.
10. Isherwood, *Ramakrishna*, p. 67.
11. *The Great Master*, p. 174.
12. *Life of Sri Ramakrishna*, p. 114.
13. Isherwood, *Ramakrishna*, p. 114.
14. *The Great Master*, p. 301-02.
15. *Life of Sri Ramakrishna*, p. 214.
16. M., *The Gospel of Sri Ramakrishna*, trans. by Swami Nikhilananda,
     Ramakrishna-Vivekananda Center (New York, 1969), p. 803.
17. *Ibid.*, p. 129.
18. *Ibid.*, p. 130.
19. *Life of Sri Ramakrishna*, p. 234.
20. *Ibid.*, p. 234.
21. *Ibid.*, p. 235; and Isherwood, *Ramakrishna*, p. 136.
22. Isherwood, *Ramakrishna*, p. 136.
23. *The Great Master*, p. 317-18.
24. *Ibid.*, p. 604; Isherwood, *Ramakrishna*, p. 103-04.
25. *Life of Sri Ramakrishna*, p. 236.
26. *The Great Master*, p. 319.
27. *Ibid.*, p. 319.
28. *The Gospel*, p. 270.
29. *The Great Master*, p. 193.
30. *The Gospel*, p. 519.
31. *Ibid.*, p. 584.
32. *Ibid.*, p. 871.
33. *Ibid.*, p. 745.
34. Isherwood, *Ramakrishna*, p. 159-60.
35. Sharat Chandra Chakrabarty, *Sadhu Nag Mahashay*, Udbodhan
     (Calcutta, 1969), p. 37.

36. *The Gospel*, p. 400.
37. *Ibid.*, p. 536.
38. *The Great Master*, p. 511.
39. Isherwood, *Ramakrishna*, p. 181-82.
40. Swami Nikhilananda, *Holy Mother*, Ramakrishna-Vivekananda Center (New York, 1962), p. 52.
41. *Life of Sri Ramakrishna*, p. 360-61.
42. Isherwood, *Ramakrishna*, p. 183.
43. *The Gospel*, p. 925.
44. *Ibid.*, p. 274-75.
45. *Ibid.*, p. 643-44.
46. Mahendra Nath Datta, *Ramchandrer Anudhyan*, (Calcutta, 1958), p. 94-95.
47. *Sadhu Nag Mahashay*, p. 74.
48. Mahendra Nath Datta, *Vivekananda Swamijir Jivaner Ghatanavali*, (Calcutta, 1964), Volume 2, p. 58.
49. *Ibid.*, Volume 3, p. 54.
50. M., *Sri Sri Ramakrishna Kathamrita* (Calcutta, 1961), Volume 1, p. 118.
51. *Vivekananda Swamijir Jivaner Ghatanavali*, Volume 2, p. 56.

LAKSHMI DEVI

1. Udbodhan, *Sri Sri Mayer Katha*, (Calcutta, 1969), Volume 1, p. 152.
2. Krishna Chandra Sengupta, *Sri Sri Lakshmimani Devi* (Cuttack, 1943), p. 60-61.
3. *Ibid.*, p. 38-41.
4. M., *The Gospel of Sri Ramakrishna*, trans. by Swami Nikhilananda, Ramakrishna-Vivekananda Center (New York, 1969), p. 379.
5. *Lakshmimani Devi*, p. 41.
6. From Swami Gauriswarananda's letter to Swami Dhireshananda (*Diary*, February 2, 1955).
7. Sister Devamata, *Days In An Indian Monastery*, Ananda Ashrama (California, 1927), p. 283-84.
8. *Lakshmimani Devi*, p. 230-31.
9. *Ibid.*, p. 12-13.
10. *Ibid.*, p. 56.
11. Swami Nirlepananda, *Ramakrishna-Saradamrita*, Karuna Prakashani (Calcutta, 1968), p. 3-12.
12. *Prabuddha Bharata*, 1929, p. 429-30.
13. *Days In An Indian Monastery*, p. 234.
14. *Ibid.*, p. 234-35.
15. *Ramakrishna-Saradamrita*, p. 4-12.
16. *Sri Sri Mayer Katha*, Volume 1, p. 305.
17. *Lakshmimani Devi*, p. 59.
18. Udbodhan, *Sri Sri Mayer Katha* (Calcutta, 1965), Volume 2, p. 98.
19. *Lakshmimani Devi*, p. 62-63.
20. *Ibid.*, p. 65-66.
21. *Ibid.*, p. 269, 54, 18.
22. *The Complete Works of Sister Nivedita*, Sister Nivedita Girls' School (Calcutta, 1967), Volume 1, p. 108.
23. *Ibid.*, p. 108.
24. *Lakshmimani Devi*, p. 109.

25. *Ibid.*, p. 145-46.
26. *Ibid.*, p. 154-55.
27. *Ibid.*, p. 187-88.
28. *Ibid.*, p. 171-72.
29. *Ramakrishna-Saradamrita*, p. 9.
30. *Lakshmimani Devi*, p. 271.

SHAMBHU CHARAN MALLIK

1. M., *The Gospel of Sri Ramakrishna*, trans. by Swami Nikhilananda, Ramakrishna-Vivekananda Center (New York, 1969), p. 647.
2. *Ibid.*, p. 934.
3. *Ibid.*, p. 234.
4. *Ibid.*, p. 894.
5. Swami Saradananda, *Sri Ramakrishna, The Great Master*, trans. by Swami Jagadananda, Ramakrishna Math (Madras, 1978), Volume 1, p. 351.
6. *Ibid.*, p. 409-10.
7. *The Gospel*, p. 845.
8. Akshay Kumar Sen, *Sri Sri Ramakrishna Punthi*, Udbodhan (Calcutta, 1949), p. 188-89.
9. *The Great Master*, p. 539-40.
10. *Ibid.*, p. 338-39.
11. *The Gospel*, p. 863.
12. *Ibid.*, p. 453.
13. *Ibid.*, p. 321.
14. *Ibid.*, p. 397.
15. *Ibid.*, p. 545.
16. *The Great Master*, p. 352-53.
17. *The Gospel*, p. 545.

RAM CHANDRA DATTA

1. Kankurgachi Yogodyana, *Ram Chandra Mahatmya* (Calcutta, 1905), p. 64.
2. *Ibid.*, p. 11.
3. Ram Chandra Datta, *Sri Sri Ramakrishna Paramahamsadever Jivanvrittanta*, Yogodyana (Calcutta, 1950), p. 104.
4. *Ram Chandra Mahatmya*, p. 13.
5. *Ibid.*, p. 14.
6. *Ibid.*, p. 16.
7. *Ibid.*, p. 16-17.
8. *Ibid.*, p. 17-18.
9. *Ibid.*, p. 18-19.
10. *Ibid.*, p. 20-21.
11. Advaita Ashrama, *Life of Sri Ramakrishna* (Calcutta, 1943), p. 303-04.
12. *Ram Chandra Mahatmya*, p. 26-27.
13. Kankurgachi Yogodyana, *Ramchandrer Vaktritavali* (Calcutta, 1938), Volume 1, p. 21-22.
14. *Ram Chandra Mahatmya*, p. 21-22.
15. *Ibid.*, p. 23-24.
16. Swami Gambhirananda, *Sri Ramakrishna Bhaktamalika*, Udbodhan (Calcutta, 1964), Volume 2, p. 304.

17.   *Ibid.*, p. 303.
18.   *Ibid.*, p. 304.
19.   *Ibid.*, p. 304.
20.   Jnanendra Nath Biswas, *Yogodyana Mahatmya*, Navabhava Library (Calcutta, 1941), p. 22.
21.   *Ibid.*, p. 23.
22.   M., *The Gospel of Sri Ramakrishna*, trans. by Swami Nikhilananda, Ramakrishna-Vivekananda Center (New York, 1969), p. 365.
23.   *Bhaktamalika*, p. 308.
24.   *The Gospel*, p. 426.
25.   *Ibid.*, p. 422.
26.   *Ibid.*, p. 566.
27.   *Ram Chandra Mahatmya*, p. 27.
28.   *Life of Sri Ramakrishna*, p. 548.
29.   *Ram Chandra Mahatmya*, p. 28.
30.   *Ibid.*, p. 28.
31.   *Paramahamsadever Jivanvrittanta*, p. 171.
32.   *Udbodhan*, Volume 45, p. 556.
33.   Advaita Ashrama, *Teachings of Sri Ramakrishna* (Calcutta, 1958), p. 108.
34.   *Ram Chandra Mahatmya*, p. 50.
35.   *Bhaktamalika*, p. 309.
36.   *Ibid.*, p. 309.
37.   Mahendra Nath Datta, *Ramchandrer Anudhyan* (Calcutta, 1958), p. 90.
38.   *Bhaktamalika*, p. 315.
39.   *Yogodyana Mahatmya*, p. 85.

MANOMOHAN MITTRA

1.   *Udbodhan*, Volume 10, p. 260.
2.   Udbodhan, *Bhakta Manomohan* (Calcutta, 1944), p. 22-24.
3.   *Ibid.*, p. 26.
4.   *Ibid.*, p. 18-19.
5.   *Ibid.*, p. 29.
6.   *Ibid.*, p. 34.
7.   *Ibid.*, p. 38-39.
8.   *Ibid.*, p. 41.
9.   *Ibid.*, p. 41.
10. *Ibid.*, p. 49.
11. *Ibid.*, p. 46-48.
12. *Ibid.*, p. 51.
13. *Ibid.*, p. 60.
14. *Ibid.*, p. 103-06.
15. *Ibid.*, p. 55.
16. *Ibid.*, p. 57.
17. *Ibid.*, p. 61-62.
18. M., *The Gospel of Sri Ramakrishna*, trans. by Swami Nikhilananda, Ramakrishna-Vivekananda Center (New York, 1969), p. 1013-15.
19. *Bhakta Manomohan*, p. 93-95.
20. *Ibid.*, p. 97-100.
21. *Udbodhan*, Volume 11, p. 513-15.
22. *Bhakta Manomohan*, p. 112.

23. *Ibid.*, p. 118-19.
24. *Ibid.*, p. 122-23.
25. *Ibid.*, p. 124.
26. *Ibid.*, p. 157.
27. *Ibid.*, p. 234.

SURENDRA NATH MITTRA

1. Ram Chandra Datta, *Sri Sri Ramakrishna Paramahamsadever Jivanvrittanta*, Yogodyana (Calcutta, 1950), p. 136.
2. Christopher Isherwood, *Ramakrishna and His Disciples*, Methuen & Co. (London, 1965), p. 172.
3. *Ibid.*, p. 172-73.
4. *Ibid.*, p. 173.
5. *Ibid.*, p. 173.
6. Vedanta Press, Hollywood, *Vedanta and the West*, Issue 177, p. 36.
7. M., *The Gospel of Sri Ramakrishna*, trans. by Swami Nikhilananda, Ramakrishna-Vivekananda Center (New York, 1969), p. 362.
8. *Vedanta and the West*, Issue 177, p. 34-35.
9. *The Gospel*, p. 566.
10. Akshay Kumar Sen, *Sri Sri Ramakrishna Punthi*, Udbodhan (Calcutta, 1949), p. 261-62.
11. Advaita Ashrama, *Life of Sri Ramakrishna* (Calcutta, 1943), p. 309-10.
12. Swami Saradananda, *Sri Ramakrishna, The Great Master*, trans. by Swami Jagadananda, Ramakrishna Math (Madras, 1979), Volume 2, p. 745.
13. *The Gospel*, p. 695-96.
14. *Ibid.*, p. 610.
15. *Ibid.*, p. 361.
16. *Ibid.*, p. 1012-13.
17. *Ibid.*, p. 210.
18. Swami Gambhirananda, *Sri Ramakrishna Bhaktamalika*, Udbodhan (Calcutta, 1964), Volume 2, p. 288-89.
19. *The Gospel*, p. 144.
20. *Ibid.*, p. 449.
21. *Ibid.*, p. 457.
22. *Ibid.*, p. 144.
23. *Ibid.*, p. 817.
24. *Ibid.*, p. 1015-16.
25. *Life of Sri Ramakrishna*, p. 561.
26. *Ibid.*, p. 573.
27. *The Gospel*, p. 954.
28. *Ibid.*, p. 961.
29. Isherwood, *Ramakrishna*, p. 308.
30. *The Gospel*, p. 975.
31. *Ibid.*, p. 976.
32. Chandra Sekhar Chatterjee, *Sri Sri Latu Maharajer Smritikatha*, Udbodhan (Calcutta, 1953), p. 291.
33. *Ibid.*, p. 292.

BALARAM BASU

1.   Swami Saradananda, *Sri Ramakrishna, The Great Master*, trans. by Swami Jagadananda, Ramakrishna Math (Madras, 1979), Volume 2, p. 935.
2.   M., *The Gospel of Sri Ramakrishna*, trans. by Swami Nikhilananda, Ramakrishna-Vivekananda Center (New York, 1969), p. 1011.
3.   Advaita Ashrama, *Life of Sri Ramakrishna* (Calcutta, 1943), p. 371-72.
4.   *Ibid.*, p. 372-73.
5.   *Ibid.*, p. 373.
6.   Swami Chetanananda, *Swami Adbhutananda: Teachings and Reminiscences*, Vedanta Society (St. Louis, 1980), p. 39.
7.   *The Gospel*, p. 724.
8.   *The Great Master*, p. 747-48.
9.   *The Gospel*, p. 490.
10. *Ibid.*, p. 305.
11. *Life of Sri Ramakrishna*, p. 375.
12. Akshay Kumar Sen, *Sri Sri Ramakrishna Punthi*, Udbodhan (Calcutta, 1949), p. 307.
13. *The Gospel*, p. 756.
14. *Ibid.*, p. 805.
15. Mahendra Nath Datta, *Saradananda Swamijir Jivaner Ghatanavali*, Calcutta, p. 95-96.
16. *The Gospel*, p. 93.
17. *Ibid.*, p. 109-10.
18. Swami Nirlepananda, *Ramakrishna-Saradamrita*, Karuna Prakaṣhani (Calcutta, 1968), p. 11-12.
19. Udbodhan, *Sri Sri Mayer Katha* (Calcutta, 1965), Volume 2, p. 103.
20. Swami Gambhirananda, *Sri Ramakrishna Bhaktamalika*, Udbodhan (Calcutta, 1964), Volume 2, p. 209-10.
21. Vaikuntha Nath Sanyal, *Sri Sri Ramakrishna Lilamrita* (Calcutta, 1936), p. 360-61.
22. *The Great Master*, Volume 2, p. 989.
23. *Ibid.*, p. 990.
24. Ramakrishna Shankarananda Sevashram, *Swami Shankaranander Galpa-Katha* (Bamunmura, 1966), p. 62.
25. *Swami Adbhutananda*, p. 39.
26. Chandra Sekhar Chatterjee, *Sri Sri Latu Maharajer Smritikatha*, Udbodhan (Calcutta, 1953), p. 110.
27   Swami Nirlepananda, *Swamijir Smriti Sanchayan* (Calcutta, 1967), p. 90.
28. Mahendra Nath Datta, *Vivekananda Swamijir Jivaner Ghatanavali* (Calcutta, 1964), Volume 1, p. 85-86.
29. *For Seekers of God*, trans. by Swamis Vividishananda and Gambhirananda, Advaita Ashrama (Calcutta, 1975), p. 268-69.

CHUNILAL BASU

1.   Swami Gambhirananda, *Sri Ramakrishna Bhaktamalika*, Udbodhan (Calcutta, 1964), Volume 2, p. 406.
2.   *Ibid.*, p. 406-07.
3.   *Ibid.*, p. 407.
4.   *Ibid.*, p. 408.

5. *Ibid.*, p. 409.
6. *Ibid.*, p. 409.
7. *Ibid.*, p. 410.
8. M., *The Gospel of Sri Ramakrishna*, trans. by Swami Nikhilananda, Ramakrishna-Vivekananda Center (New York, 1969), p. 831.
9. *Ibid.*, p. 934.
10. *Bhaktamalika*, p. 411.
11. *Ibid.*, p. 411.

YOGIN-MA (YOGINDRA MOHINI BISWAS)

1. *Mahanarayana Upanishad*, 79. 3.
2. Swami Nirlepananda, *Ramakrishna-Saradamrita*, Karuna Prakashani (Calcutta, 1968), p. 24.
3. Swami Gambhirananda, *Sri Ramakrishna Bhaktamalika*, Udbodhan (Calcutta, 1964), Volume 2, p. 461.
4. *Ramakrishna-Saradamrita*, p. 13.
5. *Ibid.*, p. 15.
6. *Ibid.*, p. 16-17.
7. *Ibid.*, p. 15-16.
8. *Ibid.*, p. 17.
9. *Bhaktamalika*, p. 460.
10. *Udbodhan*, Volume 26, p. 365-66.
11. *Ramakrishna-Saradamrita*, p. 17.
12. *Ibid.*, p. 26.
13. *Ibid.*, p. 17.
14. M., *The Gospel of Sri Ramakrishna*, trans. by Swami Nikhilananda, Ramakrishna-Vivekananda Center (New York, 1969), p. 156.
15. *Ibid.*, p. 824.
16. Swami Akhandananda, *Smriti-Katha*, Udbodhan (Calcutta, 1937), p. 42-43.
17. Swami Saradananda, *Sri Ramakrishna, The Great Master*, trans. by Swami Jagadananda, Ramakrishna Math (Madras, 1979), Volume 2, p. 720-21.
18. *Ibid.*, p. 724.
19. Vedanta Press, Hollywood, *Vedanta and the West*, Issue 110, p. 59.
20. *Ramakrishna-Saradamrita*, p. 18.
21. Swami Gambhirananda, *Srima Sarada Devi*, Udbodhan (Calcutta, 1968), p. 174-75.
22. *Ramakrishna-Saradamrita*, p. 27.
23. *Udbodhan*, *Sri Sri Mayer Katha* (Calcutta, 1969), Volume 1, p. 312.
24. *Vedanta and the West*, Issue 110, p. 57.
25. *Udbodhan*, Volume 26, p. 367.
26. *Ibid.*, p. 367.
27. *Ibid.*, p. 370.
28. *Vedanta and the West*, Issue 110, p. 54-55.
29. *Prabuddha Bharata*, 1942, p. 341.
30. *Prabuddha Bharata*, 1924, p. 415.
31. *Ibid.*, p. 415.
32. *Prabuddha Bharata*, 1932, p. 456-58.
33. *Bhaktamalika*, p. 469.
34. *Ibid.*, p. 473.

35.   *Vedanta and the West*, Issue 110, p. 62.
36.   Udbodhan, *Sri Sri Mayer Katha* (Calcutta, 1965), Volume 2, p. 336-37.
37.   *Prabuddha Bharata*, 1942, p. 344.

GAURI-MA

1.   Durga Puri, *Gauri-ma*, Saradeswari Ashrama (Calcutta, 1955), p. 1-2.
2.   Swami Gambhirananda, *Sri Ramakrishna Bhaktamalika*, Udbodhan
      (Calcutta, 1964), Volume 2, p. 492-93.
3.   *Gauri-ma*, p. 23.
4.   *Ibid.*, p. 22.
5.   *Ibid.*, p. 32.
6.   *Ibid.*, p. 33-36.
7.   *Ibid.*, p. 44-45.
8.   *Ibid.*, p. 57.
9.   *Ibid.*, p. 69.
10.   *Ibid.*, p. 70-72.
11.   *Ibid.*, p. 73.
12.   *Ibid.*, p. 74-76.
13.   *Ibid.*, p. 94.
14.   *Ibid.*, p. 95.
15.   *Ibid.*, p. 111.
16.   *Ibid.*, p. 111.
17.   *Ibid.*, p. 112-13.
18.   *Ibid.*, p. 107.
19.   *Ibid.*, p. 108-09.
20.   *Ibid.*, p. 109.
21.   *Ibid.*, p. 103.
22.   *Ibid.*, p. 104.
23.   *Ibid.*, p. 115.
24.   *Ibid.*, p. 118.
25.   Akshay Chaitanya, *Sri Sri Sarada Devi*, Calcutta Book House (1972), p. 76.
26.   Her Direct Disciples, *At Holy Mother's Feet*, Advaita Ashrama (Calcutta,
      1963), p. 130-31.
27.   *The Complete Works of Swami Vivekananda*, Advaita Ashrama (Calcutta,
      1968), Volume VI, p. 264, 267, 285.
28.   *Gauri-ma*, p. 119.
29.   *Ibid.*, p. 161.
30.   *Ibid.*, p. 162.
31.   *At Holy Mother's Feet*, p. 188.
32.   *Gauri-ma*, p. 307-08.
33.   *Ibid.*, p. 310.
34.   *Ibid.*, p. 315-17.
35.   *Ibid.*, p. 319-21.
36.   *Ibid.*, p. 318-19.
37.   *Ibid.*, p. 328-29.
38.   *Ibid.*, p. 297-99.
39.   *Ibid.*, p. 351-53.
40.   *Ibid.*, p. 265.
41.   *Ibid.*, p. 370.
42.   *Ibid.*, p. 372.
43.   *Ibid.*, p. 374.

PRATAP CHANDRA HAZRA

1. M., *The Gospel of Sri Ramakrishna*, trans. by Swami Nikhilananda, Ramakrishna-Vivekananda Center (New York), 1969, p. 270.
2. *Ibid.*, p. 536-37.
3. Akshay Kumar Sen, *Sri Sri Ramakrishna Punthi*, Udbodhan (Calcutta, 1949), p. 184-85.
4. Chandra Sekhar Chatterjee, *Sri Sri Latu Maharajer Smritikatha*, Udbodhan (Calcutta, 1953), p. 106.
5. *Ibid.*, p. 106-07.
6. *The Gospel*, p. 178.
7. *Ibid.*, p. 654.
8. *Ibid.*, p. 654-55.
9. *Ibid.*, p. 591-92.
10. *Ibid.*, p. 360.
11. *Ibid.*, p. 542.
12. *Ibid.*, p. 592.
13. *Ibid.*, p. 542.
14. *Ibid.*, p. 542.
15. *Sri Sri Ramakrishna Punthi*, p. 463-65.
16. Swami Chetanananda, *Swami Adbhutananda: Teachings and Reminiscences*, Vedanta Society (St. Louis, 1980), p. 38.
17. *The Gospel*, p. 402.
18. *Udbodhan*, Volume 67, p. 316.
19. Sharat Chandra Chakrabarty, *Sadhu Nag Mahashay*, Udbodhan (Calcutta, 1969), p. 36.
20. *The Gospel*, p. 812.
21. *Ibid.*, p. 230-31.
22. Swami Jagannathananda, *Srima Katha*, Udbodhan (Calcutta, 1941), Volume 1, p. 247.
23. *The Gospel*, p. 588.
24. *Ibid.*, p. 570.
25. *Ibid.*, p. 571.
26. *Ibid.*, p. 769.
27. *Ibid.*, p. 769.
28. *Swami Adbhutananda*, p. 38.
29. Christopher Isherwood, *Ramakrishna and His Disciples*, Methuen & Co. (London, 1965), p. 206.
30. Swami Saradananda, *Sri Ramakrishna, The Great Master*, trans. by Swami Jagadananda, Ramakrishna Math (Madras, 1979), p. 878.
31. *The Gospel*, p. 693.
32. Swami Chetanananda, *Sri Ramakrishner Sannidhey*, Ramakrishna Mission (Shillong, 1982), p. 16.
33. *The Gospel*, p. 402.
34. *Swami Adbhutananda*, p. 38.
35. *Ibid.*, p. 38.
36. *The Gospel*, p. 693.
37. *Swami Adbhutananda*, p. 38.
38. *The Gospel*, p. 567.
39. *Ibid.*, p. 765-66.
40. *Ibid.*, p. 768-69.
41. Mahendra Nath Datta, *Vivekananda Swamijir Jivaner Ghatanavali*

(Calcutta, 1964), Volume 1, p. 141.
42. *Sri Sri Ramakrishna Punthi*, p. 608.
43. *Udbodhan*, Volume 76, p. 528-29.
44. *Swami Adbhutananda*, p. 38.
45. *Prabuddha Bharata*, 1980, p. 223.
46. *The Gospel*, p. 993.
47. *Swami Adbhutananda*, p. 38.
48. Swami Jagannathananda, *Srima Katha* (Calcutta, 1953), Volume 2, p. 146.
49. Manada Shankar Dasgupta, *Yugavatar Sri Ramakrishna* (Calcutta, 1971), p. 468.
50. *Tattvamanjari*, December 1903, Volume 7, p. 214-16.

M. (Mahendra Nath Gupta)

1. Suresh Chandra Datta, *Sri Sri Ramakrishnadever Upadesh* (Calcutta, 1968), p. 92.
2. M., *The Gospel of Sri Ramakrishna*, trans. by Swami Nikhilananda, Ramakrishna-Vivekananda Center (New York, 1969), p. 81.
3. Swami Nityatmananda, *Srima Darshan*, General Printers (Calcutta, 1968), Volume 5, p. 326-27.
4. Advaita Ashrama, *Life of Sri Ramakrishna* (Calcutta, 1943), p. 492-93.
5. *Prabuddha Bharata*, 1932, p. 392.
6. *Srima Darshan*, 1970, Volume 7, p. 198.
7. *Ibid.*, 1967, Volume 1, p. 22.
8. *Ibid.*, p. 13.
9. *Ibid.*, 1967, Volume 1, The Life of M., p. (32).
10. *Ibid.*, 1965, Volume 3, p. 300.
11. *The Gospel*, p. 77-78.
12. *Srima Darshan*, 1970, Volume 7, p. 199.
13. *The Gospel*, p. 79.
14. *Ibid.*, p. 90.
15. *Bhagavatam*, X.31.9.
16. *The Gospel*, p. 359.
17. *Ibid.*, p. 359.
18. *Ibid.*, p. 381.
19. *Prabuddha Bharata*, 1932, p. 395.
20. *The Gospel*, p. 92.
21. *Ibid.*, p. 261.
22. *Ibid.*, p. 825-26.
23. Advaita Ashrama, *The Disciples of Sri Ramakrishna* (Calcutta, 1955), p. 421.
24. *The Gospel*, p. 718-19.
25. *Srima Darshan*, 1972, Volume 9, p. 43.
26. *The Gospel*, p. 331.
27. *Ibid.*, p. 331.
28. *Ibid.*, p. 331.
29. *Ibid.*, p. 591.
30. *Ibid.*, p. 800-01.
31. *Ibid.*, p. 126.
32. *Ibid.*, p. 80.
33. *Ibid.*, p. 597-98.

34. *Ibid.*, p. 128.
35. *Ibid.*, p. 256.
36. *The Disciples of Sri Ramakrishna*, p. 426.
37. *The Gospel*, p. 985.
38. *Ibid.*, p. 270; *The Disciples*, p. 419.
39. M., *Sri Sri Ramakrishna Kathamrita*, Kathamrita Bhavan (Calcutta, 1961), Volume 1, Appendix: M.'s Life, p. 5.
40. *The Gospel*, p. 973.
41. *The Disciples of Sri Ramakrishna*, p. 424.
42. *The Gospel*, p. 504.
43. *Ibid.*, p. v.
44. *Srima Darshan*, 1969, Volume 6, p. 106.
45. *Ibid.*, 1974, Volume 4, p. 290.
46. *Ibid.*, 1969, Volume 6, p. 118; Volume 1, The Life of M. p. (8).
47. *The Complete Works of Swami Vivekananda*, Advaita Ashrama (Calcutta, 1968), Volume VI, p. 204.
48. *Ibid.*, (Calcutta, 1970), Volume V., p. 140.
49. *The Disciples of Sri Ramakrishna*, p. 427.
50. *Prabuddha Bharata*, 1932, p. 444.
51. *Udbodhan*, Volume 56, p. 278.
52. *Ibid.*, p. 278.
53. *Prabuddha Bharata*, 1932, p. 497.
54. M., *Gospel of Sri Ramakrishna*, Ramakrishna Math (Madras, 1930), Volume 1, p. 15-34.
55. *Prabuddha Bharata*, 1949, p. 232.
56. *Srima Darshan*, 1965, Volume 3, p. 2-3, 30.
57. *Ibid.*, 1969, Volume 5, p. 243.
58. *Ibid.*, 1972, Volume 11, p. 130-31.
59. *Udbodhan*, Volume 67, p. 437.
60. *Udbodhan*, Volume 48, p. 456.
61. *Udbodhan*, Volume 66, p. 362.
62. *Udbodhan*, Volume 39, p. 451.
63. *The Gospel*, p. 748.
64. *Ibid.*, p. 96.
65. *Srima Darshan*, 1967, Volume 1, The Life of M., p. (11).
66. *Prabuddha Bharata*, 1932, p. 501.
67. *Udbodhan*, Volume 39, p. 452.

NAG MAHASHAY (DURGA CHARAN NAG)

1. Sharat Chandra Chakrabarty, *Sadhu Nag Mahashay*, Udbodhan (Calcutta, 1969), p. 43.
2. Advaita Ashrama, *Teachings of Sri Ramakrishna* (Calcutta, 1958), p. 116.
3. *Ashtavakra Samhita*, XVII. 5.
4. *Nag Mahashay*, p. 1.
5. *Ibid.*, p. 7.
6. *Ibid.*, p. 7.
7. *Ibid.*, p. 8.
8. *Ibid.*, p. 16.
9. *Ibid.*, p. 18.
10. *Ibid.*, p. 20.

11.   *Ibid.*, p. 20.
12.   *Ibid.*, p. 25-26.
13.   *Ibid.*, p. 31.
14.   *Ibid.*, p. 32.
15.   *Ibid.*, p. 34.
16.   *Ibid.*, p. 38-39.
17.   *Ibid.*, p. 40.
18.   *Ibid.*, p. 41.
19.   *Ibid.*, p. 44.
20.   *Ibid.*, p. 45-46.
21.   *Ibid.*, p. 51.
22.   *Bhagavatam*, XI. 8. 21.
23.   *Nag Mahashay*, p. 51.
24.   *Ibid.*, p. 47.
25.   *Ibid.*, p. 54.
26.   *Ibid.*, p. 54-55.
27.   *Ibid.*, p. 56-57.
28.   *Ibid.*, p. 65-66.
29.   *Ibid.*, p. 66-67.
30.   *Ibid.*, p. 68-69.
31.   *Ibid.*, p. 103-04.
32.   *Bhagavad Gita*, XVII. 3.
33.   *Nag Mahashay*, p. 99.
34.   *Ibid.*, p. 99-100.
35.   *Ibid.*, p. 95.
36.   *Ibid.*, p. 95-96.
37.   *Ibid.*, p. 92-93.
38.   *Ibid.*, p. 93-94.
39.   *Ibid.*, p. 95.
40.   *Ibid.*, p. 100-01
41.   *Ibid.*, p. 95.
42.   *Ibid.*, p. 101.
43.   *Ibid.*, p. 89.
44.   *Ibid.*, p. 89.
45.   Binodini Mittra, *Sri Sri Nag Mahashay*, 1923, (Teachings of Nag Mahashay, Nos. 159, 1, 161, 133), p. 582-600.
46.   First Disciples of Sri Ramakrishna, *Spiritual Talks*, Advaita Ashrama (Calcutta, 1968), p. 87-88.
47.   *Nag Mahashay*, p. 72.
48.   *Ibid.*, p. 78-79.
49.   Udbodhan, *Sri Sri Mayer Katha* (Calcutta, 1965), Volume 2, p. 390; and *Nag Mahashay*, p. 75-76.
50.   *Nag Mahashay*, p. 79.
51.   *Ibid.*, p. 42.
52.   *Ibid.*, p. 102.
53.   *Ibid.*, p. 85-86.
54.   *Udbodhan*, Volume 54, p. 226-28.
55.   *Nag Mahashay*, p. 61-62.
56.   *Ibid.*, p. 62.
57.   *Spiritual Talks*, p. 135-36.
58.   *Nag Mahashay*, p. 2-3.

59. Binodini, *Sri Sri Nag Mahashay*, p. 402.
60. *Nag Mahashay*, p. 102-03.
61. *Ibid.*, p. 103.
62. Binodini, *Sri Sri Nag Mahashay*, p. 227-28.
63. *Nag Mahashay*, p. 129-30.
64. *Ibid.*, p. 132.
65. *Ibid.*, p. 137.
66. *Ibid.*, p. 137-38.
67. *Ibid.*, p. 132.
68. *Ibid.*, p. 139.

SURESH CHANDRA DATTA

1. *Maha Nirvana Tantra*, 8.23.
2. *Prabuddha Bharata*, 1948, p. 231.
3. Sharat Chandra Chakrabarty, *Sadhu Nag Mahashay*, Udbodhan (Calcutta, 1969), p. 14.
4. *Prabuddha Bharata*, 1948, p. 233.
5. *Sadhu Nag Mahashay*, p. 36.
6. *Prabuddha Bharata*, 1948, p. 232.
7. *Ibid.*, p. 232.
8. *Ibid.*, p. 233.
9. Brajendra Nath Bandyopadhyay and Sajani Kanta Das, *Samasamayik Drishtite Sri Ramakrishna Paramahamsa*, General Printers (Calcutta, 1968), p. 119-20.
10. *Udbodhan*, Volume 14, p. 772.
11. Suresh Chandra Datta, *Ramakrishna Paramahamsadever Jivani O Upadesh*, (Calcutta, 1908), p. 30-31.
12. *Ibid.*, p. 58.
13. Advaita Ashrama, *Life of Sri Ramakrishna* (Calcutta, 1943), p. 440.
14. *Udbodhan*, Volume 14, p. 773-74.
15. *Prabuddha Bharata*, 1948, p. 233.
16. *Sadhu Nag Mahashay*, p. 53.
17. Swami Gambhirananda, *Sri Ramakrishna Bhaktamalika*, Udbodhan (Calcutta, 1964), Volume 2, p. 365.

NAVAGOPAL GHOSH AND NISTARINI GHOSH

1. *Dhammapada*, Chapter XXIII, Verses, 9-10.
2. Swami Gambhirananda, *Sri Ramakrishna Bhaktamalika*, Udbodhan (Calcutta, 1964), Volume 2, p. 373-74.
3. *Ibid.*, p. 374.
4. Advaita Ashrama, *Life of Sri Ramakrishna* (Calcutta, 1943), p. 513-14.
5. *Bhaktamalika*, p. 375-76.
6. *Udbodhan*, Volume 52, p. 295.
7. Told by Swami Ambikananda (From Swami Dhireshananda's Diary, May 30, 1953).
8. Sister Devamata, *Sri Ramakrishna and His Disciples*, Ananda Ashrama (California, 1928), p. 125.
9. *Ibid.*, p. 126.
10. Sister Devamata, *Days In An Indian Monastery*, Ananda Ashrama (California, 1927), p. 237.
11. *Ibid.*, p. 237-38.

12. *Bhaktamalika*, p. 377.
13. M., *The Gospel of Sri Ramakrishna*, trans. by Swami Nikhilananda, Ramakrishna-Vivekananda Center (New York, 1969), p. 843.
14. Vedanta Press, Hollywood, *Vedanta and the West*, Issue 109, p. 18-19.
15. *Bhaktamalika*, p. 378.
16. Devamata, *Ramakrishna*, p. 158-59.
17. *Ibid.*, p. 154.
18. *The Complete Works of Swami Vivekananda*, Advaita Ashrama (Calcutta, 1968), Volume VI, p. 512-13.
19. *Bhaktamalika*, p. 381.
20. *Ibid.*, p. 381.
21. Akshay Chaitanya, *Brahmananda Lilakatha*, Nava Bharat (Calcutta, 1962), p. 126-27.
22. *Udbodhan*, Volume 52, p. 295-96.
23. Told by Swami Ambikananda (From Swami Dhireshananda's Diary, May 30, 1953).
24. *For Seekers of God*, trans. by Swamis Vividishananda and Gambhirananda, Advaita Ashrama (Calcutta, 1975), p. 269-70.

ADHAR LAL SEN

1. *The Mahabharata*, Shanti Parvan, Chapter 175, Verse 16.
2. Swami Nityatmananda, *Srima Darshan*, General Printers (Calcutta, 1966), Volume 4, p. 123.
3 Swami Chetanananda, *Swami Adbhutananda: Teachings and Reminiscences*, Vedanta Society (St. Louis, 1980), p. 50.
4. *Udbodhan*, Volume 40, p. 399-400.
5. *Udbodhan*, Volume 52, p. 69.
6. *Ibid.*, p. 70.
7. *Ibid.*, p. 156-57.
8. M., *The Gospel of Sri Ramakrishna*, trans. by Swami Nikhilananda, Ramakrishna-Vivekananda Center (New York, 1969), p. 185-86.
9. *Ibid.*, p. 209.
10. *Ibid.*, p. 209-10.
11. Udbodhan, *Dharma Prasange Swami Brahmananda* (Calcutta, 1958), p. 36.
12. *The Gospel*, p. 258.
13. *Ibid.*, p. 261.
14. *Ibid.*, p. 273.
15. *Ibid.*, p. 413-14.
16. *Udbodhan*, Volume 52, p. 307.
17. *The Gospel*, p. 414.
18. *Ibid.*, p. 414.
19. Akshay Kumar Sen, *Sri Sri Ramakrishna Punthi*, Udbodhan (Calcutta, 1949), p. 341.
20. *The Gospel*, p. 507-08.
21. *Ibid.*, p. 509-11.
22. *Ibid.*, p. 218-20.
23. *Ibid.*, p. 617.
24. *Ibid.*, p. 434.
25. *Udbodhan*, Volume 52, p. 309.
26. *Udbodhan*, Volume 40, p. 399.

27. *Swami Adbhutananda*, p. 49-50.
28. *The Gospel*, p. 666.
29. *Swami Adbhutananda*, p. 49.
30. *Udbodhan*, Volume 40, p. 400.
31. Swami Gambhirananda, *Sri Ramakrishna Bhaktamalika*, Udbodhan (Calcutta, 1964), Volume 2, p. 246.
32. Swami Jagannathananda, *Srima Katha*, (Calcutta, 1953) Volume 2, p. 242.
33. *Udbodhan*, Volume 81, p. 304.
34. *Swami Adbhutananda*, p. 50.

GIRISH CHANDRA GHOSH

1. M., *The Gospel of Sri Ramakrishna*, trans. by Swami Nikhilananda, Ramakrishna-Vivekananda Center (New York, 1969), p. 679, 682.
2. Abinash Chandra Gangopadhyay, *Girish Chandra*, Dey's Publishing (Calcutta, 1977), p. 20.
3. *Ibid.*, p. 27.
4. Mahendra Nath Datta, *Vivekananda Swamijir Jivaner Ghatanavali* (Calcutta, 1966), Volume 2, p. 64-65.
5. *Girish Chandra*, p. 20.
6. *Ibid.*, p. 32.
7. *Ibid.*, p. 117; *Udbodhan*, Volume 14, p. 721.
8. *Udbodhan*, Volume 15, p. 138-39.
9. Achintya Kumar Sengupta, *Ratnakar Girishchandra*, Anandadhara Prakashan (Calcutta, 1964), p. 20-21; Abinash, *Girish Chandra*, p. 121-22.
10. *Udbobhan*, Volume 15, p. 139-41.
11. Advaita Ashrama, *The Disciples of Sri Ramakrishna* (Calcutta, 1955), p. 391.
12. Vedanta Press, Hollywood, *Vedanta and the West* (March-April 1953), p. 48-50.
13. *Ibid.*, p. 50.
14. *Ibid.*, p. 51.
15. *The Gospel*, p. 546.
16. *Vedanta and the West* (March-April 1953), p. 51.
17. *The Gospel*, p. 556.
18. *Girish Chandra*, p. 198.
19. Nalini Ranjan Chattopadhyay, *Sri Ramakrishna O Banga Rangamancha*, Mandal Book House (Calcutta, 1978), p. 74.
20. *Swamijir Jivaner Ghatanavali* (Calcutta, 1967), Volume 3, p. 71-72.
21. *Vedanta and the West* (March-April 1953), p. 53.
22. *Ibid.*, p. 53-54.
23. *Ibid.*, p. 55.
24. *The Gospel*, p. 677-78.
25. *Vedanta and the West* (March-April 1953), p. 55.
26. *Ibid.*, p. 55-56.
27. *Ibid.*, p. 57.
28. *The Disciples of Sri Ramakrishna*, p. 400.
29. Christopher Isherwood, *Ramakrishna and His Disciples*, Methuen & Co. (London, 1965), p. 252.
30. *Vedanta and the West* (March-April 1953), p. 56-57.
31. Ram Chandra Datta, *Sri Sri Ramakrishna Paramahamsadever*

Jivanvrittanta, Yogodyana (Calcutta, 1950), p. 144.
32. *The Gospel*, p. 1026.
33. Advaita Ashrama, *Life of Sri Ramakrishna* (Calcutta, 1943), p. 447-48.
34. *The Gospel*, p. 694.
35. *Vedanta and the West*, Issue 187, p. 58.
36. Swami Saradananda, *Sri Ramakrishna, The Great Master*, trans. by Swami Jagadananda, Ramakrishna Math (Madras, 1978), Volume 1, p. 375-77.
37. Isherwood, *Ramakrishna*, p. 254.
38. *The Gospel*, p. 706.
39. *Vedanta and the West* (March-April 1953), p. 58.
40. *The Disciples of Sri Ramakrishna*, p. 403.
41. *Udbodhan*, Volume 15, p. 292-93.
42. Swami Chetanananda, *Swami Adbhutananda: Teachings and Reminiscences*, Vedanta Society (St. Louis, 1980), p. 46-47.
43. *The Gospel*, p. 741.
44. Swami Jnanatmananda, *Mahat Smriti*, Mittra and Ghosh (Calcutta, 1977), p. 54-55.
45. *Girish Chandra*, p. 228; *Dharma Prasange Swami Brahmananda* (Udbodhan, 1958), p. 60.
46. *Vedanta and the West*, Issue 187, p. 56.
47. *Ibid.*, p. 62-63.
48. *The Disciples of Sri Ramakrishna*, p. 403.
49. *Girish Chandra*, p. 219.
50. *Minutes of the Ramakrishna Mission* (25th Meeting, October 24, 1897).
51. *The Gospel*, p. 821-22.
52. *Udbodhan*, Volume 15, p. 288-89.
53. *For Seekers of God*, trans. by Swamis Vividishananda and Gambhirananda, Advaita Ashrama (Calcutta, 1975), p. 265.
54. *Udbodhan*, Volume 15, p. 358-59.
55. *The Great Master*, p. 874.
56. *The Gospel*, p. 926.
57. *Vedanta and the West*, Issue 187, p. 61-62.
58. *Udbodhan*, Volume 15, p. 349-50, 365.
59. *The Disciples of Sri Ramakrishna*, p. 404-05.
60. Isherwood, *Ramakrishna*, p. 300.
61. Swami Gambhirananda, *Sri Ramakrishna Bhaktamalika*, Udbodhan (Calcutta, 1964), Volume 2, p. 268.
62. *Ratnakar Girishchandra*, p. 172.
63. *Udbodhan*, Volume 15, p. 353.
64. *Bhaktamalika*, p. 268; *Udbodhan*, Volume 14, p. 726.
65. *Udbodhan*, Volume 15, p. 356-58.
66. Hemendra Nath Dasgupta, *Sri Sri Ramakrishnadev O Bhakta-Bhairav Girishchandra* (Calcutta, 1946), p. 44.
67. *Udbodhan*, Volume 35, p. 347.
68. *Girish Chandra*, p. 413.
69. *Vedanta and the West*, Issue 186, p. 56.
70. *Prabuddha Bharata*, 1933, p. 190.
71. *Girish Chandra*, p. 217-18.
72. *Udbodhan*, Volume 14, p. 729.
73. *Girish Chandra*, p. 156-58.

74. *Ibid.*, p. 177.
75. *Ibid.*, p. 176-77.
76. *Udbodhan*, Volume 14, p. 123.
77. *Ibid.*, Volume 14, p. 718.
78. Sister Devamata, *Days In An Indian Monastery*, Ananda Ashrama (California, 1927), p. 268.
79. *Mahat Smriti*, p. 43.
80. *Girish Chandra*, p. 325.
81. *Ibid.*, p. 414.
82. *Udbodhan*, Volume 15, p. 351.
83. *Udbodhan*, Volume 14, p. 717-18.
84. *Ratnakar Girishchandra*, p. 6-7.
85. *Udbodhan*, Volume 14, p. 717-18.
86. *Girish Chandra*, p. 326.
87. *Days In An Indian Monastery*, p. 267.
88. *Sri Ramakrishna O Banga Rangamancha*, p. 20.
89. *Sri Ramakrishna O Bhakta-Bhairav Girishchandra*, p. 107.
90. Dhan Gopal Mukerji, *The Face of Silence*, E. P. Dutton & Co. (New York, 1926), p. 214-16.
91. Isherwood, *Ramakrishna*, p. 254.
92. *The Complete Works of Swami Vivekananda*, Advaita Ashrama (Calcutta, 1969), Volume VII, p. 271.
93. *Girish Chandra*, p. 418.
94. *Sri Ramakrishna O Bhakta-Bhairav Girishchandra*, p. 69.
95. *The Complete Works of Swami Vivekananda* (1968), Volume VI, p. 499-500.
96. *Udbodhan*, Volume 52, p. 291.
97. *Girish Chandra*, p. 419-20.
98. *Udbodhan*, Volume 15, p. 366-67.
99. *Ibid.*, Volume 15, p. 359.
100. *Vedanta and the West*, Issue 187, p. 59.
101. *Udbodhan*, Volume 53, p. 506.
102. *Sri Ramakrishna O Bhakta-Bhairav Girishchandra*, p. 102.
103. *Udbodhan*, Volume 14, p. 118.

KALIPADA GHOSH

1. M., *The Gospel of Sri Ramakrishna*, trans. by Swami Nikhilananda, Ramakrishna-Vivekananda Center (New York, 1969), p. 850.
2. *Ibid.*, p. 226.
3. *Ibid.*, p. 257.
4. *Ibid.*, p. 237.
5. *The Complete Works of Swami Vivekananda*, Advaita Ashrama (Calcutta, 1966), Volume IV, p. 418.
6. Swami Chetanananda, *Swami Adbhutananda: Teachings and Reminiscences*, Vedanta Society (St. Louis, 1980), p. 44-45.
7. Jnanendra Nath Biswas, *Yogodyan Mahatmya*, Navabhava Library (Calcutta, 1941), p. 74-75.
8. *Udbodhan*, Volume 24, p. 754.
9. *Udbodhan*, Volume 60, p. 640.
10. Swami Gambhirananda, *Sri Ramakrishna Bhaktamalika*, Udbodhan (Calcutta, 1964), Volume 2, p. 414.

11. Udbodhan, *Dharma Prasange Swami Brahmananda*, (Calcutta, 1958), p. 170.
12. Swami Saradananda, *Sri Ramakrishna, The Great Master*, trans. by Swami Jagadananda, Ramakrishna Math (Madras, 1979), Volume 2, p. 962-63.
13. *Udbodhan*, Volume 24, p. 754.
14. *The Gospel*, p. 878-79.
15. *Ibid.*, p. 879.
16. *The Great Master*, p. 997-98.
17. *The Gospel*, p. 932.
18. *Bhaktamalika*, p. 417-18.
19. *Ibid.*, p. 413.
20. Udbodhan, *Bhakta Manomohan* (Calcutta, 1944), p. 229.
21. *Bhaktamalika*, p. 418.
22. Chandra Sekhar Chatterjee, *Sri Sri Latu Maharajer Smritikatha*, Udbodhan (Calcutta, 1953), p. 399.
23. *Ibid.*, p. 411.

DEVENDRA NATH MAJUMDAR

1. Pranesh Kumar, *Mahatma Devendranath* (Calcutta, 1930), p. 34-35. (Quoted from *Sadhu Aghorenather Jivancharit*, 3rd ed., p. 31-33.)
2. *Ibid.*, p. 35.
3. *Ibid.*, p. 36.
4. *Ibid.*, p. 15.
5. *Ibid.*, p. 37.
6. *Ibid.*, p. 41.
7. *Ibid.*, p. 42.
8. *Ibid.*, p. 43.
9. *Ibid.*, p. 43.
10. *Ibid.*, p. 45.
11. *Ibid.*, p. 48.
12. *Ibid.*, p. 50.
13. *Ibid.*, p. 52.
14. *Ibid.*, p. 53-54.
15. *Ibid.*, p. 57.
16. *Ibid.*, p. 58.
17. *Ibid.*, p. 59-60.
18. *Ibid.*, p. 61.
19. *Ibid.*, p. 62.
20. *Ibid.*, p. 71.
21. *Ibid.*, p. 72-79.
22. *Ibid.*, p. 81.
23. *Ibid.*, p. 87-91.
24. *Ibid.*, p. 83-86.
25. *Ibid.*, p. 89-90.
26. M., *The Gospel of Sri Ramakrishna*, trans. by Swami Nikhilananda, Ramakrishna-Vivekananda Center (New York, 1969), p. 738-39.
27. *Ibid.*, p. 739-42.
28. *Mahatma Devendranath*, p. 109.
29. *Ibid.*, p. 110.
30. *Ibid.*, p. 111.

31. Akshay Kumar Sen, *Sri Sri Ramakrishna Punthi*, Udbodhan (Calcutta, 1949), p. 606.
32. *Mahatma Devendranath*, p. 116.
33. *Ibid.*, p. 119.
34. *Udbodhan*, Volume 13, p. 64.
35. *Mahatma Devendranath*, p. 125-26.
36. *Ibid.*, p. 126-28.
37. *Ibid.*, p. 128-29.
38. *Ibid.*, p. 154.
39. *Ibid.*, p. 165.
40. *Ibid.*, p. 174-76.
41. Mahendra Nath Datta, *Bhakta Devendranath* (Calcutta, 1956), p. 39.
42. *Mahatma Devendranath*, p. 231-32.
43. *Ibid.*, p. 233.
44. *Ibid.*, p..227-28.
45. *Ibid.*, p. 281.
46. *Ibid.*, p. 283.

UPENDRA NATH MUKHOPADHYAY

1.   *Bhagavad Gita*, 7.16.
2.   Sister Devamata, *Sri Ramakrishna and His Disciples*, Ananda Ashrama (California, 1928), p. 105.
3.   Swami Gambhirananda, *Sri Ramakrishna Bhaktamalika*, Udbodhan (Calcutta, 1964), Volume 2, p. 397.
4.   Swami Akhandananda, *Smritikatha*, Udbodhan (Calcutta, 1937), p. 182.
5.   *Bhaktamalika*, p. 398.
6.   Swami Abhedananda, *Amar Jivankatha*, Sri Ramakrishna Vedanta Math (Calcutta, 1964), p. 83.
7.   Jnanendra Nath Biswas, *Yogodyan Mahatmya*, Navabhava Library (Calcutta, 1941), p. 36.
8   *Bhaktamalika*, p. 400-01.
9.   Akhandananda, *Smritikatha*, p. 184.
10. Chandra Sekhar Chatterjee, *Sri Sri Latu Maharajer Smritikatha*, Udbodhan (Calcutta, 1953), p. 353.
11. *Bhaktamalika*, p. 404.
12. *Souvenir*, Centenary of Upendra Nath Mukhopadhyay (Calcutta, 1868-1968), p. 33-34.

HARAMOHAN MITTRA

1.   M., *The Gospel of Sri Ramakrishna*, trans. by Swami Nikhilananda, Ramakrishna-Vivekananda Center (New York, 1969), p. 493.
2.   Swami Gambhirananda, *Sri Ramakrishna Bhaktamalika*, Udbodhan (Calcutta, 1964), Volume 2, p. 383.
3.   Swami Saradananda, *Sri Ramakrishna, The Great Master*, trans. by Swami Jagadananda, Ramakrishna Math (Madras, 1978), Volume 1, p. 373-74.
4.   *The Complete Works of Swami Vivekananda*, Advaita Ashrama (Calcutta, 1970), Volume V, p. 120.

GOPALER-MA (AGHOREMANI DEVI)

1. *The Complete Works of Sister Nivedita*, Nivedita Girls' School (Calcutta, 1967), Volume 1, p. 109.
2. Swami Gambhirananda, *Sri Ramakrishna Bhaktamalika*, Udbodhan (Calcutta, 1964), Volume 2, p. 439.
3. The Vedanta Center, Boston, *The Message of the East*, 1920, p. 163.
4. Swami Saradananda, *Sri Ramakrishna, The Great Master*, trans. by Swami Jagadananda, Ramakrishna Math (Madras, 1979), Volume 2, p. 731.
5. Brahmachari Prakashchandra, *Swami Saradananda* (Calcutta, 1936), p. 267.
6. *The Great Master*, p. 734.
7. *Ibid.*, p. 735.
8. *Ibid.*, p. 735.
9. *Ibid.*, p. 735-36.
10. *Ibid.*, p. 737.
11. *Ibid.*, p. 738.
12. *Ibid.*, p. 739.
13. *Ibid.*, p. 739.
14. *Ibid.*, p. 740.
15. *Ibid.*, p. 740-41.
16. *Ibid.*, p. 753.
17. *Ibid.*, p. 753.
18. *Ibid.*, p. 754.
19. *Ibid.*, p. 755.
20. *Ibid.*, p. 750.
21. *Ibid.*, p. 751.
22. *Ibid.*, p. 751-52.
23. *Ibid.*, p. 756.
24. *Ibid.*, p. 756-57.
25. *Ibid.*, p. 757-58.
26. *Ibid.*, p. 408.
27. *Ibid.*, p. 760-61.
28. *Bhaktamalika*, p. 451.
29. *The Message of the East*, 1920, p. 165.
30. *Udbodhan*, Volume 27, p. 484-85.
31. *Works of Nivedita*, Volume I, p. 110.
32. Swami Nirlepananda, *Ramakrishna-Saradamrita*, Karuna Prakashani (Calcutta, 1968), p. 54-55.
33. *Ibid.*, p. 55.
34. *Bhaktamalika*, p. 453-54.
35. *Ibid.*, p. 454-55.
36. *Ramakrishna-Saradamrita*, p. 66.
37. Lizelle Reymond, *The Dedicated*, The John Day Company (New York, 1953), p. 304.
38. *Ramakrishna-Saradamrita*, p. 58.
39. *Ibid.*, p. 68.
40. *Prabuddha Bharata*, 1906, p. 172-73.
41. *Bhaktamalika*, p. 459.
42. *Ramakrishna-Saradamrita*, p. 62-63.

GOLAP-MA (GOLAP SUNDARI DEVI)

1. Swami Nirlepananda, *Ramakrishna-Saradamrita*, **Karuna Prakashani** (Calcutta, 1968), p. 20-21.
2. *Prabuddha Bharata*, 1925, p. 94.
3. Akshay Kumar Sen, *Sri Sri Ramakrishna Punthi*, Udbodhan (Calcutta, 1949), p. 406.
4. M., *The Gospel of Sri Ramakrishna*, trans. by Swami Nikhilananda, Ramakrishna-Vivekananda Center (New York, 1969), p. 787-88.
5. Advaita Ashrama, *The Disciples of Sri Ramakrishna* (Calcutta, 1955), p. 481.
6. Swami Nikhilananda, *Holy Mother*, Ramakrishna-Vivekananda Center (New York, 1962), p. 61.
7. *Ibid.*, p. 67.
8. Swami Saradananda, *Sri Ramakrishna, The Great Master*, trans. by Swami Jagadananda, Ramakrishna Math (Madras, 1979), Volume 2, p. 579-80.
9. *Udbodhan*, Volume 27, p. 49.
10. *Ramakrishna-Saradamrita*, p. 21.
11. *Ibid.*, p. 28.
12. *Ibid.*, p. 20.
13. *The Gospel*, p. 822-25.
14. Udbodhan, *Sri Sri Mayer Katha* (Calcutta, 1965), Volume 2, p. 181-82.
15. Udbodhan, *Sri Sri Mayer Katha* (Calcutta, 1969), Volume 1, p. 306.
16. *Ramakrishna-Saradamrita*, p. 29.
17. Nikhilananda, *Holy Mother*, p. 79.
18. Advaita Ashrama, *Life of Sri Ramakrishna* (Calcutta, 1943), p. 527.
19. *Udbodhan*, Volume 27, p. 53-54.
20. Nikhilananda, *Holy Mother*, p. 94.
21. *Ibid.*, p. 94.
22. *Sri Sri Mayer Katha*, Volume 2, p. 121.
23. Nikhilananda, *Holy Mother*, p. 101.
24. *Udbodhan*, Volume 27, p. 49.
25. *Sri Sri Mayer Katha*, Volume 2, p. 258.
26. Nikhilananda, *Holy Mother*, p. 113.
27. *Ibid.*, p. 274.
28. Sister Devamata, *Days In An Indian Monastery*, Ananda Ashrama (California, 1927), p. 278.
29. *Udbodhan*, Volume 27, p. 50-51.
30. *Ibid.*, p. 52-53.
31. *Sri Sri Mayer Katha*, Volume 1, p. 72-73.
32. *Sri Sri Mayer Katha*, Volume 2, p. 190.
33. Nikhilananda, *Holy Mother*, p. 288.
34. *Udbodhan*, Volume 57, p. 158.
35. Akshay Chaitanya, *Swami Saradanander Jivani* (Calcutta, 1955), p. 280.
36. *Udbodhan*, Volume 57, p. 158.

AKSHAY KUMAR SEN

1. *Udbodhan*, Volume 29, p. 7.
2. Pranesh Kumar, *Mahatma Devendranath* (Calcutta, 1930), p. 66.
3. *Udbodhan*, Volume 29, p. 9.
4. Akshay Kumar Sen, *Sri Sri Ramakrishna Punthi*, Udbodhan (Calcutta,

1949), p. 398.

5. *Ibid.*, p. 399.
6. *Ibid.*, p. 400.
7. Swami Gambhirananda, *Sri Ramakrishna Bhaktamalika*, Udbodhan (Calcutta, 1964), Volume 2, p. 369.
8. Akshay Kumar Sen, *Sri Sri Ramakrishna Mahima*, Udbodhan (Calcutta, 1969), p. 33-34.
9. *Ibid.*, p. 18.
10. *Mahatma Devendranath*, p. 66-67.
11. M., *The Gospel of Sri Ramakrishna*, trans. by Swami Nikhilananda, Ramakrishna-Vivekananda Center (New York, 1969), p. 742.
12. *Sri Sri Ramakrishna Punthi*, p. 607.
13. *Bhaktamalika*, p. 370.
14. *Sri Sri Ramakrishna Punthi*, p. 620-21.
15. *Ibid.*, p. 621.
16. Vaikuntha Nath Sanyal, *Sri Sri Ramakrishna Lilamrita* (Calcutta, 1936), p. 339.
17. *Bhagavad Gita*, Invocation, Verse 8.
18. Mahendra Nath Datta, *Vivekananda Swamijir Jivaner Ghatanavali*, Mahendra Publishing Committee (Calcutta, 1964), Volume 1, p. 142-43.
19. Brajendranath Bandyopadhyay and Sajani Kanta Das, *Samasamayik Drishtite Sri Ramakrishna Paramahamsa*, General Printers (Calcutta, 1969), p. 125.
20. Ramakrishna-Shivananda Ashrama, *Sri Sri Mahapurush Maharajer Smritikatha* (Barasat, 1960), p. 49-50.
21. Chandra Sekhar Chatterjee, *Sri Sri Latu Maharajer Smritikatha*, Udbodhan (Calcutta, 1953), p. 307.
22. *The Complete Works of Swami Vivekananda*, Advaita Ashrama (Calcutta, 1968), Volume VI, p. 334.
23. *Samasamayik Drishtite*, p. 125.
24. *Ibid.*, p. 129.
25. *Udbodhan*, Volume 85, p. 215-16.
26. Swami Gambhirananda, *Srima Sarada Devi*, Udbodhan (Calcutta, 1968), p. 627-28.
27. Brahmachari Akshay Chaitanya, *Sri Sri Sarada Devi*, Calcutta Book House (Calcutta, 1972), p. 155.
28. *Bhaktamalika*, p. 372.
29. *Ibid.*, p. 372.

MANINDRA KRISHNA GUPTA*

1. Swami Gambhirananda, *Sri Ramakrishna Bhaktamalika*, Udbodhan (Calcutta, 1964), Volume 2, p. 389.
2. *Udbodhan*, Volume 38, p. 468-69.
3. *Ibid.*, p. 703.
4. *Ibid.*, p. 705.
5. *Ibid.*, p. 818-19.
6. *Ibid.*, Volume 39, p. 643.
7. *Ibid.*, p. 645.
8. *Ibid.*, Volume 41, p. 669-71.
9. M., *The Gospel of Sri Ramakrishna*, trans. by Swami Nikhilananda,

Ramakrishna-Vivekananda Center (New York, 1969), p. 912.
10. *Bhaktamalika*, p. 390.
11. *Ibid.*, p. 390-91.

PURNA CHANDRA GHOSH

1. Swami Saradananda, *Sri Ramakrishna, The Great Master*, trans. by Swami Jagadananda, Ramakrishna Math (Madras, 1979), Volume 2, p. 699.
2. *Ibid.*, p. 899.
3. M., *The Gospel of Sri Ramakrishna*, trans. by Swami Nikhilananda, Ramakrishna-Vivekananda Center (New York, 1969), p. 797-98.
4. *Udbodhan*, Volume 49, p. 301.
5. *Ibid.*, p. 302-03.
6. *The Great Master*, p. 900.
7. *Ibid.*, p. 900.
8. *Ibid.*, p. 900.
9. *The Gospel*, p. 869-70.
10. *Ibid.*, p. 810.
11. *Ibid.*, p. 736-37.
12. *Ibid.*, p. 738.
13. *Ibid.*, p. 752-53.
14. Udbodhan, *Sri Sri Mayer Katha* (Calcutta, 1965), Volume 2, p. 89.
15. *The Gospel*, p. 785.
16. *Udbodhan*, Volume 49, p. 305.
17. *Ibid.*, p. 305.
18. *The Gospel*, p. 812-13.
19. *Ibid.*, p. 796.
20. *Panchadashi*, Chapter 9, Verse 84.
21. *The Gospel*, p. 839.
22. Swami Abhedananda, *Amar Jivankatha*, Ramakrishna Vedanta Math (Calcutta, 1964), p. 42-43.
23. *The Gospel*, p. 912.
24. *Udbodhan*, Volume 49, p. 362.
25. *Ibid.*, p. 364.
26. *Udbodhan*, Volume 15, p. 779.
27. *Udbodhan*, Volume 49, p. 364.
28. *Ibid.*, p. 361-62.
29. *Ibid.*, p. 365.
30. Swami Abjajananda, *Swamijir Padaprante*, Saradapith (Belur Math, 1972), p. 37.
31. *The Gospel*, p. 796-97.
32. *Udbodhan*, Volume 15, p. 779.
33. *Ibid.*, p. 780.
34. *Sri Sri Mayer Katha*, Volume 2, p. 331-32.
35. *Udbodhan*, Volume 49, p. 366.
36. *Udbodhan*, Volume 15, p. 780.
37. *Udbodhan*, Volume 49, p. 366.

Index

Numbers in parentheses indicate an entire chapter devoted to the individual. Numbers in italics indicate photographs.

427